Praise for *Another Nineteen*

"Kevin Ryan has written a book that reminds us that the attacks of September 11, 2001 and their details have never really been investigated. Kevin has laid out the historical framework in a way that has never been done before. The importance of this cannot be overstated."

> – Lorie Van Auken, member of the Family Steering Committee for the 9/11 Commission and widow of Kenneth Van Auken, who was killed at the World Trade Center

"Finally a comprehensive and meticulously researched book that thoroughly details what occurred before and on 9/11. Without a doubt, *Another Nineteen* should be required reading for those who want the real story."

> – Robert McIlvaine, father of Bobby McIlvaine, who was killed at the World Trade Center on 9/11

"There have been many books about 9/11 explaining why the official story is false. In *Another Nineteen*, Kevin Ryan has taken a unique approach, dealing with 19 men who probably actually were responsible for the attacks. Perhaps no reader will agree with everything, but Ryan has pioneered an approach that will likely move researchers closer to the truth about that fateful day in September."

> – David Ray Griffin, author of *9/11 Ten Years Later: When State Crimes Against Democracy Succeed*

Praise for *Another Nineteen*

"Over the last decade, Kevin Ryan has been one of the most intelligent and useful analysts of what happened on 9/11, on topics ranging from the scientific analyses of how the WTC towers collapsed to the broader political background of the event. It is a most welcome opportunity to have the fruits of his researches collected in a book."

> — Peter Dale Scott, author of *The Road to 9/11: Wealth, Empire, and the Future of America*

"In *Another Nineteen*, Kevin Ryan brings together a vast amount of research that connects many current and former high-level government and military officials, and business executives, to the 9/11 attacks. Kevin shows in convincing detail how these people were in positions that would allow them to affect the outcome of the attacks, benefit from them, or both. Clearly written and cogently argued, this book is filled with new information on potential 9/11 suspects, and is a must-read for any student of 9/11."

> — James Gourley, editor of *The 9/11 Toronto Report*

"Given the profound corruption of the FBI, citizens have had no choice but to become investigators. For over a decade this new CSI—civil society investigation—has taken on the responsibility of assembling evidence relating to the crime of 9/11. Kevin Ryan's superb research has now produced a list of suspects, and the investigation has been taken to a new level."

> — Graeme MacQueen, founder of the Peace Studies Centre at McMaster University and co-editor of the *Journal of 9/11 Studies*

Another Nineteen:
Investigating Legitimate 9/11 Suspects

By Kevin Robert Ryan

This book is dedicated to future generations.

First edition published by Microbloom and printed in the USA.

ISBN-10: 1489507833

ISBN-13: 978-1489507839

Library of Congress Control Number (LCCN): 2013909937

Table of Contents

More Support for *Another Nineteen*

"We need a new investigation into 9/11. The official report by Hamilton and Kean failed to research the collapse of WTC 7 and did not present a balanced narrative of the 9/11 suspects. It's time for an unbiased debate about terrorism and secret warfare."

> – Dr. Daniele Ganser, Swiss Institute for Peace and Energy Research (SIPER), and author of *NATO's Secret Armies: Operation GLADIO and Terrorism in Western Europe*

"When the United States of America failed to adequately investigate the events leading up to and occurring on the morning of 9/11/2001, it left each and every citizen of the world responsible for filling in the gaps. Kevin Ryan is doing his civic duty. That I am not competent to vet his data is clear. Who is? But his work alongside the work of others will be an important part of the mosaic that will one day be the pertinent facts of the morning of 9/11."

> – Donna Marsh O'Connor, mother of Vanessa Lang Langer, who was killed at the World Trade Center on 9/11

Preface

It's been ten years since I began studying the events of 9/11. This effort followed from my awareness that the 2003 U.S. invasion of Iraq was justified through a coordinated campaign of lies. Like many citizens who understood that, I wondered when the lying began. The answer to that question was more detailed and troubling than expected.

While learning about the early problems with the official account, I began to follow-up on information previously given to me by my employer Underwriters Laboratories (UL). Through communications with the CEO of UL and other top managers, I learned that the company had tested and certified the fire resistance of the steel components used to build the World Trade Center towers.

A year spent asking difficult questions led to the knowledge that executives at UL could not explain how the buildings could have failed so quickly due to fire. In November 2004, I wrote to the government agency investigating the WTC destruction (NIST), to get more information, and was shortly thereafter fired in retaliation.

After finding another job and relocating my family, I realized the implications of UL's willingness to falsify its record with regard to the WTC. Something was terribly wrong with the official accounts of 9/11. As those crimes continued to be the source of untold suffering and loss throughout the world, I became committed to discovering the truth.

There have been rewards in this struggle as well. I've met many great people who, like me, are convinced that the "catastrophic and catalyzing" realization that we've been deceived about 9/11 can bring us together to achieve peace and justice. In pursuit of that common objective, I've met with many people including 9/11 Commission Vice-Chairman Lee Hamilton. I've also made presentations throughout the U.S. and Canada, and appeared in many documentary films and media programs, including on National Public Radio and Colorado Public Television. Through these efforts, I've become a better communicator. In being attacked and denigrated for my questions and concerns, I've learned to see the ego-based roots that lie behind many human problems.

4

The 9/11 attacks were a wake-up call that can be used for the purpose of understanding the extent of the deception in our lives. That understanding can help us make adjustments to how we live with each other and how we prioritize the education of our children. Once we tap into this ongoing "inside job," we will have the power to make lasting positive change in our society.

Many people have worked with me in the pursuit of truth and justice and I owe a debt of gratitude to many of them. Among the most helpful have been Adnan Zuberi, Aidan Monaghan, Allan Giles, Bonnie Faulkner, Carol Brouillet, Catherine A. Fitts, Cheryl Curtiss, Chris Emery, David Chandler, David Griffin, David Kubiak, Don Paul, Dylan Avery, Elizabeth Woodworth, Frances Shure, Gregg Roberts, James Gourley, Janice Matthews, Jeremy Rys, Jim Hoffman, Jon Cole, Justin Keogh, Laurie Manwell, Matthew Everett, Michael Anderson, Michael Wolsey, Mike Berger, Niels Harrit, Paul Rea, Peter Scott, Richard Gage, Ted Tilton, Tim Boyle, Tony Szamboti, Victoria Ashley, William Bergman, the 9/11 Working Group of Bloomington, and the directors I worked with at Architects & Engineers for 9/11 Truth.

I would especially like to recognize my current and former co-editors at the *Journal of 9/11 Studies*. Steven Jones, Frank Legge, and Graeme MacQueen have joined me in making an ongoing sacrifice of personal time and energy in order to produce well-researched and reliable information about the events of 9/11.

Finally, I would like to thank my family, particularly my wife Caroline and daughter Crystal. Without their love and support this independent research would not have been possible.

As worldwide understanding of the 9/11 deception grows, there is yet hope for an honest, "official" inquiry into the events of 9/11. This book, however, is meant to be an example of what independent investigators can do. A concerted, grass-roots effort to learn as much as possible about legitimate suspects and related organizations can continue to provide a crucial history and help avoid future attacks. I hope this contribution takes us another step toward that goal.

Kevin Ryan, June 2013

Chapter 1

Introduction

The terrorist attacks of September 11, 2001 were a turning point in world history. We have been told that those crimes were planned and implemented by nineteen Arab Muslim hijackers under the direction of the leaders of al Qaeda. According to the official account, this criminal conspiracy received no help or funding from any government.

Unfortunately, this explanation fails to address a majority of the evidence and leaves most of the critical questions unanswered.[1] In fact, the reports that constitute the official account do so little to explain what happened that it is possible that, to this day, we know very little about who was behind the attacks. That fact is alarming to many people, given that so much war and unprecedented change has been driven by the official account.

On closer inspection, the *9/11 Commission Report* (the report) provides only 90 pages of discussion about what actually happened on the day of 9/11, found in Chapters 1 and 9. The remainder of the report is devoted to promoting a myth behind al Qaeda, and suggesting what to do about it.

The 9/11 Commission told us that, "Our aim has not been to assign individual blame. Our aim has been to provide the fullest possible account of the events surrounding 9/11 and to identify lessons learned."

However, author David Ray Griffin revealed that the Commission not only failed to provide the fullest possible account, it omitted or distorted many of the relevant facts.[2] The report also gave us a new explanation for one of the most alarming aspects of the attacks—the complete failure of the U.S. national air defenses. The new explanation represented the fourth, distinctly different, version of how the air defenses failed.

A number of excuses were given by Commission members for the shortcomings of the report. In their 2006 book, *Without Precedent*, the leaders of the Commission, Thomas Kean and Lee Hamilton, claimed that "we were set up to fail."[3] Hamilton said that the Commission faced too many questions, too little funding, and too little time.[4]

But the fact is that, if it had not been for 9/11 victim's family members working diligently to publicize problems with the emerging official myth, there would never have been a 9/11 Commission investigation at all. Both President Bush and Vice President Cheney actively sought to limit the investigation into the attacks.

As CNN reported in January 2002, President Bush personally asked Senate Majority Leader Tom Daschle to limit the congressional investigation. This unusual request came after a "rare call to Daschle from Vice President Cheney." Daschle stated that Cheney "expressed the concern that a review of what happened on September 11 would take resources and personnel away from the effort in the war on terrorism."[5]

When the political pressure caused by the victim's families grew too great, the 9/11 Commission was born. But the Commission was given less than one tenth of the funding that had been allotted to investigate the sexual exploits of President Clinton just three years earlier. Clearly, the U.S. government did not want an in-depth investigation into 9/11.

The Commission

There were several brief inquiries that preceded the 9/11 Commission. These included the CIA Inspector General (IG) inquiry, the Department of Justice inquiry, and the Joint Congressional Inquiry. The scope of all three of these was limited to the shortcomings of U.S. intelligence agencies related to the alleged hijackers. The 9/11 Commission, which stated its goal of presenting "the fullest possible account," built its work on the earlier inquiries and used many of the same staff for its investigation.

To lead the Commission, President Bush first appointed Henry Kissinger. As with the 14-month delay in getting started, this appointment was a strong indication that the investigation was not intended to be a fact-finding mission. Kissinger's refusal to release his client list, which was expected to include the name Bin Laden, forced his resignation and replacement by Kean and Hamilton.[6] Kean's ties to the oil and gas industry and Hamilton's history as an intelligence agency insider, along with similar conflicts of interest among the rest of the Commission members, were issues that remained unaddressed.

In November 2003, one of the 9/11 Commission members quit. This was Senator Max Cleland of Georgia, who was outraged at the process and had previously said "This is a scam" and "It's disgusting. America is being cheated." In October 2003, Cleland told the *New York Times* that, "As each day goes by, we learn that this government knew a whole lot more about these terrorists before September 11 than it has ever admitted."[7]

The Commission's report came out nine months later, in July 2004, and was hailed as a great achievement by the publicists hired to promote it. Unfortunately for the rest of us, the report failed to answer 70% of the questions provided by the 9/11 victim's families who had inspired the Commission's charter.

Throughout the report, the Commission claimed that "no evidence" existed, or could be found, to explain aspects of the 9/11 events. This was reminiscent of comments made by President Ford to his press secretary, Ron Nessen, about Ford's work on the Warren Commission that investigated the assassination of President Kennedy. Ford told Nessen that he and his colleagues on the Warren Commission – "were very, very careful when we wrote our final report not to say flatly that Lee Harvey Oswald acted alone and was not part of a conspiracy." Ford clarified that the Warren Commission was "very careful to say we 'found' no evidence of a conspiracy."[8] The strategy appeared to be that if the commission claimed to have never "found" the evidence then it could not be held accountable for ignoring it.

The 9/11 Commission took this "we found no evidence" phrase to an extreme and used some form of it 36 times within its report.[9] Four of those instances highlight the fact that the 9/11 Commission could not explain how any of the alleged hijackers entered the cockpits of any of the four hijacked planes. Other instances reflected that the Commission put almost no effort into allegations of insider trading, or how the attacks were funded, which the Commission said was "of little practical significance."[10] In an honest investigation, the funding would be seen as a strong clue to who was behind the attacks.

The WTC Reports

Although the Commission addressed the World Trade Center (WTC) in a brief, superficial manner, the detailed explanation for what happened to the Twin Towers and WTC Building 7 was left to the National Institute of Standards and Technology (NIST). This agency reported through the U.S. Department of Commerce, which at the time was under the direction of George W. Bush's old friend and oil industry colleague, Donald Evans.

Like the *9/11 Commission Report*, the NIST reports, which were issued in 2005 and 2008, each represented only the latest in a series of failed official explanations for the destruction of the WTC buildings. NIST avoided much of the evidence for what had happened to the buildings by providing only a "collapse initiation sequence" for the towers, and by performing no physical testing to support its unusual explanation for WTC Building 7.

The timing of NIST's WTC 7 report appeared to be scheduled for dual political purposes; to coincide with the seventh anniversary of 9/11 and to give the appearance of finished business at the end of the Bush Administration. That was not surprising, as the timing of NIST's other reports coincided with political events as well. These included the draft report on the towers in October 2004—just before the election; the final report on the towers—just before the fourth anniversary of 9/11; and NIST's first of several "responses to FAQs"—just before the fifth anniversary. All of them appeared to involve politically motivated release dates.

In each case, the dates allowed time for the mainstream media to quickly present the official story while public interest was high, but did not allow time for critical questioning of the related documents, which were extensive and deceptive. With the WTC 7 report, the public was given just three weeks prior to September 11, 2008 to comment on a report that was nearly seven years in the making.

It was quickly discovered that the NIST WTC 7 report was a very poor attempt at a realistic explanation for what happened to that 47-story building, which had not been hit by a plane.[11] It seemed that NIST didn't even try to present a logical explanation for what happened, but simply relied on the idea that a compliant media would help them close the public discussion quickly.

The Response to Public Skepticism

The efforts to conceal the truth were not entirely effective, however. National polls showed that many people were very skeptical of the official myth. A poll done by Scripps-Howard in 2006, for example, showed that 36% of the American public suspected "that federal officials assisted in the 9/11 terrorist attacks or took no action to stop them so the United States could go to war in the Middle East."[12]

Among those who still trusted the official account were some who insisted that, if there was much more to the story of what happened on 9/11, the media would have latched on and reported the issues diligently. The *History Commons Complete 9/11 Timeline*, which can be found online, shows that the mainstream media did, at first, report many interesting facts about 9/11 that did not end up in the official account.[13] Those facts were never followed-up or were quickly forgotten as the official myth was formed and reformed.

Attempts by some media sources to support the official accounts led to an increasing suspicion that something was being covered up. Hearst Publications magazine *Popular Mechanics*, the British Broadcasting Corporation (BBC), and *Skeptic* magazine, are examples of media that went to great lengths to stifle any questioning of the official account and divert attention from the glaring discrepancies.

Such official story champions focused their efforts around the term "conspiracy theory" and its variants, which they liberally applied to any attempts made by independent researchers.[14] Ironically, this was despite the fact that the only 9/11 conspiracy theory of any consequence had always been the official account.

The use of "conspiracy theory" to deter citizens from investigating historic events presents a paradox, to be sure. It suggests that those who commit criminal conspiracies can only be relatively powerless people who happen to live on the most strategically important lands, and conspiracies among rich, powerful people are impossible or absurd.

Our entire legal system is based on the idea of conspiracy. Despite this fact the public has been conditioned by the government and the media to blindly accept the official reports and to treat any questioning of those reports as "conspiracy theorizing." That is, you are a conspiracy theorist if you don't believe the government's conspiracy theory.

This cultural phenomenon goes back to 1967. At that time, in response to questions about the *Warren Commission Report*, the CIA issued a memorandum calling for mainstream media sources to begin countering "conspiracy theorists."[15] In the 45 years before the CIA memo came out, the phrase "conspiracy theory" appeared in the *Washington Post* and *New York Times* only 50 times, or about once per year. In the 45 years after the CIA memo, the phrase appeared 2,630 times, or about once per week.

Before the CIA memo came out, the *Washington Post* and *New York Times* had never used the phrase "conspiracy theorist." After the CIA memo came out, these two newspapers have used that phrase well over a 1,000 times. As suggested by the memo, the phrase is always delivered in a context in which "conspiracy theorists" are made to seem less intelligent and less rational than people who uncritically accept official explanations for major events.

President George W. Bush and his colleagues often used the phrase conspiracy theory in attempts to deter questioning about their activities. When questioned by reporters about an emerging scandal in September 2000, Bush said the idea that his presidential campaign was flashing subliminal messages in advertisements was absurd, and he added that "conspiracy theories abound in America's politics."[16] When in 1994, Bush's former company Harken Energy was linked to the fraudulent Bank of Credit and Commerce International (BCCI) through several investors, Bush's spokeswoman, Karen Hughes, shut down the inquiry by telling the Associated Press, "We have no response to silly conspiracy theories."

Because Bush's campaign had, in fact, been flashing subliminal messages in its advertisements, and Harken Energy was actually linked to BCCI, people began to wonder what Bush and his colleagues meant when they made diversionary comments about conspiracy theories. More importantly, that track record raised questions about Bush's statement after the 9/11 attacks, in which he said in a speech to the United Nations — "Let us never tolerate outrageous conspiracy theories concerning the attacks of September the 11th."

There is no question that criminal, government-sponsored conspiracies exist. History is replete with them and they usually involve the government claiming that the country was under attack from "terrorists." This was true of Hitler's Reichstag fire and it was true of the attacks that occurred in 20th century Western Europe under the guise of Operation Gladio. An example more relevant to 9/11 was the conspiracy behind Operation Northwoods, a plan drafted and approved in 1962 by the highest levels within the U.S. military.

Author James Bamford wrote of Operation Northwoods that it called "for a wave of violent terrorism to be launched in Washington, D.C., Miami, and elsewhere. People would be framed for bombings they did not commit; planes would be hijacked. [This would provide] the public and international backing they needed to launch their war."[17] The signed documents are available to everyone today and because of this we know that high level U.S. government representatives do conspire, on occasion, to commit terrorist crimes against the American people for the purpose of starting wars.[18]

Another claim made by those who fend off questions about 9/11 is that the official conspiracy theory is more plausible than it seems at first sight because it involves only a small group of conspirators. That is, it includes only 19 alleged hijackers directed by Osama Bin Laden (OBL). Of course, we must include Khalid Sheikh Mohammed (KSM) because the *9/11 Commission Report* called him the architect of the attacks. Over the years we have also been asked to consider the roles of Zacarias Moussaoui, Ayman Al-Zawahiri, Mohammed al Qahtani and a few others who have been discussed in the media as possible candidates for prosecution in military courts.

Proposing a Better Explanation

Today, we don't have an alternative to the official conspiracy that spells out how the events of 9/11 could be the result of a conspiracy among insiders. Yet at the same time we know it is impossible that those within the popular version of al Qaeda, the one promoted by the mainstream media, could have shut down the U.S. air defenses for two hours on 9/11 or destroyed the WTC buildings.

This book does not cover the falsity of the official account of 9/11 in great detail. That work has been done and today the information is widely available. See the bibliography for resources in that regard. Instead, this is an attempt to take next steps, by providing a preliminary investigation into another 19 suspects who had the power to accomplish what the official account has not explained.

Is it possible to propose a compelling alternative conspiracy based on the involvement of insiders? Could certain corporations, government representatives, and covert operatives have been involved? Such an alternative conspiracy should address more of the evidence and answer more of the questions about what happened, while not overly complicating the conspiracy.

If we examine the events of 9/11 in terms of what should have happened that did not, and what did happen that should not have, we can focus a little better on who might have been involved. At a minimum, the following five major, unexplained aspects must be addressed by any alternative account.

1. The many opportunities for U.S. intelligence agencies to track down and capture the alleged hijackers should have resulted in the attacks being stopped before they happened.

2. The four planes should not have been hijacked because the systems in place to prevent hijackings should have been effective.

3. The U.S. chain of command should have responded to the attacks immediately but it did not.

4. The U.S. national air defenses should have responded effectively and some, if not all, of the hijacked aircraft should have been intercepted by military jets.

5. The three WTC buildings should not have fallen through what should have been the path of most resistance.

In addition to addressing these problems, an effective alternative version of 9/11 would better explain facts related to Flight 77 and the Pentagon, Flight 93, and ancillary issues like 9/11 insider trading.

For simplicity, this alternative conspiracy should accept as much of the official account as possible, including that the alleged hijackers were on the planes. However, it should also pay attention to the question of who benefited from the attacks, which the official investigations did not address. The benefits realized by al Qaeda should be compared to the benefits realized by those within an alternative conspiracy.

The official account claims that OBL, KSM and the alleged hijackers went to great lengths to plan and implement the 9/11 operation for reasons of revenge and symbolism. This explanation does not make a great deal of sense considering that the Arab Muslim world has suffered enormously as a result of the attacks. The only ones who have benefited in that region are the ruling royal families of countries like Saudi Arabia, the United Arab Emirates (UAE), and Kuwait, who have long collaborated with the West. Those minority groups have benefited from the War on Terror because it has temporarily protected them from regional threats like that posed by Saddam Hussein and from other challenges to their positions of power.

The attacks of September 11 were an act of war meant to gain control over others. That's true no matter what conspiracy you believe. If you accept the official conspiracy theory, that 19 Arab hijackers committed these crimes under the direction of OBL and KSM but with no help from any government, then the war was a religious jihad and the jihadists wanted to control the behavior of the U.S. government.

Yet if you learn more about the facts, including that the alleged hijackers were not religious Muslims but were people who took drugs, drank alcohol and dated strippers, then you begin to see the need for another explanation.[19] Add to this an understanding of how unbelievably lucky the alleged hijackers would have had to be to even begin accomplishing everything the official account gives them credit for, and the need for better answers grows.

The Implications

If the 9/11 attacks were accomplished as a result of an insider conspiracy, then several implications become obvious. First, the evidence which was omitted or distorted by official investigators might lead to revealing the true conspiracy. Secondly, any examples of avoidance, obstruction, or false testimony to those investigations would give good leads on the true conspiracy.

Owning up to the possibility that we were so grandly manipulated is not easy though. The psychological barriers to these questions can be difficult to overcome. It doesn't get easier with the realization that the official 9/11 narrative has been the driving force behind many other crimes, including the deaths of countless innocent people.

If an insider conspiracy for 9/11 is found to be true then it was probably not the first time the American people have been so thoroughly deceived. Historical events such as the "October Surprise" holding of the hostages and the Iran-Contra crimes, both investigated by 9/11 Commission vice chairman Lee Hamilton, might shed light on a system that periodically subverts democracy for its own purposes. Other examples include Operation Gladio and the deceptions behind the first Gulf War. As readers will discover in this book, there are many links between the actors in these various events.

There has been a need for appropriate language to discuss these kinds of operations. Professor Peter Dale Scott has provided such language by defining concepts such as deep events, deep politics and the deep state. These terms refer to covert mechanisms that facilitate the strategies of the politically-minded rich, a group otherwise referred to as the "overworld."

Deep events, which Scott defines as those which are "systematically ignored or falsified in the mainstream media and public consciousness," can be seen as sharing certain features, such as cover-up of evidence and irresoluble controversy over what happened.[20] These features contribute to a suppressed memory of the event among the general public. Deep events are often associated with illegally sanctioned violence, and involve little known, but historically evident, cooperation between leaders of the state and organized crime.

Throughout this review of alternate suspects, the elements of a deep event are revealed to be present in the historical record of the 9/11 crimes. In this case, the public's suppressed memory has been helped along by a subservient press.[21]

What's more, 9/11 can be seen as not only a deep event but a "constitutional deep event." That is, the implementation of continuity of government (COG) plans as a result of 9/11 means that the U.S. constitution has been circumvented in favor of what former Assistant Attorney General Jack Goldsmith called the "Terror Presidency." That office has been exploited by an influential power group, whose major operatives are Dick Cheney and Donald Rumsfeld, to pursue long-standing goals of U.S. global domination.[22]

The question remains, however—was 9/11 not only a deep event but a deep state operation? As the suspects in this book are examined, evidence will be discussed that indicates the answer is yes. The crimes of 9/11 appear to have been a deception planned and perpetrated by powerful interests associated with a private network of deep state operatives, some of whom were embedded within U.S. political and military institutions.

Only half of the people reviewed in this book were in government or military roles at the time of the attacks. The others were private citizens working for think tanks or corporations. As will be seen, many of them have links to past crimes against democracy. These nineteen people may or may not have been consciously involved in a conspiracy to attack the United States on 9/11. But none of them are innocent and investigating them will lead to the truth about what happened.

Of course, an insider conspiracy can be seen to have had a much more believable motivation—the seizure and long-term maintenance of uncontested power. Such a conspiracy would have represented the interests of trans-national corporations and powerbrokers who have benefited, beyond imagination, from the 9/11 attacks.

Historical information is interwoven throughout this review because the old adage is certainly true that those who fail to learn their history are doomed to repeat it. Readers will find that 9/11 was not something new but, instead, was just another chapter in a long history of power plays. The 9/11 crimes were unique only in the sense that the ease of access and scope of information available to citizens today might still result in critical mass awareness and a widespread call for truth and justice.

Chapter 2

Dick, Don, and Another 19

"He's a ruthless little bastard. You can be sure of that." — Richard Nixon, describing Donald Rumsfeld

Two people stand out with regard to their ability to have influenced the events of 9/11 as those events were proceeding. Vice President Dick Cheney was in control at the White House, initially in his office and then at the Presidential Emergency Operations Center (PEOC). With the president out of the loop while traveling, Cheney was the most powerful person in Washington other than the other half of the National Command Authority, Secretary of Defense (SECDEF) Donald Rumsfeld.

In this book, Dick and Don represent the equivalents of KSM and OBL for an alternative explanation. That is, they were in positions to coordinate the work of the other nineteen and to oversee the success of the actual attacks. The two men did nothing to protect the country on the morning of 9/11, and their reported actions indicate that they were aware of a plan being implemented.

For the thirty years before 9/11, Cheney and Rumsfeld had worked together in positions of power, both in and out of government. A review of that thirty-year history is important in terms of understanding their motivations.

The history of this time period is also relevant to how 9/11 might have been organized and managed by deep state operatives. That is, previous operations which subverted democracy for the benefit of the powerful few, like Operation Gladio, the Iran-Contra crimes, and the selling of the Gulf War, lend crucial insight into the activities of Dick, Don, and their colleagues.

The History of Don

Rumsfeld's ruthless nature, the access and power that he wielded, and his inexplicable actions on 9/11, make him a primary suspect in the crimes. Another reason to begin with him is that he was a mentor to Dick Cheney in the early days of their relationship and his history suggests that both of them might have been more than simple civil servants from the start.

At Princeton, Rumsfeld's college roommate was Frank Carlucci, another future SECDEF and another person of interest in this book. Rumsfeld's senior thesis there was titled *The Steel Seizure Case of 1952 and Its Effects on Presidential Powers*. Throughout his long political career, Rumsfeld would continue to maintain a great interest in the expansion of presidential powers (which was a major result of the 9/11 attacks).

Other Princeton graduates that worked closely with Rumsfeld over the years were James Baker III, who graduated two years before Rumsfeld, and Edgar D. (Ned) Jannotta, who graduated just a year before Rumsfeld. Baker played several prominent roles in the Reagan and Bush I administrations. Jannotta, also a high school friend of Rumsfeld, later became the chairman of the Chicago-based, international investment firm William Blair & Company.

From 1954 to 1957, Rumsfeld served in the U.S. Navy as a pilot and flight instructor. Shortly thereafter, he pursued an interest in the U.S. Congress. He first worked as an assistant to David S. Dennison, Jr., a Congressman from Ohio, and then moved on to work for Congressman Robert P. Griffin of Michigan.

Although it was clear that Rumsfeld was very interested in running for Congress himself, he left his position as a congressional assistant to take a job with an investment firm called A.G. Becker. This period of Rumsfeld's life, from 1960 to 1962, is downplayed in every biography of the man. In his own memoirs, Rumsfeld mentions A.G. Becker only once, and suggests that he worked there for only one year. However, it is evident that Rumsfeld's employment at A.G. Becker was two years long and was the stepping stone to his winning a seat in the House of Representatives.

A.G. Becker was an investment firm located in Chicago. The company started under another name, as a manufacturer of paper. A junior partner, Abraham G. Becker, took over the firm after the panic of 1893 and expanded into stock and bond brokerage. One of the firm's largest deals was the $50 million financing of Sears, Roebuck & Co in 1919. The deal was a favor to Becker's friend Julius Rosenwald, one of the owners of Sears. Rumsfeld would later be on the board for a subsidiary called Sears World Trade.

It's not clear what responsibilities Rumsfeld had at A.G. Becker. However, there are other suspects investigated in this book whose careers started at investment consulting firms, including Dick Cheney and Wirt Walker. Another suspect, Benedict Sliney, was a Wall Street lawyer.

The intelligence services of the United States have always been closely connected to the world of high-dollar investment. Recalling the origins of the CIA and its predecessor organization, CIA Executive Director A.B. Buzzy Krongard once said, "the whole OSS was really nothing but Wall Street bankers and lawyers."[1] Thirteen years after the creation of the CIA, Donald Rumsfeld lucked into a job with one of the world's most powerful investment firms, headquartered in Chicago.

When the incumbent House Republican in Illinois' 13th congressional district decided to forego another term, Rumsfeld jumped at the chance to take her place. His campaign manager was his friend Ned Jannotta of William & Blair Company, who would later become a board director for AON Corporation, a WTC impact zone tenant at the time of the 9/11 attacks. Rumsfeld continued to work with Jannotta in the interim, as a fellow director of William Blair & Company.

First elected to Congress in November 1962, Rumsfeld was re-elected by large majorities in the next three elections. While in Congress, Rumsfeld became the friend and confidante of House minority leader Gerald Ford, who had campaigned for Rumsfeld during his first election. Rumsfeld finally came into his power when Ford became President of the United States in 1974.

Ford was born Leslie Lynch King, Jr, and only changed his name formally after college graduation to acknowledge the stepfather who raised him, Gerald Rudolph Ford. Ford attended the University of Michigan where he was a member of the Omicron chapter of the Delta Kappa Epsilon (DEKE) fraternity.

After graduation in 1935, the newly named Ford turned down several offers to play professional football and instead took a coaching job at Yale. While there, he graduated from Yale Law School, in 1941. During World War II, Ford was a Navy pilot and instructor, as Rumsfeld would be twelve years later. Ford represented the Grand Rapids, Michigan congressional district from 1949 until he became Vice President in 1973.

In a surprising move, Rumsfeld resigned from Congress in 1969, at the start of his fourth term, to join the Nixon Administration as director of the Office of Economic Opportunity (OEO). One surprising thing about this move was that Rumsfeld had voted against funding the agency while he was a congressman.

Observers thought that Rumsfeld took the job for the purpose of abolishing the OEO but instead he kept things running, although perhaps not as intended. Rumsfeld hired Dick Cheney as his special assistant at the OEO almost immediately, in the spring of 1969. Cheney had interviewed with Rumsfeld the year before for a congressional assistant position.

As with Cheney, the OEO under Rumsfeld was a foot in the door for several other people who would go on to fill important positions in the U.S. government for many years afterward. This included Rumsfeld's Princeton roommate Frank Carlucci, Senate Watergate investigator (and President Clinton's "private CIA" man)[2] Terry Lenzner, and the EPA administrator on 9/11, Christine Whitman.

Rumsfeld left the OEO in December 1970 to become the director of the Cost of Living Council, where he reported to Secretary of Labor George Shultz. At the same time, however, in a very unusual move, Rumsfeld was appointed as a special advisor reporting directly to President Nixon. At 38 years of age, Rumsfeld was suddenly sharing presidential power with H.R. Haldeman, John Erlichmann, and John Dean.

In February 1973, Nixon sent Rumsfeld to Belgium to serve as Ambassador to NATO. While he was there, Ned Jannotta brought his family for vacation and Rumsfeld and Jannotta spent some time together.[3] As will be further discussed in Chapter 11, Operation Gladio was in full force at this time. Gladio was run from NATO Headquarters in Brussels via a CIA-controlled organization called the Clandestine Planning Committee.

Rumsfeld was the U.S. ambassador to NATO during the 1973 Arab oil embargo, which was initiated by Arab oil-producing countries in order to punish the United States for its foreign policy activities. The embargo came just days after the U.S. arming of Israel during the Yom Kippur War, and only a month after the September 11 CIA-led coup in Chile. Regardless, the oil embargo led to a deep rift within NATO. As a result, some European nations and Japan sought to disassociate themselves from U.S. Middle East policy.[4]

In August 1974, when President Nixon resigned, Ford immediately called Rumsfeld back to Washington to serve as his transition chairman. Subsequently, Rumsfeld became Ford's White House Chief of Staff and held that position from September 1974 to November 1975.

Just three months after Ford and Rumsfeld had settled in, the *New York Times* ran a story by journalist Seymour Hersh claiming that the CIA had committed crimes over a period of years. These crimes, referred to as "The Family Jewels," included such things as the assassination of political leaders around the world, and spying on Americans at home.

Ford responded in January by initiating an investigation headed by Vice President Nelson Rockefeller to investigate some of the claims. Governor Ronald Reagan was selected for the Commission, along with Lyman Lemnitzer of Operation Northwoods fame. Congressional investigations were also launched, in both the Senate and the House of Representatives.

Although Henry Kissinger is often cited as an adversary of Rumsfeld, he used his influence to come to the rescue of the White House and the CIA. At a crucial point in these investigations, Kissinger inserted himself, his reputation, and his skills at media manipulation to turn the tide in favor of continued secrecy.[5] His actions made it clear that when the "secret government" was at risk, these men answered to the same control structure.

Throughout the following months, Rumsfeld pushed Ford to launch a Cabinet shakeup. A few months later, in October of that year, Ford obliged Rumsfeld in what became called the "Halloween Massacre." Ford named Rumsfeld as Secretary of Defense and one of Ford's former congressional associates, fellow DEKE and Navy pilot George H. W. Bush, became the Director of Central Intelligence.

The investigations and growing public awareness of CIA crimes resulted in legislation that restricted CIA activities. This in turn led the U.S. deep state to develop alternative means to accomplish what the CIA could no longer do on its own. History has revealed the creation of a private network of intelligence operatives at this time, one which would influence and alter U.S. foreign policy dramatically in the late 20th century.[6]

This private, covert network was formed at a time when many 9/11 suspects were working together in government. In fact, the number of Nixon and Ford Administration leaders who were linked to the 9/11 attacks is actually quite astounding. Dick and Don were there, as was George H.W. Bush, but so was Joseph Kasputys who owned several of the companies in the WTC towers including one in the exact impact area of the south tower.[7] Kasputys worked, from 1972 to 1977, for the U.S. departments of commerce and defense. He was also the deputy director of Nixon's White House task force that dealt with the Arab oil embargo of 1973.

Half of the alternative suspects named in this book worked for the Nixon and/or Ford Administrations in one capacity or another. Meanwhile, several others worked for the CIA or were in the military at the time. How many might have worked for the "CIA within the CIA," a phrase used to describe the private network, is not known.

Not long after the private network formed, it discovered that more secure banks were needed to distribute funding for its operations. With the blessing of CIA director Bush, Saudi Arabian intelligence chief Kamal Adham "transformed a small Pakistani merchant bank, the Bank of Credit and Commerce International (BCCI), into a world-wide money-laundering machine, buying banks around the world to create the biggest clandestine money network in history."[8]

As the CIA and its foreign partners were using BCCI to fund covert operations in the 1980s, Rumsfeld was working for the Reagan Administration in various roles, including as Special Envoy to the Middle East. One trip to Baghdad left a lasting impression when Rumsfeld personally reassured Saddam Hussein that his use of chemical weapons would not deter U.S. efforts to solidify its relationship with Iraq.[9]

At the same time, Rumsfeld was chairman of the RAND Corporation, where he worked with 9/11 suspect Brian Michael Jenkins. He was also a member of the board of Sears World Trade (SWT) when Frank Carlucci was running that company. SWT appears to have been involved in the Iran-Contra crimes as discussed in Chapter 3.

Around the time that he met with Saddam, Rumsfeld became part of a select group of people who made plans for Continuity of Government (COG) in times of crisis. Dick Cheney and Richard Clarke were also part of this group as early as 1984, along with Oliver North. Cheney, Clarke and Rumsfeld continued in this capacity, practicing to take over the functions of the U.S. government, up to the day of 9/11 when those plans were implemented for the first time.

In the late 1980s, Rumsfeld was a member of the U.S. Arms Control Committee and the National Economic Committee. Meanwhile Rumsfeld also became a director, along with 9/11 suspect Peter Janson, in a company called ABB that later sold nuclear technology to North Korea (see Chapter 10).

Although Rumsfeld was known as a corporate executive for many years, he was never far from government. While George H.W. Bush was president, Rumsfeld ran a company called General Instruments

24

while also a member of the Board of Visitors of the National Defense University. In the days of Clinton, he led Gilead Sciences and joined the board of Gulfstream Aerospace (with Colin Powell). Throughout this time he continued his role in the COG program.

In the mid-90s Rumsfeld served as a trustee for both the RAND Corporation and the American Enterprise Institute. He was also a founder and active member of the Project for the New American Century (PNAC), a neo-conservative group that pushed extremist, interventionist foreign policy. He signed the January 1998 PNAC letter to Clinton that called for "regime change" in Iraq. Several of the other suspects named in this book were PNAC signatories.

In the late nineties, Rumsfeld chaired two U.S. government sponsored commissions that would have considerable sway in policy making. The first was the Commission to Assess the Ballistic Missile Threat to the United States. This group concluded that Iraq, Iran, and North Korea had the ability to develop intercontinental ballistic missile capabilities and that U.S. intelligence capabilities would not be able to adequately warn of such developments. The second was the "Rumsfeld Commission" on the national security uses of space. Rumsfeld was joined by his protégé Stephen Cambone and 9/11 suspect Duane Andrews in that endeavor.

At his confirmation hearing in January 2001, Rumsfeld warned of a surprise attack on the United States. "We know that the thing that tends to register on people is fear, and we know that that tends to happen after there's a Pearl Harbor, tends to happen after there's a crisis. And that's too late for us," he said.[10] A few days later, Rumsfeld's commission on the national security uses of space issued its report that warned of a "Space Pearl Harbor."[11]

Soon after Rumsfeld was sworn in as SECDEF for the second time, he announced a series of sweeping reviews meant to transform the U.S. military into a force capable of fighting wars in multiple venues simultaneously. These reviews were led by Pentagon analyst Andrew Marshall.

In the months prior to 9/11, Rumsfeld continued to hint that a surprise attack was imminent. He also obsessed over Iraq. He asked, "Imagine what the region would look like without Saddam and with a regime that's aligned with US interests. It would change everything in the region and beyond it. It would demonstrate what U.S. policy is all about."[12]

All things considered, no one person can be said to have had more influence over the events leading up to and including 9/11 than Donald Rumsfeld. The only person who comes close to such status is Rumsfeld's long-time colleague Dick Cheney.

The History of Dick

Dick was the Vice President of the United States on September 11, 2001. As the events began to unfold that day, Cheney was reported to have been whisked away by Secret Service personnel to a secure location in the White House basement levels.

It is a revealing fact that this process of securing the vice president, without asking if he agreed with the process, was not followed for the president at the same time. Instead, George W. Bush was left sitting in an elementary school classroom—a location that had been widely publicized for days before 9/11. Instead of being protected, the Secret Service allowed Bush to go on reading with children while Dick handled the "response" to 9/11.

It seemed that someone wanted the President of the United States out of the way while the 9/11 attacks were occurring. Dick's history and his critical role on 9/11 make him a prime suspect. Therefore he should be examined closely.

After graduating from high school in Wyoming, Cheney went to Yale University with the recommendation of Casper oilman and Yale alumnus, Tom Stroock. But Cheney did not do well and had to drop out after three semesters. He returned to Wyoming in 1960 and took a job with a local power company.

Although Cheney was classified as available for military service in February 1962, and the Vietnam War raged for more than another decade, he never served in the military. In terms of his age, Cheney remained eligible for the draft until 1967, but he was able to avoid serving due to his successful application for five separate deferments over that five year period. The excuse he gave later was that he "had other priorities than military service during the sixties."

Many have speculated that these deferments and Cheney's response to questioning about them makes him a "chickenhawk." That is, he was not courageous enough to serve in the military yet he was later behind hawkish efforts to start wars around the world. An alternate explanation for Cheney's actions, however, is that he was already in a different kind of service, perhaps having been recruited by deep state interests. In any case, Dick Cheney has shown throughout his career that he is anything but a coward.

Cheney was arrested for drunk driving twice, in 1962 and 1963. Neither those arrests, nor his lengthy record of avoiding the draft, caused any problem for him in his later, meteoric rise in politics.

He married his high school sweetheart Lynne Vincent in 1964. For the next four years, Dick and Lynne kept busy while having two children. He served as an intern in the Wyoming State Legislature, received an M.A. in political science, and they both pursued Ph.D.s at the University of Wisconsin. While at Wisconsin, Dick worked for Governor Warren Knowles but did not finish his doctorate.

In 1968, Cheney won a congressional scholarship to work with Wyoming congressman William Steiger. As part of his assigned duties with the congressman, Cheney traveled to college campuses to report on student protests. That same year, Cheney interviewed for a position as an assistant to Rumsfeld, who was running for his fourth term as U.S. Representative from Illinois. Cheney did not get the job although the interview is often cited in historical accounts of both men.

It seems plausible that Rumsfeld didn't hire Cheney immediately because he knew that he would likely be getting a job in the Nixon Administration but could not let the record reflect that fact while he was running for Congress. In any case, Rumsfeld quit his congressional seat just a few months later and immediately hired Cheney as his personal assistant at the OEO.

Because Rumsfeld was also granted the title of Assistant to the President, he and his "Assistant's assistant," Cheney, had access to the White House. This was an incredible stroke of luck for the politically ambitious pair, but their astonishing streak of fortune was just beginning.

At this time, opposition to the Vietnam War was increasing dramatically, with more and more Americans attending anti-war demonstrations and demanding that the U.S. withdraw from Vietnam. It seems possible that the timing of Rumsfeld's special appointment at the White House, and Cheney's entrance directly from reporting on protests, was part of a high-level response to the threats posed by the war opposition.

Between 1969 and 1972 the war escalated. However, the June 1972 break-in of the DNC headquarters in the Watergate Hotel led to the removal of Nixon from the presidency. Author Russ Baker has proposed that Americans have fundamentally misunderstood the truth about Watergate. In fact, Baker suggests that Watergate may have been a CIA operation to set-up and take down Nixon so that he could not expose potential links between the CIA and the assassination of President Kennedy.[13]

When Nixon sent Rumsfeld to Europe as ambassador to NATO, Cheney left government to join the investment advisory firm Bradley Woods & Company. He spent the next year and a half writing opinion papers on energy-related topics and Nixon policies.

The firm was started by Bruce Bradley and Alan Woods. Bradley is now a board director at Lancaster Systems & Solutions (LS2) with 9/11 suspect Barry McDaniel, who is covered in Chapter 13. Woods, who filled a number of interesting roles in the Ford Administration, would later become a vice president at Sears World Trade with Carlucci.

Bradley and Woods, therefore, associated with a number of people who are suspected of having engaged in deep state operations. Nixon's demise was brewing when Cheney worked with them. And both Dick and Don were soon back at the White House when, on August 8, 1974, Nixon resigned.

Cheney immediately joined Rumsfeld on Ford's transition team, and then he was named assistant to Rumsfeld, who became White House Chief of Staff. Cheney was also appointed as deputy assistant to the president. During this time, Cheney was responsible for some very important duties and was "widely acknowledged to have participated in every major administration decision."[14]

After the Ford Administration shake-up in 1975, Cheney, at the age of 34, became Ford's chief of staff. During the next two years, Cheney was given enormous power within the executive branch. He wrote or reviewed many of the presidents' speeches, and fought the president's battles. Those battles included some historic contests over the recently revealed covert activities of the CIA.

The difficult times that Dick and Don experienced in the Nixon and Ford administrations came to a head in late 1976. The painful loss in Vietnam, brought about in part by U.S. citizen protests, and the embarrassing public scrutiny of CIA activities was shortly followed by a loss that Dick and Don would remember. The defeat of Ford's re-election hopes culminated in what appeared to a life-long motivation for these two men to protect and expand presidential powers.

Dick and Don would also spend much of their political careers increasing the clout of the military-industrial complex, apparently in response to those early political losses. Their desires were finally satisfied by way of the 9/11 attacks. Along the way, they both made a lot of money.

After Ford's presidency was over, Cheney went back to work for Bradley Woods. He soon decided to run for Congress, however, as a representative from Wyoming. During the campaign, in the summer of 1978, he suffered his first of five heart attacks that would lead to heart transplant surgery. Later that year, he was elected to the first of six terms as a congressman from Wyoming.

In 1981, Cheney became the Chairman of the Republican Policy Committee, a position that he held for the next six years. During that time, he was criticized for voting against a House resolution calling for the release of Nelson Mandela and the recognition of the African National Congress.

During the Iran-Contra hearings in the mid-1980s, Cheney vigorously defended his COG colleague Oliver North. Accused of illegally selling arms to Iran, at the time a designated terrorist state, and using the proceeds to illegally arm the Contras in Nicaragua, North himself kept silent. Although it was clear that Reagan Administration officials had broken the law, and that Vice President Bush was likely behind some of it, indictments of Bush and Reagan did not occur. That was because the leader of the investigation, future 9/11 Commission vice chairman Lee Hamilton, uncritically accepted excuses from the White House that were later found to be untrue.

Cheney was elected House minority whip in 1988. He was soon suspected of being behind the attacks on Speaker of the House Jim Wright that forced Wright's resignation. Wright was the first ever sitting Speaker of the House to be forced out through scandal. The attacks later turned out to be driven by false accusations. The same year, Cheney underwent quadruple by-pass heart surgery.

Author Michael Parenti attributed the political attacks to the questions Wright was raising with regard to Reagan-supported CIA covert actions in Nicaragua.[15] Wright not only criticized Reagan's policy, but took steps to enter into negotiations with the Nicaraguan government.

In 1989, after the election of George H.W. Bush, Cheney became Secretary of Defense when Bush's first choice, John Tower, was rejected by the Senate for personal misconduct. There is reason to believe Cheney was behind the demise of Tower's nomination as well.

During the run-up to the 1990-91 Persian Gulf War, Cheney was briefed by General Norman Schwarzkopf about Iraqi threats against Kuwait. Iraq invaded Kuwait soon after.

Cheney responded to the threat to U.S. interests in Kuwait by flying to Saudi Arabia to ask King Fahd to allow U.S. troops into his country. To convince the King, Cheney's staff at the Pentagon claimed that 250,000 Iraqi troops with 1,500 tanks were massed on the Saudi border. The photographic evidence, however, was never made public and Soviet satellite imagery taken that day showed no troops near the border. Cheney was getting his intelligence at the time from 9/11 suspect Duane Andrews, who is covered in Chapter 15.

Early the next year, journalist Jean Heller learned about the contradiction in the Soviet satellite imagery and revealed it to Dick Cheney's office at the Pentagon. Cheney and his staff ignored Heller's story, as did most of the media. The aerial bombardment of Iraq, initiating Operation Desert Storm, began days later.

Along with Israel, the U.S. government had promoted and exacerbated the eight-year long Iran-Iraq War that had ended just two years earlier. The U.S. had provided chemical weapons to Saddam Hussein, a fact that was emphasized by Rumsfeld's 1984 visit to Iraq and his famous handshake with Saddam.

Despite having supported Iraq, hypocritical claims of the dangers posed by such Iraqi weapons were used to petition the American public for intervention in 1990. Also used was the televised testimony of Kuwaitis such as the fifteen-year old Nayirah, who was coached to tell lies by the public relations firm Hill & Knowlton. Meanwhile, Nayirah's cousin Mish'al Al-Sabah was running KuwAm Corporation with 9/11 suspect Wirt Walker (see Chapter 12).

When the Gulf War ended, Cheney hired a company called Halliburton to put out 320 oil well fires, and he hired the Halliburton subsidiary Brown and Root to rebuild infrastructure in Kuwait. A few years later, Cheney would become CEO of Halliburton.

In 1992, Cheney's Defense Department paid Halliburton nearly $9 million to evaluate how to downsize the U.S. military. The same year, Halliburton was selected by the U.S. Army Corps of Engineers to provide all the logistics services for the military for five years. This massive and unprecedented "LOGCAP" contract resulted from a plan that Halliburton itself had drawn up.

Cheney's term as Secretary of Defense was over a few months later when Bill Clinton was elected president. The defeat of George H.W. Bush in his re-election bid could be seen as another political loss for

Cheney. However, the militaristic policies of the Bush/Cheney team would soon be vindicated by a new threat.

Shortly after Clinton's victory, in December 1992, a terrorist group called al Qaeda was blamed for a series of bombings in Yemen. Just two months later, the WTC was bombed. Although the WTC bombing was not initially blamed on al Qaeda, prior to 9/11 three other attacks would be attributed to that group. The others were the shooting down of U.S. helicopters in Somalia in 1993, the bombings of U.S. embassies in Africa in 1998, and the *USS Cole* incident in 2000.[16]

Meanwhile the Mujahideen in Afghanistan, which had been funded and trained by the CIA and the Pakistani ISI to fight against the Soviets, was dispersing. And the holdings of the covert operations network BCCI were bought up by the government of the United Arab Emirates (UAE). The U.S. counterterrorism guru, Richard Clarke, would soon become a personal friend and representative of the UAE government, as discussed in Chapter 6.

In 1994, Cheney was offered the job of Halliburton's CEO. Although he had no experience in business management, he did have experience securing government contracts for the company.

Clinton signed an embargo order that same year, prohibiting U.S. companies from doing business that would benefit the Iranian oil industry. A year later this became a near total U.S. embargo on Iran, just as Cheney took the Halliburton job. Although the company was awarded $2.3 billion in federal contracts during Cheney's five years as CEO, Halliburton didn't pay much attention to the laws regarding business with Iran.

For example, in 1997 an Iraqi-Canadian named Abdulamir Mahdi ordered $41,000 worth of Halliburton spare parts for an oil processing facility in Iran. Halliburton went ahead and violated the U.S. embargo and the equipment was shipped to Iran. Mahdi was later arrested and received a four-year sentence but Halliburton was never charged.[17] While Cheney was still CEO, Halliburton opened an office in Tehran and ended its presence in Iraq.

Cheney negotiated Halliburton's 1998 purchase of Dresser Industries for $7.7 billion. Dresser was the industrial-intelligence front that gave George H.W. Bush his start in business.[18] Suspect L. Paul Bremer, discussed in Chapter 11, was a director for another company in partnership with Dresser Industries that had patented a thermite demolition device in 1996.[19]

After the Halliburton-Dresser merger, a number of asbestos-related lawsuits were filed against the company. The claims ultimately caused the value of the company's stock to fall 80 percent in one year.[20]

In 1999, Dick Cheney and Donald Rumsfeld joined the advisory board of Salomon Smith Barney (SSB). On September 11, 2001, that investment firm occupied all but ten floors of WTC building 7.

When George W. Bush decided to run for president shortly thereafter, he asked Cheney to help him find a vice-presidential running mate. Cheney put unusual amounts of effort into "screening" all the candidates for the job. The process appeared to be akin to the collection of sensitive information on potential political enemies. Ultimately, Bush told the press that he had chosen Cheney, who had side-stepped the vetting process, to be his running mate. All the sensitive information that Cheney had collected on the others was stored away for future use.

Cheney quit Halliburton in August to campaign as Bush's vice-president. He left the company with a stock payoff worth $30 million. Just two months later, Halliburton announced layoffs and that it was under a grand jury investigation for over-billing the government of California.

Cheney suffered his fourth heart-attack in November, 2000, just before the election. A week after the vote, it was reported that Halliburton stock had lost between $3 and $4 billion of its total market value due to the Dresser Industries asbestos problem.

During Cheney's tenure as CEO, Halliburton sold millions of dollars in supplies to Iraq's oil industry. The deals were done through old subsidiaries of Dresser Industries and under the oversight of the United Nations Oil for Food Program. Halliburton worked with Iran and Libya as well, via subsidiaries, despite those countries being identified as sponsors of terrorism.[21]

Nonetheless, Cheney was sworn in as Vice President of the United States on January 19, 2001. He and Rumsfeld had to resign from their board positions with SSB, the major WTC building 7 tenant, due to their new positions.

Eight days later, President Bush announced the formation of what would be a secret energy task force (the National Energy Policy Development Group) led by Cheney. The group held meetings with oil and gas industry representatives, which included discussion of dividing up the oil reserves of the Iraqi nation.[22]

Cheney's energy task force presented a report in May which recommended the adoption of a specific national energy policy. That same month, President Bush announced that he was putting Cheney in charge of a new Office of National Preparedness that would work closely with the federal Emergency Management Administration (FEMA). This new office was to direct a number of federal agencies, including the Department of Defense, to prepare for "consequence management" related to attacks against the nation.[23]

A month later, in response to a request from the U.S. Government Accountability Office (GAO) about his secret energy task force, Cheney released some miscellaneous documents. The documents were not responsive to the specific request, however, and further requests by the GAO for additional information were denied by Cheney's office.[24]

Conflict continued over the lack of transparency regarding the energy task force. Seeking to deflect an inquiry, Cheney sent a letter to Congress stating that the GAO's demand for documents compromised "the confidentiality of communications among a President, a Vice-President, the President's other senior advisors, and others."[25]

Cheney's war with the GAO over the public's right to know was interrupted on September 11, when the energy task force's plan suddenly became viable.

Dick and Don on 9/11

Cheney was at the White House on the morning of 9/11. That morning, he had an unusual meeting with Sean O'Keefe, who was deputy assistant to the president and Deputy Director of the Office of Management and Budget. O'Keefe had been a close colleague of Cheney at the Pentagon and served as Secretary of the Navy under George H.W. Bush.

The meeting with O'Keefe was remarkable in that, unlike Cheney's normal meetings, it was unscheduled and lasted longer than Cheney normally allowed, even pushing out another scheduled appointment. Although the conversation seemed urgent, "In time, neither man would be able to recall what it was that had been so important."[26]

The attacks began as Cheney and O'Keefe were meeting in Cheney's office. O'Keefe then left and Cheney began another meeting with his speechwriter. It was reported that other members of the White House staff began to congregate there until the Secret Service came in to move the vice president to the lower levels.

When questioned by the 9/11 Commission, Secretary of Transportation Norman Mineta testified that he came to the PEOC in the basement of the Pentagon around 9:20 a.m., and Cheney was already there. Mineta said that Cheney had an exchange with a "young man" who came in and out over a period of time, giving Cheney updates about an incoming plane and asking if "the orders still stand."[27]

Mineta's testimony indicated that Cheney was aware of Flight 77 as it was approaching Washington, before the official account says that anyone knew, and that he had issued orders about that incoming plane. What those orders were has never been revealed but Mineta has consistently stood by his testimony.

As the attacks were beginning, SECDEF Rumsfeld was finishing a breakfast meeting with Pentagon leaders. Attendees said that at this meeting Rumsfeld predicted that a "shocking" world event would occur in the near future, one that would remind people of the need for a strong U.S. military.[28]

By the time that the second plane hit the WTC, Rumsfeld had moved on to a meeting with his CIA briefer. Reports vary on where he was after that, but national security advisor Condoleezza Rice claimed that she could not reach him.[29]

Some said that Rumsfeld continued with regularly scheduled meetings after the second strike, and that he was on a roll with his predictions that morning. Apparently, he told Congressman Christopher Cox "Believe me, this isn't over yet. There's going to be another attack, and it could be us."[30] Minutes later, the Pentagon was hit.

Regardless of where he was between the WTC and Pentagon strikes, it is clear that throughout the attacks Rumsfeld failed to lead the defense of the nation. And that failure continued. After the Pentagon was hit, Rumsfeld wandered out to the parking lot for approximately 30 minutes. His presence there showed that he was not concerned about the remaining planes that were reported to have been hijacked and that he was not considering the danger to other potential targets. It was as if he knew what to expect.

To explain his behavior, Rumsfeld later stated; "I wanted to see what had happened. I wanted to see if people needed help. I went downstairs and helped for a bit with some people on stretchers. Then I came back up here and started—I realized I had to get back up here and get at it."[31]

Rumsfeld would have been expected to immediately concern himself with the work of his direct subordinate, NORAD commander Ralph Eberhart. However, Rumsfeld did not appear to be worried about the nation's air defenses at all. As discussed in Chapter 8, NORAD's inexplicable failures and Eberhart's lying to Congress afterward left much to be concerned about.

Rumsfeld should also have been very concerned about the defense communication failures that were occurring on 9/11. Those problems will be discussed in the chapter on Duane Andrews.

Dick and Don were running the show on 9/11 and for that reason alone they should be top suspects in the crimes. But they also led the response to 9/11, and their actions in that regard give further evidence that they were involved from the start.

Following 9/11, Rumsfeld led the military planning and execution of the U.S. invasion of Afghanistan and the 2003 invasion of Iraq. Rumsfeld pushed hard to send as small a force as possible to both conflicts. This limitation of force was referred to as the Rumsfeld Doctrine.

Although he can claim to have been acting under orders from the President, Rumsfeld was fully aware that the justifications for both the Iraq and Afghanistan wars, which were largely based on the official narrative of 9/11, were false. That the U.S. had apparently planned to invade both Iraq and Afghanistan in advance of 9/11 was a subject that Rumsfeld did not discuss.

Cheney was a central character in production of the false, warmongering claims. For example, in August 2002, he told an audience of veterans, "There's no doubt that Saddam Hussein now has weapons of mass destruction [and that he will use them] against our friends, against our allies and against us." The world soon discovered that this was untrue and that the Iraq War was built entirely on lies. Dick and Don were behind a lot of it.[32]

Rumsfeld was also responsible for putting in place the people who destroyed Iraq after the 2003 invasion. Two such people, L. Paul Bremer and Bernard Kerik, will be discussed in later chapters. Moreover, Rumsfeld was primarily responsible for the immoral and illegal torture techniques used at prison facilities such as Abu Ghraib and Guantanamo Bay.[33]

The other 9/11 suspects are all connected to Dick and Don in some way, and a number of them have been close colleagues for many years. Together they represent a convergence of organizations like the RAND Corporation, PNAC, SAIC, the Carlyle Group, and the COG program players. Some of these suspects appear to have played roles in the Iran-Contra crimes and in the false justifications for the Gulf War.

The next chapter reviews some important history related to the private network of operatives that formed in the late 1970s, and how that history evolved. Two men played significant roles in that evolution and they both just happened to be linked in suspicious ways to the events of 9/11.

Chapter 3

✈

Carlucci, Armitage, and the Deep State

People who were closely associated with Dick and Don should be investigated for 9/11 crimes if they were in positions to be involved. Richard Armitage and Frank Carlucci are two such people. They each played important roles with respect to the events of September 11, 2001 and, prior to that, both had a colorful history of covert operations which intertwined and was aligned with the careers of Dick and Don. Armitage and Carlucci also benefited from the War on Terror by way of profits made after 9/11.

For the twelve years prior to the attacks, Frank Carlucci ran the Carlyle Group, an investment firm with close ties to the most powerful members of the Reagan and Bush I administrations, and to the Saudi Arabian oil industry. The two major operating subsidiaries of that company were BDM international, for which Carlucci was chairman, and the Vinnell Corporation. Working for Carlucci at BDM from 1989 to 1996 was its vice president, Barry McDaniel, who left to become the chief operating officer (COO) for an alarmingly suspicious company called Stratesec. That was the security company that had contracts for so many of the facilities associated with the 9/11 attacks.

On September 11, 2001, Carlucci was meeting with Carlyle investors at the Ritz Carlton Hotel in Washington, DC, along with the brother of Osama bin Laden.[1] Former president George H.W. Bush had been meeting with them the previous day. Today, McDaniel is business partners with one of Dick Cheney's closest former colleagues, Bruce Bradley, whose colleague Alan Woods is mentioned below.[2]

Armitage was one of the signatories of a 1998 letter to President Clinton from PNAC, calling for military intervention against Saddam Hussein in Iraq. In 2001, Armitage was the Deputy Secretary of State reporting to Colin Powell. He was involved in the secure video teleconference run by Richard Clarke that failed to respond to the hijacked airliners. The week of 9/11, in Washington, Armitage met with General Mahmud Ahmed, the head of Pakistani Inter-Services Intelligence (ISI) who reportedly ordered $100,000 to be wired to the alleged hijackers.[3] Moreover, Armitage was a director at ChoicePoint, which provided DNA testing on 9/11 victims through its subsidiary, Bode Technology.

At the time of the attacks, Armitage was the boss of Marc Grossman, Undersecretary of State for Political Affairs, and Grant S. Green, Undersecretary of State for Management. It has been reported that Grossman met with General Ahmed as well, prior to 9/11.[4] As Undersecretary of Management, Green was responsible for administration of U.S. embassies abroad as well as coordination with the president on key management issues, and he supervised the State Department's Office of White House Liaison.

Green's position in the State Department put him in control of the Bureau of Consular Affairs, which issued visas to foreign nationals. The Bureau's new express visa program, instituted under the leadership of Armitage and Green, provided visas to five of the alleged 9/11 hijackers. Ten of the other alleged hijackers had previously received their visas in the same U.S. consulate office in Saudi Arabia. The express program made an already bad system worse because the new process was one in which "The issuing officer has no idea whether the person applying for the visa is actually the person (listed) in the documents and application."[5] That is, in terms of the visas anyone could have taken the place of the alleged hijackers and Armitage and Green were in a position to supervise that dubious process.

Therefore Carlucci, Armitage and Green had noteworthy connections to 9/11. Furthermore, Green's background recalls the secret history of Armitage and Carlucci, two men who greatly influenced U.S. government policy in the three decades before 9/11.

Some History

Frank Carlucci was one of the oldest and closest friends of Donald Rumsfeld, whose role as Secretary of Defense on 9/11 was central to the events of that day. They were college roommates together at Princeton and Rumsfeld brought Carlucci into his first position in the federal government at the Office of Economic Opportunity (OEO). Carlucci went on to become Deputy Director of Nixon's Office of Management and Budget (OMB), and was later appointed ambassador to Portugal by President Ford.

Like Richard Clarke, Robert Gates, and Paul Wolfowitz, Carlucci's career as a powerbroker in the U.S. federal government transcended political affiliation. That might be due to his charm and ability to work with others, or it might be that he worked on behalf of a deep state structure that transcended political parties. His history suggests the latter.

Before joining the Carter Administration as Deputy Director of the CIA in 1977, Carlucci had a long history of being implicated in world-changing covert operations. According to the *London Times*, he was "accused of plotting the 1961 assassination of Patrice Lumumba, who won independence for the Congo; the overthrow of Chilean president Salvador Allende; coups in Brazil and Zanzibar; and numerous other covert actions."[6]

Carlucci denied these accusations and none were proven, but such claims continued. It was reported that Carlucci "was also accused by Italian communists of being behind the kidnapping of Aldo Moro, and subverting the revolutionary process in Portugal." In Central America, the spokesman for the Sandinista Front in Nicaragua told reporters that Carlucci "has been a specialist in dirty work and coup attempts in the Third World."[7]

Carlucci was also "very close friends" with Ted Shackley, a man who was at the center of the private network of covert operatives created after the U.S. government began to cut back CIA activities in the mid-1970s.[8] Shackley and his associate Thomas Clines knew Carlucci from the 1973 U.S-led coup in Chile, for which Carlucci arranged funding via his role in the OMB. It was Shackley, with help from George H.W.

Bush, who maneuvered Carlucci into the position of Deputy Director of the CIA.[9]

Shackley had a long, close working relationship with Richard Armitage as well. While Carlucci was working in the Nixon Administration and later in Portugal, Shackley and Armitage were funding covert operations from Southeast Asia by way of drug trafficking. Vast amounts of cash were smuggled out of Vietnam via this operation, along with military armaments, by Clines and another associate, Richard Secord.[10]

In 1975, Secord was transferred to Iran as chief of the Air Force's Military Advisory Assistance Group. With Shackley, Clines and others, Secord established an arms sales company called Egyptian American Transport and Service Corporation (EATSCO). Later EATSCO was convicted of embezzling millions of dollars from the Pentagon. In the mid-1980s, Secord worked for The Vinnell Corporation, a fact which surfaced during the Iran-Contra investigations.[11]

Another person referred to as a "silent partner" in EATSCO was Erich Von Marbod, who later became Carlucci's special assistant at a company called Sears World Trade (SWT). Von Marbod was also the long-time mentor of Richard Armitage, having supervised him in operations in Vietnam and Iran. In September 1975, when Secord was relocated there, Von Marbod went to Tehran as the personal representative of defense secretary James Schlesinger. Armitage followed with his own "entourage."[12]

In 1979, as the Shah was falling from power, Von Marbod negotiated (or extorted) a memorandum of understanding from the Iranian government which essentially gave power of attorney to the United States government to terminate all of Iran's military contracts. The document put Iran in a difficult situation with respect to armaments just as it was facing a potential war with Iraq.[13]

Unofficial U.S. aid to the Mujahideen in Afghanistan also began in the summer of 1979. Proxy agents coordinated by the Safari Club, a private network formed by representatives from several countries, had been invading Afghanistan for about a year prior to that. The U.S. aid to the Mujahideen, a coalition of rebel groups from which al Qaeda originated, officially did not start until 1980 but went on for many years under the name Operation Cyclone. This operation relied heavily on using the Pakistani ISI as an intermediary for funds and weapons distribution, military training, and financial support.

With help from the CIA, the ISI armed and trained over 100,000 insurgents between 1978 and 1992.[14] The Mujahideen, and therefore ultimately al Qaeda, was supported by the U.S. and the ISI during the time when Frank Carlucci was working as Deputy Director of the CIA, leading the Department of Defense, and acting as CEO of SWT, which was discovered to be an arms sales consultant firm. During this time, Armitage was a major driver of this policy, traveling to Pakistan and Afghanistan and even meeting directly with Mujahideen leaders.[15]

In 1980, Secord helped plan the efforts to rescue the U.S. hostages held in Iran. Although Secord's involvement has only been cited for the second plan, which was never attempted, concerns were raised that the original plan was sabotaged for political purposes.

Coincidentally, David Rubenstein, the founder of The Carlyle Group, had access to the first, secret plan that resulted in a failed rescue attempt when he was "shuffling through some papers in the president's inbox." Rubenstein was actually in the president's office by himself one night, supposedly looking for a memo. Dan Briody wrote that "President Carter questioned Rubenstein about his late-night foray into his office, asking him pointedly and repeatedly what he had seen while he was there."[16]

The rescue operation appears to have failed through a hard to believe sequence of mechanical problems with the helicopters. It was a challenging plan but it never really got off the ground at all.[17] Initially, one of six helicopters failed due to rotor blade malfunction, then a second failed in a sandstorm (the common notion is that all of them failed in this way), then a third helicopter failed by way of a faulty hydraulic pump. Finally, a ground-based refueling accident resulted in the deaths of nine people. It was at this time that "Carter's presidency did not recover."[18]

Sears World Trade

Considering the Kuwaiti links of Stratesec CEO Wirt D. Walker, including his leadership of Stratesec's Kuwaiti-based parent company starting in 1982,[19] it is interesting that Ted Shackley also began working in Kuwait in the early 1980s. It was George H.W. Bush, whose family has many ties to Walker, who helped Shackley get established in Kuwait in the oil business.[20]

Back in the U.S. at this time, Frank Carlucci was one of the most powerful people in government. He was Deputy Secretary of Defense from 1981 through 1982, while Armitage served as deputy assistant secretary and then assistant secretary. Despite having this important job, Carlucci left government to run the mysterious SWT for a few years at the height of his government career. After SWT lost tens of millions of dollars in apparently aimless endeavors, Carlucci returned to become Reagan's National Security Advisor (NSA), and then Secretary of Defense.

Just before leaving his position as Deputy Secretary of Defense, in 1982, Carlucci did a favor for Secord. After being suspended from his DOD job for three months while he was being investigated by the FBI about his links to EATSCO, Secord was reinstated by Carlucci. Secord retired a year later and established Stanford Technology Trading Group International, which used a complex web of secret Swiss bank accounts and shell corporations to build "a lucrative Enterprise from covert-operations business assigned to them by Lt. Col. Oliver L. North."[21]

It was at this time that Carlucci left his DOD post for SWT, a company which was ostensibly meant to be a simple trading company. Through review of the company's operations, however, Fortune Magazine suggested that SWT was actually "providing cover jobs for US intelligence operations." The accusation was supported when the *Washington Post* revealed the existence of a secret SWT subsidiary called IPAC.

Carlucci joined SWT when Roderick M. Hills, former Chairman of the U.S. Securities and Exchange Commission, was its chairman. Hills quickly noticed that he was no longer in charge. In an interview with author Joseph Trento, Hills remarked that he was — "shocked to see that Carlucci hired Von Marbod when we all knew he was under criminal investigation… When I went down to the Sears World Trade Washington office across from the National Archives, the place looked like spook central. Carlucci was answering to a higher authority, and I don't think it had anything to do with world trade for profit."[22] Hills resigned in April 1984, leaving SWT to Carlucci.

Carlucci hired Von Marbod at a salary of $200,000 per year. The company had 1,100 employees in offices around the world but Von Marbod worked with Carlucci in Washington, DC. Carlucci hired some other interesting people to run this "spook central" operation. There was:

- S. Linn Williams, a Princeton graduate who was the Vice President and General Counsel for SWT. For many years after his stint there, Williams was with Gibson Dunn & Crutcher, the law firm that employed U.S. Customs Commissioner Robert Bonner, who played an important role in the identification of the alleged 9/11 hijackers; and Ted Olson, whose testimony was critical to the official story about Flight 77.[23]

- Arthur P. Ismay was SWT's Director of Countertrade. An important function for SWT, countertrade was also critical to Iran's ability to obtain the arms it needed at the time. From July 1962 to June 1964 Ismay was the Officer-In-Charge of the presidential yacht USS Sequoia. President Kennedy held strategy meetings on the Sequoia during the Cuban Missile Crisis, and had his last birthday party on the yacht. Ismay later said he had information implicating a colleague in the Kennedy assassination.[24] He was never questioned about it and, instead, he was told to destroy the ship's logbook.[25] Ismay went on to become a swift boat commander in Vietnam. After military service, he worked for Rockwell International, the company that was the predecessor to Stratesec's sister companies, Aviation General and Commander Aircraft.[26]

- Alan Woods was Vice President of Technology for SWT from 1983 to 1985. In his book, Dick Cheney mentioned the importance of the firm Bradley Woods to his own career in the 1970s. And recall that Stratesec COO Barry McDaniel is now in close business partnership with Woods partner, Bruce Bradley. Woods had previously served in the Ford DOD as Assistant Secretary for Public Affairs; Special Assistant to the Secretary (Rumsfeld); and as Deputy Director of Presidential Personnel at the White House. After his time with SWT, Woods became a U.S. Trade Representative in the Reagan Administration.

SWT is also where Grant Green comes into the picture. As stated before, Green's role as Undersecretary of Management in 2001, under Armitage, put him in a position to supervise the issuance of visas to a number of the alleged 9/11 hijackers.

Green worked for SWT during the same four years as Carlucci, from 1983 through 1986. In fact, he was Carlucci's assistant at SWT and then followed Carlucci to the Reagan Administration, serving as Special Assistant to the President on National Security Affairs while Carlucci was Reagan's National Security Advisor (NSA).[27] In December 1987, Reagan nominated Green as Assistant Secretary of Defense and Green served in that role for two years under Carlucci, who became Secretary of Defense.

For some reason, Green has made a point of being secretive about his connection to another company created and run by Frank Carlucci. His resume does not list the company name but only refers to it as a "Major Consulting and Marketing Company."[28] From 1989 to 1996, Green was Executive Vice President and Chief Operating Officer of this mysterious firm. Through his political contributions, we can see that this was IPAC, or the International Planning and Analysis Center.[29]

As author Dan Briody wrote, "Using a subsidiary of SWT called the International Planning and Analysis Center, Carlucci consulted on the buying and selling of anti-aircraft missiles, radar, jets, and other military equipment for the United States and Canada. IPAC was loaded with ex-military, and also provided consulting to Third World countries. But nobody within SWT even knew about it."[30] And although SWT lasted only four years after suffering huge, inexplicable losses, IPAC went on for years after that and conducted business in a secret way similar to that used to accomplish the Iran-Contra crimes.

Given the fact that anti-aircraft missiles were just the kind of arms that Iran was being sold through the Iran-Contra deals, and that SWT was conducting this consulting at the very same time, it is highly likely that Carlucci's company was coordinating the arms sales to Iran. The *Philadelphia Inquirer* suggested exactly that, saying "this hallowed American institution [Sears] served as consultant in the Iranian arms sale."[31] Furthermore, the SWT-consulted arms sales were said to be accomplished with "funding from the State Department's Agency for International Development." The leaders of the U.S. State Department at the time included Paul Wolfowitz, who was deputy secretary of defense on 9/11.

A Familiar Failure to Investigate and Prosecute

In November 1986, just a month after SWT was dissolved, the Tower Commission was appointed by President Reagan to investigate the Iran-Contra scandal. The commissioners included Senator John Tower, former NSA Brent Scowcroft, and former Secretary of State Edmund Muskie. Stephen Hadley, who would be Deputy NSA on 9/11, was counsel for the commission. It was revealed that military arms including TOW anti-tank missiles and Hawk anti-aircraft missiles were sent to Iran with the help of two middlemen: Manucher Ghorbanifar and Adnan Khashoggi. CIA Director William Casey was thought to have conceived the plan, although Ted Shackley and Michael Ledeen were also central characters. Casey was reported to be stricken ill hours before he would testify and he died under mysterious circumstances just six days later.

In November 1987, a report was issued by the "Congressional committees investigating the Iran-Contra Affair," led by Democrat Lee Hamilton and Republican Dick Cheney. The report stated that Reagan's administration exhibited "secrecy, deception and disdain for the law." Hamilton chose not to investigate Reagan or Vice President Bush, however, saying that he did not think it would be "good for the country" to put the public through another impeachment trial.[32]

Hamilton's report mentioned that the missiles involved "were sold from Israeli stock with U.S. approval. The remaining materiel came from U.S. stocks." In other words, at least some of the weapons sold to Iran as part of the Iran-Contra crimes came through the Army

Materiel Command (AMC), at the time managed by Barry McDaniel and his colleagues.

During the years when Carlucci was running SWT and IPAC, McDaniel was the Deputy Director for Readiness at the U.S. AMC. McDaniel was the main logistics administrator for AMC's commanding general, Richard H. Thompson. McDaniel was responsible for procuring and fielding all of the weapons systems for the Army — a job that entailed spending tens of billions of dollars to buy and maintain tanks, helicopters, missiles, sensors, and communications equipment.

In an interview as he was leaving the job in 1988, McDaniel recalled his supervision of the military's acquisition officers worldwide.[33] He also made mention of the importance of the Southwest Asia Petroleum Distribution Project (SWAPDOP) during his tenure. Apparently, pipelines and petroleum in this area of the world, which includes the Middle East, Afghanistan, Iran and Pakistan, had something to do with the deployment of U.S. Army materiel during the mid 1980s. What McDaniel's role in that deployment was, and what it might have had to do with arming the Mujahideen, is not yet clear.

Independent counsel Lawrence Walsh continued the appearance of an investigation into Iran-Contra until issuing his final report in 1993. It gradually emerged that Secord, Armitage, Casey, Clines, Shackley, Oliver North, John Singlaub, and Edwin Wilson were involved in the conspiracy to provide arms to the Contras. Walsh accused Armitage of providing false testimony during the investigation.

Although NSA John Poindexter and Oliver North were convicted in the case, those convictions were ultimately overturned. And none of the investigations pursued links between Frank Carlucci, SWT, or IPAC in the Iran-Contra affair. Ironically, Carlucci came back to the Reagan Administration just as these investigations were beginning as a replacement for Poindexter, in order to calm public concerns. Carlucci was backed for the job by defense secretary Caspar Weinberger, Secretary of State George Shultz, and CIA director Casey.[34]

When George H.W. Bush became president he set about rewarding those who had helped cover-up the Iran-Contra crimes. Bush appointed Armitage as a negotiator and mediator in the Middle East.

Brent Scowcroft became his NSA and John Tower was nominated to be Secretary of Defense. When the Senate refused to confirm Tower, Bush gave the job to Cheney. Later, six people who had been charged with offenses related to Iran-Contra, including PNAC members Weinberger and Elliott Abrams, were pardoned by Bush.

Carlucci's tenure as Secretary of Defense resulted in an investigation into vast corruption at the Pentagon, called Operation Ill Wind. This investigation initially focused on Melvyn Paisley, who was a Navy contracts specialist in DOD and a consultant for BDM International. Not long afterward, the Carlucci-run Carlyle Group bought BDM and Carlucci became chairman of the company. He immediately brought in former Kissinger assistant Phillip Odeen and future Stratesec COO Barry McDaniel.

Ultimately, the lack of thorough investigation and prosecution of those responsible for Iran-Contra led to "strengthening the very institutions that made their abuses possible."[35] As a result, long-time covert operatives like Richard Armitage and Frank Carlucci were able to carry on with the same kinds of special operations that subvert democracy through secrecy and abuse of the public trust.

Years later, Armitage and Carlucci, along with Cheney, McDaniel, Green and Rumsfeld, were in positions to make the attacks of September 11 an extraordinary sequel to the Iran-Contra crimes. These men should certainly be among those investigated for their possible roles in the attacks 9/11.

With regard to al Qaeda, it appears that Carlucci and Armitage both worked with al Qaeda's predecessor, the Mujahideen, when that alliance was being funded and trained by the CIA and ISI. Armitage was later in a position to oversee the provision of visas to the alleged hijackers.

The next two chapters review evidence suggesting that leaders of the U.S. intelligence community facilitated terrorism by failing to investigate, and therefore protecting, terrorist suspects in the years leading up to 9/11.

Chapter 4

Louis Freeh and the FBI

In the summer of 2001, Federal Bureau of Investigation (FBI) agent Robert Wright, a counterterrorism expert from the Chicago office, made some startling claims about the Bureau in a written statement outlining the difficulties he had doing his job. Three months before 9/11, he wrote: "The FBI has proven for the past decade it cannot identify and prevent acts of terrorism against the United States and its citizens at home and abroad. Even worse, there is virtually no effort on the part of the FBI's International Terrorism Unit to neutralize known and suspected terrorists residing within the United States."[1]

Revelations since 9/11 have confirmed Wright's claims. FBI management did little or nothing to stop terrorism in the decade before 9/11 and, in some cases, appeared to have supported terrorists. This is more disturbing considering that the power of the FBI over terrorism investigations was supreme. In 1998, the FBI's strategic plan stated that terrorist activities fell "almost exclusively within the jurisdiction of the FBI" and that "the FBI has no higher priority than to combat terrorism."[2]

A number of people are suspect in these failures, including the leaders of the FBI's counterterrorism programs. But at the time of Wright's written complaint, which was not shared with the public until May 2002, the man most responsible was Louis Freeh, Director of the FBI from 1993 to 2001.

Agent Wright was not FBI leadership's only detractor, and not the only one to criticize Freeh. The public advocacy law firm Judicial Watch, which prosecutes government abuse and corruption, rejoiced at the news of Freeh's March 2001 resignation.[3] Judicial Watch pointed to a "legacy of corruption" at the FBI under Freeh, listing the espionage scandal at Los Alamos National Laboratories, as well as "Filegate, Waco, the Ruby Ridge cover-up, the Olympic bombing frame-up of Richard Jewell, [and] falsification of evidence concerning the Oklahoma City bombing."[4]

Judicial Watch said that Director Freeh believed he was above the law. The group went on to say that Freeh was "a man so corrupt he destroyed the office he led, and a man so cowardly he refuses to face the music for the illegalities he has allegedly committed."[5] To this was added a claim that the FBI under Freeh was being directed by sinister yet unknown forces. "In case after case throughout the 1990's, the FBI seems to have tailored its investigative efforts to fit somebody's pre-arranged script. The question is, who wrote that script—and why?"

Freeh became FBI Director on July 19, 1993, just five months after the first WTC bombing, three months after the Waco siege, and one day before the alleged suicide of Hillary Clinton's former Rose Law Firm associate, deputy White House counsel Vincent Foster. Freeh's predecessor was William Sessions.

Prior to his appointment by President Clinton, Freeh was a federal judge. He had been selected for that position by President George H.W. Bush in 1991. Before that, Freeh had been an Assistant District Attorney for the Southern District of New York and an FBI field agent.

Freeh was involved with U.S. counter-terrorism efforts for many years prior to his appointment as FBI Director in 1993. As an FBI agent he worked for the New York Field Office, which led the FBI's counterterrorism effort. It was later the lead field office for Bin Laden investigations and was the first to establish a Joint Terrorism Task Force (JTTF) of state and federal law enforcement and intelligence personnel. Freeh worked there for seven years until he was promoted to Assistant U.S. Attorney in 1981. Throughout the 1980s, Freeh worked with or for U.S. Attorney Rudy Giuliani, who was mayor of New York City on 9/11.

Although Clinton was a Democrat, after his appointment as FBI Director Freeh immediately began forming alliances with Republicans in Congress. This apparently caused difficulty between the FBI and Clinton's White House. Freeh also developed a secret relationship with his former supporter, former President George H. W. Bush. He used that relationship to communicate with the Saudi royal family without Clinton's knowledge.[6]

Ignoring or Facilitating Domestic Terrorism

Just five months before Freeh's appointment as FBI Director, the World Trade Center (WTC) was bombed in an attack that killed six people and wounded a thousand others. It was blamed on a Pakistani-Kuwaiti by the name of Ramzi Yousef, along with about half a dozen others. However, as the *New York Times* reported, it was clear that the FBI was somehow involved as well.

> "Law-enforcement officials were told that terrorists were building a bomb that was eventually used to blow up the World Trade Center, and they planned to thwart the plotters by secretly substituting harmless powder for the explosives, an informer said after the blast.
>
> The informer was to have helped the plotters build the bomb and supply the fake powder, but the plan was called off by an F.B.I. supervisor who had other ideas about how the informer, Emad A. Salem, should be used, the informer said."[7]

The 1993 WTC bombing was a terrorist operation that had been infiltrated by the FBI but the role that the FBI played in trying to prevent that operation, or allow it to go forward, has never been revealed. What has been revealed is that forensic data was falsified and "conclusions were altered to help the government's case."[8] These facts were revealed by Frederick Whitehurst, the chemist and supervisory special agent in charge of the FBI's crime lab who became a whistleblower. The altered conclusions that Whitehurst described were made under the leadership of Louis Freeh.

A similar case occurred in April 1995, when the Murrah Federal Building in Oklahoma City (OKC) was bombed, killing 168 people including 19 children. Investigators have since learned that the FBI played a role in that bombing as well. Reasons that the OKC bombing was suspicious include the fact that there were secondary explosives found in the building that were not reported as part of the official account. And as with the events of 9/11, the FBI immediately confiscated, and refused to release, security videos that would have revealed what actually happened.[9]

Freeh's colleague and personal friend, Larry Potts, was the FBI supervisor who was responsible for the tragedies at Ruby Ridge in 1992 and Waco in 1993. Potts was then given responsibility for investigating the Oklahoma City bombing.[10] Later it was claimed by one of the convicted conspirators that lead bomber Timothy McVeigh was actually acting under the direction of Potts.[11] As an apparent reward for Potts' performance, in May 1995 Freeh promoted him to be his number two man as Deputy Director of the FBI. Two months later, Freeh removed Potts from that position due to public outrage at the appointment.

On the FBI links to the OKC bombing, Peter Dale Scott wrote, "One such case of a penetrated operation 'gone wrong' in 1993 might be attributed to confusion, bureaucratic incompetence, or the problems of determining when sufficient evidence had been gathered to justify arrests. A repeated catastrophe two years later raises the question whether the lethal outcome was not intended."[12]

The result of the OKC bombing in governmental terms was the passage of a new anti-terrorism law in April 1996. This was a bill that would be mirrored by the USA Patriot Act six years later, and it was described as representing an assault on civil liberties. *The Houston Chronicle* called the bill a "frightening" and "grievous" attack on domestic freedoms. But Louis Freeh supported it.

Because many Congressional representatives opposed the bill, it was passed only after having been watered down. In Freeh's words, it had been "stripped… of just about every meaningful provision."[13] Freeh's call for this legislation to be more restrictive of civil liberties must be considered with the fact that his agency was accused of facilitating the event that precipitated the legislation.

One of the obstacles often cited as a root cause for the FBI not doing its anti-terrorism job effectively was "the Wall." This was a set of procedures that restricted the flow of information between law enforcement officers pursuing criminal investigations and officers pursuing intelligence information via the Foreign Intelligence Surveillance Act (FISA). The procedures, set out in a 1995 memo from Deputy Attorney General (and future 9/11 Commissioner) Jamie Gorelick, were seemingly intended to prevent the loss of evidence, due to technicalities, that might be obtained via a FISA warrant.[14] Because such losses were never actually experienced, later claims about "the Wall" appeared to be weak excuses to explain why information was not shared or actions were not taken.

In July 1996, TWA Flight 800 crashed into the Atlantic Ocean just after taking off from JFK Airport in New York, killing all 230 people on board. Freeh later claimed that "No one knew what brought it down."[15] Curiously, the FBI took over the investigation despite the fact that the National Transportation Safety Board (NTSB) had the authority as established by law. FBI agents then blocked attempts by the NTSB to interview witnesses.[16]

One month after the explosion, chemists at the FBI crime laboratory in Washington found traces of PETN, an explosive component of bombs and surface-to-air missiles, in the wreckage.[17] Despite this, in November 1997, the FBI closed its investigation and announced that "No evidence has been found which would indicate that a criminal act was the cause of the tragedy of TWA flight 800."[18]

This reversal of findings was led by Freeh and Jamie Gorelick. After meeting with Freeh and Gorelick, James Kallstrom, the agent in charge of the New York office where the TWA 800 investigation was being handled, produced several unlikely explanations for the detection of the PETN. Although none of these hypotheses was probable, the FBI was able to convince the media to change the story.[19]

Louis Freeh was leading the FBI during the investigation into the 1993 WTC bombing, at the time of the OKC bombing, and at the time of the crash of TWA Flight 800. All of these events suggest the facilitation, or cover-up, of terrorist acts by the FBI. However, these were not the only indications that Louis Freeh was leading an agency that facilitated terrorism.

Ignoring or Facilitating "Islamic" Terrorism

Before leaving his position in the summer of 2001, Freeh was responsible for overseeing more than a dozen failures related to "Islamic" terrorism and the alleged 9/11 hijackers. Here are the first nine.

1. Between 1989 and 1998, Ali Mohamed was an FBI informant. He was also a U.S. Army Special Forces sergeant and al Qaeda's primary trainer.[20] According to U.S. Attorney Patrick Fitzgerald, Mohamed "trained most of al Qaeda's top leadership – including Bin Laden and Al-Zawahiri – and most of al Qaeda's top trainers. He gave some training to persons who would later carry out the 1993 World Trade Center bombing."[21] Mohamed had been an FBI informant, since at least 1992, and was previously a CIA "contract agent." In a move indicative of U.S. oversight, he transitioned directly from the U.S. Special Forces to fighting and training the Mujahideen in Afghanistan.[22] When he was arrested in 1998, Mohamed was allowed to plea bargain and he has never been brought to trial.

2. In May 1995, FBI agents wrote a memo about what they had learned in their interrogation of Abdul Hakim Murad, a Kuwaiti who allegedly helped bomb the WTC in 1993. Murad told the FBI about another plan to hijack multiple airliners in Asia and crash them into buildings in the U.S., including the WTC. Inexplicably, the FBI memo omitted all of the details the agents had learned about this plot, called Operation Bojinka.[23] In 1996, Murad was convicted of crimes related to Bojinka yet, as author Peter Lance wrote, the FBI seemed to be "go out of its way to avoid even a hint of the plot that was ultimately carried out on 9/11."[24]

3. Gregory Scarpa Jr. was an organized crime figure who, when imprisoned for an unrelated crime in 1996, was located in a cell between Ramzi Yousef and Abdul Hakim Murad. Working

undercover for the FBI, Scarpa was able to gain significant information about an active al Qaeda cell in New York City, and a "treasure trove of al Qaeda plans." After working closely with Scarpa to gain the intelligence, Freeh and his subordinates ended up calling the whole thing a "hoax" and buried the information.[25]

4. On May 15, 1998, an FBI pilot sent his supervisor in the Oklahoma City FBI office a memo, warning that he had observed "large numbers of Middle Eastern males receiving flight training at Oklahoma airports in recent months." The memo went on to suggest that these people were planning terrorist activities. It was sent to the Bureau's Weapons of Mass Destruction unit but no action was ever taken.[26]

5. In July 1999, the FBI was given evidence that KSM was living in the United Arab Emirates.[27] Having been indicted by a U.S. court in January 1996, for the Bojinka plot, KSM was one of the world's most wanted terrorists at the time. The FBI failed to request extradition from the UAE government however, despite the UAE being a "valued counterterrorism ally of the United States."[28]

6. In September 1999, FBI agents showed up at Airman Flight School in Norman, OK, to investigate the school's training of Ihab Ali Nawawi. A suspect in the 1998 embassy bombings who was allegedly the personal pilot of Osama bin Laden, Nawawi had been arrested in Orlando four months before.[29] He has been in U.S. custody ever since but has never been brought to trial. Despite the investigation of Nawawi and the 1998 warning from an OKC FBI pilot, the FBI apparently never thought to keep a closer eye on Airman Flight School. Zacarias Moussaoui and several alleged 9/11 hijackers trained or were seen at the school in 2000 and 2001.

7. In October 1999, Hani El-Sayegh, a suspect in the 1996 Khobar Towers Bombing, was deported from a prison in Atlanta to Saudi Arabia. This was the result of an agreement between Freeh and Prince Naif, Saudi Arabia's interior

minister. After his deportation, El-Sayegh was reportedly tortured as FBI agents watched and submitted questions to his Saudi interrogators. David Vine from the *Washington Post* remarked, "Such practices are sharply at odds with Freeh's oft-stated message about the FBI's need to respect human dignity and the tenets of democracy while fighting crime."[30] Another problem with this incident was that the U.S. had control over a suspect in the 1996 terrorist murder of 19 U.S. servicemen and yet, instead of bringing that suspect to trial, they sent him back to Saudi Arabia. A reporter from *TIME* magazine expressed the problem this way: "Run that one by again: The United States doesn't want to try a man suspected of a bomb attack that killed Americans—and they're sending him home?!"[31] It is presumed that El-Sayegh was ultimately executed by the Saudis.[32]

8. In April 2000, a Pakistani from England named Niaz Khan told the FBI that he was recruited by al Qaeda, trained in Pakistan to hijack planes, and sent to the U.S. for a terror mission, as were several pilots. Khan said that he told the FBI, about a year before 9/11, that al Qaeda planned to hijack airliners in the United States.[33] The FBI confirmed that Khan passed two polygraphs. Yet FBI headquarters supposedly didn't believe Khan and sent him home to London.

9. When two of the alleged 9/11 hijackers, Khalid Al-Mihdhar and Nawaf Al-Hazmi, came to the U.S. in January 2000, they immediately met with Omar Al-Bayoumi, a suspected Saudi government spy and an employee of a Saudi aviation company. Al-Bayoumi, who had been the subject of an FBI investigation in 1998 and 1999, became a very good friend to the two alleged hijackers, setting them up in an apartment and paying their rent.[34] Al-Mihdhar and Al-Hazmi then moved in with a long-time FBI asset, Abdussattar Shaikh, who had been working closely with the Bureau on terrorism cases since 1994. Apparently the FBI was not able to make a timely connection between its suspect Al-Bayoumi or its informant Shaikh and the two alleged 9/11 hijackers they supported for two years prior to 9/11. In 2003, the FBI gave Shaikh $100,000 and closed his contract.[35]

From these nine incidents, we know that FBI management under Freeh was not working to prevent "Islamic" terrorism in the years before 9/11. These examples also suggest that the FBI was suppressing and ignoring information about terrorism, perhaps for the purpose of protecting or co-opting the related terrorist networks. As for al Qaeda, author Lawrence Wright wrote that, in the late 1990s, "Director Freeh repeatedly stressed in White House meetings that al Qaeda posed no domestic threat. Bin Laden didn't even make the FBI's most wanted list until June 1999," nearly a year after the embassy bombings.[36]

In February 2001, Robert Hanssen, a veteran FBI counterintelligence agent, was arrested for espionage.[37] Freeh claimed the CIA and FBI worked very well together to catch Hanssen. Apparently there was no difficulty, of the type later cited by the 9/11 Commission, that supposedly prevented collaboration between the two agencies.

It was claimed that Hanssen, while betraying his country for financial gain, sold a special software program, called PROMIS, to the Russians. William Hamilton, the president of Inslaw—the company that manufactured PROMIS—said that the Russians then sold the program to Osama bin Laden and that it might have played a part in facilitating the 9/11 attacks.[38] This claim was also reported by *The Washington Times* and it was said that the software would have given Bin Laden the ability to monitor U.S. efforts to track him down and also the ability to monitor electronic-banking transactions, enabling money-laundering operations.[39]

PROMIS had a history going back over two decades. In the 1980s, Oliver North of Iran-Contra fame had used the software to create lists of national security threats in conjunction with the secretive Continuity of Government (COG) program. In an interesting coincidence, before his death British Foreign Secretary Robin Cook told the House of Commons that "Al Qaeda" was not really a terrorist group but a database of international Mujahideen and arms smugglers used by the CIA and Saudis.[40]

The Justice Department oversight committee on the use of PROMIS included Rudy Giuliani and, therefore presumably, Louis Freeh. The lawyer for Inslaw, in its legal dealings with the Justice Department, was

Roderick M. Hills, who would shortly thereafter be Frank Carlucci's boss at Sears World Trade.

Investigator Michael Ruppert and his colleagues have proposed that software programs evolving from PROMIS were used on 9/11. The hypothesis involves Mitre Corporation and its contractor PTech, which were known to be operating at the Pentagon on projects that affected the operability of Federal Aviation Administration (FAA) systems.[41]

After 9/11, the FBI did not report known links between PTech and its Saudi investor Yassin al Qadi to the U.S. Customs Department investigation into terrorist financing. This concealment was despite PTech having contracts with many U.S. agencies controlling sensitive information, including the FBI, and Al-Qadi being declared a terrorist financier. It was also known that PTech director Yaqub Mirza had contacts at high levels within the FBI.[42]

Working for the Bush Administration

The month before Hanssen's arrest, George W. Bush was inaugurated as President. The only cabinet-level figure to be retained from the outgoing Clinton administration was CIA Director George Tenet, who was said to be a long-time friend of George H. W. Bush. But Freeh stayed on as well until his unexpected resignation in May that year. Freeh did not give specific reasons for leaving at the time and he remained in the position until June 25.

Having been FBI Director for eight years, Freeh had put most of the FBI's leadership in place. This included his deputy as of 1999, Thomas Pickard, who would go on to be acting director of the FBI from June to September 2001. It also included Dale Watson, head of the FBI's counterterrorism program as of 1999, and the people in his organization. Watson had worked with Freeh in the New York FBI office years before and had worked on the investigations into the U.S. embassy bombings and the bombing of the *USS Cole*. Between FBI assignments, in 1996 and 1997, Watson had been the Deputy Chief of the CIA's Counterterrorism Center.

Working for Watson in the FBI's counterterrorism division was Michael Rolince, the head of the International Terrorism Operations Section (ITOS). Under Rolince were the heads of the Usama Bin laden Unit (UBLU) and the Radical Fundamentalism Unit (RFU).

These men worked with Freeh during the early months of 2001, when three major FBI failures in prevention of terrorism occurred.

1. The first was on March 7, 2001 when, during trial proceedings for the 1998 U.S. embassy bombings in Africa, FBI agent Stephen Gaudin read aloud in court a phone number that had been used by the alleged al Qaeda plotters to plan and execute the embassy attacks.[43] This was the phone number of the "Yemen Hub," which doubled as the home phone of Ahmed Al-Hada, the father-in-law of alleged 9/11 hijacker Khalid Al-Mihdhar. According to U.S. officials, the same phone was purportedly used for planning the *USS Cole* bombing and, later, the 9/11 attacks. The phone number was also published in the British weekly the *Observer*, just five weeks before 9/11. As author Kevin Fenton wrote: "Any of the *Observer's* readers could have called the number and asked for a message to be forwarded to Osama bin Laden."[44] This widely reported FBI gaffe should have alerted al Qaeda to U.S. knowledge of its secret Yemen operations center while also ensuring that anyone listening would know the exact al Qaeda phone number being monitored by U.S. intelligence. Despite this major tip-off, al Qaeda continued to use the phone to plan the 9/11 attacks, until "only weeks before 9/11."[45] Why did the Bureau not work to intercept the calls made in the months and weeks before 9/11 and use them to help stop the attacks?

2. The FBI had Mohamed Atta and one of his colleagues under surveillance in early 2001, according to an FBI informant. The informant later said he was a "million percent positive" that the 9/11 attacks could have been stopped if the FBI had gone after Atta at the time. Instead, FBI handlers steered the informant away from Atta.[46]

3. Several FBI agents, including Dina Corsi, Margaret Gillespie, Doug Miller and Mark Rossini, were involved in a concerted attempt to hide information about Al-Mihdhar and Al-Hazmi from other intelligence officers who almost certainly would have captured the suspects. These acts of inexplicable secrecy included not sharing cables on the subject, not sharing photographs of the suspects, misrepresenting "the Wall" restrictions, and misrepresenting comments from the National Security Law Unit.[47]

The FBI agents noted in the last example were all assigned as liaisons to the CIA's Alec Station unit, focused on Osama Bin Laden. It is surprising that neither Richard Blee, the head of that unit at the time, nor Rodney Middelton, the head of the FBI's UBLU, were ever interviewed by independent journalists about these critical issues. Middleton left the FBI the day before 9/11, and Blee went on to be named CIA station chief in Kabul as the U.S. invasion of Afghanistan began.

Between April and September 2001, several major changes occurred in the FBI's counterterrorism program. In May, the head of the RFU was replaced by Dave Frasca, who would go on to be a central character in the obstruction of opportunities to identify and capture the alleged hijackers. At the same time, Louis Freeh announced his resignation despite not having another job.

Freeh left the FBI on June 25, 2001 with nowhere to go. It was said that he approached acting New Jersey Governor Donald DiFrancesco and offered to serve, without salary, as the state's anti-terrorism "czar." This would have brought Freeh close to the 9/11 attacks in New York City but it didn't happen. Instead, Freeh was apparently doing nothing for the three months before 9/11, or at least doing nothing that we know about. Freeh then took a job as director, counsel, and ethics officer at credit card issuer MBNA.

The final three 9/11-related failures that can be attributed to Freeh, through the subordinates he put in place, are as follows. If any of these had been handled appropriately, the alleged 9/11 hijackers would have been caught and their alleged plans foiled.

1. On July 10, 2001, Phoenix FBI counterterrorism agent Ken Williams sent FBI headquarters what is called the "Phoenix Memo," warning that Osama bin Laden was sending students to U.S. flight schools. Williams listed cases of suspected Arab extremists training in Arizona flight schools and urged the FBI to search for such cases in other cities. The FBI failed to respond to the memo at all and it was dismissed as speculative. As 9/11 Commissioner Bob Kerrey would later point out about the memo, "had it gotten into the works at the — up to the highest possible level, at the very least, 19 guys wouldn't have gotten onto these airplanes with room to spare."[48]

2. In mid-August 2001, Zacarias Moussaoui was arrested in Minnesota. The FBI agents who made the arrest called Moussaoui a "suspected airline suicide attacker." The agents requested permission to search Moussaoui's belongings, including his laptop computer, but they were denied that permission. A week later the FBI supervisor in Minneapolis, trying to get the attention of those at FBI headquarters, said he was trying to make sure that Moussaoui—"did not take control of a plane and fly it into the World Trade Center."[49] Still, FBI headquarters denied the field agents' requests. In May 2002, one of the agents, Coleen Rowley, described this obstruction. She wrote that FBI headquarters personnel "continued to, almost inexplicably, throw up roadblocks and undermine Minneapolis' by-now desperate efforts to obtain a FISA search warrant, long after the French intelligence service provided its information and probable cause became clear. HQ personnel brought up almost ridiculous questions in their apparent efforts to undermine the probable cause. In all of their conversations and correspondence, HQ personnel never disclosed to the Minneapolis agents that the Phoenix Division had, only approximately three weeks earlier, warned of Al Qaeda operatives in flight schools seeking flight training for terrorist purposes! Nor did FBIHQ personnel do much to disseminate the information about Moussaoui to other appropriate intelligence/law enforcement authorities. When, in a desperate 11th hour measure to bypass the FBIHQ roadblock, the

Minneapolis Division undertook to directly notify the CIA's Counter Terrorist Center (CTC), FBIHQ personnel actually chastised the Minneapolis agents for making the direct notification without their approval!"[50]

3. Finally, on August 23, 2001, less than three weeks before 9/11, the CIA formally told the FBI that Al-Mihdhar and Al-Hazmi might be in the United States. But even though the two alleged hijackers had their names listed in the San Diego phone book and had been living with an FBI informant, the Bureau supposedly could not find them.

   FBI agent Robert Fuller, only recently transferred to UBLU, claimed to take the August information and use it to search databases looking for Al-Mihdhar and Al-Hazmi but he said he found nothing. Fuller had another JTTF officer help him search a database run by ChoicePoint, the company known for purging Florida voters in the 2000 presidential election.[51] The Justice Department IG report says Fuller did an NCIC criminal history check, credit checks, and a motor vehicle records search. But the *9/11 Commission Report* clearly contradicted this, saying "Searches of readily available databases could have unearthed the drivers licenses, the car registration, and the telephone listing" all of which were in Al Mihdhar and Al Hazmi's names.[52]

Later it was noted that "the hijackers had contact with 14 people known to the FBI because of counter-terror investigations prior to 9/11."[53] This was known to the 9/11 Commission as its staff director made a clear statement about how close the FBI was to catching the alleged hijackers. "Rather than the hijackers being invisible to the FBI, they were, in fact, right in the middle of the FBI's counterterrorism coverage," said Eleanor Hill. "And yet, the FBI didn't detect them."[54]

All of this certainly seems to suggest that FBI headquarters and Director Freeh had sufficient information to track and capture the alleged 9/11 hijackers. Freeh's close association with the Saudis is also troubling considering the role of suspected Saudi spy Al-Bayoumi. The company Al-Bayoumi worked for, Dallah Al-Baraka, was owned by

Saleh Abdullah Kamel, an alleged member of the "Golden Chain" financiers of Osama bin Laden. And the wife of Freeh's friend Prince Bandar was reported to have sent funding to the alleged hijackers through Al-Bayoumi's wife.[55]

In his resignation speech, Freeh praised the integrity of George W. Bush and the dedication of Dick Cheney. "President Bush has brought great honor and integrity to the Oval Office. It was equally an honor to be appointed by his father to serve as a federal judge. I also wish to thank Vice President Dick Cheney for conducting an effective transition process and for his dedication to duty in serving the Nation," said Freeh.[56]

Going on, Freeh thanked his colleagues at the CIA and emphasized how well the two agencies had worked together. "Through the leadership of Director George Tenet, we have forged an unprecedented relationship with the men and women of the Central Intelligence Agency in the counter-intelligence and counter-terrorism arenas," he claimed. "This, in turn, has enabled us to place greater emphasis on counter-intelligence [and] counter-terrorism."[57]

These remarks are in direct contradiction to the *9/11 Commission Report*, which placed blame for the failure to track down and capture the alleged hijackers on two root causes. The first was that, although the "system was blinking red," the intelligence communities were not working well together, partly because of "the Wall" of procedures that supposedly prevented adequate information sharing between the agencies. The second presumed root cause was that the information needed to stop the attacks did not rise high enough within the FBI and CIA to ensure action would be taken. Neither of these excuses is believable, given the examples already reviewed.

At the end of Freeh's tenure as director, the FBI was under severe criticism from all directions. Patrick Leahy, the chairman of the Senate Judiciary Committee whose office would a few months later be one of the targets of the anthrax attacks, said, "There are some very, very serious management problems at the FBI."[58] Richard Durbin, a Democrat from Illinois, said, "It's hard to believe the situation has deteriorated and disintegrated the way it has. How did this great agency fall so far so fast? The FBI has been starved for leadership."[59]

Nine days after Freeh announced his retirement, the FBI told Timothy McVeigh's attorneys that it had failed to give them about 3,000 pages of documents related to the OKC bombing investigation. "Self-righteous and sanctimonious, Freeh never admitted a personal mistake. He never pointed out his own role in the McVeigh debacle."[60]

If There Is Nothing to Hide, Why Hide It?

Testifying before the 9/11 Congressional Inquiry in October 2002, Freeh said: "I am aware of nothing that to me demonstrates that the FBI and the intelligence community had the type of information or tactical intelligence which could have prevented September 11th. In terms of the FBI's capability to identify, investigate and prevent the nineteen hijackers from carrying out their attacks, the facts so far on the public record do not support the conclusion that these tragic events could have been prevented by the FBI and intelligence community acting by themselves."[61]

This assessment contradicts that of FBI agent Robert Wright, whose written warning prior to 9/11 was ignored. Wright later stated that: "September the 11th is a direct result of the incompetence of the FBI's International Terrorism Unit. No doubt about that. Absolutely no doubt about that. You can't know the things I know and not go public." Agent Wright was prohibited by the U.S. Justice Department from telling all he knew about the pre-9/11 FBI failures. But he added: "There's so much more. God, there's so much more. A lot more."[62]

Why did the FBI, if it had nothing to hide, go into full-blown cover-up mode immediately after the attacks? For example, FBI agents confiscated all of the surveillance videos which would have shown what happened at the Pentagon.[63] The Bureau harassed witnesses in Florida who suggested that the alleged hijackers were not the devout Muslims the official account made them out to be.[64] In Pennsylvania, FBI agents took control of the United 93 crash site and intentionally ignored eyewitness testimony that contradicted the official account.[65]

At the WTC debris collection site, FBI agents were caught stealing evidence.[66]

The FBI also went to great lengths to avoid cooperating with the Joint Congressional Inquiry. For example, the Bureau refused to allow the interviewing or deposing of Abdussattar Shaikh, the FBI informant who had lived with alleged hijackers Al-Mihdhar and Al-Hazmi.[67] Through the FBI's maneuvering, Shaikh was never required to testify. The FBI also tried to prevent the testimony of Shaikh's FBI handler, which occurred only secretly at a later date.

The protection of Abdussattar Shaikh by the FBI makes no sense considering that the Bureau encouraged the torture of other suspects, like Hani El-Sayegh. Alleged al Qaeda associate Abu Zubaydah, who was later found to have nothing to do with al Qaeda, had already been tortured many times to gain information related to 9/11 while Shaikh was allowed to negotiate his entire removal from the 9/11 investigation.[68]

The FBI also failed to cooperate with the 9/11 Commission. According to author Philip Shenon, the FBI was "as uncooperative with the 9/11 Commission as it had been in the Congressional investigation" and was "painfully slow to meet the Commission's initial request for documents and interviews."[69]

The only reasonable explanation for FBI management's behavior in the decade before 9/11 and in the ensuing investigations is that they were somehow complicit in the attacks. But why would Freeh and the FBI want to support the activities of alleged terrorists?

We know that the accused 19 hijackers could not have accomplished most of what needs explaining about 9/11. They could not have disabled the U.S. air defenses, they could not have made the U.S. chain of command fail to respond appropriately, and they could not have caused the destruction of the three tall buildings at the WTC. However, the myth of al Qaeda was a necessary part of the official account and was able to provide a grain of truth in an otherwise unbelievable story.

In 2006 Freeh joined George Tenet on the board of a company that had been flagged, but never investigated, for 9/11 insider trading.[70] He also became the personal attorney for Saudi Prince Bandar who, as stated before, was implicated through his wife in financing of the alleged hijackers. More recently, Freeh was trotted out to pass judgment on the late coach Joe Paterno. But he is in no position to pass judgment on others.

Under Louis Freeh, the FBI failed miserably at preventing terrorism when preventing terrorism was the FBI's primary goal. Moreover, the actions of FBI management suggest that it was facilitating and covering-up acts of terrorism throughout the time that Freeh was the Bureau's director. Fifteen examples have been cited here from the time of Freeh's tenure and three other examples were given from the time just after he left, when it was unclear why he left or what he was doing. Add to these examples the fact that the FBI took extraordinary measures to hide evidence related to the 9/11 attacks and it becomes startlingly clear that Mr. Freeh should be a prime suspect in any honest investigation.

Chapter 5

George Tenet and the CIA

"Everybody assumed that it was Al Qaeda, because the operation looked like Al Qaeda, quacked like Al Qaeda, seemed like Al Qaeda." – Condoleezza Rice[1]

On the morning of 9/11, Director of Central Intelligence (DCI) George Tenet was having breakfast with his long-time mentor, former United States Senator David Boren. According to Tenet's memoirs, Boren had "plucked" him "from obscurity in 1987 to serve as Chief of Staff of the Senate Select Committee on Intelligence (SSCI), which he chaired."[2] Tenet had actually served as the legislative director for Republican Senator John Heinz for several years and had joined the SSCI staff in 1985 before becoming the SSCI staff director.

Tenet certainly was not living in obscurity after getting Boren's endorsement. He quickly moved from SSCI staff director in the Bush I era to join the Clinton transition team and was named a member of the National Security Council when the new president took over. This led to his appointment as Deputy Director of the CIA in 1995, under DCI John Deutch. After Deutch's abrupt resignation in December 1996, Tenet became acting DCI and was officially appointed to the position in July 1997. He was one of the longest-serving agency directors in history, staying in the position twice as long as other DCIs with the only exceptions being Richard Helms (1966 to 1973) and William Casey (1981 to 1987).

David Boren was a Yale graduate and member of Skull & Bones, like George W. Bush would be five years later. After serving four years as Governor of Oklahoma and 15 years in the U.S. Senate, he became the President of the University of Oklahoma, a position he has held since 1994. Boren lives in the suburb of Norman, which is just outside of Oklahoma City (OKC).

There are many connections between the alleged 9/11 hijackers and the area where Boren lives. A motel just outside OKC was frequented by Mohamed Atta, Marwan Al-Shehhi (both alleged suicide pilots), and their alleged accomplice, Zacarias Moussaoui. Curiously, just a few years earlier, convicted OKC bombers Timothy McVeigh and Terry Nichols had stayed at the same motel, "interacting with a group of Iraqis during the weeks before the bombing."[3] Louis Freeh's FBI didn't seem to want this information which was repeatedly provided by the motel owner. In August 2001, the same owner testified that he saw Moussaoui, Atta, and Al-Shehhi at his motel when they came late one night to ask for a room.

Between February and August of 2001, Moussaoui lived in Norman and attended flight school there. According to Moussaoui's indictment, Atta and Al-Shehhi had visited the same flight school in July 2000, but did not take classes.

FBI summary documents, prepared for the 9/11 investigations, state that Mohamed Atta was also spotted at nearby Wiley Post Airport in Bethany, Oklahoma within six months of the 9/11 attacks. An employee at private aviation company Million Air witnessed Atta flying at the airport along with two other alleged 9/11 hijackers, Marwan Al-Shehhi and Waleed Al-Shehri.[4] Other FBI summary documents indicate that Saeed Al-Ghamdi was also seen flying in to Wiley Post Airport on an unspecified date and that Hani Hanjour had made inquiries to a company in The Netherlands that ran a flight school there.[5]

These are startling revelations considering that Hangar 8 of that airport was the home of Aviation General, the aircraft company owned by KuwAm Corporation and run by Wirt Walker, the CEO of KuwAm's subsidiary Stratesec.[6] Walker and Stratesec had pre-9/11 security contracts with the WTC, United Airlines, which owned two of the planes that were destroyed on 9/11, and Dulles Airport where American Airlines Flight 77 took off.

According to a University of Oklahoma librarian, a ticket for one of the alleged hijackers on Flight 93 was purchased by a white American male on one of the University's computers.[7] It has been speculated that the white male was Nick Berg, the American who was supposedly a student in Norman and who was later the victim of a famous al Qaeda kidnapping and beheading. In an alarming coincidence, investigators discovered that Zacarias Moussaoui used Berg's email account to send messages. An implausible story was concocted that Berg had let Moussaoui use the account and his laptop during a 5-minute encounter on a bus.[8]

More on the OKC connection will be found in Chapter 12, which addresses Wirt Walker. But it is important to recognize that the hometown of George Tenet's mentor, David Boren, appears to have been a center of activity related to the alleged 9/11 hijackers.

On 9/11, Boren went from his breakfast meeting with Tenet to join former DCI James Woolsey in producing the media story. Although the U.S. intelligence community claims to have been far from able to reveal and stop the 9/11 plot in advance, Boren seemed to know what the attacks were all about as they happened.

While being interviewed on September 11, Boren said:

> "I think you have to have bin Laden on the suspect list. You probably have some nation states that ought to be on the suspect list as well [Iraq, for example]. You know, looking at this, it's very clear—and I think this hopefully will give us leads to trace back and find and affix responsibility—the training that had to have been there by those who took over the aircraft, the ability to pilot the aircraft. It appears that perhaps they were piloting the aircraft, the knowledge to turn off the transponders that would make it very difficult to trace these aircraft from the ground and through our air control system.
>
> These were people that were highly trained; they knew what they were doing. It was all very carefully coordinated. So we're dealing with people with a lot of sophistication here. Some of that training and some of that preparation is bound to have left clues that hopefully we'll be able to thread through pretty quickly."[9]

There certainly were a lot of clues, and many of them seemed to implicate David Boren and his university. Boren had no intention of mentioning those clues, however. He didn't mention that the airport run by the university where he was president had been training Zacarias Moussaoui to fly. He also failed to point out that Mohamed Atta and other alleged 9/11 hijackers had called, emailed and visited his airport in the two years before 9/11. Additionally, it might have been of interest to listeners that the FBI had showed up several times over the years to talk to the people at Airman Flight School, located at Boren's airport, about the training of terrorism suspects.

Another relevant point of interest was that, just the month before, Boren had personally brought the former CIA Station Chief in Berlin to the university to teach in the Political Science department. David Edger, who had been involved in orchestrating another September 11th tragedy, the Coup in Chile, joined the faculty at the University of Oklahoma at Boren's invitation. Edger's most recent responsibility at the CIA was the monitoring of the Hamburg al-Qaeda cell, which included Mohamed Atta, Marwan Al-Shehhi, Ramsi bin Al-Shibh, and Ziad Jarrah.[10]

According to George Tenet, he immediately understood what was happening, even as he was having breakfast with Boren. He claimed that he "instantly thought that this had to be al-Qa-ida" when he heard about the first plane. Boren recalled George "mentioning Bin Ladin and wondering aloud if this is what Moussaoui had been involved with." Tenet "immediately thought about the Bojinka plot" and a subsequent plan to fly a small plane into CIA headquarters that was broken up in 1994. It wasn't until he arrived at CIA headquarters that he learned about the second plane hitting the WTC.[11]

In his book, Tenet wrote about how Pakistani ISI General Mahmud Ahmed was meeting with Congressmen Lindsey Graham and Porter Goss that morning as the first plane struck the WTC. Ahmed's itinerary showed that Paul Wolfowitz was also meeting with Ahmed.[12] Thirty minutes after the second plane hit, Ahmed was being chauffeured along Constitution Avenue in Washington when smoke from the Pentagon became visible. Goss showed up at the Pentagon too.

Tenet also wrote about how Shafiq Bin Laden, Osama's bother, had been attending the Carlyle Group's investor conference in Washington at the same time. Rounding out a series of stunning coincidences that morning, Tenet also remarked about Kirk Lippold's meeting at CIA headquarters as the attacks began. Lippold, the captain of the *USS Cole*, had predicted at that very moment that a seminal event would be needed to raise awareness of the al Qaeda threat.[13]

Tenet went on to describe what happened next.

> "Although in our collective gut we knew al-Qa-ida was behind the attacks, we needed proof, so CTC [CIA's Counterterrorist Center] requested passenger lists from the planes that had been turned into weapons that morning." [After we got the passenger manifests] an analyst from CTC raced over to the printing plant. 'Some of these guys on one of the planes are the ones we've been looking for in the last few weeks.' He pointed specifically to two names: Khalid Al-Mihdhar and Nawaf Al-Hazmi. That was the first time we had absolute proof of what I had been virtually certain of from the moment I heard about the attacks: we were in the middle of an al-Qa-ida plot."

Tenet was not being truthful about his agency's search for Al-Mihdhar and Al-Hazmi. The CIA was aware that the two suspects had come to the U.S. in January 2000 and it had been tracking their movements both before and after that time. As stated earlier, the two alleged hijackers had been sponsored by an FBI suspect and had lived with an FBI informant for months after their January 2000 arrival in the United States.

The best account of the CIA and FBI misdeeds related to Al-Mihdhar and Al-Hazmi is revealed in Kevin Fenton's book, *Disconnecting the Dots*. Fenton describes the problems with the official account in relation to known facts about the tracking of these two alleged hijackers.

Fenton wrote about several revelatory subjects, including the CIA's attempts to hide from the intelligence community information about Al-Mihdhar having a U.S. visa. Before focusing on those late opportunities to capture two alleged hijackers, however, it is useful to examine how many early chances the CIA had to find out about the 9/11 plot.

Hyping the Terrorist Threat While Facilitating Terrorism

After being appointed CIA Director, Tenet did exactly what Louis Freeh had done after his appointment as FBI Director. He began to cultivate close personal relationships with officials in Saudi Arabia. Like Freeh, Tenet grew especially close to Prince Bandar, the Saudi ambassador to the United States. Bandar and Tenet often met at Bandar's home near Washington. For unknown reasons, Tenet did not share information from those meetings with his own CIA officers who were handling Saudi issues at the agency. The CIA's Saudi specialists only learned about Tenet's dealings with the Saudi authorities inadvertently, through their Saudi contacts.[14]

As Deputy Director for the CIA, in 1996, Tenet had worked to install one of his closest friends and confidants, John Brennan, as CIA station chief in Saudi Arabia. In this role, Brennan often communicated directly with Tenet, avoiding the usual chain of command. At the time, as an apparent favor to the Saudis, CIA analysts were discouraged from questioning Saudi relationship to Arab extremists.[15]

The unusual relationship that both George Tenet and Louis Freeh had with Saudi intelligence (and George H.W. Bush) recalls the private network that was created in the mid-1970s to accomplish covert actions though means of proxies. This private network included disgruntled CIA officers who had been fired by President Carter, as well as the group known as The Safari Club, and BCCI.

The Safari Club resulted from an agreement between Saudi Arabian intelligence chief Kamal Adham, Anwar Sadat of Egypt, the Shah of Iran, and French intelligence director Alexandre de Marenches.[16] The BCCI network grew, with the blessing of CIA director George H.W. Bush, through the guidance of the Safari Club, which needed a network of banks to help fund proxy operations, including off-the-books operations required by the CIA.[17] As discussed in Chapter 3, this private network was utilized in the arming of the Mujahideen, the precursor to al Qaeda.

Evidence suggests that this private network continued to exist twenty years later, when Tenet began leading the CIA, and that terrorist operations were among those which were funded.

Under George Tenet's leadership, the CIA failed miserably to detect and prevent al Qaeda terrorism. This might make sense in light of British Foreign Secretary Robin Cook's claim that al Qaeda was not originally a terrorist group but a database of operatives used by the CIA.[18] In any case, it was almost as if Tenet wanted al Qaeda to not only remain viable, but to be seen as an ever-looming threat.

For example, in February 1998, Al Qaeda made public its second fatwah, repeating its declaration of holy war against the United States and its allies. It included the signatures of Osama bin Laden and Ayman al-Zawahiri, head of the Jihad Group in Egypt.[19] What did George Tenet and the CIA do in response?

- According to CIA officer Michael Scheuer, "The Agency's Bin Laden unit was ordered disbanded" in April 1998. Although Tenet rescinded the order later, Scheuer commented that "the on-again, off-again signals about the unit's future status made for confusion, distraction, and much job-hunting in the last few weeks" before the embassy attacks.[20]

- In May 1998, Tenet traveled to Saudi Arabia to meet with Saudi Crown Prince Abdullah. Tenet and Abdullah made a secret agreement that Bin Laden, if captured, would not be given to the U.S. for trial but instead given to the Saudis. Recommending that the Saudis bribe the Taliban to turn Bin Laden over, Tenet canceled the CIA's own operation to get Bin Laden.[21]

- Michael Scheuer claimed that, between May 1998 and May 1999, U.S. leaders passed up ten opportunities to capture Bin Laden. According to Scheuer, it was George Tenet and his deputies who rejected the proposals.[22]

Apparently two declarations of holy war by al Qaeda were not enough to compel George Tenet to increase his agency's focus on Bin Laden. Not only that, Tenet seemed to intentionally back off pursuing Bin laden in 1998 and 1999, obstructing U.S. attempts to capture al Qaeda's leader.

The result was the August 7, 1998 bombings of two U.S. embassies in Africa. This was an attack "in which hundreds of people were killed in simultaneous truck bomb explosions at the United States embassies in the East African capitals of Dar es Salaam, Tanzania, and Nairobi, Kenya. The date of the bombings marked the eighth anniversary of the arrival of American forces in Saudi Arabia."[23]

Just months before the bombings, the CIA had been warned by the Kenyan Intelligence Service that the embassy in Nairobi was going to be attacked by al Qaeda. But the CIA ignored the warning.[24] Not only that, but the embassy bombings were "carried out by a cell that U.S. agents had already uncovered."[25]

After the 1998 bombing, the mainstream media began to acknowledge that Bin Laden's early organization had been funded by the CIA. U.S. Senator Orrin Hatch, a member of the SSCI, said at the time that if he had it to do all over again, he would still have armed, trained and supplied Bin Laden and his organization.[26]

Late that year, in a memo to the CIA, George Tenet declared war against al Qaeda. He wrote that "Our work to date has been remarkable and in some cases heroic" but "we must now redouble our efforts against Bin Ladin himself, his infrastructure, followers, finances, etc with a sense of enormous urgency." He said, "We are at war.... I want no resources or people spared... either inside CIA or the [U.S. intelligence] community."[27]

Although meetings were held, Tenet did not attend them and his deputy went to only one meeting despite Tenet having put him in charge. The meetings were attended by "few if any officers" from other agencies and quickly stopped discussing the fight against al-Qaeda. No other effort was made at the CIA or elsewhere in the U.S. intelligence community, as a result of this declaration of war by Tenet, to make a plan to defeat al-Qaeda.[28]

In 1999, the CIA under the direction of Tenet began a new venture called In-Q-Tel. Through the CIA's Directorate of Technology, this semi-private corporation sought to find and purchase companies with applications related to intelligence work. Among those working with Tenet at In-Q-Tel was:

- Paul Kaminski, the former Air Force colonel and undersecretary of defense who was associated with the RAND Corporation. Kaminski later worked with Hugh Shelton and Mike Canavan (See Chapter 7) at Anteon Corporation.

- Stephen Friedman, a senior principal with WTC impact zone company Marsh & McLennan and former partner at Goldman Sachs who later became George W. Bush's top economic advisor. Friedman also had belonged to a Cornell University society called Quill and Dagger, the membership of which included Paul Wolfowitz, Clinton's national security advisor Sandy Berger, George W. Bush's Deputy NSA Stephen Hadley, and Jules Kroll, the founder of Kroll Associates.

- Norman Augustine, the CEO of Lockheed Martin. A director at the Center for Security Policy and at Riggs Bank, Augustine was also a member of a RAND Corporation task force led by Frank Carlucci that outlined "A Global Agenda" for incoming President George W. Bush.[29] Augustine is now a senior advisor for the investment company Frontier Group, where he works with Carlucci.

Despite the attempts by Tenet and others to hype the threat from al Qaeda, as of August 1999 not even *The Washington Post* appeared to be convinced of the threat. Two reporters at the *Post* questioned the emerging legend of al Qaeda by writing, "for all its claims about a worldwide conspiracy to murder Americans, the government's case is, at present, largely circumstantial. The indictment never explains how bin Laden runs al Qaeda or how he may have masterminded the embassy bombings."[30]

Behind the scenes, Tenet's lack of action suggested that he was unconcerned. An example was given in March 1999 when German intelligence provided to the CIA the mobile phone number and first name of one of the alleged 9/11 hijackers—Marwan Al-Shehhi.[31] The

CIA did nothing with the information. Although Tenet later dismissed its importance, others said that the number could have been easily traced, leading to the capture of Al-Shehhi.

Additionally, the CIA appeared "to have been investigating the man who recruited the [alleged 9/11] hijackers at the time he was recruiting them."[32] Although there is no evidence that the CIA took actions to stop the plot as it was unfolding, there were many interesting leads to follow.

For example, in the summer of 1999 Bin Laden was reportedly given $50 million by a group of oil-rich sheikhs. The *New York Times* reported on this gift which came via a single bank transfer: "The Central Intelligence Agency has obtained evidence that Mr. bin Laden has been allowed to funnel money through the Dubai Islamic Bank in Dubai, which the United Arab Emirates Government effectively controls."[33]

For unknown reasons, the UAE is often disregarded by 9/11 investigators despite the fact that it appears to have more ties to the accused terrorists than any other country. As will be discussed in the next chapter, the UAE had a good friend and representative in the one man in U.S. government who was specifically tasked with leading the fight against terrorism, Richard Clarke.

An example of the UAE links was that the alleged plot architect KSM was reported to be living in Sharjah, UAE as of 1999. Sharjah was reportedly a major center of al-Qaeda activity at the time.[34] One of the alleged hijackers, Fayez Ahmed Banihammad, was from Sharjah as was plot financier Mustafa Ahmed al-Hawsawi. All of the alleged 9/11 hijackers traveled through the UAE on their way to the United States, other than Mohamed Atta, Nawaf Al-Hazmi and Khalid Al-Mihdhar, the latter of whom was said to be the one to facilitate the travel of the others.

Accused hijacker pilot Ziad Jarrah was detained and questioned in January 2000 at Dubai Airport. However, CIA and UAE officials failed to warn German intelligence about Jarrah, who traveled on to Hamburg.

Overall, the lack of communication and action taken by DCI Tenet regarding the men who would be accused of perpetrating the 9/11 attacks was reflective of the same attitude exhibited by FBI Director Louis Freeh. With the strong ties between Tenet's good friend Clarke and the UAE, it would seem that much could have been done to stop the 9/11 attacks long before they happened.

The CIA's tracking of two 9/11 suspects has been reported extensively. This began with the monitoring of a January 2000 meeting in Malaysia attended by KSM and several other alleged al Qaeda leaders. The meeting also included the two alleged 9/11 hijackers who did not travel to the U.S. via the UAE, Khalid Al-Mihdhar and Nawaf Al-Hazmi. These are the two suspects who, in his book, Tenet claimed the CIA had been looking for only in the few weeks before 9/11. Chapter 4 covered the fact that these two had been living in San Diego with an FBI asset.

With regard to the CIA's failed communications, author Kevin Fenton lets Tenet off the hook, saying that there is "no evidence of [Tenet] doing anything intentionally wrong before the attacks.[35] Fenton acknowledges that Tenet lied extensively in testimony to the Joint Congressional Inquiry, and that he gave "a string of evasive answers" to the 9/11 Commission.[36] Yet Fenton's premise is that low-level CIA and FBI officers kept a secret plan [the hiding of evidence about the two suspects] from their superiors.[37]

The facts presented, however, suggest that senior level CIA leadership was behind the orders to hide the evidence about Al-Mihdhar and Al-Hazmi. Examples include the failure of the CIA station in Bangkok to communicate that the two suspects had left Thailand for the U.S., and the order referenced by the CIA station chief in Kuala Lumpur when he said "I'm not supposed to show these photographs."[38] Although that order was disobeyed, and the surveillance photos of the Malaysia meeting were shared with FBI officers, such an order to a CIA station chief could not have come from low-level officers. Control of multiple CIA stations could only come from the top.

While the CIA withheld information about Al-Mihdhar and Al-Hazmi living in the United States, Tenet simultaneously kept the threat hype going. A month after the Malaysia meeting, he told the U.S. Senate that OBL was planning "to strike further blows against America." [39]

Despite this presumed threat, Tenet had not ordered a National Intelligence Estimate on terrorism in his entire tenure, the last one having been produced in 1997. Finally recognizing this need in late 2000, according to the 9/11 Commission, Tenet charged the CIA's CTC with making a strategic assessment. But as with so many other coincidences, the person who was to lead the assessment didn't start work until the day before 9/11.[40]

U.S. intelligence officers later said they were told to back-off investigation of Bin Laden and the Saudis.[41] After the Bush Administration took over in January 2001, there was a "major policy shift" at the National Security Agency in that OBL could still be investigated, but they could not look at where he got his money.[42]

This was the environment which led to Tenet having breakfast, as the attacks began, with David Boren, whose university and hometown had so many links to the alleged hijackers. Four days later, on September 15, 2001, Tenet presented the Worldwide Attack Matrix, a blueprint for what became known as the War On Terror.[43]

As the new war was implemented, George Tenet failed to cooperate with the official investigations into the events of 9/11. Moreover, during the Joint Congressional Inquiry proceedings, he lied to representatives of the U.S. Congress, which means that he is another suspect who can be brought up on 9/11-related charges today.

Tenet also failed to cooperate with the 9/11 Commission while, at the same time, his CIA was lying about and then destroying videotapes that constituted a major part of the evidence upon which the official account was built.

Failure to Cooperate, Destruction of Evidence, and Other Hints

Tenet began being uncooperative when he refused to be interviewed by the Joint Inquiry. As the Joint Inquiry later reported, it had "attempted to schedule an interview of DCI George Tenet in order to solicit his recollections, understandings and opinions regarding a host of questions relating to policy, resource, organizational, authority, priorities, and other issues that had been developed during the Inquiry. Such an interview was at first delayed and then made conditional on further discussions with DCI staff. Ultimately, the DCI testified at length in closed and open sessions before the Joint Inquiry and the interview was denied on that basis."[44]

The Joint Inquiry also noted that the CIA refused to allow investigators to receive important cables that would later form the basis for the Inquiry's findings. Instead, "CIA took the position that so-called 'operational cables' from the field and certain other documents it deemed to be sensitive could be subject to Joint Inquiry review at CIA Headquarters, but that no copies could be brought to the Joint Inquiry's office."[45]

Nine months after 9/11, one major assumption about the leaders of al Qaeda was questioned in the mainstream press. KSM, the alleged mastermind of the attacks, was reported by the *Los Angeles Times* to have spent years engaging in behavior that was far from that of a devout Muslim. "He met associates in karaoke bars and giant go-go clubs filled with mirrors, flashing lights and bikini-clad dancers. He held meetings at four-star hotels. He took scuba-diving lessons at a coastal resort." No one suspected him "of being dangerous to anything but his bank account."[46] Unfortunately, this contradictory information did not make it into the official reports.

Investigative reporter Daniel Hospicker contributed a considerable amount of evidence showing that the lifestyles of many of the alleged hijackers were far from Islamic. Furthermore, these suspects associated with drug-traffickers and frequented an area in Florida that was known for CIA operations.[47] In fact, the evidence gathered from witnesses in Florida where the suspects trained indicated that Atta, Al-Shehhi and company appeared to be drug-abusing, alcohol-consuming gangsters who spent a lot of time in nude bars.[48] Obviously, this evidence didn't fit with the official account.

In December 2002, the Joint Inquiry concluded that certain high-level people in U.S. government were guilty of significant failures with respect to stopping the attacks. Senator Richard Shelby, vice chairman of the Inquiry, said these people had "failed in significant ways to ensure that this country was as prepared as it could have been." The people cited were DCI Tenet; former DCI John Deutch; former FBI

Director Louis Freeh; NSA Director Michael Hayden; and former NSA leaders Lieutenant General Kenneth Minihan and Barbara McNamara.[49] The Inquiry report clarified, however, that these people were not responsible for 9/11, which was caused entirely by "the 19 alleged hijackers and the terrorist infrastructure that supported them."[50]

However, Senator Shelby continued to be highly critical of George Tenet. In fact, Shelby publicly called for Tenet's resignation, saying "There have been more failures on his watch as far as massive intelligence failures than any CIA director in history. Yet he's still there. It's inexplicable to me."[51] When Tenet did resign in 2004, Shelby commented "This is not a surprise to me at all. What was a surprise was that he held onto the job as long as he did."[52]

Shortly afterward, Shelby was accused of leaking classified information related to the 9/11 investigation. Vice President Dick Cheney threatened termination of the White House's cooperation with the congressional inquiry unless its leaders pushed for an investigation of Shelby. Although Shelby denied it, the investigation suggested that he had revealed classified information to Carl Cameron, a correspondent for Fox News. The information consisted of two messages intercepted by the National Security Agency on September 10, 2001, but were only translated the day after the attacks—"the match is about to begin" and "tomorrow is zero hour."[53]

Senator Orrin Hatch, who was a big supporter of both Tenet and Freeh and who was involved with arming al Qaeda's precursor organization, was known to have leaked information in a similar way but was not referred to the Justice department. Observers saw the hidden hand of George Tenet in the accusations against Shelby.[54]

Tenet had less trouble with the 9/11 report from the CIA's Inspector General (IG). The IG report originally suggested a need for accountability but, in 2004, it was revised at request of Porter Goss, to remove accountability. Instead, "accountability boards" for further assessment were recommended. These accountability boards were to be focused on Tenet and several others including CIA executive director Buzzy Krongard, CTC chief Cofer Black, Alec Station chief Richard Blee, and Blee's deputy Tom Wilshire. In the end, the accountability boards were dropped too and Tenet was let off the hook entirely.

The 9/11 Commission investigation was also not a challenge for Tenet or the CIA. When the agency refused to cooperate, for example by not allowing the Commission in to interview the alleged al Qaeda detainees, the Commission acquiesced and did not issue subpoenas. When the CIA suspected that other witnesses might accidentally reveal information that would threaten the agency, it forced the Commission to accept the use of witness "minders." That is, the CIA insisted that agency representatives – usually legal counsel – be present to monitor all interviews of agency personnel. The minders would intimidate the witnesses and, in some cases, the minders actually responded on behalf of the witnesses.[55]

The Commission ultimately built much of its account on testimony obtained through the torture of alleged al Qaeda operatives, including KSM, Ramsi bin Al-Shibh, and Abu Zubaydah. This was despite the fact that the Commission was denied the ability to interview the suspects, or even the interrogators.

It was Zubaydah who was first captured, and his reported torture testimony led to the capture of KSM and Bin Al-Shibh. The CIA moved these victims to secret "black sites" around the world in order to stay ahead of international authorities and continue the torture. The Commission simply received summaries of the torture testimonies from the CIA and used them over 440 times as sources to support the *9/11 Commission Report.*

Tenet and his deputies, including John Brennan, were instrumental in driving the torture policy. And despite the detainees' torture testimony forming a large basis for the Commission's work, Tenet, like Donald Rumsfeld, did not want the detainees to be interviewed by the Commission. In fact, the CIA refused to let the Commission speak with them or the interrogators. What was used to form the official account was taken third or fourth hand.

The CIA also failed to tell the Commission that its agents had told Abu Zubaydah during his interrogation that they discovered he was not an al-Qaeda fighter, partner, or even a member.[56] In 2009, this fact was confirmed as the U.S. government stated officially that it no longer considered the suspect Abu Zubaydah to have ever been associated with al Qaeda in any way.[57] The result was that after years of imprisonment and brutal torture, Zubaydah began to be airbrushed out of history, despite his having initiated the accusations against supposed 9/11 architect KSM. In his 2007 book, Tenet went further, claiming that "interrogating Abu Zubaydah led to Ramsi bin al Shibh."[58] The torture testimony of KSM and Bin Al-Shibh was cited hundreds of times by the 9/11 Commission to frame the myth behind the 9/11 attacks.

It was later revealed that the CIA destroyed its videotapes of the interrogations of al Qaeda operatives, many of which featured Abu Zubaydah. Kean and Hamilton wrote in a 2008 article for the *New York Times* that "Those who knew about these videotapes – and did not tell us about them – obstructed our investigation." They clarified that Mr. Tenet, in a December 2003 meeting with the Commissioners, alluded to "several documents he thought would be helpful to us, but neither he, nor anyone else in the meeting, mentioned videotapes."[59] In a January 2004 follow-up meeting, Tenet again failed to mention the existence of the videotapes.

June 2004, just weeks before release of the *9/11 Commission Report*, Tenet resigned. Supportive reactions came from Porter Goss and Senator Hatch, who said "When the dust settles, I think people will recognize the many contributions George Tenet made to the war on terror. I understand why the president had confidence in him."[60]

In 2006, Tenet joined the board of Viisage Corporation, a security products company that had been flagged for 9/11 insider trading by the SEC but was never investigated.[61] Shortly thereafter, Louis Freeh joined the board of Viisage as well.[62] Although the two men most responsible for the intelligence failures that led to 9/11 had both joined a company suspected from having profited from the attacks, there was still no investigation into the SEC concerns.

That same year, Tenet also joined QinetiQ, a company partly owned by the Carlyle Group and run by Duane Andrews.[63] A former protégé of

Dick Cheney, Andrews is reviewed as a 9/11 suspect in Chapter 15. Donald Rumsfeld's protégé Stephen Cambone also joined Andrews and Tenet at QinetiQ.

The facts show that, as DCI from 1997 to 2004, Tenet was responsible for an agency that had, at the very least, failed miserably to perform its duties related to counterterrorism. Overall the evidence suggests that, as with Louis Freeh and the FBI, some of those failures were intentional. Concerns that Tenet and Freeh had developed secret paths of communication with Saudi authorities, and that they might have disrupted plans to capture or investigate al Qaeda suspects, were never addressed. Therefore, areas of inquiry for an ongoing investigation into George Tenet's 9/11-related activities should include the following.

- His relationship to David Boren and the OKC area where several 9/11 suspects had trained or visited, and where the aviation companies of Wirt Walker were located

- His role in the CIA's tracking of Al-Mihdhar and Al-Hazmi, and the communications failures related to that tracking

- His relationship to Saudi Prince Bandar and any part he had in discouraging CIA officers from questioning Arab extremism

- His role in the decision to disband the CIA's OBL unit in April 1998, just two months after al Qaeda's second fatwah against the United States

- His role in rejecting or cancelling more than ten opportunities to capture OBL in the few years before 9/11, as described by Michael Scheuer

- Any foreknowledge he had of the 1998 embassy bombings, including any warnings or pre-bombing investigations of the suspects who were accused

- His lack of actual action against terrorism, including the absence of a National Intelligence Estimate on the threat

- His failure to cooperate with the official investigations and his lying to members of Congress during the investigations

- His part in the concealment and destruction of the videotape evidence that formed the basis for the official account

- His relationship to suspected 9/11 insider trading and Viisage Corporation

In the next chapter, Tenet's good friend Richard Clarke will be reviewed. The CIA's collaboration with the United Arab Emirates, and its failure to investigate that country's possible role in 9/11, is something that should be kept in mind throughout that review.

Chapter 6

Richard Clarke, COG, and the UAE

In the summer of 2011, an interview with former "Counterterrorism Czar" Richard Clarke made a splash in the alternative media.[1] In the interview, Clarke speculated about CIA malfeasance related to the pre-9/11 monitoring of two alleged hijackers. This was interesting due to Clarke's suggestion that the CIA had courted 9/11 suspects as sources, but it was far more interesting for what was not said with regard to Clarke's personal history and associations.

The seeming point of the new statements from Clarke was that the CIA might have withheld information from him, the FBI, and the Department of Defense (DOD) in the twenty months leading up to the 9/11 attacks. Clarke was not suggesting that the CIA did this maliciously, but only that his good friend, George Tenet, and two others made a mistake in their approach. Clarke said of these CIA leaders, "They understood that al Qaeda was a big threat, they were motivated, and they were really trying hard." The mild twist that Clarke put on the story was that the CIA's diligent effort to secure much needed sources within al Qaeda was pursued without any suspicion that those sources might turn out to be "double agents."

Clarke claimed that if the CIA had simply told him, the FBI, and the DOD about Khalid Al-Mihdhar and Nawaf Al-Hazmi, "even as late as September 4th, [2001]" they would have conducted a massive sweep. "We would have conducted it publicly," he said, "We would have found those assholes. There's no doubt in my mind. Even with only a week left."

There were serious problems with Clarke's new claims. For one thing, evidence indicates that FBI headquarters worked to protect the alleged 9/11 hijackers in the months leading up to 9/11. Another obvious problem is that those "assholes" lived with an FBI asset for at least four months and there are reasons to believe the FBI knew that.

More importantly, Richard Clarke personally thwarted two of the attempts the CIA had made to capture Osama bin Laden (OBL) in the two years before 9/11. It seems disingenuous at best that Clarke would say that he didn't have enough information to capture two of OBL's underlings in 2000 when he was responsible for preventing the capture of OBL just the year before.

Although Clarke apologized to the 9/11 victims' families for government failures that led to 9/11, there are reasons to take his input with a healthy level of skepticism. One reason is that Clarke has made a number of false statements with regard to 9/11 and terrorism. Additionally, Clarke's personal history suggests that he protected terrorist suspects and may have been in league with a terrorist network.

Not Just Another COG

After graduation from the University of Pennsylvania, where he was a member of the Sphinx Society, Clarke began his government career in the Ford Administration. He worked as a defense department nuclear weapons analyst and shared a Pentagon office with Wayne Downing, who later became a leader of Science Applications International Corporation (SAIC) as will be reviewed in Chapter 15.

At the time, White House chief of staff Dick Cheney and defense secretary Donald Rumsfeld were fighting a war of public perception to preserve the increasingly unpopular aspects of the CIA. Nuclear policy was a big issue then, and at least one of Clarke's closest colleagues in later years, Paul Wolfowitz, worked to present false "Team B" information.

After getting his Master of Arts degree from MIT, Clarke went on to become President Reagan's Deputy Assistant Secretary of State for Intelligence. In this role, Clarke negotiated U.S. military presence in Egypt, Bahrain, Kuwait, Oman, the United Arab Emirates (UAE), Qatar, and Saudi Arabia. He asked these foreign governments for "access" agreements and the right to enhance existing facilities. As a result, the U.S. moved large numbers of contractors into Saudi Arabia.

One such contractor, Bernard Kerik, the New York City police commissioner on 9/11, signed on for a three year tour as the "the chief investigator for the royal family of Saudi Arabia."[2]

During his first half dozen years in Reagan's State department, Clarke called Morton Abramowitz, the Assistant Secretary of State for Intelligence and Research, his boss and mentor. Abramowitz, who was said to be influential in the career of Clarke, had worked as assistant secretary for defense under Donald Rumsfeld in the seventies when Clarke worked in the DOD. Abramowitz left his position at State in 1989 to become the ambassador to Turkey. The next person for whom Abramowitz was boss and mentor was his deputy ambassador, Marc Grossman.[3]

In 1984, Clarke was selected to take part in one of the most highly classified projects of the Reagan Administration. This was the secret Continuity of Government (COG) program run by the National Program Office that continued up to and after the attacks of September 11.[4] Other than Clarke, the members of the COG group included Dick Cheney, Donald Rumsfeld, George H.W. Bush, Kenneth Duberstein, and James Woolsey.[5] If not a formal member of the group, Oliver North reported to it and acted on its behalf. Although Cheney and Rumsfeld were not government employees throughout the twenty years that Clarke participated in this official government program, they both continued to participate.[6]

COG was developed to install a shadow "government in waiting" to replace the U.S. Congress and the U.S. Constitution in the event of a national emergency like a nuclear war. The first and only time that COG was put into action was when Richard Clarke activated it during the 9/11 attacks. As of 2002, that shadow government continued to be in effect as an "indefinite precaution."[7]

In 1998, Clarke would revise the COG plan for use as a response to a terrorist attack on American soil. Apparently, COG and the shadow government these men created are still in play to this day.[8]

In 1989, Clarke was appointed by George H.W. Bush to be the Assistant Secretary of State for Politico-Military Affairs, under James

Baker. Clarke was in this position until 1992, and his role was to link the DOD and the Department of State by providing policy in areas related to international security and military operations. One important aspect of his job during this time was that Clarke coordinated State department support of Operation Desert Storm and led the efforts to design the region's security structure after the Gulf War.

Throughout the years of the George H.W. Bush Administration, Clarke worked with defense secretary Cheney and State Department "Foreign Policy Consultant" Rumsfeld. Others he worked closely with at the time included:

- James Baker, the Secretary of State who went on to join the Carlyle Group
- Paul Wolfowitz, the Undersecretary of Defense for Policy who, in the week before 9/11, led meetings with Pakistani ISI General Ahmed
- Duane Andrews, the Assistant Secretary of Defense for Intelligence who left to run SAIC
- Robert Gates, the CIA Director who was implicated in the Iran-Contra crimes and later also worked with SAIC
- Senate Intelligence Committee representatives George Tenet and William Cohen, the latter of whom sponsored the 1997 Quadrennial Defense Review that dramatically reduced the number of jet fighters protecting the continental Unites States[9]
- And Reagan advisor Richard Armitage, who was responsible for granting visas to some of the alleged hijackers and participated in the failed air defense teleconference on 9/11

According to his book, Clarke remembers that "Wolfowitz and I flew on to Bahrain, Abu Dhabi and Salaleh" to coordinate relations with the UAE, at Cheney's request. Over the following decade, Clarke negotiated many deals with the Emirates, essentially becoming an agent of the UAE, and he was "particularly close to the UAE royal family."[10]

Not long after Clarke began going there, the royal family of Abu Dhabi took over full ownership of the Bank of Credit and Commerce International (BCCI). As discussed earlier, BCCI is significant relative to 9/11 because it was involved in funding terrorists and was in partnership with the Pakistani intelligence network from which several alleged 9/11 conspirators came, including KSM.[11] In fact, *TIME* magazine reported that, relative to BCCI, "You can't draw a line separating the bank's black operatives and Pakistan's intelligence services."[12]

More importantly, there is strong evidence that the CIA was involved in the founding of BCCI.[13] The CIA connection to the origins of the BCCI terrorist network are revealing because the royal family of the UAE was also said to have played a primary role in the creation of BCCI. As the official U.S. government report on the subject pointed out, "There was no relationship more central to BCCI's existence from its inception than that between BCCI and Sheikh Zayed and the ruling family of Abu Dhabi."[14]

Clarke's friends in the UAE royal family not only created the BCCI terrorist network, they took it over when the Bank of England shut it down. "By July 5, 1991, when BCCI was closed globally, the Government of Abu Dhabi, its ruling family, and an investment company holding the assets of the ruling family, were the controlling, and official 'majority' shareholders of BCCI—owning 77 percent of the bank. But since the remaining 23 percent was actually held by nominees and by BCCI's alter-ego ICIC, Abu Dhabi was in fact BCCI's sole owner."[15]

Not long after this, in 1992, Bush named Clarke to the National Security Council staff as Special Assistant to the President and he became chairman of the Interagency Counterterrorism Committee. One might think that Richard Clarke's close relationship to the royal family of the UAE, and this new role as the NSC head of counterterrorism, might have posed a slight conflict of interest. But no one seemed to notice.

Likewise, few have noticed that the attacks attributed to al Qaeda began just after the first Bush Administration left office. It was in December of 1992 that al Qaeda is said to have first committed an act of terrorism by bombing U.S. troops in Yemen. Attacks and plots in Somalia, Saudi Arabia, and many others places located near the production and transport routes of fossil fuels have been attributed to al Qaeda since that time.[16]

Continuing as "Counterterrorism Czar" in the Clinton Administration, Clarke was not interested in pursuing the remnants of the BCCI terrorist network. Instead, he had a different approach to combating terrorism. In 1993, the United States began a practice known as "rendition." Throughout the rest of the world, rendition is known as torture. The policy behind this program was proposed by Clarke, who worked to get "snatch teams" in place to kidnap suspects for torture. The success of Clarke's rendition proposal led to the post-9/11 U.S. program of secret kidnappings and torture around the world.

In the summer of 1994, Clarke played a leading role in the international failure to intervene in the Rwandan genocide. People who worked to stop the slaughter before it happened cite Clarke as a heartless, malicious man who was "scandalously oblivious" to the evidence of the looming genocide.[17] Although the U.S. could have taken many steps to prevent the tragedy, it did not due to Clarke's "structurally empowered skepticism and stonewalling."[18] Instead, over a period of 100 days, approximately 800,000 people were killed.

Clarke and the UAE

In September 1994, high-ranking UAE and Saudi government ministers, such as Saudi Intelligence Minister Prince Turki al-Faisal, began frequent bird hunting expeditions in Afghanistan. It was reported that, "They would go out and see Osama, spend some time with him, talk with him, you know, live out in the tents, eat the simple food, engage in falconing, some other pursuits, ride horses." Two members of the UAE royal family that participated in these trips were Sheikh Mohammed bin Rashid Al-Maktoum and Sheikh Zayed bin Sultan Al Nahyan, ruler of the UAE.[19]

As these UAE meetings with OBL occurred, Clarke's relationship with the UAE royals blossomed. At the same time, he engaged in preparations for terrorist events on U.S. soil. In 1998, he chaired a tabletop exercise in which a Learjet filled with explosives would be flown on a suicide mission into a target in Washington, DC. At a conference in October 1998, Clarke predicted that America's enemies "will go after our Achilles' heel" which is "in Washington. It is in New York." That was quite a prediction.

Clarke updated the COG plans, in early 1998, so that they could be utilized in the event of a terrorist attack like the one that he predicted that year (and that occurred in 2001). National Security Advisor Sandy Berger, who was later caught stealing documents that had been requested by the 9/11 Commission, was the one to suggest that Clinton create the new Counterterrorism Czar position that Clarke would fill at the time of his prediction.[20] Berger was also the one to introduce Clarke's COG partner, James Woolsey, to Clinton. Woolsey went on to become Clinton's CIA director.

In early February 1999, Clarke met with Al-Maktoum, one of the UAE royals known to hunt with Bin Laden, in the UAE. Al-Maktoum was a big supporter of the Taliban and al-Qaeda. And although people often forget, two of the 9/11 hijackers were citizens of the UAE and the funding that supported the attacks flowed through the UAE, according to the official account.

Just a few months after Clarke's UAE visit, in July 1999, the CIA claimed that Bin Laden had "been allowed to funnel money through the Dubai Islamic Bank in Dubai, which the United Arab Emirates Government effectively controls." Apparently Bin Laden "had a relationship with the bank, which they believed had been arranged with the approval of the officials who control the bank."[21]

Bin Laden was not the only al Qaeda link to Clarke's friends in the UAE. Reportedly, KSM was living in the city of Sharjah, UAE at the time of Clarke's trip. Sharjah was reportedly a major center of al Qaeda activity then. The plot's alleged money man Mustafa Ahmed al-Hawsawi was also based in Sharjah.[22] Saeed Sheikh, known as the 9/11 paymaster, was said to have established an al Qaeda base in the UAE while openly working with the Pakistani ISI. Some have suggested that Hawsawi and Sheikh were the same man.[23]

Al-Maktoum, who Clarke met with in 1999, later tried to take over the management of six major U.S. ports. George W. Bush lobbied on his behalf but the deal fell through.[24]

The *9/11 Commission Report* has six references to the UAE, most of which can be found on page 138. One of these suggests that "but for the cooperation of the UAE, we would have killed Bin Ladin two years in advance of September 11."

Therefore it is difficult to understand why the leading authority on counterterrorism in the U.S. would be meeting, and maintaining close personal relationships, with the UAE friends of Bin Laden just two years before 9/11. This was three years after Bin Laden had first declared holy war against the United States,[25] and one year after his more recent such proclamation.[26]

It is far more difficult to understand why Clarke was personally behind the failure of two CIA attempts to kill or capture Bin Laden in 1999. The first of these occurred just a few days after Clarke's visit to the UAE. The CIA obtained information that OBL was hunting with UAE royals in Afghanistan at the time, and President Clinton was asked for permission to attack the camp. Clarke voted down that plan, and others within the U.S. government speculated that his ties to the UAE were behind his decision.[27]

The next month, when the CIA had tracked Bin Laden's location again and was prepared to take him out during another of the Afghanistan hunting trips, Clarke took it upon himself to alert his UAE friends about the CIA monitoring their meetings with Bin Laden. Of course, the UAE royals tipped off Bin Laden and the U.S. lost another opportunity to kill or capture its number one enemy.[28] Considering that CIA plans are top secret national security priorities, and that OBL was wanted for the bombings in East Africa, Clarke's action should have been seen as treason.

When questioned by Congressman Richard Burr as part of the Joint Congressional Inquiry into 9/11, Clarke was evasive about his actions to protect his UAE friends and bin Laden. The fact that Clarke was allowed to testify without being under oath, in a special agreement in which his comments were considered only a "briefing," was itself telling.

Regarding the second attempt that Clarke had foiled, Burr asked, "Did the CIA, in fact, brief you that the camp was an ideal situation, that they did have real time intelligence, that the collateral damage would be extremely limited, involving only the camp facility? And as a follow-up [to] my last question, Mr. Clarke, did, in fact, you call the royal family and inform them of the information we had about the intelligence of that camp and that exercise?" Clarke replied, "I think those facts are slightly wrong," clarifying that the information the CIA had was not exactly real-time yet essentially admitting that he tipped off the UAE royals.[29]

Somehow, Clarke's two efforts to keep OBL from being captured or killed in 1999 slipped his mind when he testified to the 9/11 Commission. Apparently, these events were also not important enough for Clarke to mention when recently discussing the two "asshole" hijackers whose presence in the U.S. he now says the CIA kept from him and the FBI.

Who Knew About Al-Mihdhar and Al-Hazmi?

The 2011 interview with Clarke began with discussion of the CIA's monitoring of a January, 2000 meeting in Malaysia among top al Qaeda operatives. Khalid Al-Mihdhar and Nawaf Al-Hazmi attended the meeting, as did KSM and several other al Qaeda leaders. Clarke claimed in the interview that the CIA followed the alleged 9/11 hijackers out of the meeting in Malaysia but then lost them in Bangkok.

Two months later, Al-Mihdhar and Al-Hazmi arrived in Los Angeles, according to the CIA, and Clarke said many CIA agents knew about this. Clarke recalled that the CIA "stopped [information about Al-Mihdhar and Al-Hazmi] from going to the FBI and the Defense Department." He then cryptically stated, "We therefore conclude that there was a high level decision, in the CIA, ordering people not to share that information" and "I would have to think it was made by the Director [Tenet]". To clarify why he suddenly thought this lack of information sharing was unusual, Clarke said of Tenet, "You have to understand...we were close friends, he called me several times a day, and shared the most trivial of information."

But it was not only the CIA that knew about this meeting and the attendees. According to the Director of the National Security Agency (NSA), Michael Hayden, "In early 2000, at the time of the meeting in Kuala Lumpur, we had the Al-Hazmi brothers, Nawaf and Salem, as well as Khalid Al-Mihdhar, in our sights. We knew of their association with al-Qaeda, and we shared this information with the [intelligence] community." The NSA knew about these suspects well before that, however, because an early 1999 NSA communications intercept referenced "Nawaf Al-Hazmi," so it was clear that the NSA knew about him for more than two years before 9/11. Oddly enough, the *Washington Post* reported that Al-Hazmi, Al-Mihdhar and four of the other alleged hijackers were "living, working, planning and developing all their activities" near the entrance to NSA headquarters in Laurel, Maryland, in the months prior to the 9/11 attacks.[30]

Al-Hazmi had been seen in San Diego as early as 1996 and he traveled extensively throughout the US, spending time in Cody, Wyoming and Phoenix, Arizona, and making a truck delivery to Canada. He and Al-Hazmi lived openly in the United States, using their real names and credit cards. They had season passes to Sea World and the San Diego Zoo and liked to hang out at a nude bar in San Diego. They went to a flight school there and said they wanted to learn how to fly Boeings. Instructor Rick Garza of Sorbi's Flying Club turned down that request because he said they were "clueless," didn't even know how to draw an airplane, and could not communicate in English.[31]

Al-Hazmi even worked at a Texaco gas station, although he didn't need the money because someone in the UAE was regularly sending him thousands of dollars.[32]

The money Al-Hazmi received was said to come from a UAE citizen named Ali Abdul Aziz Ali (a.k.a. Ammar al Baluchi), who was the nephew of KSM and cousin of Ramzi Yousef. Apparently, a majority of money that came to the hijackers was transferred through Ali Abdul Aziz Ali or Mustafa al-Hawsawi. The 9/11 Commission reported that Ali "helped them with plane tickets, traveler's checks, and hotel reservations," and "taught them about everyday aspects of life in the West, such as purchasing clothes and ordering food."

Whether he was protecting his UAE friends or not, Clarke failed to act on information about al Qaeda operatives living in the U.S., just one month before the meeting in Malaysia. After an al Qaeda "millennium plot" was said to be broken up in Jordan, Clarke authorized an investigation of one of the plotters, Khalil Deek, who lived in Anaheim, California for most of the 1990s. The investigative team reported to Clarke and the NSC directly in December, 1999, stating that Deek's next door neighbor was operating an al Qaeda sleeper cell in Anaheim. No action was taken by Clarke or the NSC.

A few months later, in April 2000, Clarke was quoted in the *Washington Post* as saying that terrorists "will come after our weakness, our Achilles Heel, which is largely here in the United States." Although this was a bold statement, it was unfortunate that Clarke did not have time to track down and capture the terrorists that he knew were living and plotting in the United States.

The bombing of the *USS Cole*, which took the lives of 17 American sailors, occurred in October, 2000. *The Washington Post* reported that Al-Mihdhar had received training in Afghanistan in 1999 along with the operatives who were responsible for the *Cole* bombing. According to *The Guardian*, the Prime Minister of Yemen had accused Al-Mihdhar of being "one of the *Cole* perpetrators."

Like 9/11, there are numerous unanswered questions about the *Cole* bombing and, as with 9/11, no justice has been done. A senior Yemeni security official claimed that "there was evidence that the U.S. itself was responsible for the explosion as part of a conspiracy to take control over the port of Aden."[33] The President of Yemen repeated a similar claim, saying on national television that the U.S. had plans to invade and occupy Aden after the bombing.[34]

At the time of the attack, Clarke was part of a high level meeting to discuss the response, along with William Cohen, George Tenet, the State Department coordinator for counterterrorism, Michael Sheehan, and several others. In this meeting, Clarke was the hawk, proposing attacks throughout Afghanistan in response. None of the voting attendees supported Clarke's plan and, after the meeting, Sheehan asked Clarke: "What's it going to take to get them to hit al-Qaeda in Afghanistan? Does al-Qaeda have to hit the Pentagon?"[35] Once again, that was quite a prediction.

In late May 2001, Clarke wrote a memorandum to Condoleezza Rice and her assistant, Stephen Hadley. The title of the memo was "Stopping Abu Zubaydah's Attacks."[36] Cited as part of the evidence that the "System was Blinking Red," the 9/11 Commission said the memo claimed that Zubaydah was preparing to launch "a series of major terrorist attacks" and, when they occurred, "we will wonder what more we could have done to stop them."[37]

Clarke went on to write in his 2004 book that Zubaydah, whose torture testimony presumably led to the capture of KSM and others, was one of "al Qaeda's top operational managers."[38] Apparently, all of these claims were false as the U.S. government said in 2009 that Zubaydah was never associated with al Qaeda in any way.[39]

Also in May 2001, the CIA gave its photos of the January 2000 Malaysian meeting to an intelligence operations specialist at FBI headquarters. One of the photos was of Al-Mihdhar, who FBI Director Mueller would later say was likely responsible for coordinating the movements of all the non-pilot hijackers. In June 2001, FBI and CIA officials discussed these photos and one FBI agent remembers that Al-Mihdhar was mentioned in these discussions.

Phoenix FBI agent Ken Williams wrote a memo to FBI headquarters, in July 2001, saying that Bin Laden's followers were going to flight schools to train for terrorist attacks. If the FBI had followed through on this, it would have found Al-Hazmi very easily. He was reportedly staying in Phoenix with Hani Hanjour between January and June 2001. The memo was reviewed by the agency's Bin Laden and Islamic extremist counterterrorism units, but it has been reported that neither Attorney General John Ashcroft nor newly appointed FBI Director Robert Mueller briefed President Bush and his national security staff about these revelations. Of course, this was well before the September

4th date that Clarke claims was the best chance for him and the FBI to have first found out.

Zacarias Moussaoui visited Malaysia as well, and stayed at the same condominium where the January 2000 meeting took place. The owner of the condo even signed letters that convinced U.S. authorities to allow Moussaoui into the country. Al-Hazmi and Al-Mihdhar were referenced in papers that the FBI confiscated from Moussaoui when he was arrested in August 2001. FBI headquarters refused multiple requests from the FBI agents pursuing the case to search Moussaoui's possessions. Those confiscated possessions and papers would have immediately led the FBI to Atta, Al-Mihdhar, Al-Hazmi and the other alleged hijackers.

But the FBI had to know about these alleged hijackers well before that, because Al-Hazmi and Al-Mihdhar lived with an FBI informant, Abdussattar Shaikh, for at least four months in late 2000. Shaikh was a "tested" asset working with the local FBI. Shaikh had regular visits from Mohammed Atta and Hani Hanjour as well and even introduced Hanjour to a neighbor.[40]

Newsweek reported that, once, when Shaikh was called by his FBI agent handler, Shaikh said he couldn't talk because Al-Mihdhar was in the room. This suggests that the FBI knew full well that this future 9/11 hijacker was living with an FBI asset. But a more damning fact is that the FBI refused to allow the 9/11 Congressional Inquiry to interview either Shaikh or his FBI handler.

The FBI absolutely knew about the movements of these alleged 9/11 hijackers. In January, 2001, it was the FBI that gave information to the CIA about how *USS Cole* bombing operatives had delivered money to al Qaeda planners at the time of the January 2000 Malaysia meeting. CNN reported, in 2002, that "At that point, the CIA – or the FBI for that matter – could have put Al-Hazmi and Al-Mihdhar and all the others who attended the meeting in Malaysia on a watch list."

In the new interview, Clarke further speculates that the reason that the CIA information was not shared with him, the DOD, and the FBI was because the CIA (i.e. Cofer Black as of June, 1999) was courting these two as sources within al Qaeda. Some might wonder why Clarke never thought of his good friends within the UAE royal family, who met with OBL regularly, as sources on al Qaeda. Surely people who met with OBL personally in the two years before 9/11, and were big supporters of al Qaeda like Clarke's friend, Al-Maktoum, might have had some information to provide!

In any case, Clarke went on in his 2011 interview to suggest that Tenet and Black might have recruited Al-Hazmi and Al-Mihdhar (who had been accused of perpetrating the *USS Cole* bombing) as inside sources on al Qaeda. To the CIA's chagrin, Clarke implied, they at some point became double agents. It is amazing that Clarke insinuated that Black and Tenet were too dim-witted to see that these two Saudis might also be working for the Saudi government. Clarke appeared to be making the absurd suggestion that a CIA director could not predict that the suspected Saudi agent who arranged housing for Al-Hazmi and Al-Mihdhar, arranged payments for them, and arranged to move them to San Diego, might have turned them into Saudi agents.

When Al-Hazmi and Al-Mihdhar arrived in Los Angeles in early 2000, they were met by a strange benefactor named Omar Al-Bayoumi who brought them to Parkwood Apartments in San Diego. It is Al-Bayoumi that Clarke was referring to when he suggested the "Saudi has connections to the Saudi government, and some people believe that this guy was a Saudi intelligence officer. If we assume that this Saudi intelligence officer was the handler for these two, then presumably he would have been reporting to the CIA office in Los Angeles. There was a strong relationship between the CIA director and the minister of intelligence of Saudi Arabia [Prince Turki al Faisal]."[41]

Although only two of the alleged 9/11 terrorists were said to be from the UAE, those being Marwan al-Shehhi and Fayez Banihammad, nearly all of the alleged hijackers arrived in the United States by traveling through the UAE.

Questions for Richard Clarke

Ignoring Clarke's strong relationship to the UAE, as well as the UAE's ownership of the BCCI network, and its support for the Taliban, al

Qaeda, and OBL, Clarke was asked: "How long do you think it would take [the CIA] to decide—this isn't working"? Clarke replied: "I don't know. I do know that in August of 2001 they decide they're gonna tell the FBI."

This remark referred to the idea that it was not until August 21 that the FBI figured out that al Qaeda operatives were in the United States. This claim was transparently false because the FBI was, at the very least, already aware of Moussaoui and the Phoenix memo saying that terrorists were taking flight lessons in the United States. But in August, it was said that an FBI analyst assigned to the CIA's Counter-Terrorism Center suddenly determined that Al-Hazmi and Al-Mihdhar had entered the U.S. back in January 2000.

The U.S. government was, in the months before 9/11, warned by a dozen foreign governments to watch for a major terrorist attack being planned for inside the United States. It was reported that, on August 23, 2001, the Israeli Mossad gave U.S. officials an urgent warning in the form of a list of terrorists known to be living in the U.S. and panning to carry out an attack in the near future. The list included the names of Al-Hazmi, Al-Mihdhar, Al-Shehhi and Atta.[42]

An "all points bulletin" was issued that same day, instructing the FBI and other agencies to put Al-Hazmi and Al-Mihdhar on the watch list. Doing so would have made certain that these two were caught before the attacks. The FBI did not do so, however. The FBI also failed to use this information to thoroughly check national databases of bank records, drivers license records or the records of the credit cards that were used to purchase the 9/11 tickets. These facts render Clarke's vague insinuations moot, because the FBI clearly wasn't going to act on any relevant information it received.

In yet another example, on August 28, a report was received by the New York FBI office requesting that an investigation be conducted "to determine if Al-Mihdhar is still in the United States." FBI headquarters immediately turned down the request. An FBI agent wrote an email in response, saying "someday someone will die [because of this]. Let's hope the [FBI's] National Security Law Unit will stand behind their decisions then, especially since OBL [Osama bin Laden] is now getting the most protection."

All this was before September 4—the date that Clarke says would have given plenty of time for him and the FBI to catch Al-Hazmi and Al-Mihdhar—if only they had known the two were in the United States.

Hopefully Clarke's next interview will be part of legal proceedings in which he is a defendant answering for his failures related to 9/11. When that happens, questions that should be posed to him include the following:

1. Is the COG plan that you and Dick Cheney, Donald Rumsfeld, George H.W. Bush, Kenneth Duberstein, and James Woolsey created, and that you implemented on 9/11, still in effect?

2. Do you have any information on how your friends in the UAE royal family used the terrorist network BCCI after they bought it?

3. Do you have any explanation for how you could have predicted in 1998, at the same time that you updated the COG plan to be a response to a terrorist attack, that America's enemies "will go after our Achilles' heel" which is "in Washington. It is in New York."?

4. When you met with UAE Defense Minister Al-Maktoum in February 1999, just days before the CIA planned to kill or capture Bin Laden as he was meeting with UAE royals, who else did you meet with?

5. Why did you vote down the CIA plan to kill or capture Bin Laden while he was hunting with UAE royals in February 1999?

6. Why did you expose the CIA's secret plan, without approval from the CIA or the president, to kill or capture Bin Laden in March 1999 as he was meeting with UAE royals again?

7. Don't you think those two actions on your part were far more detrimental to the United States than any of your recent, vague speculations?

8. Did you communicate with NSA Director Michael Hayden between January 2000 and the attacks of 9/11? If so, why did you not, in your 2011 interview, accuse him of withholding information on Al-Hazmi and Al-Mihdhar? He has spoken openly of having known about their presence in the U.S. and said that he did share it with the intelligence community.

9. Why did you, as Counterterrorism Czar, take no action in December 1999 when you and the NSC were given the evidence that Khalil Deek's next door neighbor was operating an al Qaeda sleeper cell in Anaheim, CA?

10. You appear to suggest that neither you nor the FBI knew that Al-Mihdhar and Al-Hazmi lived with Abdussattar Shaikh, a tested FBI asset, for at least four months in the year 2000. Is that correct and, if so, don't you think that contradicts your claim that – "I know how all this stuff works, I've been working it for 30 years. You can't snowball me on this stuff."?

11. On what evidence did you base your May 29, 2001 memo and your 2004 book, both of which claimed that Abu Zubaydah was a major al Qaeda terrorist? What do you say now that the U.S. government has abandoned those claims?

12. Do you know why the FBI would not allow Abdussattar Shaikh or his FBI handler to be interviewed as part of the 9/11 investigation?

13. These days, when you're talking with your UAE friends in your offices in the UAE, do you ever discuss 9/11, the hijackers and plotters who spent their time there, and the UAE money that financed the 9/11 attacks?

Clarke now works with his COG partner, former CIA Director James Woolsey, at Paladin Capital, which has offices in New York and the UAE. Clarke is also the chairman Good Harbor Consulting, where he is in partnership with many people who are making a fortune off the War on Terror.

Additionally, Clarke stands out prominently as the only American on the board of trustees of the UAE government-sponsored Khalifa University.[43] Good Harbor Consulting has an office in Abu Dhabi as well, and Clarke is known to have a "big footprint" in the UAE.[44]

Chapter 7

Canavan, Sliney and the FAA

Among the most important unanswered questions about the attacks of September 11 is: Why were none of the four planes intercepted? The failure of the U.S. air defenses can be traced to a number of factors and people but some of the most startling root causes have to do with the utter failure of communications between two agencies responsible for protecting the nation's airspace. At one of them, the Federal Aviation Administration (FAA), two people stood out in this failed chain of communications. One was a lawyer on his first day at the job, and another was a U.S. Special Operations commander who was never held responsible for his critical role, or even questioned about it.

The 9/11 Commission reported that:

> "On 9/11, the defense of U.S. airspace depended on close interaction between two federal agencies: the FAA and the North American Aerospace Defense Command (NORAD)."[1]

According to the Commission, this interaction began with air traffic controllers (ATCs) at the relevant regional FAA control centers, which on 9/11 included Boston, New York, Cleveland, Washington, and Indianapolis. In the event of a hijacking, these ATCs were expected to "notify their supervisors, who in turn would inform management all the way up to FAA headquarters. Headquarters had a hijack coordinator, who was the director of the FAA Office of Civil Aviation Security or his or her designate."

The hijack coordinator's responsibility was to "contact the Pentagon's National Military Command Center (NMCC)" and "the NMCC would then seek approval from the Office of the Secretary of Defense to provide military assistance. If approval was given, the orders would be transmitted down NORAD's chain of command [to the interceptor pilots]."[2]

The *9/11 Commission Report* (the report) indicated that the military was eventually notified about all the hijackings but none of those notifications came in time to intercept the hijacked aircraft. The report also contradicted a good deal of testimony given on the subject by suggesting that earlier statements made by military leaders, in testimony to the Commission, were "incorrect." The corrections to these statements led to a reassessment of how much time the military actually had to respond to requests for assistance that it received from the FAA. Ultimately, the report stated that NORAD's North East Air Defense Sector (NEADS) "air defenders had nine minutes' notice on the first hijacked plane, no advance notice on the second, no advance notice on the third, and no advance notice on the fourth."[3]

The report does not place blame for the failure to intercept on any specific people in the chain of communications, but it specifically exonerates "NEADS commanders and officers" and "[i]ndividual FAA controllers, facility managers and Command Center managers." In fact, the report goes so far as to praise these people for how well they did.[4] Curiously, the hijack coordinator at FAA headquarters was not mentioned in the list of those who were exonerated.

The ATCs did notify their management as required, but further notification to FAA headquarters (FAA HQ) was supposedly riddled with delays. FAA HQ ultimately got plenty of notice of the four hijacked planes but failed to do its job. Perhaps the most glaring example was demonstrated by the failure of FAA HQ to request military assistance for the fourth hijacking, that of Flight 93.

On page 28, the report says: "By 9:34, word of the hijacking had reached FAA headquarters." Despite this advance notice, Flight 93 was said to have crashed in Pennsylvania, never having been intercepted, sometime between 10:03 and 10:07.

To put this in perspective, FAA notification at 9:34 a.m. EST was over 30 minutes after a second airliner had crashed in the World Trade Center. At that time it was known that a third plane was hijacked and that plane was just about to crash into the Pentagon. Everyone knew the country was under a coordinated terrorist attack via hijacked aircraft because, as of 9:03 a.m., mainstream news stations had already been televising it.

That was the situation when FAA HQ was notified about a fourth hijacking. Given those circumstances, an objective observer would expect the highest level of urgency throughout all levels of government in response to that fourth hijacking. But that was not what happened. FAA management did not follow the protocol to ask for military assistance. The 9/11 Commission contends that FAA HQ gave air defenders no notice whatsoever of the hijacking of Flight 93 until after the plane had been destroyed. For whatever reasons, the FAA's Command Center (located in Herndon, VA) did not request military assistance either. In fact, neither the Command Center nor FAA HQ contacted NMCC to request military assistance for any of the hijacked planes.

Therefore it seems reasonable to look at the people whose roles were most important in this failed chain of communications. Once the entire country was aware that a terrorist attack was underway and that planes were being hijacked and used as weapons, the two people who were most important to the FAA's response were the person running the FAA's national Command Center and the hijack coordinator at FAA headquarters.

It turns out that these two people were both new to their jobs. In fact, it was the first day on the job for Benedict Leo Sliney, the national operations manager at FAA's Command Center.

Benedict Sliney

Benedict Sliney was an ATC in the U.S. Air Force during the Vietnam War and, after that; he worked at the FAA for the first half of his professional career. In the 1980s, Sliney went on from the FAA to work as an attorney and continued in that career throughout the 1990s. He worked for several law firms during this time, handling various kinds of cases, and he was a partner in some of those firms.

Sliney's clients included financial investors who were accused of Securities and Exchange violations. In one 1998 case, he represented Steven K. Gourlay, Jr., an employee of Sterling Foster. It was reported that Sterling Foster was "secretly controlled" by Randolph Pace and was at the center of "one of the most notorious scams ever."[5] Sliney got Gourlay's charges dropped in 1998[6] but, in a related 2002 case, Gourlay pled guilty to conspiracy to commit securities fraud, mail fraud and wire fraud, and was sentenced to six months in prison.[7]

In the summer of 2000, Sliney represented Merrill Lynch in a case in which the delay of the transfer of clients' funds to Smith Barney was said to have "caused their investments with Merrill, Lynch to lose some $638,000 in value." Sliney was able to get Merrill Lynch off the hook.[8]

For whatever reasons, Sliney decided to leave his lucrative law career just months before 9/11 in order to return to the FAA. It was reported that Jack Kies, FAA's manager of tactical operations, offered Sliney the job of Command Center national operations manager. Instead, Sliney asked to work as a specialist and he started in that role. Kies offered Sliney the national operations manager position again six months later and Sliney accepted.[9] His first day on the job was September 11, 2001.

On 9/11, others present at the FAA's Command Center outranked Sliney. Interviews of those others, however, including Linda Schuessler and John White, confirm that Sliney was given the lead in the Command Center's response to the hijackings that day. Despite that critical role, Sliney is mentioned only one time in the narrative of the *9/11 Commission Report.*

According to the summary of his interview for the investigation, Sliney was first notified of "a hijack in progress" sometime between 8:15 and 8:20 a.m. EST. This was about the same time as communications were lost with American Airlines Flight 11, the first of the planes to be hijacked, and it was about 30 minutes before that plane crashed into the north tower of the World Trade Center (WTC). It was nearly two hours before Flight 93 was destroyed in Pennsylvania. Incredibly, according to Sliney's interview, it was not until after a second confirmed hijacking occurred and two planes had crashed into the WTC (nearly an hour after he learned about the first hijacking) that Sliney "realized that the hijackers were piloting the aircraft."[10]

After the second tower was hit, Sliney responded by asking for a military response via the special military unit assigned to the FAA's Command Center, the Air Traffic Services Cell (ATSC). This was at approximately 9:06. At the time, one of the three military officers in the ATSC called the NMCC and that officer was told that "senior leaders" at the NMCC are "in a meeting to determine their response" to the attacks, and would call back.[11] As this example shows, there are as many unanswered questions about what went on at the NMCC that morning as there are about what happened at the FAA.[12]

Several of the FAA's top people confirmed that the military was engaged and knew about the hijackings early on. This included Jeff Griffith at the Command Center and Monte Belger, the FAA's acting Deputy Administrator, who was present at FAA Headquarters. According to Belger, "there were military people on duty at the FAA Command Center, as Mr. Sliney said. They were participating in what was going on. There were military people in the FAA's Air Traffic Organization in a situation room. They were participating in what was going on."[13]

Sliney's interview summary is full of phrases like he "did not recall" and "was not aware," although he did recall being informed that interceptors were eventually launched (too late). Apparently, Sliney didn't know what the fighters would do if they were launched. He recalled thinking: "Well, what are they going to do?" In an apparent defensive posture, Sliney claimed, "definitively that he did not receive a request to authorize a request to the military for assistance."[14]

One might think that the national operations manager for the FAA's Command Center would not need a "request to authorize a request for military assistance" and that he might know what military assistance would entail. But Sliney's interview summary suggests that he did not even know what the protocol was for requesting military assistance in the event of a hijacking. Sliney's understanding on 9/11 and two years later, when the interview was conducted, was that an FAA request for military assistance "emanates from the effected Center...directly to the military." That is, Sliney supposedly was not aware of any role that the FAAs' Command Center or FAA HQ might have had in the request for interception of hijacked aircraft. This is in contradiction to the protocol given by the *9/11 Commission Report* and it is definitely in contradiction to the concept of a "hijack coordinator."

In addition to the confusion about the Command Center's role in requesting military assistance, it seems there was only one person at FAA headquarters who was authorized to request military assistance – the hijack coordinator. On 9/11, Benedict Sliney was told that no one could find that one person. Sliney later recounted his experience learning of that fact in this way:

"I said something like, 'That's incredible. There's only one person. There must be someone designated or someone who will assume the responsibility of issuing an order, you know.' We were becoming frustrated in our attempts to get some information. What was the military response?"[15]

Michael Canavan

The hijack coordinator at FAA headquarters, Lt. Gen. Michael A. Canavan, had been in his position for only nine months and would leave the job within a month after 9/11. Surprisingly, although Canavan was mentioned in the *9/11 Commission Report*, he was not cited for his role as the FAA's hijack coordinator, a role that was at the center of the failure to intercept the planes on 9/11.

Instead of being mentioned as the hijack coordinator, Canavan was in the report because he had been the commander of the Joint Special Operations Command (JSOC), which ran the military's counterterrorism operations and covert missions. The report described Canavan's part in the failure to follow-through on a carefully laid-out 1998 CIA plan to capture Osama bin Laden (OBL) in Afghanistan. Canavan was quoted as saying that the plan put tribal Afghanis at too much risk and that the "operation was too complicated for the CIA."[16] Ironically, after 9/11, few if any U.S. leaders would express concern for tribal Afghanis while engaging in a war of aggression in Afghanistan.

Nearly the entirety of Canavan's career was in military special operations. He was a Special Forces soldier for many years and, before he was JSOC Commander, he was Special Operations Commander for the U.S. European Command (SOCEUR), which included operations throughout Africa as well. Canavan was SOCEUR from 1994 to 1996 and JSOC Commander from 1996 to 1998.

JSOC is a successor organization to the Office of Policy Coordination (OPC), which was a secret government-funded organization authorized by the National Security Council in 1948. The OPC was led by CIA director Allen Dulles and Frank Wisner, a State Department official who wielded unprecedented power due to his position in New York law and financial circles. The JSOC was created in 1980 by the

Pentagon and run by Ted Shackley's OPC colleague, Richard Stillwell. According to author Joseph Trento, JSOC quickly became "one of the most secret operations of the U.S. government."[17]

Creation of the JSOC was, ostensibly, a response to the failed 1980 hostage rescue attempt in Iran called Operation Eagle Claw. JSOC immediately went on to engage in an "array of highly covert activities" by way of "black budgets."[18] This included operations in Honduras and El Salvador which supported the illegal wars associated with the Nicaraguan rebels called the Contras.

In 1987, JSOC was assigned to a new military command called the U.S. Special Operations Command (SOCOM) that came about through the work of Senator William Cohen. Senator Cohen went on to become the Secretary of Defense from 1997 to 2001 and it was he who led the Quadrennial Defense Review of 1997 that reduced the number of jet fighters actively protecting the continental U.S. from 100 to 14.[19] Cohen is now chairman of The Cohen group, where he works with his vice chairman Marc Grossman, who FBI whistleblower Sibel Edmonds says figures prominently in the information she has attempted to provide.

Hugh Shelton was the commander of SOCOM during the same years that Canavan was the commander of JSOC. Shelton went on to become the Chairman of the Joint Chiefs of Staff (CJCS), which is the highest position in the U.S. military. He was in that position on September 11th and was, like Canavan, curiously absent for just the morning hours on that day.[20]

In any case, it seems odd that Michael Canavan occupied what turned out to be the most important position relative to the failure to intercept the hijacked planes on 9/11 and was also involved in evaluating plans to capture OBL just three years earlier. Apart from the coincidence that he was selected as the most qualified person for both of those very different positions, he was also a central figure in these two different reasons why the 9/11 attacks were said to have succeeded.

When he first started the job as FAA's hijack coordinator, just nine months before the attacks, Canavan was in charge of running training exercises that were "pretty damn close to [the] 9/11 plot," according to John Hawley, an employee in the FAA's intelligence division.[21] In his comments to the 9/11 Commission, Canavan denied having participated in such exercises and the Commission apparently didn't think to reconcile the conflicting comments it had received from Hawley and Canavan on this important issue.

That's not surprising in light of the fact that Canavan's treatment by the 9/11 Commission was one of uncritical deference. Reading through the transcript of the related hearing gives the impression that the Commission members were not only trying to avoid asking the General any difficult questions—they were fawning over him.

Lee Hamilton began his questioning of Canavan by saying "You're pretty tough on the airlines, aren't you?"[22] As with many of the statements and reports made by Hamilton, the evidence suggests that the opposite is true.

In May 2001, Canavan wrote an internal FAA memorandum that initiated a new policy of more lax fines for airlines and airports that had security problems. The memo suggested that, if the airlines or airports had a written plan to fix the problem, fines were not needed. For whatever reason, the memo was also taken to mean that FAA agents didn't even have to enforce corrections as long as the airline or airport said they were working on it.[23] Canavan's memo was repeatedly cited as a cause of failure to fix security problems in the months leading up to 9/11.[24]

The FAA's office of Civil Aviation Security, which Canavan led, was also responsible for the "Red Teams." These teams were responsible for covertly conducting airport security testing in order to identify vulnerabilities. The Red Teams were intended to test all of the hijacking prevention systems that the alleged hijackers defeated on 9/11. In his position as leader of that office, Canavan quickly learned all the weaknesses of those systems.

One of Canavan's Read Team Leaders, Bogdan Dzakovic, later testified to the 9/11 Commission that airports had begun to be warned by the FAA before the Red Teams got there. He also claimed that FAA officials knew something like 9/11 was going to happen and that they purposefully ignored the evidence. Dzakovic indicated that his team "repeatedly warned the FAA of the potential for security breaches and hijackings but was told to cover up its findings." A Department of

Transportation inquiry into the claims revealed that, prior 9/11, the "Red Team program was grossly mismanaged and the result was a serious compromise of public safety."[25]

Canavan's job as hijack coordinator was clearly the most important link in the communications chain between the FAA and the military. But the 9/11 Commission did not address this hijack coordinator position, and did not mention the alarming fact that we don't know who actually handled the job of hijack coordinator on the day of 9/11. We don't know because Canavan said he was in Puerto Rico that morning and claimed to have missed out on everything that happened that day.[26]

Here is Canavan's exact statement to the Commission, in response to an unrelated question from Commissioner Richard Ben-Veniste, whose questions were, like Hamilton's, rather submissive.

> "Here's my answer — and it's not to duck the question. Number one, I was visiting the airport in San Juan that day when this happened. That was a CADEX airport, and I was down there also to remove someone down there that was in a key position. So when 9/11 happened, that's where I was. I was able to get back to Washington that evening on a special flight from the Army back from San Juan, back to Washington. So everything that transpired that day in terms of times, I have to — and I have no information on that now, because when I got back we weren't — that wasn't the issue at the time. We were — when I got back it was, What are we going to do over the next 48 hours to strengthen what just happened?"[27]

One might think that the Commissioners would have expressed surprise at Canavan's rambling, incoherent claim that he was just not available during the events of 9/11. We would certainly expect the Commissioners to have followed up with detailed questions about who was in charge that day with respect to the most important role related to the failed national response. But that was not the case. Instead, Ben-Veniste redirected the discussion while "putting aside the issue." None of the other Commissioners said a word about Canavan being missing that day or even asked who was filling in for him as the primary contact between the FAA and the military with regard to hijackings. And, of course, the *9/11 Commission Report* did not mention any of it at all.

Canavan's assistant and back-up, Lynne Osmus, just happened to be out sick that day. It was not clear who the back-up to the back-up would have been, but someone from another department was vaguely cited. This was Lee Longmire, a veteran U.S. Army counterintelligence officer who on 9/11 was in charge of Airport Compliance and Field Operations. But Longmire was apparently not aware that he was filling in for Canavan because the notes from his 9/11 Commission interview did not reflect it.[28]

Longmire suggested that the Commission talk to one of his assistants, Mike Weikert, who he believed was more involved. Weikert is of further interest because FAA intelligence officer John Hawley, who claimed that Canavan had led table top exercises that "were pretty damn close to the 9/11 plot," also stated in his Commission interview that Weikert had helped to lead those exercises.[29]

In the interest of finding out more about what happened, investigators should return to the failure of FAA HQ to request military assistance for Flight 93. The question should be asked — what was FAA HQ doing for those 30 minutes after being informed of a fourth hijacking, and in the absence of the one person who was charged to do something about it? Apparently, for fifteen minutes nothing was done. But after that, according to the official account, the conversations were going nowhere.

At 9:49 a.m., according to the report, this was the exchange between the FAA Command Center and FAA HQ:

> Command Center: Uh, do we want to think, uh, about scrambling aircraft?
>
> FAA HQ: Oh, God, I don't know.
>
> Command Center: Uh, that's a decision somebody's gonna have to make probably in the next ten minutes.
>
> FAA HQ: Uh, ya know everybody just left the room.

The report says that ineffectual discussions about scrambling aircraft were still occurring at FAA HQ twenty minutes after it had received notification of the fourth hijacking.

At 9:53 am, "FAA headquarters informed the Command Center that the deputy director for air traffic services was talking to Monte Belger about scrambling aircraft." This contradicts Benedict Sliney's testimony that an FAA request for military assistance "emanates from the effected Center…directly to the military." Moreover, the Deputy Director of Air Traffic Services that day was Jeff Griffith and Monte Belger was the Deputy Administrator for the FAA. And Belger and Griffith denied they ever had a conversation about scrambling aircraft, despite the 9/11 Commission stating this as fact.

Jane Garvey was also present during the failed response at FAA HQ. She was the FAA Administrator from 1997 to 2002 and coincidentally, in the years before that, had been the director of Logan International Airport in Boston, where two of the flights took off on 9/11. Apparently Garvey's record as director for the Logan airport, which had for many years the worst security record of any major airport, was not a problem for her nomination to the top job at FAA. It was Garvey who appointed Canavan to his role as Associate Administrator for Civil Aviation Security, commonly known as the hijack coordinator.

In any case, in the absence of the hijack coordinator the FAA was completely incompetent in terms of communicating the need to intercept the hijacked planes on 9/11. Officially, the only notice of the hijackings to the military came directly from the FAA centers, bypassing both the Command Center and FAA HQ. Boston Center reached NEADS at 8:37 to request help with the first hijacking, and New York Center notified the military of the second hijacking at 9:03. NEADS only found about the third hijacking at 9:34 by calling the Washington Center to ask about Flight 11, and the military was said to have first learned about the hijacking of Flight 93 from Cleveland Center at 10:07. Nevertheless, none of the planes were intercepted.

9/11 and Special Operations

Although Michael Canavan was unavailable to perform his critical job on 9/11, he was fully involved in the response to the attacks. Just two days later, he attended a "Principals Committee Meeting" chaired by Condoleezza Rice that included all of George W. Bush's "war cabinet."[30] This meeting set the stage for how the new War on Terror would be conducted.

Canavan later cashed in on the windfalls of the resulting wars and the privatization of military operations when he was hired on at Anteon

International Corporation as president of its Information Systems Group. In doing so he joined a number of prominent defense department alumni, including his former special operations colleague Hugh Shelton, who was on the board of directors at Anteon.

Since 9/11, covert activities have been authorized frequently but, prior to that, SOCOM was not supposed to conduct covert operations. Therefore, JSOC had worked intimately with the CIA's clandestine group called the Special Activities Division. Canavan led those kinds of operations in northern Iraq, Liberia and Bosnia. He ran special operations in Croatia in 1996 and, according to President Clinton, was the one who identified Secretary of Commerce Ron Brown's body after Brown's plane crashed there.[31]

JSOC regularly works with foreign intelligence agencies, including the Mossad.[32] It has been involved with hijackings, for example that of the *Achille Lauro* and TWA Flight 847. It has also operated from bases in foreign countries, such as Saudi Arabia, for many years.[33] Presidential Decision Directive PDD-25, gave JSOC one of the rare exemptions from the *Posse Comitatus* Act of 1878, which meant that JSOC could legally conduct its missions within the United States.[34]

In the War on Terror, the special mission units of JSOC have been given the authority to pursue secret operations around the world. JSOC effectively operates outside the law, capturing and killing people with or without the knowledge of the host countries in which it operates. JSOC missions are always low-profile and the U.S. government will not acknowledge any specifics about them.

Investigative journalist Seymour Hersh has discovered that an assassination squad of the JSOC was under the command of Vice President Cheney after the 9/11 attacks.[35] Hersh also claimed that the leaders of JSOC "are all members of, or at least supporters of, the Knights of Malta" and that "many of them are members of Opus Dei."[36] The ties between the Knights of Malta and high-level U.S. intelligence personnel, including William Casey and William Donovan, have been well-documented.[37] Such accusations have also been made of Louis Freeh, who would have worked closely with Canavan and Shelton in the pursuit of special operations targets.

Other special operations leaders who were involved in the lack of response on 9/11 included Richard Armitage, who supervised the Bureau of Consular Affairs that granted express visas to the alleged hijackers. Armitage was present on the secure video teleconference with Richard Clarke during the attacks.[38]

As reviewed in Chapter 3, Armitage was involved in special operations in Vietnam and later was party to several of the most well-known covert operations in U.S. history, including the Phoenix Program and the Iran-Contra crimes.[39] After the invasion of Iraq, Armitage was identified as the one who betrayed CIA agent Valerie Plame by revealing her identity, apparently in retaliation for her husband's attempt to set the record straight on weapons of mass destruction. Armitage admitted that he revealed Plame's identity but claimed it was done inadvertently.[40]

Another special operations soldier who testified to the 9/11 Commission and played a significant role with regard to the airlines and facilities prior to 9/11 was Brian Michael Jenkins. While Shelton and Canavan were running SOCOM and JSOC, Jenkins was the deputy chairman of Kroll Associates when that company was designing the security system for the World Trade Center (WTC) complex.[41]

Jenkins was appointed by President Clinton to be a member of the White House Commission on Aviation Safety and Security, where he collaborated with James Abrahamson of WTC security company Stratesec, and FBI director Louis Freeh. As will be discussed in Chapter 11, Jenkins served as an advisor to the National Commission on Terrorism, led by L. Paul Bremer, who went on to be an executive of WTC impact zone tenant Marsh & McLennan and then the Iraq occupation governor. Jenkins returned to the RAND Corporation where he had previously worked with Donald Rumsfeld, Condoleezza Rice, Frank Carlucci of The Carlyle Group, and Paul Kaminski of Anteon.

Lieutenant Colonel John Blitch was yet another special operations soldier who played a big part in the events immediately following 9/11. Blitch spent his career in the U.S. Army's Special Forces and was said to have retired just the day before 9/11 to become an employee of Science Applications International Corporation (SAIC). Immediately following the attacks, he was put in charge of the team of robotic machine operators that explored the pile at Ground Zero, using devices that had previously been used for elimination of unexploded ordnance.

Conclusions

Despite being given plenty of notice about the four planes hijacked on 9/11, FAA HQ did not request military assistance to ensure the planes were intercepted before they crashed. The 9/11 Commission attributed this to a string of gross failures in communication between the FAA and the military. However, the report placed no blame on any of the people who were involved and didn't even mention the one person who was most important to this chain of communications.

One of the most important people involved was Benedict Sliney, who had, just before 9/11, left a lucrative law career defending Wall Street financiers to return to work as a specialist at the FAA. It was his first day on the job. With regard to ensuring military interception of the hijacked planes, he said he did not receive a "request to authorize a request." Sliney also claimed to not know that FAA management at the Command Center, where he was in charge, or at FAA HQ, had any role in requests for military assistance. This is in contradiction to the stated protocol in the *9/11 Commission Report* and also the idea of an FAA hijack coordinator.

The FAA hijack coordinator was Michael Canavan, a career special operations commander who had come to the civilian FAA job only nine months before 9/11. According to an FAA intelligence agent, one of the first things Canavan did in that job was lead and participate in exercises that were "pretty damn close to the 9/11 plot." He was also known within the FAA for writing a memo just a few months before 9/11 that instituted a new leniency with regard to airport and airline security.

With regard to the communication failures, Canavan offered the unsolicited excuse that he was absent during the morning hours of 9/11, in Puerto Rico. The 9/11 Commission did not pursue this excuse nor did it ask who was filling the critical hijack coordinator role in Canavan's absence. In fact, the *9/11 Commission Report* didn't address the hijack coordinator role at all. The report mentioned Sliney only once in the entire narrative and did not refer to Canavan in his role as hijack coordinator.

Independent investigators should look into why a lawyer, who knew how to handle evidence and get financiers off the hook, was experiencing his first day on the job as national operations manager at the FAA. And if 9/11 was a "special operation" as some people now suspect, investigators might consider that a number of special operations specialists were in place to ensure that the operation went off without a hitch and was not discovered. Long-time special operations leaders like Michael Canavan, Brian Michael Jenkins, and Richard Armitage played critical roles with respect to the facilities, events, and official story of 9/11. These facts seem worthy of further scrutiny.

Chapter 8

Ralph Eberhart and NORAD

In a 2004 U.S. Senate hearing, Senator Mark Dayton remarked that "this country and its citizens were completely undefended" for "109 minutes" on 9/11.[1] Dayton went on to clarify that officials within the North American Aerospace Defense Command (NORAD) had covered up the facts about the lack of air defenses by lying to the 9/11 Commission, to Congress, and to the American people. And they were not held accountable.

One man was most responsible for both the air defense failures and the lying that covered it up. U.S. Air Force General Ralph E. Eberhart had taken over command of NORAD from General Richard Myers in February 2000. The position included leadership of all air defense operations in North America and, also, the U.S. Space Command. Therefore, on 9/11, Eberhart was responsible for the failure to intercept the four hijacked aircraft over a period of nearly two hours.

NORAD is the joint U.S.-Canadian military organization charged with monitoring and defending the airspace over North America. Long-standing operating procedures at NORAD, for dealing with airliners that have gone off-course or been hijacked, were not followed on 9/11. Each of the four flights involved in the 9/11 attacks should have been intercepted when they lost radio contact, deviated from their course, or turned off their transponders.[2]

The procedures for interception were automatic and required no special orders to implement.[3] Through these procedures, interceptor jets had been scrambled 129 times in the year 2000 and 67 times in the year prior to June 2001. A 1994 government report stated, "Overall, during the past four years, NORAD's alert fighters took off to intercept aircraft (referred to as scrambled) 1,518 times, or an average of 15 times per site per year. Of these incidents, the number of suspected drug smuggling aircraft averaged ... less than 7 percent of all of the alert sites' total activity. The remaining activity generally involved visually inspecting unidentified aircraft and assisting aircraft in distress."[4]

On 9/11, the NORAD interception system failed completely and we have been given multiple, conflicting explanations for why that happened. Considering that there is strong evidence for an alternative hypothesis of insider involvement in 9/11, it is reasonable to assume that an intentional compromising of the U.S. air defenses might have occurred that day. Adding to this suspicion is the fact that guilt tends to be reflected in false testimony. And as Senator Dayton said, NORAD officials "lied to the American people, they lied to Congress and they lied to your 9/11 Commission."[5]

Exactly *which* NORAD statements were lies and which were not is a matter that is still not clear to this day. This is partly because the explanations and testimony that are now said to have been false were far more damning to NORAD than the final account, which exonerates NORAD entirely. Why would NORAD leaders want to lie so as to make their performance look worse?

In order to determine the facts, investigators should begin with at least three areas of inquiry: 1) the times at which NORAD was notified (or made aware) of the hijackings, 2) the times at which NORAD responded in the form of scrambling jets to intercept, and 3) the instructions given to the interceptor pilots in terms of speed and direction.

NORAD's Ever-changing Story

The military's explanations began with a short description of the response to the hijackings. Two days after the attacks, General Richard Myers gave this account to the Senate Armed Services Committee, in an official hearing for his confirmation as Chairman of the Joint Chiefs of Staff (CJCS). He said that no fighter jets were scrambled to intercept any of the hijacked 9/11 flights until after the Pentagon was hit.[6]

Although Myers was not in command of NORAD on 9/11, he should have known two days later if normal procedures had been followed. As

Acting CJCS on 9/11, and as vice chairman otherwise, his role was to ensure the president and secretary of defense were informed of critical military matters.

A second story was given a week after the attacks, when NORAD provided a partial timeline of the notifications it had received from the Federal Aviation Administration (FAA) and the responses that followed. General Eberhart reiterated this timeline in testimony to the U.S. Senate a few weeks later and for over two years it stood as the official account.[7] This timeline said that NORAD had received notification about three of the hijacked planes with plenty of time left to ensure interception and had scrambled jets from multiple bases as the attacks proceeded.

The timeline showed that NORAD was notified about the hijacking of Flight 175 at 8:43 am, a full twenty minutes before it impacted the south tower of the World Trade Center (WTC). Moreover, F-15 interceptor jets from Otis Air Force Base (AFB) were said to be airborne by 8:52, having been scrambled in response to the first hijacking. This allowed twice the time needed for the jets to reach New York City before Flight 175 crashed.

Eberhart added that NORAD was notified about the hijacked Flight 77 coming into Washington at 9:24 am, fourteen minutes before it impacted the Pentagon. He told the Senate Armed Services Committee (repeatedly) that this was a "documented notification."[8] If true, interceptor jets from Andrews AFB, only ten miles from the Pentagon, could have easily reached the errant airliner given this lead time.

Although the military might use the excuse that Andrews AFB was not technically under the command of NORAD, the 9/11 Commission said that Eberhart's statement was simply not true. In fact, both Commission counsel Dan Marcus and team leader John Farmer were later very blunt about this being false.[9] Therefore, it is clear that Eberhart should be charged with the related crime. It is illegal to make any materially false statement or representation in testimony to the Unites States Congress.[10] And that was not the only false statement that Eberhart apparently made to the senators.

In May 2003, Eberhart's subordinates General Arnold and Colonel William Alan Scott presented a slightly revised version of NORAD's timeline. They contradicted the timeline for Flight 175, saying that NORAD was not notified of the hijacking until 9:05, three minutes after the aircraft crashed into the south tower. This was despite the fact that when asked by a U.S. Senator about "the second hijacked plane somewhere up there" (Flight 175), Eberhart had previously said "Yes, sir. During that time, we were notified."[11]

Arnold and Scott also revealed for the first time that NORAD was notified about the hijacking of Flight 93 at 9:16 am. This was 47 minutes before that flight allegedly crashed in Pennsylvania, at 10:03 am. Obviously, interceptor jets could have easily reached and escorted Flight 93 given this revised timeline.

The fourth and final story from NORAD was the official account given by the *9/11 Commission Report*, now supported by NORAD. In this explanation NORAD received "no advance notice" on any of the last three hijacked airliners.[12] Instead of 20 minutes of notice on Flight 175, and 14 minutes notice on Flight 77, and 47 minutes notice on Flight 93, we were told that NORAD was not notified about any of them until it was too late. The military was off the hook entirely.

All the evidence for notifications and response, which had constituted the official account for nearly three years, had been thrown out the window. In place of these documents and testimonies, new explanations were given for why the scrambled aircraft never reached the hijacked airliners. These included unbelievable claims of communication failures and misdirection of the scrambled jets, as well as the introduction of a never-before mentioned "Phantom 11" scenario.[13]

The official account was supported two years later by an article in *Vanity Fair*. [14] Allegedly, the author of the article was given privileged access to audio tapes that were not available to the public. Although the newly revealed "NORAD tapes" ostensibly bolstered the Commission's new timeline, credible explanations were never given for throwing out the years of testimony and evidence that had supported entirely different timelines.

The changing stories given by NORAD led to placing more blame for the failed air defenses on the FAA. After NORAD's 2003 timeline was issued, however, the FAA publicly stated that NORAD had in fact been informed throughout all the developments that morning. FAA official Laura Brown wrote a memo to the 9/11 Commission in which she stated that the FAA had shared "real-time information" with NORAD about "loss of communication with aircraft, loss of transponder signals, unauthorized changes in course, and other actions being taken by all the flights of interest, including Flight 77."[15]

FAA leadership certainly did fail that morning and there are shocking questions to be answered in that regard.[16] Not the least of these questions is why evidence that might have helped was destroyed by an FAA official after the attacks.[17] But the multiple stories given by the military indicate that NORAD was at least as culpable as the FAA in the inexplicable lack of air defense. And the facts indicate that NORAD was in the loop earlier than its 2003 timeline suggested, meaning that there is no reasonable explanation for why NORAD-controlled jets did not intercept most, if not all, of the planes hijacked on 9/11.

When questioned by the 9/11 Commission, Eberhart confirmed that if NORAD had been in the loop as the FAA said it was, his people would have been able "to shoot down all three aircraft—all four aircraft."[18]

Reasons to Suspect Eberhart

Investigation of NORAD and its commander Eberhart is warranted, apart from the evidence for lying to Congress. Additional reasons to focus on Eberhart include the following nine facts.

1. As Commander in Chief of the U.S. Space Command (CINCSPACE), Eberhart was responsible for setting Infocon levels.[19] Infocon is an alert system that defends against attacks on communications networks within the DOD. Just 12 hours before the 9/11 attacks, an order was given to lower Infocon to its least protective level.[20] Setting Infocon at a lower level made

it easier for people to hack into or compromise the DOD computer networks, including the air defense system.[21]

2. As both CINCSPACE and Commander in Chief of NORAD (CINCNORAD), Eberhart was in charge of many of the highly coincidental military exercises (i.e. war games) that were going on that morning.

3. Eberhart did nothing effective in response to the 9/11 hijackings, despite being present in the military's teleconference as those hijackings were in progress. He did not order the scrambling of jets, he did not order an escort for Air Force One, and he did not provide leadership.

4. Eberhart also failed to implement military control over U.S. airspace until well after the attacks were over. Although it was his prerogative to do so, Eberhart did not implement SCATANA, the process of assuming military control over the U.S. airspace, until an hour after the last plane had been destroyed. Eberhart later said that he had waited until it finally became "obvious" to him that a coordinated terrorist attack was underway.[22] He told the 9/11 Commission that, although people were telling him to take control of the airspace earlier, he didn't feel that the military could "provide traffic de-confliction like the FAA has."[23]

5. In the middle of the 9/11 attacks, Eberhart decided to drive between Peterson Air Force Base and NORAD's Cheyenne Mountain Operations Center (CMOC). Normally this 12-mile drive takes 30 minutes but it took Eberhart between 45 minutes and an hour to make the drive that morning. No reason was ever given (or requested) for why Eberhart did not fly directly to CMOC from Peterson, making use of the Cheyenne Mountain helicopter port. Eberhart made conflicting statements about his reasons for making this trip, saying that he stayed for a while at Peterson because he "did not want to lose communication."[24] Nevertheless, Eberhart lost communication at the most important time by leaving at approximately 9:30 am (EST), when two of the hijacked planes were still flying wildly

off-course. His reason for doing this was that things had "quieted down."[25]

6. While on his way to the CMOC he was in the U.S. military's air threat call via cell phone. In this call, at 9:49 am, Eberhart "directed all air sovereignty aircraft to battle stations, fully armed."[26] Although this might sound like decisive action, the command apparently grounded all interceptor jets that had not yet taken off due to the fact that "battle stations" is a grounded status. Other military leaders later gave orders to actually scramble the jets. And despite his involvement, Eberhart portrayed himself as being out of the loop entirely. For example, he told the 9/11 Commission that he had "no knowledge of the circumstances that initiated the scramble" of fighter jets from Langley AFB and that he had just "recently" been made aware that it happened (in March 2004).[27]

7. Eberhart failed to explain the multiple changes in the account of 9/11 that were given by NORAD. In fact, he seemed to tell his staff to change the NORAD timeline as much as was needed in order to prevent further questioning about the military's performance.[28]

8. For whatever reasons, Eberhart also gave false information about the NORAD response to others. General Richard Myers, acting CJCS that morning, said that Eberhart told him there were "several hijack codes in the system." Yet none of the four planes had squawked the hijack code on 9/11 and therefore it is not clear how such codes could have been in the system.[29]

9. NORAD failed to cooperate with the 9/11 Commission. Even as late as March 2004, the Commission was struggling to get basic documents about 9/11 performance from Eberhart's organization.[30] In some cases, such as with the after-action reports that follow all military actions, the Commission never received the NORAD documents.

Of all these concerns, it is the military exercises that NORAD was conducting on 9/11 that have drawn the most attention from concerned citizens. When questioned about them, Eberhart claimed that the impact of the 9/11 exercises on NORAD's response was that they "at most cost us 30 seconds."[31] That was clearly not the case.

NORAD's Coincidental Exercises

After several government officials had made incorrect statements about the military's preparation for hijackings and the use of planes as weapons, General Myers responded to a pointed question on the subject. He reported that NORAD had practiced "five exercise hijack events," between November 1999 and October 2000, all of which "included a suicide crash into a high value target."[32] Records released since that time show that NORAD had practiced 28 hijack exercise events in the 20 months leading up to 9/11. At least six of these were focused on hijackings located entirely within the Unites States, which puts to rest the excuse that NORAD was only looking for threats coming from outside of U.S. borders.[33]

One of these exercises, Vigilant Guardian in October 2000, practiced interception of an airliner hijacked for a suicide attack against the 39-story United Nations building in New York City, just a few blocks from the WTC.[34] Another air defense exercise, called Amalgam Virgo and practiced just three months before 9/11, was accompanied by a planning document that had a picture of Osama bin Laden on the cover.[35]

Many of the military exercises or war games that were occurring on the day of 9/11 were run under the control of CINCNORAD Eberhart. In fact, Eberhart was in command of the war games that had the greatest impact on the nation's air defenses. Of course, he had help.

NORAD is divided into several large areas that cover the U.S. and Canada, one of which is the region of the continental U.S. called CONR, headed on 9/11 by General Larry Arnold. Within CONR there are three sectors. The 9/11 attacks took place in the airspace monitored by CONR's Northeast Air Defense Sector (NEADS). Personnel at NEADS were therefore primarily responsible for trying to coordinate the NORAD response to the hijackings. CMOC was also an important facility in the response failures.

At NEADS, Colonel Robert Marr was in charge. Marr had been in the U.S. Air Force for over 20 years until 1994, at which time he spent a few months in Saudi Arabia as "director of combat operations."[36] He then left the military to work two years for a private company called Phoenix Air. Coincidentally, Phoenix Air provided aircraft for the Amalgam Virgo exercises.[37] There is also reason to believe that Phoenix Air is associated with Huffman Aviation where the alleged 9/11 hijackers had trained.[38] After his stint at Phoenix Air, Marr returned to the military as the exercise coordinator at NEADS and, by 9/11, had risen to the position of commander of the facility.

NORAD exercise planners stated that several exercises were "planned" on 9/11.[39] These included Vigilant Guardian and Vigilant Overview, both command post exercises (CPX), and Amalgam Virgo and Amalgam Warrior, which were field training (or FTX) exercises. All four of these exercises were CJCS-approved and sponsored by CINCNORAD Eberhart.[40]

It is clear that at least one of these planned exercises, Vigilant Guardian, was actually being conducted on 9/11. Additionally, another war game called Apollo Guardian was running on 9/11. This was an exercise conducted by the U.S. Space Command, meaning Eberhart was in control of that too.

FTX exercises are sometimes what are referred to as SPADEs, meaning "a track is taken out of radar coverage and then re-introduced as an unknown track."[41] This exercise feature is interesting given that Flight 77 was lost on radar for a period of time on 9/11 and then reappeared in a way that has not yet been explained.[42]

Amalgam Virgo 02 was a modification of Twin Star, a live-fly joint FAA/NORAD exercise conducted in 1995. This was described by NORAD exercise design manager Ken Merchant and Major Paul Goddard, the Canadian who was NORAD exercise chief.[43] According to Goddard, the Twin Star plan was to have interceptor jets scramble and escort a hijacked airliner. During this exercise, "the fighters never got off on the appropriate heading, and it took them forever to catch up."[44]

It seems worthwhile to consider that Amalgam Virgo 02, which was ostensibly only in the planning stages on 9/11, might actually have been in play that morning. One reason to consider this is that, on 9/11, the fighters "never got off on the appropriate heading, and it took them forever to catch up." Another reason is that 9/11 Commissioner Richard Ben-Veniste showed considerable interest in Amalgam Virgo 02, as did the 9/11 Commission staff in its request for documents.[45] According to Ben-Veniste, this was a case in which "NORAD had already in the works plans to simulate in an exercise a simultaneous hijacking of two planes in the United States."[46] The plan for Amalgam Virgo 02 was therefore similar to the 9/11 attacks, with multiple, simultaneous hijackings.

Another large-scale exercise being conducted on 9/11 was Global Guardian, a joint nuclear war simulation run by the U.S. Strategic Command (Stratcom) in conjunction with NORAD. This was essentially a practice for Armageddon that involved live nuclear bombs and at least three airborne command and control airliners called E-4Bs.[47] The E-4B that was seen circling the White House during the 9/11 attacks might have been part of this exercise.[48]

The 9/11 Commission did not mention most of these exercises in its report. To the contrary, the report mentioned only Vigilant Guardian and then only once, in a deceptively stated footnote that said "On 9/11, NORAD was scheduled to conduct a military exercise, Vigilant Guardian, which postulated a bomber attack from the Soviet Union."[49] This statement is false in several ways, not the least of which is that NORAD was involved in multiple exercises on 9/11. And Vigilant Guardian was not simply an exercise involving one bomber from the former Soviet Union.

Vigilant Guardian 01 (VG) had been in play for several days as of 9/11. On September 9, it included a scenario in which terrorists hijacked an airliner and planned to attack New York City. The exercise presented a number of other scenarios based around airliner hijackings and in one of these, the fictitious terrorists threatened to "Rain Terror from the Skies."[50]

According to the VG planning documents, the 9/11 exercise was to be conducted "sim over live," meaning the simulated hijackings were to be inserted into the live air control system. This was repeated in the instructions – "Ensure all tracks of interest (sim or live) are input on the live chart."[51] Furthermore, the VG plan was that "All expansions will be Real World." Although frequently misunderstood, the term "Real World" does not refer to an actual hijacking, it refers to the use of real aircraft in live-fly exercises.[52]

Due to these confusing circumstances, NEADS staff confused the actual hijackings on 9/11 with the exercises. As researcher Matthew Everett explained, "What is remarkable is that at a time when it should have been obvious to them that the U.S. was in the middle of a major terrorist attack, these key personnel [at NEADS] were uncertain whether what was happening was real or simulated."[53] The confusion caused much more than a "30 second" problem as Eberhart suggested, because NEADS personnel thought the exercises were continuing well after the attacks.

On 9/11, VG was scheduled to include a simulated hijacking at 9:40 a.m., within an hour of when Flight 11 struck the WTC. When they first learned that Flight 11 was hijacked, NEADS staff noted that the "exercise" appeared to be starting an hour early that morning. The evidence indicates that everyone at NEADS, including Colonel Marr, thought the actual hijackings were exercises. They even joked about it.[54] That might have been due to the VG plan stating that the NEADS building where Colonel Marr and company were located was a planned "exercise play area" and everyone there, knowingly or not, was "subject to exercise play."[55]

NEADS radar scopes were displaying simulated information at least until the time of the Pentagon attack. The same problem was going on at CMOC, another exercise play area, with radar screens showing false tracks as late as 10:12. In fact, personnel at CMOC called NEADs in an attempt to stop the exercise inputs.[56] Because those inputs did not stop, it appeared that someone wanted the NEADS and CMOC radar scopes to continue showing false information until after the four planes had been destroyed.

Ken Merchant added that the NMCC, located at the Pentagon, regularly participated in NORAD exercises by interjecting emergency action messages (EAMs).[57] On 9/11, the performance of the NMCC, which plays a critical role in establishing the military chain of command and communicating orders, was remarkably poor. Officers there lacked any sense of urgency and were completely ineffective with regard to communications.[58]

The disruptive effect of the ongoing NORAD exercises that morning continued until after all the hijacked planes had crashed. One military newspaper said VG continued until 30 minutes after attacks.[59] Similarly, Global Guardian was "formally terminated" at 10:44 a.m. but certain actions taken after that time, including that the CMOC's blast doors were closed (a needless action in response to hijacked airliners), suggested that the exercise continued.[60]

Examining the details of how the interceptor jets were managed with respect to the different hijacked flights gives a better understanding of what questions are most important. Jets from Otis AFB were the first to respond and it seemed that those jets had the best chance of catching up with Flight 175.

The Otis Interceptor Jets and Flight 175

The FAA was aware of the hijacking of Flight 11, the first plane, as early as 8:15 a.m. when radio communication was lost. The *9/11 Commission Report* says that the FAA's Boston Center notified NEADS of this hijacking at 8:38. This suggests that the FAA waited 23 minutes to notify NORAD about the hijacking, despite the fact that the military had a communications liaison office (the ATSC) located at FAA's Herndon Command Center.

According to the first timeline provided by NORAD J3, the executive officer for which was Lt. Col. Thomas Browning, FAA notified NEADS of the Flight 175 hijacking at 8:43.[61] This gave the military twenty full minutes to scramble and intercept, and Otis fighters were airborne at 8:52. The F-15 interceptor jets should have needed only six minutes to travel the 192 miles to New York City at the aircraft's maximum speed (Mach 2.5).

The official account now says that NORAD found out about Flight 175 at 9:05, after it crashed. The reasoning given to Colonel Marr by 9/11 Commission staffers as they were trying to convince him of the new timeline was that Flight 175 was not hijacked until 8:46 a.m., so therefore NORAD could not have been notified of it at 8:43.[62] This, however, is not convincing as the *9/11 Commission Report* says the "likely takeover" of Flight 175 was between 8:42 and 8:46 a.m., not exactly at 8:46. If the FAA was aware of the hijacking occurring at 8:42, and with everyone on high alert due to the first hijacking notice at 8:38, the FAA could have notified NORAD a minute later as was originally claimed. This reasoning for the change is therefore not credible.

The Otis fighters therefore should have reached New York City (NYC) before Flight 175 crashed. Instead, the fighters engaged in some strange detours en route to NYC. The Otis fights first flew in a "holding pattern" over the Atlantic.[63] Then they made a sharp turn to the east, away from NYC, and the pilots were told "Remain in current position until FAA requests assistance."[64] Why the Otis pilots flew as they did has did not been revealed.

According to the final account, Flight 175 never turned off its transponder and therefore was clearly visible and fully identified on radar. Nonetheless it lost radio contact with controllers at 8:42 a.m., and it flew without being intercepted for nearly twenty minutes after Flight 11 had crashed into the WTC. Meanwhile, those in charge of national air traffic and defenses watched the airliner the entire time as it flew to New York City and crashed into the WTC.

Just after Flight 175 hit the WTC, an Air National Guard (ANG) commander in Syracuse, New York told Marr, "Give me 10 min. and I can give you hot guns. Give me 30 min. and I'll have heat-seeker [missiles]. Give me an hour and I can give you slammers [Amraams]." And Marr replied, "I want it all." Apparently, this means that Marr wanted to wait for another hour before responding with interceptor jets after two hijacked aircraft had already crashed.

Critics of this interpretation might say that Marr was only trying to ensure the jets would be able to do something when they arrived. But this is contradicted by the fact that other fighters scrambled that day were, according to Commissioner Ben-Veniste and General Craig McKinley, authorized "to use their airplanes to bring down Flight 77 or 93 if they could interdict them. That means to clip their wings, crash into them, perhaps the pilots at the risk of their own lives [*sic*]."[65]

After the 9/11 Commission released its report, Commission staff seemed to make a lot of fuss about the idea that "certain NORAD and FAA" officials might have been deceptive in their testimony.[66] Ultimately this charge seemed to focus on Colonel Marr, but General Eberhart would have been as guilty of the same crimes and he was not criticized. The Commission memo on the subject claimed that the "chat logs" were suddenly more authoritative than all other primary source data including interviews and documented timelines. Could it be that the Commission used the idea that Marr had been deceptive to re-frame the entire NORAD timeline to their own liking? If so, this would mean that the original timelines for Flights 175 and 93 might have been correct but were changed to "no notification given."

The Langley Interceptor Jets and Flight 77

The January 2004 interview of Colonel Marr by five 9/11 Commission staff members, including U.S. Army intelligence officer Miles Kara, suggests that Marr was being coerced into accepting a revised NORAD timeline that had been created by the Commission staff. On the other hand, Marr might not have needed much coaxing. It could be that he simply did not know how he would be viewed according to the new explanations. The interview memorandum says that "Commission staff presented to Marr that it appears Langley was launched in response to AA 11 [Phantom 11]." Marr simultaneously "agreed" yet "did not concede" the point.[67]

According to the long-standing timeline prior to the *9/11 Commission Report*, the FAA notified NORAD about the Flight 77 hijacking at 9:24. Commissioner Ben Veniste interrogated Arnold's deputy Colonel William Alan Scott and General McKinley, who was substituting for Eberhart, about this notification. Ben Veniste said the Commission had evidence that NORAD was in a teleconference with FAA and was receiving real-time information, as Laura Brown from the FAA said. This meant that when FAA learned of Flight 77's hijacking, at around

9:02 a.m., so did NORAD.[68] Eberhart "was not pleased with the hearing" in which Ben-Veniste challenged NORAD so strongly.[69] It was after this, and after the refusal of NORAD to cooperate in providing documents to the Commission, that the timeline began to change to "no notifications."

In the 2003 hearing that Eberhart didn't attend and was unhappy about, Ben-Veniste went on to grill McKinley and Scott about Eberhart's previous statements to the Senate Armed Services Committee (he mistakenly called it the House Committee). Ben-Veniste had, just the day before, found that FAA Commissioner Jane Garvey was clueless about the major questions that Eberhart had asked the 9/11 Commission to put to the FAA 18 months before.[70] Ben-Veniste wanted clarification, twenty months after 9/11, and the answers were even more confusing.

It is interesting that when McKinley gave his testimony in May 2003, providing a narrative that has since been entirely abandoned, he began by saying "I'd like to thank the Commission staff, especially Miles Kara, for his help in preparing for this."[71] That is, 9/11 Commission staff including Miles Kara prepped at least this one witness from NORAD before the Commissioners had a chance to interview him. It appears that Kara helped to create NORAD's early, presumably false, story by helping General McKinley to prepare. As with the "minders" used in Commission interviews and the apparent production of a new timeline by Commission staff, this practice seems to reflect a manipulation that has not been thoroughly considered by investigators.

In any case, at Langley AFB on 9/11, the 119th Fighter Wing of the District of Columbia (DC) ANG was on duty. The Detachment Commander there, Lt. Col. Michael Connor, was on leave but fighter pilots were on alert and ready for air defense. Lead pilot Captain Dean Eckmann and his wingman Major Brad Derrig were the assigned alert pilots. They had been given a "battle stations" order at 9:09, presumably because NORAD wanted them to be ready for anything. At 9:24 a.m., the time that NORAD was originally said to be notified of the hijacking of Flight 77, Eckmann and Derrig were given a scramble order.

Minutes later, the Supervisor of Flying (SOF) at Langley, Captain Craig Borgstrom, was mysteriously ordered via phone, by some unknown person at NEADS, to launch along with the two alert pilots.[72] This was an unprecedented order and to this day no one knows why the SOF, who was needed to coordinate activities from the ground, was scrambled in a spare jet that just happened to be there. Borgstrom called his Wing Commander in Fargo to communicate the order which was "something that had never been done on alert, ever."[73]

Borgstrom said that Mark "Fifi" Lafond was the "ground guy that coordinated a lot of the initial movements."[74] One of Borgstrom's instructors from his training days in Mississippi, Lafond later went on to run a company called Skyblazer Aviation out of Georgia.

Borgstrom doesn't recall the exact heading they were given. He wrote "020" in his logbook but others in the loop remembered it as "010" with an altitude of 29,000 feet. The scramble order would have sent the jets directly to Washington, DC but, after they launched, someone changed their order to "090 for 60," sending them out over the Atlantic Ocean. This new heading was supposedly recorded in a flight strip generated by the Langley tower.

The fact that the scramble order was different than the flight strip was a serious point of concern that was discussed by many people in the 9/11 Commission interviews. But it was ultimately said that the air traffic controllers at the Langley tower, Master Sergeant Kevin Griffith and Senior Airman Raymond Halford, had used this heading on the strip because it was more typical than the scramble order and would get the jets off in a safe way. Why the jets remained going east for so long, when the flight strip was meant to simply get them into the air safely, is another unanswered question.

Griffith and Halford were interviewed along with their commander in the tower, Captain Jay Scherer. They were shown a "duplication" of the flight strip from 9/11 (redacted in the released document) with an odd reason given. Another odd thing is that all of these people from the Langley tower are listed as coming from "Norfolk Tower," which if anything would seem to be referring to the Naval Air Base at Chambers Field, not Langley.

The staff at Norfolk TRACON, an FAA radar control tower in Virginia Beach to which such fighters were automatically relayed after takeoff, were confused by the "090 for 60" order. The supervisor there, John Harter, said that "All they could figure out was that someone through secure communications changed the scramble order to which they were not privy."[75]

The Langley jets were given yet another unprecedented order when they were ordered to go "max-subsonic," meaning they were not to break the sound barrier. Borgstrom told an interviewer that "I've never heard of [max-subsonic] before in my short career, but I don't think anybody has ever heard that order before."[76] Eckmann made the point that he "had never heard a speed given in any of his previous scrambles." The order resulted in the jets flying at less than half their maximum speed but, since they were headed in the wrong direction anyway, this was simply another factor in a series of delays.

The Langley jets were handed off again, this time from Norfolk TRACON to "Giant Killer," a military station that was in control of the airspace over the Atlantic coast. When interviewed, the staff at Giant Killer also expressed that the "090 for 60" flight strip was a problem, although the flight strip was not available for any of them to see. Instead, as with Norfolk TRACON and the Langley tower staff, they were presented with a "replication" during their interviews.[77]

Interviews with those at Giant Killer showed that they never talked to the Langley fighters (NEADS had control) and they were not able to explain why the scramble order was different than the flight strip. Additionally, they could not explain a further set of unprecedented orders given to the Langley pilots. These were the orders delivered as the jets finally started heading toward Washington—to squawk "Quad 7s" and defer to "AFIO control."

Both of these orders were given by the military controller called Huntress at NEADS.[78] The reason for the order to squawk "Quad 7s" was never explained, but AFIO is an FAA procedure that is apparently not used within the continental United States.[79] Neither the pilots nor anyone at Giant Killer or Norfolk TRACON had ever heard of these orders before.

There are, therefore, several important issues that need to be investigated with regard to the Langley fighters that were scrambled on 9/11. Among these are:

- Why was the SOF scrambled from Langley, leaving no one to coordinate further orders from the base, and who gave that order?
- Why did the heading for the Langley jets get changed to "090 for 60" and why did they continue to go east?
- Why did they get the unprecedented "max-subsonic" order which caused them to go much slower than they were capable?
- Why were the Langley jets ordered to squawk "Quad 7s" and defer to "AFIO control"?

Note also that the Langley fighters were scrambled at the same time that CINCNORAD Ralph Eberhart decided to drive for nearly an hour between Peterson AFB and Cheyenne Mountain, despite Cheyenne Mountain having its own helicopter port.

The Andrews Interceptor Jets

Many people have wondered why NORAD scrambled jets from Langley when there was another base with jets at the ready that was much closer to Washington. Although interceptor jets were eventually scrambled from Andrews AFB after all the hijacked aircraft had been destroyed, the official reason for not turning to Andrews first was that the jets there were not under NORAD command.

Eberhart stated, in his Commission interview, that Andrews jets "were not under our command and control." Air Force Public Affairs Officer Don Arias reiterated the claim, saying "Andrews was not part of NORAD."[80] This disclaimer was confusing considering that the website for Andrews and its DC Air National Guard unit claimed that its mission was "to provide combat units in the highest possible state of readiness." What's more, Colonel Marr had ordered his staff to "Call every Air National Guard unit in the land. Prepare to put jets in the air. The nation is under attack."[81]

Regardless, interceptor jets did not launch from Andrews, which was only ten miles from the Pentagon, until 10:38 a.m., and those were not armed. This was more than an hour after the Pentagon was hit, almost two and a half hours after the first plane was known to be hijacked, and approximately 90 minutes after Andrews personnel had first offered assistance (see Chapter 9).

General Arnold stated in testimony, "It is my understanding that the Secret Service asked [Andrews] to get anything they could airborne, and I think the quote was "to protect the House."[82] The official account confirmed that the Secret Service was behind the order and added a disclaimer for the military.

> The President and the Vice President indicated to us they had not been aware that fighters had been scrambled out of Andrews, at the request of the Secret Service and outside the military chain of command. There is no evidence that NORAD headquarters or military officials in the NMCC knew-during the morning of September 11-that the Andrews planes were airborne and operating under different rules of engagement.[83]

The man in charge of Andrews AFB that day was General David Wherley. In an interesting and unique situation, it was the 9/11 Commission's executive director Philip Zelikow who prepared the interview summary for General Wherley, based on his recollection of a conversation the two men had the same day. According to the document, Zelikow's same-day recollection was helped out by the presence of Ernest May, his collaborator on the early outline for the *9/11 Commission Report*. In so many words, Zelikow and May blamed everything on Wherley and said, "All of this was separate from NORAD."[84]

It is no longer possible to confirm this claim. That's because General Wherley died in an extraordinary train wreck, in the Washington DC metropolitan area, in June 2009.[85]

The Destruction of Flight 93

Colonel Marr repeated, several times, in his January 2004 interview with 9/11 Commission staff members, that he recalled monitoring

Flight 93 during the time that it was hijacked. That would be impossible given the Commission's finding that NORAD was never notified about the hijacking of Flight 93 until after it crashed. But again, Marr's interview suggests that the Commission had come up with a new NORAD timeline and just needed to convince NORAD personnel to buy into it in order to calm the storm of public outcry over the lack of air defense.

It was not only Marr who remembers monitoring Flight 93 in the NEADS battle cab. NEADS intelligence officer Lt. Col. Mark Stuart, who was standing right next to Marr during the crisis, reported the same thing.[86] Both of them said that they were tracking Flight 93. And many air traffic controllers made clear in their handwritten notes from that day, and their personal statements afterward, that Flight 93 was known as a hijacking long before it was destroyed.[87]

General Arnold clarified in testimony to the Commission that, "It was our intent to intercept United Flight 93. And in fact my own staff, we were orbiting now over Washington, D.C. by this time, and I was personally anxious to see what 93 was going to do, and our intent was to intercept it. But we decided to stay over Washington, D.C., because there was not that urgency. So we elected to remain over D.C. until that aircraft was definitely coming towards us."[88]

Eberhart also detailed how Flight 93 was being tracked. The summary of his Commission interview stated that "He believes he reported to Cheyenne Mountain as UAL 93 was ongoing."

It appears that, in order to explain away the considerable evidence for knowledge about the hijacking of Flight 93, the Commission decided to use the false report of another hijacking as a point of confusion. This was Delta Airlines Flight 1989, which was reported hijacked that morning despite the pilot of that aircraft saying that he was not hijacked.[89]

In his interview with the Commission in 2004, Eberhart "commented that Delta 1989 and UAL 93 may have been interchanged. He commented that he understands that there is 'support' for this theory."[90] These flight confusion remarks are remarkable given that there is reason to believe that Delta Flight 1989 was actually a "live-fly" aircraft in of one of Eberhart's exercises that day.[91]

One problem with this new explanation, however, is that General Arnold made clear, in an interview with 1st Air Force public relations writer Leslie Filson, that NORAD was tracking both United 93 *and* Delta 1989. Filson said that she was told they were tracking United 93 specifically.[92] Since NORAD was aware of both, it could not be that Delta 1989 was mistaken for United 93.

Eberhart and others remarked that the vice president had given a shoot down order with respect to Flight 93. Eberhart stated that "the VP order occurred slightly prior to his arrival at the mountain." He said that he "assumed that the order was passed to the level of the fighter pilot." Eberhart went on to describe the challenges with shooting down an airliner.[93]

This disagrees with remarks made by Commission vice-chairman Lee Hamilton in the May 23, 2003 hearing, when he said, "As of September 11th, only the president had the authority to order a shootdown of a commercial aircraft." The *9/11 Commission Report* gave a confused picture of exactly who gave the order. Although saying the vice president "authorized fighter aircraft to engage the inbound plane," this was somehow based on "his earlier conversation with the President."[94] Unfortunately, the Commission said there was "no documentary evidence for this call."

Exactly when the order was received was also a point of confusion. For example, General Arnold couldn't recall when he got the shoot down order and he didn't have it recorded. This was despite the fact that it was the first time that it had ever happened.

Moreover, it was claimed that Marr decided not to pass on the order to shoot down aircraft.[95] Commissioner Timothy Roemer called this decision "so surprising, so shocking to some people."[96] When questioned about this, Eberhart first said that he would have to speculate as to why Marr made that decision. Yet, when pressed, he said that Marr was asked about it.[97]

The physical evidence and eyewitness testimony indicates that Flight 93 was, in fact, shot down. This includes the wide debris field generated around the crash site and eyewitness testimony to a military-type jet at the scene.[98] Additional evidence suggests that electrical disturbances in the area at the time might have contributed to the demise of the aircraft.[99]

In 2013, Cheney admitted that he was actually making the decisions on 9/11. He said in an interview for a documentary that he told the president not to be in one location, causing Bush to fly around the country aimlessly. Cheney also said that he made the decision to shoot down United 93.[100] This further explains why the chain of command failed on 9/11, and points to an additional need to investigate Cheney and his colleagues.

Investigating Eberhart

Investigation of Ralph Eberhart and his subordinates would almost certainly reveal more of what the public needs to know. Whether Eberhart or others were part of a conspiracy to attack the United States is not the only reason. The main purpose would be to understand how such an inexplicable failure to follow the long-standing and most critical procedures of the U.S. defense system could be followed by a string of lies about that inexplicable failure.

Eberhart was among those who lied and he was in charge of NORAD at the time. Was he lying to make himself and his organization look bad, as the 9/11 Commission suggests? Or is he lying now, along with the 9/11 Commission, in order to remove NORAD's responsibility and eliminate questioning about 9/11?

Eberhart and the military as a whole definitely benefited from the 9/11 attacks. In the few years before 9/11, the ongoing Base Realignment and Closure program continued to close bases and cut back defense programs, and NORAD was affected by that. After 9/11, of course, the U.S. military saw the greatest boom in funding it has ever seen. Eberhart himself was rewarded by being placed in charge of the new NORTHCOM organization.

He has more recently been praised and honored for his great work on 9/11. Called a "9/11 hero" despite having been a disastrous failure on that day, he was honored by having the new NORTHCOM headquarters at Peterson AFB named after him.[101]

Eberhart personally benefited from the 9/11 attacks as well. He continued on as head of NORAD and NORTHCOM through 2004. After that he went on to become the chairman for more than half a dozen stock or bond equity funds, and a board director for a similar number of companies profiting from increased military expenditures, oil and gas services, and "Homeland Security."[102]

NORAD officials working for Ralph Eberhart covered up the facts about the lack of air defenses on 9/11 by lying to the American people and by failure to cooperate with the 9/11 investigations. For those reasons alone, Eberhart's performance that day and the related statements should be thoroughly investigated. Considering the nine facts presented above about Eberhart's activities on 9/11, and that Eberhart appears to have violated U.S. law by lying to Congress, that investigation should be performed with the utmost legal authority including the use of subpoenas and formal charges.

Chapter 9

✈

Carl Truscott and the U.S. Secret Service

The U.S. Secret Service failed to do its job on September 11, 2001 in several important ways. These failures could be explained if the Secret Service had foreknowledge of the 9/11 events as they were proceeding. That possibility leads to difficult questions about how the behavior of Secret Service employees might have contributed to the success of the attacks. Answering those questions will require the release of existing interview transcripts as well as follow-up questioning, under oath, of a few key people within the agency.

The most glaring example of Secret Service failure on 9/11 was the lack of protection for the President of the United States after it was well known that the country was facing terrorist attacks on multiple fronts. The interesting thing about this was that it was not a consistent approach. That is, the president was protected by the Secret Service in many ways that day but he was not protected from the most obvious, and apparently the most imminent, danger.

President Bush had been at risk earlier that morning when Middle-Eastern-looking journalists appeared at his hotel in Sarasota, Florida claiming to have an appointment for an interview. A Secret Service agent turned them away in a move that might have saved Bush from an assassination attempt.[1]

Bush then traveled to an elementary school for a community outreach photo opportunity which had been well-publicized for several days. It was reported that "Police and Secret Service Agents were on the roof, on horseback and in every hallway" at the school.[2] Every visitor at the school was required to attend a preparation meeting two days before, and all the phone lines had been tapped. The school's principal stated, "It was the safest place in the world. If you blew your nose and it wasn't time for you to blow your nose, they knew it."[3]

The agency was protecting Bush very well, but not from terrorists in hijacked airplanes. Bush entered the classroom at 9:03 a.m. EST that day, when the world was learning that the country was under attack. Many in the U.S. government were already aware of this fact, as stated by authors Allan Wood and Paul Thompson:

> "By that time, the Federal Aviation Administration (FAA), the North American Aerospace Defense Command (NORAD), the National Military Command Center, the Pentagon, the White House, the Secret Service, and Canada's Strategic Command all knew that three commercial airplanes had been hijacked. They knew that one plane had been flown deliberately into the World Trade Center's North Tower; a second plane was wildly off course and also heading toward Manhattan; and a third plane had abruptly turned around over Ohio and was flying back toward Washington, DC."[4]

Given the widespread knowledge that terrorists were hijacking planes and that planes were crashing into buildings, the Secret Service should never have let the president enter the building where he was scheduled to be located. The situation got worse, however, because shortly after Bush sat down, he was informed by his Chief of Staff that the World Trade Center had been hit again, by a second plane. Still there was no intervention by the Secret Service to remove the president from this well-publicized location.

The Special Agent in Charge (SAIC) of the Secret Service's Presidential Protective Division (PPD) on 9/11 was Carl J. Truscott. Therefore it is Truscott who should be investigated first, but there are others who were involved as well.

Either Failure to Protect the President, or Knowledge That He Was Not a Target

Bush remained at the school until 9:35 a.m., more than 35 minutes after he arrived. He even gave a televised speech during that time, letting the world know he was still there. The actions of Bush and his Secret Service detail indicate that they were not worried at all about a terrorist attack against the school. Philip Melanson, author of a book

143

on the Secret Service, described how odd this was by writing that, in an "unfolding terrorist attack, the procedure should have been to get the president to the closest secure location as quickly as possible."[5]

This failure to follow Secret Service standard procedures remains an unexplained discrepancy to this day and it leads to a number of important questions. Who was responsible for making the decision to leave the president and everyone in the building at risk? Were the Secret Service agents traveling with the president in contact with the agency's offices in Washington or New York? The largest Secret Service field office in the country was located in WTC Building 7, which was evacuated by the time Bush was entering the classroom.

The Secret Service supervisor traveling with the president, who was in charge of the president's movements that day, was Edward Marinzel. Although Truscott was Marinzel's superior, it was Marinzel who was in charge of the execution (or non-execution) of the emergency action protocols carried out with respect to the security of the traveling president.[6]

In an attempt to explain the failure to follow Secret Service procedures, the 9/11 Commission said in its report that Bush "told us his instinct was to project calm, not to have the country see an excited reaction at a moment of crisis," and that the Secret Service "told us they were anxious to move the president to a safer location, but did not think it imperative for him to run out the door." These official responses from the Secret Service, given in the *9/11 Commission Report*, were taken from an as-yet unreleased 2004 interview with Edward Marinzel.[7] However, the Commission said nothing about why Bush entered the classroom in the first place, when so many people in government knew that the country was under attack.

It seems possible that Marinzel's authority was somehow overridden, because reporters noticed that it was White House spokesman Ari Fleischer who appeared to be calling the shots while Bush sat there doing nothing. As Bush's Secret Service detail failed to protect him, Fleischer maneuvered to get his attention without alerting the press. Several reporters noticed that Fleischer had written the words "DON'T SAY ANYTHING YET" in big block letters on a paper sign and was mouthing these words to Bush as he sat there.[8]

Another apparent failure of the Secret Service was that it did not immediately request air cover for either the president's motorcade as it traveled to the airport, or for Air Force One, which took off at about 9:54. This seems to be another indication that the Secret Service knew that Bush was not in danger.

The lack of immediate request for air cover for the president's escort becomes more difficult to understand considering the 9/11 Commission's claims of an "unnerving false alarm" which was a "threat against Air Force One itself." This threat was later "run down to a misunderstood communication in the hectic White House Situation Room."[9]

The *9/11 Commission Report* did not explain the failure to request immediate air cover, but it did attempt to address the circuitous travels of Air Force One after it left Sarasota. Air Force One was redirected throughout the day, first to Barksdale AFB in Louisiana and then on to Nebraska. The Commission reported that the reason for this wandering about the country was that the "Lead Secret Service agent felt strongly that the situation in Washington was too unstable for the President to return there," and although Bush "strongly wanted to return to Washington," the Secret Service won the argument. Again, the 9/11 Commission got its information on this subject from the unreleased 2004 interview with Edward Marinzel.

Exactly why Edward Marinzel's interview has not been made publicly available is not clear. Given that it was the primary basis for the official account with regard to the failure to protect the president, it seems that the public has a right to see it. Did the Secret Service know that the president was not in danger and, if so, how did it know that? Was Marinzel in contact with Truscott, who was the lead agent aware of the situation in Washington?

Whatever the case might be, Marinzel's actions or lack thereof were considered appropriate because his role in protecting the president continued. On Thanksgiving in 2003, Marinzel led the team that planned and executed President Bush's secret visit to Baghdad which, at the time, "was the first operation in history that took a President of the United States into an active war zone."[10]

Today, Marinzel works at a consulting company with Ralph Basham, the former Director of the Secret Service (2003-2006), as well as another person who played a critical role in George W. Bush's travel, communications and protection. This was Joseph W. Hagin, who was Bush's Deputy White House Chief of Staff for Operations (2001-2008). Mr. Hagin had previously been an assistant to Vice President George H.W. Bush, from 1981 to 1985, and then Assistant to President Bush from 1989 to 1991.

Hagin came to the George W. Bush administration after eight years as a vice president for Chiquita Brands International. Formerly called United Fruit Company, the company was mired in scandal at the time of Hagin's departure, due to an exposé by the *Cincinnati Enquirer* which claimed that it mistreated the workers on its Central American plantations, polluted the environment, allowed cocaine to be brought to the United States on its ships, and bribed foreign officials.

On 9/11, Mr. Hagin had oversight responsibility for Air Force One, the White House Communications Agency, and the Secret Service PPD. Despite these far reaching responsibilities, his name does not appear in the *9/11 Commission Report*. Hagin was later "one of the principals responsible for planning the formation of the U.S. Department of Homeland Security."[11] When Hurricane Katrina occurred, Hagin was the White House point person in terms of overseeing response efforts.

Either Failure to Protect the Vice President, or Reconstruction of the Timeline

The *9/11 Commission Report* states that when the Secret Service first learned of the second plane hitting the World Trade Center, it immediately initiated a number of precautionary "security enhancements around the White House complex."[12] This would have begun at 9:03, when the entire nation witnessed Flight 175 hit the south tower on live television.

This information was obtained from the interview of Carl Truscott, who was SAIC of the PPD. Truscott had primary responsibility for supervising all protective matters relating to the president, the first family and the White House. Although Truscott's interview was not released in transcript form, a summary of the interview was made available as part of several random documents released via FOIA request to 9/11 investigator Aidan Monaghan.[13]

When the second plane hit the WTC, the Secret Service agent responsible for coordinating with the FAA, Nelson Garabito, called his FAA counterpart, Terry Van Steenbergen. At the time, Garabito was at the Secret Service's Joint Operations Center (JOC), located in the White House.

It was reported that Van Steenbergen told Garabito that two other planes were possibly hijacked, which caused Garabito to ask someone to run upstairs and pass the information on to other Secret Service agents. The 9/11 Commission found that this information was "either not passed on or was passed on but not disseminated."

This failure relates to the question of when the vice president was evacuated from his office. If Van Steenbergen's information, given to Garabito just after 9:03 a.m., was passed on to those protecting the vice president, then it would become important to know why the vice president was not moved to a safer location until 9:36, as stated by the *9/11 Commission Report*. If the information was passed on immediately, and the vice president was moved to a secure location just after 9:00 as several witnesses have suggested, then his early presence at the Presidential Emergency Operations Center (PEOC) would substantiate the important testimony of transportation secretary Norman Mineta. According to Mineta, Cheney was being given regular updates on the progress of the hijacked Flight 77 as it came toward Washington.[14]

The documents released by FOIA request include a timeline of "Actions of TSD" on 9/11. TSD is the Secret Service's Technical Services Division which, among other things, operates the Secret Service's Tigerwall air surveillance system. The TSD timeline states that, at 9:18 a.m., "SAIC Truscott learned that an aircraft had been identified en-route to the Washington area." Therefore, we have officially prepared documentation that indicates Truscott was aware of a hijacked plane heading for Washington at least 18 minutes before the official account says the vice president was moved from his office. If this is true, the public deserves to know why the vice president was not moved to safety immediately. On the other hand if he was moved earlier, that fact supports Mineta's astonishing and important testimony.

Failure to Request Interceptor Jets in a Timely Manner

As described by author Michael Ruppert, the Secret Service was getting information about the ongoing hijacking events at the same time, or before, the FAA was. This was because there was a "parallel command system in play."[15] This parallel command system was also described by Richard Clarke, who was leading one of the response teams in the White House Situation Room (WHSR). Clarke later wrote that Brian Stafford, the Director of the Secret Service, was in the WHSR with him and was passing him information. That information, according to Clarke, came from the fact that the Secret Service had "a system that allowed them to see what FAA's radar was seeing."[16]

The authoritative command system appeared to be below ground in the PEOC, where Dick Cheney was leading the activities. The TSD document released by FOIA shows that when Assistant Division Chief Spriggs arrived in the PEOC, at 9:30 a.m., Cheney and Rice were already there along with ten other "Presidential and Vice Presidential staff."[17] Truscott was the lead Secret Service agent in the PEOC, the one who was in coordination with Garabito, and the one who was most closely coordinating with Dick Cheney.

The FOIA-released 9/11 Commission summary of Truscott's interview says that he escorted Condoleezza Rice from the Situation Room to the "White House Shelter Area" where they met Cheney, who was on the phone, and Mrs. Cheney.[18] The official account gives a contradictory account, stating that Mrs. Cheney did not arrive at the White House for another 30 minutes or more. The FOIA documents say that Truscott led the Cheneys and Rice to the PEOC sometime before 9:30. SAIC Anthony Zotto, who was specifically responsible for the vice president's safety, was in the PEOC at the time. This means that Cheney was in the PEOC at least eight minutes before Flight 77 crashed into the Pentagon.

The documents released by the Secret Service via FOIA indicate that the Secret Service had knowledge of Flight 77 and Flight 93 and that those flights were headed toward Washington, DC. One of these documents, not clearly identified but apparently a timeline created by one agent to relate his experiences, indicates that the Secret Service had knowledge of "two more outstanding aircraft, not responding to the Tower, considered suspect and at least one was headed toward DC." This was several minutes before the agent arrived at "Room 552 en route to the JOC" where the agent learned that "one of the two planes, believed to be hijacked, was approximately 5 minutes out from DC."

These documents confirm that the Secret Service knew that two hijacked planes were headed toward Washington during the time that Cheney and SAIC Truscott were in the PEOC, and well before Flight 77 was reported to have crashed into the Pentagon. Cheney seemed to confirm the same when he later said, on NBC's *Meet the Press* — "The Secret Service has an arrangement with the FAA. They had open lines after the World Trade Center was" — and then cut himself off.

There remains some confusion over whether the Secret Service ordered, or had the authority to order, the scrambling of interceptor jets from Andrews AFB in response to the knowledge about the incoming hijacked aircraft. Author Lynn Spencer, who NORAD Commander Ralph Eberhart said "tells it all and tells it well," wrote that "the Secret Service also has certain authority over the military and, in this case, the DC Guard."[19] That is, the Secret Service had the authority to order the scrambling of interceptor jets on 9/11. And of course, with the president and secretary of defense both indisposed for a brief period, the vice president had appointed himself to be the effective commander in chief of the military.

Official reports now suggest that the Secret Service made such a request, although very late in the chain of events, but that Andrews commander General David Wherley did not respond rapidly enough. The reason given is that Wherley did not recognize the Secret Service as having the authority to order jets to scramble and therefore he waited until someone in the military chain of command gave him the order. Unfortunately, General Wherley is no longer available for comment as he died in an extraordinary accident which was "the most deadly train crash in the history of the Washington Metropolitan Area Transit Authority."[20]

However, it is clear that staff from Andrews AFB had reached out to the Secret Service well before Wherley ever got involved.[21] Just after

9:05, Major Daniel Caine, the supervisor of flying at Andrews AFB, called his Secret Service contact, Kenneth Beachamp. Caine asked "Are you guys going to need some help?" Agent Beauchamp replied "No, but I'll call you back if that changes." Beauchamp, whose 9/11-related interview is still "national security classified," never called back. Nearly 30 minutes later, when Flight 77 was coming into Washington, someone else from the Secret Service finally returned Caine's call to accept the offer of assistance. Upon answering the phone, Caine stated that he "could hear plain as day the vice president talking in the background."[22] That was when Caine's newly arrived superior, General Wherley, began spending another 80 minutes or more being confused about the chain of command, according to the official account.

Interceptor jets did not launch from Andrews AFB, which was only ten miles from the Pentagon, until 10:38 a.m. (and those jets were not armed). This was more than an hour after the Pentagon was hit, almost two and a half hours after the first plane was known to be hijacked, and approximately 90 minutes after Major Caine had first offered assistance to the Secret Service.

On 9/11, the Secret Service was also coordinating a terrorism-focused meeting at WTC Building 7 in New York City. As will be discussed in Chapter 13, the agency had invited explosive disposal units from several military units to attend that meeting, which was scheduled at the very time that the attacks began.

SAIC Truscott continued as the leader of the Secret Service PPD through 2005, during times when a prostitute came to the White House for overnight visits, and during the period when Jack Abramoff was visiting the White House. The White House later tried to hide the records for these visits. Truscott was also in charge during the period when the Secret Service adopted its secretive processes for visitor records management.

Like Marinzel, Truscott's performance on 9/11 was apparently well received as he was later promoted to Director of the ATF, another major agency of the U.S. Department of Treasury. In the end he was forced to resign in a scandal related to multiple abuses of power including sexist orders given to female employees. Truscott had friends in high places, however, and he was protected from prosecution by order of the White House.[23] Truscott went on to join ASERO Worldwide, an international security and risk management firm run by Doron Bergerbest-Eilon, who was formerly the most senior-ranking official at the Israeli Security Agency.[24]

Overall, the response of the Secret Service to the 9/11 attacks suggests foreknowledge of the events in that the agency failed to protect the president from the obvious danger posed by terrorists. That foreknowledge, combined with the failure of the Secret Service to follow-up on the offer of air support from Andrews AFB, leads to the suspicion that the agency was complicit in the attacks. Revealing the truth behind the suspicion will require that the central players from the Secret Service and the White House, including Edward Marinzel, Joseph Hagin, Ari Fleischer, and most importantly Carl Truscott, be examined under oath by prosecutors with subpoena power.

Chapter 10

John, Paul, Peter, and the Pentagon

"I have no desire to attack the Pentagon; I want to liberate it. We need to save it from itself." — Donald Rumsfeld, September 10, 2001

The official account of what happened at the Pentagon on 9/11 leaves many questions unanswered.[1] The work of independent investigators has also failed to address those questions. In an attempt to find answers, an alternative account of the Pentagon attack should be considered.

An alternative account would be more compelling than the official account if it explained more of the evidence without adding unnecessary complications. Considering means, motive and opportunity might allow us to propose a possible insider conspiracy while maintaining much of the official account as well.

A few of the more compelling unanswered questions are as follows.

1. How could American Airlines Flight 77 have hit the building as it did, considering that the evidence shows the alleged hijacker pilot, Hani Hanjour, was a very poor pilot?[2]

2. Why did the aircraft make a 330-degree turn just minutes before hitting the building?

3. Why did the aircraft hit the least occupied one-fifth of the building that was the focus of a renovation plan and how was it that the construction in that exact spot just happened to be for the purpose of minimizing the damage from a terrorist explosion?[3]

4. Why was the company that performed the renovation work, just for that one-fifth of the building, immediately hired in a

no-bid contract to clean up the damage and reconstruct that area of the building? (Note: The same company was also immediately hired to clean up the WTC site within hours of the destruction there.)[4]

5. What can explain the damage to the building and the aircraft debris or lack thereof?

6. Why were the tapes from the surveillance videos in the area immediately confiscated by the FBI and never released?

These questions should be considered along with the fact that U.S military and "Homeland Security" expenditures since the 9/11 attacks have totaled approximately $8 trillion.[5] This paints a picture that calls for an in-depth investigation into the people running the Pentagon, to see if they might have had the motivation and ability to plan and execute the attack.

What happened during the Pentagon renovation project should be of great interest. A preliminary investigation raises the possibility that the work done during that time could have provided the cover for an effective insider conspiracy. We should examine the people involved in planning the renovation project in order to begin answering the question of who might have benefited from the attack.

The History of the Renovation Project

Construction of the Pentagon began on September 11, 1941. It was completed in February 1943, and was called The Pentagon because it was a five-sided building that had five concentric rings (A through E) and five floors. Truly massive, with over 6 million square feet of gross area, the building met the basic needs of the Department of War, later ironically called the Department of Defense (DOD), for the next fifty years.

The renovation project was originally planned during the first Bush Administration, when Dick Cheney was Secretary of Defense (SECDEF). Because of this, Dick knew enough about the scope of the project that he could have, in later years, incorporated it into plans for an insider attack. It also happens that the ownership of the building was transferred, in November 1990, from the General Services Administration to the DOD, keeping the renovation project under full control of the military establishment.

The work began in 1993 with the construction of a power plant and then moved on to the basement levels of the building where the new National Military Command Center (NMCC) was being built. Over the ensuing four or five years the project was fraught with cost overruns and unexpected delays.

Early in the project, oversight was provided by John Deutch, the Deputy Secretary of Defense (DEPSECDEF). Deutch came to the job after a career in academics and at the Department of Energy. He was associated with Mitre Corporation, which in 1999 was in collaboration with a company called PTech to "look at interoperability issues the FAA had with NORAD and the Air Force, in case of an emergency."[6] Investigator and author Jamey Hecht has written that "The Ptech story is a crucial piece of 9/11 because the software was used to simultaneously coordinate the FAA with NORAD and the Secret Service."[7]

Deutch also worked with Science Applications International Corporation (SAIC), which has many connections to 9/11.[8] After his tenure as DEPSECDEF, in May 1995, Deutch became Director of the CIA. He left the CIA almost two years later and became a director at Citigroup, a company that was saved in 1998 by Prince Alwaleed of Saudi Arabia in a deal brokered by The Carlyle Group.[9] Deutch was allowed to keep his top-secret clearance for nearly three years after leaving the CIA (until August 1999), while he was being investigated for leaks of classified information.[10] Attorney General Janet Reno refused to prosecute Deutch and he was ultimately pardoned by President Clinton. During this time, Deutch also became a director of Raytheon and a member of the Bilderberg Group.

Throughout the Pentagon renovation project, oversight continued to be provided by the DEPSECDEF. The next in line for the job was John White, a Marine Corps officer whose career had included nine years with the RAND Corporation.[11] After his work at the DOD, he went on to join Deutch and others at Global Technology Partners, which was described by one of its senior partners as "an exclusive affiliate of Rothschild North America."[12]

In the summer of 1997, the renovation project was turned over to White's successor, John J. Hamre. As the Undersecretary of Defense for Acquisitions and Technology, Hamre had already been involved and was a powerful figure in the department. Procurement was among the most important roles in the DOD.

After his time as DEPSECDEF, Hamre became a trustee of Mitre Corporation at the time of its collaboration with PTech. Later, Hamre would become a director for ChoicePoint and SAIC. Coincidentally, the ChoicePoint subsidiary, Bode Technologies, was hired to do DNA testing of victims after the 9/11 attacks. Richard Armitage, the Deputy Secretary of State who was among those who failed to protect the nation on 9/11, was also a director at ChoicePoint and an advisor at Raytheon.

Therefore the backgrounds of the people who first planned and managed the renovation project suggest that some of them could have formed an effective Pentagon conspiracy. Of course, the Pentagon is the center of the U.S. military industrial complex and therefore the people running its programs would have stood to benefit from the extraordinary increase in military spending after 9/11.

The New Plan and the Environment in Which It Was Drafted

In 1997, a new plan for the renovation project was crafted by Hamre, reportedly in response to the mid-1990s terrorist attacks in Oklahoma City and abroad. This new plan appeared to be an effort to improve the resistance of the exterior of the building to an explosive impact, with additional actions taken to reduce the possibility of fire damage. The following improvements to the building were planned:

- Reinforcement of the exterior walls with steel

- Backing of the exterior walls with Kevlar, to minimize shrapnel effect

- Installation of blast-resistant windows

- Installation of fire sprinklers and automatic fire doors

- Construction of a building operations and control center[13]

To manage the project, Hamre created a new position called the Pentagon Renovation Program Manager. The person selected for the job was Walker Lee Evey, a former Vietnam combat commander and NASA contract negotiator. Evey had been with the 1st Infantry Division in Quan Loi, Vietnam, in 1968 and 1969. He was later a top procurement officer with Air Force Systems Command but left the military in 1987 to join NASA. He returned to the Air Force in 1996 as a high-ranking acquisitions official working for Darleen Druyun, who later went to prison for conspiring with Boeing to defraud the American people.[14]

Immediately before being hired to manage the Pentagon renovation project, Evey worked on a top-secret Air Force "black project" in California that involved satellites.[15] Although reports don't identify the project, descriptions match the Milstar satellite system, a cooperative effort between the Air Force, Boeing, Lockheed Martin, and the U.S. intelligence center at Fort Belvoir.

Milstar is primarily a communications system that allows "satellites to communicate globally without using a ground station."[16] Theoretically, onboard Milstar terminals could have been used on 9/11 to communicate changes to the flight plans of the hijacked aircraft. Milstar operates with a low risk of detection or interception, was designed to operate for weeks without ground contact, and is "used to relay the most sensitive information between the President and the armed forces."[17]

In late 1995, Druyun had boasted about all the new DOD projects related to precision guidance of aircraft and munitions. These projects included Milstar, Peace Shield (a Saudi airspace control project with Boeing) and the nationwide Global Positioning System (GPS).[18]

Although Evey knew about satellites, surprisingly he did not know anything about construction when he was hired to lead the Pentagon project. It was in November 1997 that Druyun asked Evey about the job, although Evey made it clear that he "didn't know how to do construction."

Evey's education was in psychology and he had no experience related to the renovation of buildings. After a discussion with Druyun, and having resigned himself to the assignment, he thought, "Gee, if I'm going to do design and construction, I'd better start learning about this stuff."[19] It seems reasonable to suggest that Evey was hired for his abilities to maintain costs and control suppliers but also to maintain secrecy and control psychological reactions. The latter skills would come in handy for someone in the lead position of providing official answers to questions about the 9/11 attack, given that it was an inside conspiracy.

Note that 1997 was the year that the think tank called The Project for a New American Century (PNAC) was born. A *Statement of Principles* was published by PNAC in June of that year, which called for the U.S. government to actively work at shaping a new century favorable to American principles and interests. Key to PNAC objectives was a "need to increase defense spending significantly."[20]

This was also the same year that SECDEF William Cohen suggested that Andrew W. Marshall, the long-time director of the Pentagon's Office of Net Assessment, might be ready for retirement. Marshall had been appointed to that role in 1973, effectively serving as the leader of a private think tank that drove policy within the Pentagon. He has been reappointed by every president since then and, through the 1990s, he was the leading figure in the calls for a revolution in military affairs (RMA).[21]

Cohen's attempt to push Marshall out was unsuccessful due to backlash from a cadre of Marshall's loyal protégés, who were also PNAC members. That group included Donald Rumsfeld, Dick Cheney, Paul Wolfowtiz and Richard Armitage, all of whom played leading roles in the defense failures on 9/11. When asked about 9/11, Marshall said nothing had changed for him because – "It was obvious that we were wide open to attack."[22]

At the time of the planning and implementation of the Pentagon renovation, Marshall and his allies were aggressively advocating their RMA but neither the public nor the government was supportive. Marshall's colleagues at the RAND Corporation were decrying reductions in U.S. military spending with respect to the ability to secure U.S. dominance in a new world order.[23]

Central to the RMA was the call to increase the production and use of satellite, weapons-guiding, and communications technology.[24] PNAC's report of September 2000, called *Rebuilding America's Defenses*, strongly aligned the objectives of the group with the RMA plan, and made clear that the much needed transformation would not occur "absent some catastrophic and catalyzing event—like a new Pearl Harbor."[25]

At the time of the 9/11 attack, a dozen PNAC signatories worked in leadership positions at the Pentagon, including members of the Defense Policy Board like Fred Ikle and Richard Perle. It was known that Rumsfeld deferred to Perle on many issues in 2001, sometimes in an obsequious manner.[26] Coincidentally, Shelton Lankford, a leading voice in the call for truth about the Pentagon attack, worked for Ikle and a "who's who" of Perle associates at Telos Corporation from 1990 to 2002.[27]

The dramatic change in policy that the RMA represented, and the huge increase in military spending it required, was made possible due to the 9/11 attacks, which were very much like a "new pearl Harbor." Therefore those who benefited from the attack on the Pentagon were people like Cheney, Rumsfeld, Wolfowitz and Armitage who achieved the backing for their PNAC objectives and the proposed RMA.

The People Who Implemented the New Plan

After securing his commitment, Darleen Druyun told the new renovation project manager, Lee Evey, to wait for word from John Hamre. Evey's position had been created by Hamre, who could best express the intent.

For the new project plan, which was approved in early 1998, Evey and Hamre decided to begin the new renovation specifically with Wedge 1, a section comprising one-fifth of the building on the west side. The project's new emphasis on the external walls of Wedge 1 meant that the work was focused on a very small fraction of the building, exactly where the aircraft would hit on 9/11.

The project continued for 44 months with essentially all the work being performed in that one area of the building. At the time of the 9/11 attack, the renovation was to continue with Wedge 2, where the employees had only recently been relocated.

In March 2000, Hamre stepped down to become CEO of the Center for Strategic and International Studies (CSIS), which had been the long-time employer of Rumsfeld's special assistant, PNAC signatory Stephen Cambone. CSIS had played a role in planning exercises similar to those used by the continuity of government (COG) program during the Reagan, Bush I and early Clinton administrations. [28] Cheney and Rumsfeld were key players in the COG exercises, as they practiced to replace the United States government in time of crisis. The first and only time that COG was implemented was on 9/11.[29]

Hamre was replaced as DEPSECDEF by Rudy De Leon, another Undersecretary of Defense who had joined the DOD along with Hamre in 1993. When the new Bush Administration came in a year later, De Leon went on to become Senior Vice President at Boeing.

In the eight months leading up to the 9/11 attacks, completing Wedge 1 was the primary focus of the Pentagon renovation. During this time, Lee Evey served as principal advisor to SECDEF Rumsfeld but he reported directly to DEPSECDEF Wolfowitz, who was then in charge of the renovation.[30] Cambone came to the Pentagon as well, as Special Assistant to Rumsfeld and Wolfowitz.

The actual construction work for the renovation was handled by a company called AMEC Construction, a subsidiary of the British conglomerate AMEC. The parent company provided "engineering and project management services to the world's energy, power and process industries."[31] AMEC had a significant presence in Saudi Arabia dating back to the late 1970s, providing support to the national oil company Saudi Aramco, which is the richest company in the world.[32] To this day, AMEC remains a major international player in the oil and gas industry, as well as in other natural resource industries.

AMEC was also immediately hired to cleanup and reconstruct Wedge 1 and to lead the cleanup of the WTC site. The company's role in controlling the structural evidence from the 9/11 attacks was further emphasized by the fact that it managed the "Hudson River barging operations to transport debris from the entire WTC site to a Staten Island landfill and to steel recycling operations in New Jersey."[33]

AMEC Construction was previously called Morse Diesel and was briefly a subsidiary of a company called AGRA until it was purchased by AMEC. The subsidiary was run out of Toronto, Ontario by a man named Peter Janson.[34] It had offices in New York, Fort Lauderdale, and Phoenix.

From 1990 to 1999, Janson was president and CEO of U.S operations for the Swiss-Swedish engineering company ABB. During this period, and until February 2001, Donald Rumsfeld was a director at ABB throughout the time that Janson was CEO and a director.[35] Rumsfeld helped ABB sell nuclear technology to North Korea in 2000 and, in an alarming turnabout two years later, declared the same country a terrorist state and part of the "axis of evil."[36] In any case, Rumsfeld had a relationship with Janson, who managed the Wedge 1 renovation company, for many years before 9/11.

Janson had also been the president and CEO of an ABB predecessor, the Swedish company ASEA, which had used the swastika as its logo until the 1930s. During World War II, the other predecessor of ABB, Brown Boveri, supplied parts for German U-boats. ABB directors represented companies that had similar backgrounds, including Gerhard Cromme of ThyssenKrupp, a company that "used slave laborers during World War II to advance the Nazis' war campaign."[37] ABB director Jürgen Dormann was CEO of Hoechst AG, a predecessor (and successor) of the infamous IG Farben conglomerate that cooperated closely with the Nazis.

Today, Janson is enjoying the fruits of the War on Terror as a director of Teekay Corporation, an oil and gas transport company that operates throughout the world. Both Janson and AMEC were heavily involved in the oil and gas industries, but additionally the company was strongly linked to the highest levels of government in the U.S. and elsewhere. Janson's high level links, apart from his association with Rumsfeld, included that he "reports to the Prime Minister of Canada in his role as a member of the National Advisory Board on Science and Technology."[38]

AMEC subcontracted much of the Wedge 1 work to Facchina Construction, which was founded by Paul V. Facchina. It was reported that Facchina Construction was a "major subcontractor" in the Pentagon renovation.[39] The company functioned as the heavy civil contractor under AMEC, for Wedge 1 specifically. Facchina's project manager, Ken Wyman, described the initial phase of their work as "selective demolition." Later on, "crews worked six to seven days a week pouring concrete and renovating the structure."[40]

In another interesting coincidence, Facchina Construction was hired to construct American Airlines Arena in Miami. Furthermore, the project manager for that $213 million project was AMEC and the structural engineering firm was Thornton Tomasetti, which later supervised the removal and destruction of WTC debris. As Facchina Construction worked on the Pentagon in 1998 and 1999, it simultaneously worked on the American Airlines Arena project, which, oddly enough, was sponsored by the company that owned the airplane that hit the Pentagon.

Another company that was founded by Paul Facchina is Facchina Global Services (FGS) which does intelligence work and builds secure video teleconferencing (SVTS) capabilities for the DOD. FGS provided such secure video teleconferencing capabilities for "the President of the United States, the National Security Council, Secretary of Defense, agency directors, and combatant commanders."[41] It is unclear what role FGS played in the significant problems experienced by those using the White House SVTS on 9/11.[42]

According to William Viner, a project estimator working for the contracting venture called DMJM-3DI, there was a change of plans just two years before 9/11. Viner said that the design for the "blast wall" of

Wedge 1 was modified at that time. "It wasn't part of the original design," Viner said. "It was a change order that we worked through and put in." and "We started negotiating it about two years ago, May-June 1999. We started receiving materials for it in December and started constructing it as we were coming through the outer and inner shell." When asked why this change was made so late in the project, Viner replied, "Oklahoma City." Of course, this was more than four years after the bombing of the Murrah Federal Building and that incident had already been considered in the plans drafted in 1997.[43]

On the Day of 9/11

On the day of the attack, the instant of impact was witnessed by another Vietnam combat veteran, Frank Probst, who just happened to be in the exact area outside the building when it occurred. Probst was a West Point graduate and retired Army lieutenant colonel. He worked with Evey in the Pentagon Renovation Program Office as a communications specialist.

In 1973, after his combat experiences in Vietnam, Probst joined the U.S. Army Signal Corps. He continued as a career Army communications officer, serving in places like Panama from 1973 to 1977 and the 5th Signal Corps in Germany from 1981 to 1984. Probst retired in 1986 from the Defense Communications Agency (DCA) in Arlington, VA.[44] The 5th Signal Corps managed the worldwide U.S. satellite program.[45] The DCA, now called the Defense Information Systems Agency, is the satellite communications leader for the DOD and was responsible for developing the system architecture.[46]

Probst had worked on the renovation project since 1995, before Evey joined. Six years later, as one of the few people who witnessed the impact and the one who saw it from the closest vantage point, Probst's testimony was critical to establishing the official account of what happened.

Twelve minutes before impact, at 9:25 a.m., Frank Probst was said to be completing an inspection of computer room air conditioning equipment and a first floor telephone closet just inside the west wall.[47] Afterward, he stopped at a construction trailer outside, near where the plane was about to hit. Images of the scene taken in May 2001 show the construction trailers and other materials located around the point of impact.[48] For some unknown reason, three of the construction trailers that were located immediately outside the impact area were left out of diagrams in the report published by the American Society of Civil Engineers (ASCE).[49]

At one of the construction trailers, Probst watched the news about the WTC with others there and together they remarked how the Pentagon would be a good target. Probst left the trailer around 9:35 am and the aircraft, originally piloted by long-time Pentagon employee Charles Burlingame but allegedly taken over by Hani Hanjour, came right at him.

It was reported that, "The pilot seemed to be aiming for a window on the first floor, almost exactly where Probst had been checking the air conditioning ten minutes earlier."[50] Another witness said the aircraft appeared to be "nothing more than a guided missile at that point," and by most accounts it was going full throttle approximately six feet off the ground.[51]

Probst hit the ground as the aircraft passed just a few feet above him, and he observed the end of the right wing cut through the portable electrical generator that provided backup power to Wedge 1.[52] It is amazing, given this account, that Probst was not injured by the turbulence from the wake of the aircraft. Such aircraft wakes are known to be highly dangerous.[53]

It is also remarkable that Frank Probst was checking equipment in the exact location of impact just 12 minutes before it happened. It seems unlikely that this lieutenant colonel from the DCA was the air conditioning guy, but for Probst to have wandered away to discuss how the Pentagon would be a good target for the next hijacked aircraft, and then come back to be nearly hit by that next aircraft, makes his story worthy of further investigation.

Lt. Col. Probst's presence at the impact site is not in question due to another witness who saw him there—AMEC employee Don Mason. For the purposes of this alternative account, the question to be answered is why Probst was there and what he was doing. His presence in the building just before it hit, then in the construction trailer a few minutes later, and then just below the aircraft as it impacted the building, does not seem to be accidental.

Support for the idea that there is more to Probst's story is given by the 2003 U.S. Department of Justice (DOJ) restrictions on 9/11 Commission interviews for certain witnesses. Only four Pentagon witnesses, out of the many who said they saw something, were on the DOJ-sensitive list. Those four included two Pentagon police officers, cleanup project engineer Allyn Kilsheimer (mentioned below), and Frank Probst. The restrictions that the DOJ insisted upon were that a DOJ attorney must be present during these interviews, a five day warning must be given in each case, and no record could be made, of any kind.[54]

Regardless of why Probst was there, reports state that Flight 77 crashed through the windows of rooms 1E462 and 1E466. Jack Singleton, the president of Wedge 1 electrical subcontractor Singleton Electric, said, "Where the plane came in was really at the construction entrance."[55]

The ASCE report states that the fuselage hit "at or below the second floor slab," which was about 14 feet off the ground, and it then "slid between the first-floor slab on grade and the second-floor slab for most of its distance of travel after striking the building." As it slid, the aircraft "burst through Army accounting offices on the first floor of the E ring, continued through the Navy Command Center on the D ring, and slammed into a Defense Intelligence Agency office in the C ring."[56]

The aircraft was said to have punched through three rings of the building, which essentially represented three separate structures, the outer ring (ring E), the D ring and the C ring, before coming to rest.[57]

Unfortunately, although there were many videotape recorders in the vicinity that recorded the moment of impact, all of the videotapes were confiscated by the FBI within minutes and have never been released.[58] We are therefore left with only eyewitness testimony and photographic evidence, from before and after the attack, to try and piece together the moment of impact.

First responders from local fire departments arrived at the scene within 5 minutes as did the FBI's National Capital Response Squad. Other federal, state, and local responders arrived within minutes as well, including FEMA's Urban Rescue and Search team from Virginia. Because it was terrorism, the federal plan implemented in January 2001, known as the Interagency Domestic Terrorism Concept of Operations Plan (CONPLAN), made it clear that the FBI was in charge. Personnel from the FBI and other government agencies immediately began collecting evidence at the scene.[59]

If not for the construction project, thousands of people would have been working in Wedge 1 at the time of impact. Because the aircraft hit that low occupancy section of the building, only 125 people were killed. Of those killed, none were high-level officials and none of the ten or more PNAC members with offices in the building were injured or killed. Donald Rumsfeld was safe in his office on the opposite side of the building.

The targeting of Wedge 1 guaranteed the safety of the Pentagon's top leaders, which is not what anyone would expect from al Qaeda.[60] Limitation of Pentagon deaths is, however, what we might expect from an insider conspiracy.

Instead of rushing to the NMCC to lead the national defense and ensure that no other parts of the attack were successful, Rumsfeld went out to the parking lot and the lawn and could not be reached for approximately 30 minutes. In explanation, he said, "I wanted to see what had happened. I wanted to see if people needed help. I went downstairs and helped for a bit with some people on stretchers. Then I came back up here and started—I realized I had to get back up here and get at it."[61]

It could be that Rumsfeld was personally concerned about the welfare of specific individuals, but it does not seem reasonable that he would forsake his duties and the rest of the country for 30 minutes during the most critical time of his tenure. An alternative explanation for

Rumsfeld's negligent visit to the southwest wall is that he was part of the conspiracy and he rushed to the scene due to concern that something might not have gone exactly to plan. For example, the aircraft might not have hit precisely where he had hoped, or he might have been trying to make sure that any unwanted evidence was removed before it was found by the wrong people. Or, he might simply have wanted an excuse to be out of a position of command for another 30 minutes.

Of the 45 people working in the Army office located immediately within the impact zone, 34 died. More than half of the victims worked in the Pentagon's Naval Command Center, and many of them had been moved into the facility shortly before the attack. In addition to the people in the building, there were 54 victims on the airliner, as well as the five alleged hijackers, all of whom perished.[62]

As for AMEC Construction, which was still working in the area, its vice president Ron Vermillion reported that 230 company employees were in Wedge 1 that morning. Other reports said it was less than 100 AMEC employees, doing "final, touch-up work on wedge one."[63] Regardless of the number, although AMEC had many employees in the area that was hit, all of them survived.

Including the building occupants, aircraft passengers, and alleged hijackers, 184 people died. This was a national tragedy, but it could have been much worse. The relatively low loss of life at the Pentagon could be seen as evidence that the perpetrators of the crime wanted to minimize casualties. The number of deaths among military personnel and DOD leadership was very low relative to what would have happened if any other part of the building was hit.

In his final assessment, Lee Evey remarked, "This was a terrible tragedy, but I'm here to tell you that if we had not undertaken these efforts in the building, this could have been much, much worse. The fact that they happened to hit an area that we had built so sturdily was a wonderful gift."[64]

What Might Have Been Done to Facilitate the Attack?

To help answer the question of how Flight 77 might have hit Wedge 1, flying at high speed and just barely off the ground, we might consider what aircraft guidance systems would allow such flight. Advanced automated control could explain how Flight 77 maneuvered as it did given the poor piloting skills of the alleged hijacker Hani Hanjour.

Researcher Aidan Monaghan has written a compelling article entitled *Plausibility Of 9/11 Aircraft Attacks Generated By GPS-Guided Aircraft Autopilot Systems.*[65] Monaghan hypothesizes that the precision automated flight control systems, and related commercial aviation technology that emerged just prior to 9/11, might have been utilized to accomplish the 9/11 attacks.

Monaghan explains that, in 2001, technology was available to remotely alter aircraft flight plan data in 757 and 767 aircraft, causing the planes to take a different route using autopilot functions. Combined with the Wide Area Augmentation System (WAAS), an augmented GPS signal system, and associated technology, aircraft like those used in the 9/11 attacks could be flown remotely through "highways in the sky" that are navigated by the autopilot systems.

As Monaghan reported, companies involved in implementing such technology in the late 1990s included Boeing and Raytheon. In fact, Raytheon was the primary developer and provider of WAAS technology. The Mitre Corporation provided specialists to the WAAS Integrity Performance Panel to help with the implementation of WAAS.[66]

Just a few weeks after 9/11, another company called Cubic Defense Systems filed for a patent on technology that "removes control of an aircraft from its pilot and utilizes an aircraft's auto-pilot system to implement an uninterruptable pre-programmed auto-pilot flight plan" and can terminate "an aircraft's ability to communicate."[67]

The information we have about Flight 77 as it was being flown toward the Pentagon comes largely from the flight path study provided by the National Transportation Safety Board (NTSB).[68] An interesting feature of the official account is that the aircraft was not seen on radar for 8 minutes and 13 seconds starting at the time of the hijacking. This was the period from when the transponder was turned off at 8:56 to 9:05, while it was within the domain of Indianapolis Center. Due to this radar data gap, the NTSB flight path was reconstructed using other radar data and information retrieved from the Flight Data Recorder (FDR).

The official account tells us that Flight 77 was hijacked at approximately 8:55 a.m. and the autopilot was functioning throughout that time, including during the radical change in course back to Washington. Due to the technical skills required, disabling the autopilot and re-programming a new flight plan would be very difficult tasks for an unskilled hijacker. Of course, finding a specific target after flying the plane for hundreds of miles without autopilot would be an astonishing feat for an inexperienced pilot as well.[69] All of these problems are solved by positing a remote control hijacking.

Remote control of a large airliner using WAAS, which operates using satellites and a system of 20 ground-based reference stations spread across North America, was successfully tested in the 1990s along with ancillary landing systems. One landing system developed by Raytheon just before 9/11 was the military's all weather, anti-jam Joint Precision Approach and Landing System (JPALS).[70] To operate, JPALS needs ground-based GPS receivers which send signals to a central location at the landing site. This data is then sent to the approaching aircraft via a VHF data link so that flight path adjustments can be made.

Extensive flight testing of JPALS was conducted by Raytheon and the U.S. Air Force, in the three months before 9/11, at Holloman AFB in New Mexico.[71] Like Milstar, priority use of JPALS was given to special, covert missions conducted by U.S. Special Operations. The hardware for tactical JPALS operations consists of a communications console the size of a large microwave oven, a VHF transmission antenna twice the height of an average person, and a GPS receiver the size of a camera tripod.[72]

Insiders could have located such a console in the telephone closet that Probst was checking, along with a transmission antenna on the roof of the building, and additional receivers in the construction trailers. This would seem to provide a plausible explanation for how the necessary hardware for precision approach and "landing" of Flight 77 might have been present without detection.

It might not have been necessary for additional landing system equipment to be included in such a scenario, however. By late 2001, WAAS could function for precision guidance of aircraft and targeting of structures entirely on its own. In fact, at the time, military researchers were writing that "WAAS provides such a high accuracy positioning that the Oval Office itself would be a plausible target."[73]

It is the unusual flight pattern of the aircraft that suggests a separate landing system might have been employed. If WAAS alone was used, the flight path of the aircraft would not be expected to include several disruptions of the autopilot system and a last minute, 330-degree turn.

After the plane was headed back to Washington, the autopilot stayed on until approximately 9:08 when it was shut off for three minutes and turned on again. At 9:29, within minutes of Frank Probst's inspection of equipment within the impact area, "the autopilot on American 77 was disengaged [again]; the aircraft was at 7,000 feet and approximately 38 miles west of the Pentagon."[74] And at 9:34, just before Probst left the construction trailer, the plane was "5 miles west-southwest of the Pentagon and began a 330-degree turn. At the end of the turn, it was descending through 2,200 feet, pointed toward the Pentagon."[75]

This descending, 330-degree turn might have been similar to a "circling to land" maneuver used in order to better align the aircraft for a landing approach.[76] Alternatively, the turn might have been a non-standard entry into a holding pattern, like a teardrop turn. That is, it could be that something was not ready at the time that the aircraft was about to arrive and, therefore, arrival had to be delayed for a few minutes. It is also possible that control of the aircraft was switched from one system (WAAS) to another, requiring a delay.

The turn might also have been a spectacular demonstration of new technology related to the RMA, meant for certain people who needed convincing. If the JPALS system was located in or near the building, the suspicious activities of Probst could be explained in that he was using his expertise in advanced (DCA) communications to make the necessary last minute adjustments.

Further evidence for a last-minute adjustment is given by the distress shown by Vice President Cheney when he was being asked by a young naval officer if "the orders still [stood]." Cheney and his colleagues were apparently tracking Flight 77 as it came in to Arlington from approximately 50 miles out, and he seemed very distressed at the time, from what Norman Mineta has testified.[77]

Probst was finishing his inspection of equipment within the impact zone of the building at 9:25. This was just one minute before Cheney got the "50 miles out" notice, at 9:26 a.m., according to several accounts.[78]

The NTSB flight path study says that Flight 77 was about 35 miles west of the Pentagon at 9:29. The aircraft would have flown the final 35 miles in about five minutes, impacting at about 9:34 a.m., if it had not started the 330-degree turn. Instead, according to the NTSB study, the aircraft did not finish its wide turn until shortly after 9:34. This was just about the time that Probst was reported as having left the construction trailer, at 9:35.

Therefore the suspicious coincidences regarding DCA Lt. Col. Frank Probst's activities before impact might be considered with the fact that those activities were happening at the same times as notices were being given to Cheney. Probst's activities also appear to correlate with major changes to the flight path of the incoming aircraft.

This raises the question of what was being removed from the Pentagon site just after impact, and if any of it might have been related to aircraft guidance technology. It is possible that if transmitters or receivers that were part of a landing system were located at the site they could have been hidden within the building or in the construction trailers as suggested earlier.

The aircraft was reported to have impacted an area that was outlined almost exactly by the three construction trailers that were immediately in front of the impact zone.[79] Since the impact area and some of the trailers were said to have been completely destroyed, and teams of FBI and other first responders were removing evidence immediately after the attacks, we would never know.

Georgine K. Glatz, who was referred to as the chief engineer for the Pentagon Renovation Program Office, reported to Lee Evey's deputy, Mike Sullivan. Some interesting remarks were made by Dr. Glatz when she was interviewed by the Pentagon historian, Alfred Goldberg, in December 2001. For example, Glatz expressed doubts about a truck bomb being the scenario of interest in planning the renovation. She said that it was odd considering that, at the time, "everything was guided." Glatz went on to say, "Little did I know that the remote control would be the person flying the plane."[80]

In addition to the use of new aviation technology and guidance systems, there is reason to believe that explosives were planted in the building. This evidence includes witness testimony to a strong shockwave indicative of an explosion. Other witnesses with military experience testified to the strong smell of cordite, a low-grade military explosive, at the scene.[81]

Cordite is a low explosive, but it was not likely to have been present since its use is long-outdated. Today, it is a cliché to talk of the smell of cordite when one is referring to something with an aroma like that of explosives. One of the witnesses to have remarked on it was General Hugh Shelton, who claimed to have visited the scene in the early afternoon.

Whether it was cordite or something else, there were a number of highly credible witnesses that reported secondary explosions going off in and around the impact hole for nearly an hour after the aircraft crashed.[82] One of these was the CIA agent turned Florida congressman, Porter Goss, in whose district the alleged hijackers received their training. Goss went on to lead the first official inquiry into the events of 9/11.[83]

The use of well-timed explosives at the moment of aircraft impact could explain why so few parts of the aircraft were visible outside the building. Some eyewitnesses testified that the aircraft "seemed to simply melt into the building," or that it "sort of disappeared." One witness said that the plane went into the building like a "toy into a birthday cake," and another said "it was in the air one moment and in the building the next."[84]

These witness accounts suggest that explosives were placed in the building in such a way that, when triggered, they created an opening to absorb and destroy the body of the aircraft. The renovation project would have been perfect cover for placing the explosives in such an exact configuration. Again, the three officially unrecognized and completely destroyed construction trailers, located immediately in front of the impact area, might have served a role in triggering the explosives upon impact.

The Building Investigation and Those Who Controlled the Site

Evidence that something needed to be covered-up at the Pentagon was provided by the selection of those who led the official investigation into the building damage. The leader of the investigation, nominally sponsored by the American Society of Civil Engineers (ASCE), was Paul Mlakar. He had graduated from West Point (the year after Frank Probst) and Purdue University. Mlakar had ties to the U.S. deep state in that he married the daughter of Col. Robert P. Halloran, a former intelligence agent and acting director of the NSA under Allen Dulles (1960-61).

For the 11 years prior to 1996, Mlakar was vice president of a defense contractor located in San Diego, called JAYCOR. JAYCOR was an unofficial spin-off of SAIC, the company that has so many connections to 9/11.[85] As a company, JAYCOR specialized in defense-related technologies, but was primarily a radar systems provider. While working there, Mlakar filed for a number of patents on explosive containment devices for aircraft.[86]

In 1996, Mlakar joined the U.S. Army Corps of Engineer's Engineer Research and Development Center (ERDC), in Mississippi, where he was technical director for airfields, pavements and structures. Two years later, in 1998, Mlakar's unit "performed classified simulations" that measured "the damage the Pentagon would suffer from a truck bomb."[87] Mlakar's involvement in those pre-9/11 simulations to test

172

explosive effects on the external wall of the Pentagon is not well known and represents yet another amazing coincidence.

Despite being the leader of the building investigation, Mlakar was not given access to the Pentagon crash site until September 14. Through the following week, he was allowed limited access to the site although the other members of his investigation team were not. On October 4, the team was allowed to inspect the damage accompanied by Gene Corley, Mlakar's colleague from the Oklahoma City bombing investigation. But they were only allowed in for four hours.[88] That fact suggests that whoever was driving the investigation was not really interested in evidence. However, the access Mlakar and Corley were given was better than what they had gotten in Oklahoma City, when they performed their entire physical investigation from two hundred feet (half a city block) away.[89]

A few years after 9/11, a professor from the University of California publicly accused Mlakar of obstructing the investigation into the physical damage caused by Hurricane Katrina. In a letter to ASCE, the professor claimed that Mlakar had even admitted his role as an obstructionist.[90]

All things considered, the evidence suggests that Mlakar and his Pentagon building assessment was intended to be a cover-up. Furthermore, if the attack on the Pentagon had anything to do with explosives, remote targeting of objects near the ground, or airfields, Mlakar's experience at JAYCOR and ERDC would have helped him to know what evidence to avoid.

AMEC and Facchina Construction came to the site immediately after the attack. Paul Facchina described that, "AMEC called us within an hour and a half of the attack. We were asked to provide support services and logistical support to FEMA, the FBI, and DOD— whatever they needed. We had 50 people on site right away. We built roads to the site, providing shoring for areas in distress, cleared areas, and built fences to secure the area."[91]

Those who had unlimited access to the Pentagon crash site included Allyn Kilsheimer, an engineer who was often hired by the government to clean up after terrorist incidents. Kilsheimer was put in charge not only after the Pentagon attack, but also at the site of the Oklahoma City bombing in 1995 and the first terrorist attack on the World Trade Center in 1993. When given such an assignment, Kilsheimer expected to have total control over the site, even when the FBI and military were involved, and he usually got it.[92]

Kilsheimer, one of the DOJ-sensitive witnesses mentioned above, is the son of a concentration camp survivor. He gave his reasons for working at the Pentagon attack site by saying that, after September 11, he felt he was repaying America for what it had done to help his family during World War II.[93]

It was reported that Ron Vermillion of AMEC requested Mr. Kilsheimer's services immediately after the attack. Vermillion's boss was Mack McGaughan, who reported to Rumsfeld's long-time colleague, Peter Janson. But Glatz said it was a man named Jack Kelly who called in Kilsheimer because Kelly knew him from the past. Glatz said Kilsheimer had secured a $15 million contract within 5 minutes.[94]

An interview of Jack Kelly occurred as an interruption to the interview of William Viner, when Viner was describing the unplanned addition to the renovation plan. The Kelly interview included some difficulty determining exactly who he was and who he worked for. After request for clarification, Kelly remarked that there was no one else like him. He was on "a personal services contract" and was reporting directly to Lee Evey.[95]

In any case, it was said that Kilsheimer and Kelly ran the show during the cleanup operation.[96] When interviewed, Kelly told the interviewers they could learn more of the truth about what happened from Kilsheimer or Garret McKenzie of the FBI. McKenzie was in charge of photographing the evidence. At one point, he pulled together a dozen photographers for a briefing, and told them: "We don't need to photograph all the plane parts, only unique airplane parts or something specific. Like the pilot's yoke, or anything with part of a serial number on it. If we have to prove what kind of plane this was, the serial numbers will be what we need."[97]

Summary and Conclusions

In summary, the Pentagon renovation project was excellent cover for an insider conspiracy to attack the Pentagon. The people running the project were, at the same time, calling for a revolution in military affairs that, without the 9/11 attacks, they would not have been able to realize. These people included Donald Rumsfeld, Paul Wolfowitz, and others like Raytheon's director John Deutch and its advisor Richard Armitage. Others who were involved with the project profited from the seizure of oil and natural gas resources, like Rumsfeld's longtime fellow director Peter Janson and his colleagues at AMEC.

Through this review, more probable answers (a) to the questions mentioned at the beginning of this chapter can be proposed. It is important to keep in mind that these are simply proposed answers that require further investigation.

1. How could American Airlines Flight 77 have hit the building as it did, considering that the evidence shows the alleged hijacker pilot, Hani Hanjour, was a very poor pilot?

   a. Hani Hanjour was not flying the plane. It was remotely hijacked and controlled by the autopilot through WAAS guidance until it reached a point near the Pentagon. WAAS and its complementary system, JPALS, were capable of guiding the aircraft in the way that it was flown.

2. Why did the aircraft make a 330-degree turn just minutes before hitting the building?

   a. This was a maneuver used to better align the aircraft and reduce altitude prior to the "landing" approach. Alternatively, it might have been needed due to transfer of control of the aircraft between the WAAS and the JPALS system. The activities of Frank Probst could have involved adjustments to related equipment within the impact zone at the time of system transfer, as well as further adjustments in the construction trailer at the time that the turn began. These delicate moments in execution of the plan would help explain the distress exhibited by Dick Cheney at those same moments.

3. Why did the aircraft hit the least occupied, small fraction of the building that was the focus of the renovation plan and how was it that the construction in that exact spot just happened to be for the purpose of minimizing the damage from a terrorist explosion?

   a. This was done to limit the death toll, which is not what al Qaeda would have done. Efforts to reduce casualties among military personnel and leadership were taken by conspirators operating from within the Pentagon itself, including Donald Rumsfeld and Paul Wolfowtiz, and possibly other PNAC signatories who worked there. These casualty limiting efforts included the modifications to Wedge 1 and the targeting of that least occupied area.

4. Why was the company that performed the renovation work, just for that small fraction of the building, immediately hired in a no bid contract to clean up the damage and reconstruct that area of the building? (Note: The same company, AMEC Construction, was also immediately hired to clean up the WTC site within hours of the destruction there.)

   a. In this scenario, AMEC was part of the conspiracy, through Rumsfeld's colleague Peter Janson, and arrangements were made to ensure that renovation and cleanup of evidence were done by personnel managed by this trusted colleague.

5. What can explain the damage to the building and the aircraft debris, or lack thereof?

   a. The use of explosives could explain the damage done to the building, as well as the limited amount of recognizable aircraft debris at the site. It might also explain the FBI's desire to limit photography of the aircraft parts, which would otherwise have provided evidence for explosive effects. Explosives could have been planted under cover of the renovation project in such a way as to be triggered as the aircraft approached or impacted and create an opening that absorbed a majority of the aircraft.

6. Why were the tapes from the surveillance videos in the area immediately confiscated by the FBI and never released?

   a. The videos were confiscated and withheld because they provide evidence that further confirms the use of explosives.

An insider conspiracy answers the question of who benefited much better than does the official account. An historic power grab, a change in global policy direction, and a huge increase in military spending together constitute a much more compelling motivation than the purely symbolic gesture of hitting the Pentagon with an airplane—the objective attributed to the alleged hijackers. The massive seizure of resources, primarily oil and gas, represented by the wars in Iraq and Afghanistan, provided further, incalculable benefits to those within such an alternative conspiracy.

This particular hypothesis suggests that Dick Cheney, Donald Rumsfeld, Paul Wolfowitz, John Deutch and/or John Hamre, and Peter Janson could have played parts in the attack on the Pentagon, resulting in achievement of the RMA that they and their colleagues had sought. Some of them, like Cheney, Rumsfeld, and Janson, also benefited from the seizure of oil and gas resources. Others, including Lee Evey, Frank Probst, Paul Mlakar, and one or more FBI agents, might have had knowledge that they were participating in something deceptive but they did not necessarily need to know the entire plan.

Many West Point graduates, like Mlakar and Probst, hold honor above other values and therefore would not be expected to participate in dishonorable activities leading to terrorism against citizens of the United States. On the other hand, Operation Northwoods was approved and recommended for implementation when Probst was a freshman at West Point, by Chairman of the Joint Chiefs of Staff and West Point graduate Lyman Lemnitzer. Other West Point graduates, including Anastasio Somoza (1946) and Richard Secord (1955), have been implicated in crimes against democracy.

The alleged 9/11 hijackers are also important to the investigation. If Americans were involved, how can we reconcile that with the reports about the threats of "Islamic terrorism" that have been exclaimed for so many years? As seen in Chapters 4, 5, and 6, people who were charged with investigating and stopping terrorism in the decade before 9/11 appeared to have actually been facilitating or covering-up terrorism. The next chapter reviews the important history related to terrorist threats and how that history evolved. Two men played significant roles in that evolution and they both just happened to show up at the World Trade Center.

Chapter 11

Bremer, Jenkins and Terrorism Propaganda

"Terrorism is theater." — Brian Michael Jenkins

For many years prior to 9/11, two Americans were in unique positions to originate and frame the national conversation about terrorism. Those same two people, Brian Michael Jenkins and L. Paul Bremer, played extraordinary roles related to aviation security and World Trade Center (WTC) security in the few years before the 9/11 attacks. Could Bremer and Jenkins have been front men for a program that was hyping the threat of terrorism while at the same time manufacturing terrorist events for political purposes?

If so, it would not have been the first time that the American people were subject to the hard sell of a threat to national security only to discover that the threat was overblown or non-existent. The Soviet military threat to the U.S. after World War II is now widely known to have been a fabrication that was hyped for political and financial gains.[1]

The propaganda that drove the Cold War was effective in establishing government policy primarily because it was effective in framing the national conversation about what threats were important to consider, and in controlling the media. The same has been true for the propaganda driving the War on Terror. A short review of the people and reports that promoted the Soviet communist threat is helpful in understanding the "Islamic terrorist" threat that has evolved from it.

The Communist Threat and State-sponsored Terrorism

One man, Paul Nitze, was behind the three most important reports that promoted the perception of a Soviet threat against the United States after World War II. The first of these reports, NSC68, was instrumental in changing the policies of the Truman Administration, which initially did not perceive the Soviets as a major threat. The second Nitze report was the Gaither Report that, in 1957, said the U.S. had fallen behind the Soviets in nuclear weaponry.

As an investment banker turned top government policy maker, Nitze was clearly a powerful man. Author Burton Hersh has said that Nitze was one of two people who met quarterly in Frank Wisner's office to select the missions that would be approved for The Office of Policy Coordination, the CIA's early covert operations group.[2]

Nitze was also the founder of the Committee on the Present Danger (CPD). This was a political action group that brought about the remilitarization of the U.S. in the 1950s by promoting the ideas in NSC68. CPD was resurrected in 1975 and 1976 by Cold War hawks, including Donald Rumsfeld, who wanted to eliminate the policy of détente and Soviet containment in favor of another military build-up. The group was resurrected yet again in 2004 to promote a more aggressive War on Terror.[3]

Peter Dale Scott noted a significant difference in process between the first incarnation of the CPD and the second. As Scott wrote, the first CPD was created by a consensus within the state to mobilize against a Soviet threat that was open to misunderstanding at the time. The second iteration, however, "was mounted in opposition to a government policy that threatened to establish a more peaceful and less militarized world. In short, the interests being defended were not those of the nation but of the military-industrial complex itself."[4]

Nitze became the Secretary of the Navy in 1963, serving until 1967, and therefore he was in that position at the time of the 1964 Gulf of Tonkin incident. The resulting Gulf of Tonkin Resolution brought the U.S. military into Vietnam based on claims about an attack on U.S. Navy vessels. Government records produced as early as 1968 indicate that Nitze was responsible for suppressing documents that proved the Gulf of Tonkin claims made by the U.S. Navy were false.[5] The U.S. ships were never attacked.

Despite these troubling facts, Nitze went on to serve as Deputy Secretary of Defense from 1967 to 1969. His boss, Secretary of Defense Clark Clifford, essentially left the management of the department to Nitze.[6] But it was Clifford who authored the official report on the 1967 attack on the USS *Liberty*. Clifford's report found that the Israeli military was negligent but that the aggression against the *Liberty* was not pre-meditated.[7] Many of the survivors maintain that it was deliberate.[8]

Clifford went on to infamy as a leading figure in the terrorist-financing Bank of Credit and Commerce International (BCCI). It was Clifford, in fact, who first approached Saudi Arabian intelligence director Kamal Adham with the proposal to create such a network to fund off-the-books intelligence operations internationally.[9]

In 1969, Nitze and his mentor, Dean Acheson, began to tutor aspiring bureaucrats who had been recommended by their colleague Albert Wohlstetter of the University of Chicago and the RAND Corporation. Under Nitze's supervision, Richard Perle and Paul Wolfowitz had their introduction to the workings and power structure of the U.S. government.[10]

The Gulf of Tonkin non-event was undoubtedly an example of false flag manipulation for political purposes and the *Liberty* incident appears to have been a major cover-up of an attack upon U.S. servicemen. State-sponsored terrorism was already a well-established fact by then, however. For example, the U.S. Joint Chiefs of Staff (JCS) approved a plan called Operation Northwoods in 1962.

Operation Northwoods called "for a wave of violent terrorism to be launched in Washington, D.C., Miami, and elsewhere. People would be framed for bombings they did not commit; planes would be hijacked. [This would provide] the public and international backing they needed to launch their war."[11] The signed documents are available today and because of this we know that high level U.S. government representatives conspire, on occasion, to commit crimes against the American people for the purpose of starting wars.[12]

Although Operations Northwoods was rejected by President Kennedy, the plan becomes more interesting historically when one considers the ensuing activities of the members of the JCS who approved that plan. For example, JCS chairman Lyman Leminitzer went directly from approving Operation Northwoods in 1962 to become Supreme Allied Commander in Europe (SACEUR), from 1963 to 1969, putting him in charge of NATO forces. According to author Daniele Ganser, the SACEUR ran an agency called the Clandestine Planning Committee (CPC) that was responsible for coordinating Operation Gladio.[13]

Gladio was a well-coordinated covert campaign of terrorism directed by the U.S. and other Western governments against their own populations. Hundreds of innocent people were killed or maimed in terrorist attacks which were then blamed on leftist subversives or other political opponents. General Paolo Inzerilli commanded the Italian forces of Gladio from 1974 to 1986 and he later said that "the omnipresent United States dominated the secret CPC that directed the secret war."[14]

From NATO and CPC headquarters in Paris, and later Brussels, the U.S. played a leading role in arming and coordinating the terrorist groups in various European countries from 1960 into the late 1980s. Run largely by the U.S., Britain and Belgium, other NATO countries involved included Germany, France, Italy, Denmark, Norway, The Netherlands, Portugal, Turkey, and Greece. The terrorist attacks of Gladio were coupled with terror propaganda in order to drive public and political will to fund and support ever-increasing military preparation and response to the perceived communist threat.

Incidentally, Donald Rumsfeld was the U.S. Ambassador to NATO in 1973 and 1974 and was living and working amidst the Gladio planners in Brussels during the height of that program's operations. Alexander Haig became SACEUR as Rumsfeld left Brussels, and he remained in that position until 1979. Haig was a White House colleague of Bremer, Jenkins, and Rumsfeld before and after his time as SACEUR.

Paul Nitze got his chance to oversee the third major report that hyped the Soviet threat thanks to another Operations Northwoods signatory. The project known as Team B was initiated through the actions of President Ford's Foreign Intelligence Advisory Board, led by Operation Northwoods signatory George Anderson. Team B was a re-evaluation of existing CIA (or Team A) data, by a small group of "outside experts," led by Richard Pipes, that falsely portrayed the

Soviet military threat as persistent and growing when all objective evidence said the opposite. The initiative was approved by CIA Director George H.W. Bush, and Nitze and Wolfowitz were among the lead advisors.

While Rumsfeld was in Brussels, a European "network of private-sector spies," called Cercle Pinay, decided to export its propaganda techniques to the United States. Cercle Pinay operated during the Cold War era to provide "covert funding, black propaganda, and connections to planned coups de etat" for a private intelligence network that was composed of "rogue agents of the international Right."[15]

In 1974 the British part of the Cercle complex worked to create an American copy of its propaganda front, the Institute for the Study of Conflict (ISC), called the Washington Institute for the Study of Conflict (WISC). In April 1975, WISC was formally founded. ISC, staffed by former MI6 agents, "put over the intelligence community's views to the press under the guise of a neutral academic research body." WISC followed suit in the States.

WISC joined forces with an existing propaganda machine based in New York, founded by William Casey and CPD member Frank R. Barnett, called the National Strategy Information Center (NSIC). At the same time, the roles of Nitze and the other Team B champions of the military-industrial complex grew under the Ford and Reagan administrations.

The last meeting of Cercle Pinay occurred in December 1979, and was attended by William Colby, Federal Reserve Bank chairman Paul Volcker, and Heritage Foundation president Edwin Feulner. The operations of the Cercle complex were redirected by the new head of the French SDECE, Alexandre de Marenches. It was de Marenches who then led the formation of the Safari Club. De Marenches also recommended William Casey as CIA director to Ronald Reagan, and became friends with the Belgian-American propagandist Arnaud de Borchgrave, who was later a shareholder in Stratesec.[16]

As with Nitze's leadership of the three primary reports on the Soviet threat, two men were primary leaders of the terrorism-related commissions in the years leading up to 9/11. These men were Brian Michael Jenkins and L. Paul Bremer. With the help of Nitze and others, Bremer and Jenkins transformed the Soviet threat into a threat of "international terrorism" in the 1970s and 1980s, and further transformed that threat into today's widely held belief in "Islamic terrorism." To better understand the roles that Bremer and Jenkins played related to 9/11, and as terror propagandists, we should examine their personal histories.

Brian Michael Jenkins

From 1989 to 1998, Jenkins was the deputy chairman of Crisis Management for Kroll Associates. Kroll directed the response of the Port Authority of New York and New Jersey (PANYNJ) to the 1993 WTC bombing in terms of security upgrades. As stated by the PANYNJ program manager for WTC security systems, Douglas G. Karpiloff, "After the bombing, we had the top security consultants in the nation, Kroll Associates, do a complete security analysis for us, and we followed their recommendations."[17]

During this time, Jenkins reviewed the possibility of airliners crashing into the Twin Towers.[18] As the leader of the WTC threat assessment, Jenkins was later questioned about plans that might have been made to avoid what happened on 9/11. "We knew there was no realistic way to protect the skyscrapers from a suicide mission," Jenkins said. "We couldn't very well mount missile batteries above the Windows on the World restaurant."[19]

Jenkins and his Kroll Associates colleagues worked with a company called Stratesec, discussed in the next two chapters, and other subcontractors, to design and implement the new security system for the WTC complex. This meant that he had the ability to influence or control the installation of equipment in the WTC buildings and it is possible that he could have been involved with the installation of "backdoor" access systems.

Jenkin's history as a Special Operations officer and long-time right-wing political advisor contributed to criticism of his role at the WTC. Not long after the 1993 bombing it was reported that Jenkins was "trotted out" to explain the threat we faced. Described as one of "the hoariest holdovers from the era of Reagan 'roll, back,' RAND's Brian Jenkins was both an apologist for and one of the architects of the contra war against Nicaragua – a terror war aimed primarily at the civilian population and infrastructure."[20]

Jenkins played a critical role in planning for future terrorist events at the WTC, including having reviewed the possibility of airliner crashes before they actually happened on 9/11. Coupled with the claims that he participated in planning and implementing a "terror war" in Central America during the 1980s, these facts should make him a subject of considerable interest with respect to 9/11.

Born in 1942 and commissioned in the infantry at the age of 19, Jenkins was a Special Forces soldier who saw action in many covert operations of the 1960s. He was in Guatemala in 1965, the year that U.S. security adviser John P. Longan arrived and, "along with a Guatemalan Army élite, launched Operation Cleanup, a death squad operation that throughout 1966 effected kidnappings and assassinations that killed the leaders of Guatemala's labor unions and peasant federations."[21]

Jenkins was also part of the 7th Special Forces occupation of the Dominican Republic, in which only "around 75 members of E company of the 7th Special Forces Group were deployed."[22] Jenkins then went on to serve with the 5th Special Forces Group in Vietnam where he lived in the countryside among villagers, "trying to recruit as many as possible into a pro-U.S. counter-guerrilla force."[23]

During this time Jenkins signed on as a field consultant for the RAND Corporation. He became well known for a confidential 1968 paper that he wrote for RAND entitled "The Unchangeable War."[24] Jenkins cited nine obstacles to a U.S. victory in Vietnam and suggested the war could be lost due to these symptoms of the military's "institutional rigidity." He also pointed out that his boss, General Creighton Abrams, was in charge of a pacification program run by Robert Komer, who was credited with managing the mass murder project known as the Phoenix Program and later became a WISC member.[25] It is likely that Jenkins was also part of the Phoenix Program, although documentation of that fact has not yet been revealed.[26]

In a 1971 paper that described the last ditch effort to "Vietnamize" the war, Jenkins thanked his RAND colleagues Komer and Fred Ikle.[27] As a pioneer in psychological operations, Ikle had written reports and memoranda for RAND through the 1960s. This association gives more reason to wonder if Jenkins was also a psychological operative and if he was part of the Phoenix Program, as is suspected of Richard Armitage.

In 1972, at the age of 30, Jenkins launched RAND's terrorism research program. He was "summoned to Washington by the Nixon administration and asked to help set up a Cabinet-level committee to deal with the terrorism threat."[28] Two years later, Jenkins wrote that terrorism sometimes works. He also made clear that the ability to engage in terrorism was not limited to foreigners, but that even U.S. soldiers could be seen as terrorists if they killed civilians. Jenkins wrote about "government terror" and how national governments would begin to employ terrorists as surrogates.[29]

Jenkins further explained that "Terrorism is aimed at the people watching, not at the actual victims. Terrorism is theater."[30] He believed that one objective of terrorism was "to enforce obedience and cooperation. This is the normal objective of state or official terrorism" and that "success demands the creation of an atmosphere of fear and the seeming omnipresence of the internal security apparatus."[31]

Jenkins wrote papers with WISC member George K. Tanham and was published not only by RAND but also through Crane Russak Company, which published papers by WISC member James Theberge, NSIC propagandist Frank R. Barnett, and Paul Nitze.

A 1976 paper by Jenkins described a RAND summit meeting on terrorism that included such luminaries as Andrew Marshall. In this paper, Jenkins argued for the more flexible military that Rumsfeld later promoted, and he called for the creation of a new kind of special operations unit, just like the Joint Special Operations Command

(JSOC) that succeeded the OPC a few years later, to collaborate with the CIA to address terrorism. It was also suggested that U.S. counterterrorism collaboration with the British, West Germans and Israelis should continue.[32]

In 1981, Donald Rumsfeld became Chairman of the Board for the RAND Corporation, a role he remained in until 1986 and filled again from 1995 to 1996. As Rumsfeld took over at RAND, Jenkins reviewed media exaggeration of terrorist events and the psychological impact of that coverage. He wrote, "The media exaggerate the strength of the terrorists, creating the illusion of their omnipresence." At the same time, he reviewed public support, via poll responses, for a "special world police force" to combat terrorism.[33]

Around this time, Jenkins began to advocate for using terrorism to psychologically manipulate civilian populations. As an advisor in the construction of a counterinsurgency program in El Salvador, Jenkins recommended that traditional methods be supplemented by the use of propaganda to discredit insurgents as "terrorists." In another 1984 paper, Jenkins recommended that the U.S. engage in low-intensity warfare against Nicaragua through a proxy army. Such actions fall within Jenkins' own definition of state sponsored terrorism.[34]

By 1986, Jenkins was among a small group that advised Secretary of State George Shultz on matters of terrorism. It was said that "his trips to Washington became more frequent. He also spent time with CIA Director William J. Casey, Defense Secretary Caspar Weinberger and other administration advisors."[35] That same year, Bremer became the new Ambassador at Large for Counter-terrorism and Armitage was working as the lead counter-terrorism representative for the Department of Defense.

In 1988, it was beginning to become clear that the image of a Soviet threat could no longer be sustained. The Soviet empire was crumbling economically and that fact could not be glossed over. At the time, Jenkins began suggesting that long-proclaimed Soviet responsibility for terrorism was not based on evidence but was politically required in the Reagan era. Jenkins believed that blaming the Soviets going forward could only hurt anti-terrorism efforts. A new enemy was needed.

The problem was that a new enemy of Soviet caliber was not evident at the time. Libya was blamed for the December 1988 Lockerbie bombing, but the predecessors to al Qaeda were still working for the CIA in Afghanistan. In fact, Richard Armitage was meeting and working with the Pakistani ISI and the Mujahideen, parts of which would later be known as al Qaeda.[36]

Simultaneously, a private intelligence organization continued to evolve from the Safari Club, Cercle Pinay, and the actions taken by a network of disgruntled CIA operatives who were close to George H.W. Bush. This organization grew to become a parallel CIA that worked as a partnership between right-wing Europeans, the Pakistani ISI, and oil-rich royals from the Middle East—particularly Saudi Arabia, Kuwait and the United Arab Emirates. The secret operations in which this parallel CIA engaged were funded largely by the BCCI network, and BCCI's secret subsidiary, First American Bank in the United States. From such operations, al Qaeda was born.[37]

Between 1988 and 1998, the U.S.-al Qaeda connection grew, as evidenced by the recruiting done in U.S. centers like al-Kifah in New York, and by the revelations about al Qaeda's operative Ali Mohamed. Known as a key planner for the first WTC attack in 1993 and a trainer for the 9/11 plot, Mohamed was a U.S. Army drill sergeant and an informant for the FBI. He was allowed to move freely in and out of the U.S. for many years and when detained, he was allowed to plea-bargain.[38]

U.S. protection of operatives like Mohamed was one way to ensure an increase in terrorism. But to transform the primary threat from one of a monolithic Soviet or communist empire to a more flexible, non-state terrorist organization like al Qaeda, significant amounts of inter-government communication coupled with public propaganda was required. That is, we needed official commissions to assess and report on the new threat.

In 1996, Jenkins was appointed to the White House Commission on Aviation Safety and Security, joining Vice President Gore, Stratesec director James Abrahamson, former CIA director John Deutch, and FBI director Louis Freeh. One recommendation of the Commission urged all-civilian implementation of Global Positioning System (GPS) devices provided by the Defense department.[39] Other recommendations focused on the passenger profiling and technology related to hijacking prevention.

In 1999 Jenkins co-authored a book entitled *Aviation Terrorism and Security* with British professor Paul Wilkinson.[40] Wilkinson was a terrorism propagandist for the Cercle Pinay and ISC, the parent organization of WISC.[41] He often made public presentations with ISC leaders, including Brian Crozier, Robert Moss and Hans Josef Horchem, head of the German terror propaganda outlet.

As a primary terrorism advisor for Margaret Thatcher, Wilkinson was invited to speak at the Jerusalem Conference on International Terrorism (JCIT) in July 1979, along with Benjamin Netanyahu, Team B members Richard Pipes and George Keegan, Senator Henry (Scoop) Jackson, and George H.W. Bush. The JCIT "established the ideological foundations for the 'War on Terror.' The JCIT's defining theme was that international terrorism constituted an organized political movement whose ultimate origin was the Soviet Union".[42]

Later, in 1999 and 2000, Jenkins served as an advisor to the National Commission on Terrorism, led by L. Paul Bremer, otherwise known as the "Bremer Commission." Details of that Commission's findings are related below.

Jenkins was also made a primary advisor to the Hart-Rudman Commission, another of the major terrorism-focused commissions chartered to evaluate the new threat. Members of the Hart-Rudman Commission included Lee Hamilton, who would later become vice-chairman of the 9/11 Commission, and Lynne Cheney, who would quit the commission due to other members not agreeing with her claim that a war with China was the biggest threat to the United States.[43]

The Hart-Rudman Commission reported in January 2001 that "America will become increasingly vulnerable to hostile attack on our homeland, and our military superiority will not help us." The Commission also predicted that "Space will become a critical and competitive military environment" and called for "the creation of a new independent National Homeland Security Agency."[44]

After 9/11, in a 2002 pamphlet called "Countering al Qaeda," Jenkins wrote "Al Qaeda constitutes the most serious immediate threat to the security of the United States." He thanked his colleague L. Paul Bremer.

L. Paul Bremer

Bremer is most well known for being the Iraq Occupation Governor after the 2003 U.S. invasion and for having made many of the decisions that drove Iraqi society into a spiraling downturn. But the man can easily be seen as the most important figure in the U.S. assessment of terrorism prior to 9/11.

Oddly enough, Bremer was at the WTC on 9/11. His employer at the time of the attacks, insurance giant Marsh & McLennan, occupied the exact eight floors of the north tower impact zone. In October 2000, Bremer took a job as the CEO of Marsh Political Risk Practice and he had an office in the south tower. Exactly what political risks he was assessing at the time are not known, but he was in precise position to help take advantage of the political windfall on 9/11.

On the day of the attacks, Bremer was interviewed on NBC television and he stated that Osama bin Laden was responsible and that possibly Iraq and Iran were involved too. He called for the most severe military response possible. Google removed the interview video from its servers three times, and blocked it once.[45]

Bremer was born in Hartford, Connecticut in 1941, making him just a year older than Jenkins. He was educated at Ivy League prep schools including Phillips Academy a few years before George W. Bush. Like Bush, Bremer also graduated from Yale University, in 1963. He went on to earn a Certificate of Political Studies in 1964 from the Institut D'Etudes Politiques of the University of Paris, and then went to Harvard for an MBA.

In 1966 he joined the Foreign Service, which sent him first to Kabul, Afghanistan as a general services officer. He was later assigned to Blantyre, Malawi, as economic and commercial officer, from 1968 to 1971.

At the time, the CIA was putting its agents in Foreign Service offices in order to ensure diplomatic immunity, and to provide security for the files and communications. History had led to the "establishment of small to very large contingents of American intelligence officers in most of our embassies and consulates throughout the world."[46]

Bremer was in Malawi when it was essentially a police state, and only a few years after Frank Carlucci was assigned to the same general area. Carlucci had been urgently expelled from Tanzania by that country's president after the U.S. was accused of using white mercenaries to attack from neighboring regions.[47] Carlucci was formally referred to as a "Foreign Service" agent, yet was also expelled from both Congo and Zanzibar for subversive activities.

During the 1970s, Bremer held various domestic posts with the State Department, including as an assistant to Henry Kissinger from 1972 to 1976. He was Deputy Chief of Mission in Oslo from 1976-79, during the time that Alexander Haig was SACEUR.

Bremer returned to the U.S. to take a post of Deputy Executive Secretary of the Department of State from 1979 to 1981. A letter sent to Bremer during this period was seized in the U.S. embassy in Tehran during the revolution. The letter, written two months before the hostages were taken, assured Bremer that "our interest in continued access to Iran's oil should be safeguarded by the new government's ability to maintain order in the oil fields and its need for earnings."[48]

In 1981, Bremer was made Executive Secretary and Special Assistant to Alexander Haig. Shortly after Haig's resignation in June 1982, senior officials in the State Department were told by Bremer, who "runs the nuts-and-bolts operations of the department," to prepare brief memos on key issues to bring Mr. Shultz up to date.[49] As Shultz settled in as the new Secretary of State, he specifically chose to retain Bremer and Lawrence Eagleburger among his top aides.

Ronald Reagan appointed Bremer as Ambassador to The Netherlands in 1983 and Bremer stayed in that position until 1986. The secret wars of Gladio proceeded in The Netherlands while Bremer was there, as they had in Norway when he was Deputy Chief of Mission in that country.[50]

In 1986, Reagan brought Bremer back to the U.S. by appointing him Ambassador-at-Large for Counterterrorism as well as Coordinator for Counterterrorism. William Casey and the others in the Reagan administration had been meeting with Brian Jenkins that year on the terrorist threat. At the time, Libya's leader Muammar Qaddafi was cited as the greatest purveyor of terrorism. This might have had something to do with Qaddafi's attempts to convert his oil trade from U.S. dollars to a new African gold dinar. But the bombing of a Berlin discotheque was blamed on Libya and the U.S. bombed the country in response.

While Bremer was the Ambassador to The Netherlands and then the State Department's counterterrorism lead, Paul Nitze was Special Advisor to the President and Secretary of State on Arms Control. Nitze went on to serve in a similar role for George H.W. Bush, but Bremer resigned to join Kissinger Associates as Managing Director.

As Bremer resigned, the *New York Times* reported that Reagan's Clint Eastwood-style talk about fighting terrorism had come to little or nothing in terms of justice. During Bremer's tenure only one terrorist was ever brought to the U.S. for trial, and he was small potatoes. Abu Nidal was cited as the "most notorious practitioner of terror in the Middle East" yet no indictment for Nidal was issued.[51]

Kissinger Associates had a number of meetings with BCCI representatives while Bremer worked there. BCCI was involved in funding terrorists and was linked to the Pakistani intelligence network from which several alleged 9/11 conspirators came, including KSM. In fact, *TIME* magazine reported that, "You can't draw a line separating the bank's black operatives and Pakistan's intelligence services."[52] As the BCCI scandal peaked, Bremer and his colleagues at Kissinger Associates refused to provide documents requested by the Senate investigators.[53]

At the time of the February 1993 WTC bombing, Bremer made a remark similar to that which Jenkins made, in terms of the difficulty in preventing terrorism at the WTC. "There is just going to be less security at a place like the World Trade Center than at the Congress, the White House or the Supreme Court," said Bremer. "It is easier to move around in New York, and it is easier to create a great amount of terror there."[54]

Again, it seems odd that the American who knew the most about terrorism would remark about the danger to the WTC and then be located in exactly that dangerous spot on 9/11. It is also curious that his colleague Jenkins, who was perhaps the second most well-known U.S. terrorism expert and who designed the security system for the WTC complex, would make a similar statement about the inability to protect the WTC.

In 1996, while still working for Kissinger Associates, Bremer wrote a scathing article about Clinton's lack of focus on terrorism. In this article, Bremer called on Clinton to enforce a strong, ten-step plan to address terrorism through uncompromising action. "These are not options," he wrote.[55] Apparently Bremer did not see the irony in his comment about options with respect to his own company's refusal to cooperate with the Senate investigation into BCCI, a major terrorism financing network.

In 1996, the Khobar Towers in Saudi Arabia, located near the headquarters of Saudi Aramco, were bombed. Contrary to claims that al Qaeda was behind the bombing, the U.S. blamed Hezbollah al-Hejaz for the attack. That same year, a company for which Bremer was a director patented a thermite demolition device, which is a topic of interest with regard to the destruction of the WTC.[56]

According to a 2002 State Department list that was re-published in 2004, the U.S. government had attributed only four terrorist attacks to al Qaeda prior to 9/11.[57] Those attacks were a series of bombings in Yemen in December 1992; the shooting down of U.S. helicopters in Somalia in 1993; the bombings of U.S. embassies in Africa in 1998; and the USS Cole incident in 2000.

The African embassy bombings were attributed to Osama bin Laden and the as-yet unreported group called al Qaeda. The U.S. government responded with bombings of Sudan and Afghanistan and, with help from the *New York Times*, began to drum up an intense myth about OBL and al Qaeda.

- "This is, unfortunately, the war of the future," Secretary of State Madeleine Albright said. "The Osama bin Laden organization has basically declared war on Americans and has made very clear that these are all Americans, anywhere."

- Clinton's national security advisor Samuel Berger said, "This is an evil that is directed at the United States. It's going to persist."

- Under Secretary of State Thomas. Pickering remarked, "We are in this for the long haul."[58]

- State Department representative James Foley added, "A new era, in effect, is upon us. It's imperative that the American people understand and prepare themselves for facing this kind of a threat into the 21st century for as long as it's necessary to face the threat."

In retrospect, it is surprising that this was the first reference to al Qaeda in the *New York Times*, coming only three years before 9/11. The newspaper's first reference to "Ussama [*sic*] bin Laden" had been in April 1994.

However, the first media reference to "al Qaida" was six months after the CIA's Alec Station started, in August 1996, by United Press International (led by Arnaud de Borchgrave). Alec Station, which focused on the pursuit of OBL, began operations in February 1996. But the 9/11 Commission suggested that the CIA had knowledge about al Qaeda four or five years before that. It is not clear why the *New York Times* did not pick up on al Qaeda as a threat until just a few years before 9/11, and many years after the CIA had.

More surprising is that *The Washington Post* did not report on al Qaeda until June 1999, and its reporting was highly speculative about the power behind this new threat.

"The indictment describes bin Laden as the leader, or 'emir,' of al Qaeda, a "global terrorist organization" with tentacles that allegedly reach from his hideout in the mountains of Afghanistan to followers in Texas, Florida and New York.

...But for all its claims about a worldwide conspiracy to murder Americans, the government's case is, at present, largely circumstantial. The indictment never explains how bin Laden runs al Qaeda or how he may have masterminded the embassy bombings. Only eight of the 17 suspects are alleged to have been in Kenya and Tanzania around the time the embassies were bombed."[59]

These statements should be compared to those of Bremer made a year earlier. Where *The Washington Post* was skeptical, Bremer was completely confident as he claimed that defeating OBL would be like another Cold War.

"This is a crusade he's on," said Bremer.

"There is a quantum difference in the way bin Laden looks at terror," he said. "What we are seeing is a shift to terrorism on a more theological basis, to groups that are not after precise political goals. When you start to embrace goals as broad as bin Laden's, you are no longer constrained by the number of casualties you incur. You are now in a different game."

"There's no such thing as eliminating terror, any more than eliminating crime. What we're in for, if we're serious about it, is the kind of sustained effort it took during the cold war — not months, not years, but decades."[60]

As of that moment, the U.S. had found its new Soviet caliber threat on which to base a new militarization of the country. It is interesting, however, that Bremer made sensationalist claims of a "crusade" and a "quantum difference" yet a year later *The Washington Post* was reporting that the government's case against this new terror group was "largely circumstantial."

195

In any case, Bremer was selected for a leading role in several of the ensuing terrorism commissions. First, he was appointed to the Gilmore Commission, chaired by Virginia Governor James Gilmore. Donald Rumsfeld was originally a member of the Gilmore Commission as well.[61] The vice chairman was James R. Clapper, who would later be director of national intelligence. Coincidentally, James Abrahamson, director of WTC security company Stratesec, hired Clapper as his fellow director at the satellite spy company GeoEye.

The Gilmore Commission was a federally-sponsored effort with RAND oversight that was chartered to assess readiness, and evaluate the terrorism response programs and coordination between federal, state, and local governments. In total the Commission ultimately "made 164 recommendations regarding the domestic response to terrorism. Of those 164 recommendations, all have been adopted in whole or in part by the Congress and the Federal Government."[62]

Unfortunately, despite the Commission's 1999 claim that "All terrorist acts are crimes," the greatest terrorist attack on American soil would happen two years later and would not be treated as a crime.[63] This could be because the Gilmore Commission excluded "acts of violence committed by bona fide state agents" and therefore we were all free to assume what the 9/11 Commission eventually concluded – that no government supported the 9/11 conspirators.

The Gilmore Commission found no evidence of U.S. sponsored terrorism or state manipulation of policy through violence despite the 1990 revelations of Operation Gladio, the 1997 revelations about Operations Northwoods, and the Gulf of Tonkin non-event, which was widely known to be false as of the mid-1990s.

Bremer was then appointed Chairman of the National Commission on Terrorism by House Speaker Dennis Hastert. Other members of the Commission included Jenkins, Fred Ikle, James Woolsey, Maurice Sonnenberg, and Jane Harman. In July 1999, the sole Muslim nominee for Bremer's commission was removed after complaints from certain political action groups.[64] Apparently, the practical outcome of equating Islam with terrorism was already a foregone conclusion.

The "Bremer Commission" based its report on interviews with a number of people who were seen as experts on terrorism. This included Richard Armitage, Marion Bowman, Richard Clarke, Stephen Cambone, FBI director Louis Freeh, Robert Gates, Jenkins' RAND cohort Bruce Hoffman, Lewis (Scooter) Libby, soon-to-be acting FBI director Thomas Pickard, Michael Rolince, Michael Sheehan, CIA director George Tenet, and Jenkins' fellow propagandist and JCIT attendee, Paul Wilkinson.

To clarify how oddly coincidental this interview list was, one should remember that the number of U.S. intelligence failures to capture the alleged 9/11 hijackers was astounding.[65] And many of the people mentioned above, including Richard Clarke, George Tenet, Louis Freeh, Marion "Spike" Bowman, Michael Rolince and Thomas Pickard played critical roles in those astounding failures. Others on the list, like Armitage, Casey's protégé Gates, Rumsfeld's sidekick Cambone, and Cheney's assistant Libby, benefited from the 9/11 attacks through unprecedented political gain. Wilkinson's presence is simply evidence that the Bremer Commission was a propaganda operation from the start.

Surprisingly, according to the Commission's vice chairman Maurice Sonnenberg, the Bremer Commission essentially wrote the USA Patriot Act. Sonnenberg boasted that 20 of the Commission's 25 recommendations made it into that controversial and poorly reviewed legislation.

A member of what has been referred to as the closest thing America has to a "formal aristocracy," Sonnenberg described the reasons for terrorism against the U.S. very simply. "And why do some people out there hate America? We're the top dog," Sonnenberg said. "Everybody hates the top dog."[66]

Sonneberg's company, Bear Stearns, went on to be at the center of the 2008 financial meltdown, requiring tens of billions in bailout money, and later faced a number of securities and investment fraud charges.[67] Such irregularities point to what could be called financial terrorism, as well as the fact that, occasionally, the "top dog's" formal aristocracy needs to be bailed out by the little people.

The Bremer Commission recommendations included a plan to transfer power to the Department of Defense "during a catastrophic terrorist attack or prior to an imminent attack." Another recommendation was to prepare a manual on how to implement legal authority at the federal, state and local levels in case of a catastrophic terrorist attack. Yet another was to institute annual exercises under the direction of the national coordinator for terrorism (Richard Clarke) to develop counterterrorism and consequence management responses during such an event.

Journalist James Risen noted, just after the Bremer Commission's report was issued, that one of the recommendations called "on the Central Intelligence Agency to drop its human rights guidelines on the recruitment of terrorist informants."[68] That recommendation was clarified by propagandist (and Stratesec stockholder) Arnaud de Borchgrave, who said, "It is clear also that FBI and CIA guidelines about recruiting terrorists as informants must be simplified to make it easier to recruit terrorists to provide information."[69]

As the report from the Bremer Commission was being issued, Bremer appeared on PBS' *Frontline* television program to discuss the report's claim that international terrorism was an increasingly lethal threat to the United States.[70] Joining Bremer was Larry Johnson, a former CIA covert operative and State Department expert on terrorism.

Johnson's remarks during this program were revealing: "What has happened is once the threat of the Soviet Union disappeared, we've got a lot of national security bureaucracies and other bureaucracies that are looking for a way to justify their existence, and many are scrambling to get the counter terrorism bonanza."

On the same program the year before, Johnson was asked if the U.S. government was hyping the threat of terrorism. Johnson replied, "They're grossly exaggerating the problem. They are hyping it. They shouldn't be talking about rising terrorism. What they should be saying is, 'There's one individual out there that really doesn't like us.'" Johnson named OBL as that individual and clarified that "the problem is this: the Saudi Arabian government, not just Osama bin Laden but many people in Saudi Arabia, have been sending money to radical Islamic groups for years."[71]

Only two months before 9/11, Johnson was even clearer, saying, "Americans are bedeviled by fantasies about terrorism. They seem to believe that terrorism is the greatest threat to the United States and that it is becoming more widespread and lethal. They are likely to think that the United States is the most popular target of terrorists. And they almost certainly have the impression that extremist Islamic groups cause most terrorism. None of these beliefs are based in fact."[72]

Of course, the 9/11 Commission came to the opposite conclusions that Johnson had espoused. Perhaps Johnson has changed his opinion too as he now works with Barry McDaniel, the former COO of Stratesec.[73]

In October 2000, Bremer took his new job as CEO of Marsh Political Risk. There are few coincidences more startling than this – the man most responsible for fomenting the fear of terrorism in the United States went directly to a job working in the WTC towers less than a year before 9/11. Bremer's office was in the South Tower. In an interview with CNN after the Sept 11 attacks, Bremer claimed that his office was located "above where the second aircraft hit."

Just days after the 9/11 attacks Bremer was chosen to co-chair the Heritage Foundation's Homeland Security Task Force, which created a blueprint for the White House's Department of Homeland Security. On this task force was Edwin Meese and, again, Fred Ikle. The report called for considerable increases in military spending that were not related to terrorism, including much of what Cheney and Rumsfeld had desired before 9/11.

Bremer also started a new division of Marsh & McLennan called Marsh Crisis, and Marsh went on to purchase Kroll Associates, Jenkins' former employer. At the same time, a company called Control Risks merged with Bremer's Marsh Crisis.[74] Based out of London, Control Risks had been one of the most prominent "terrorism research" outlets supported by Cercle Pinay and its propaganda branch, the ISC.[75]

In 2003, Bremer was selected by Donald Rumsfeld to become the Administrator of the Coalition Provisional Authority of Iraq (i.e. Iraq Occupation Governor). His "mistakes" there were monumental and, to many innocent people, fatal.[76] Bremer's closest aides during his tenure in Iraq included Clayton McManaway, previously an operative within Robert Komer's Phoenix Program.

Rudy Giuliani's associate Bernard Kerik, who was New York City Police Commissioner on 9/11, was appointed by George W. Bush to be Minister of the Interior for Iraq and Senior Policy Advisor to Bremer. Assigned to train the new Iraqi police, Kerik's work in Iraq was widely recognized as a dismal failure. By the time his remarkably short assignment was over, he had offended the U.S. military and left the newly forming Iraqi police force in shambles.

Bremer was not without his small successes, however. At the time of the wildly sensationalized capture of Saddam Hussein from a "spider hole," Bremer proclaimed, "Ladies and gentlemen… we got him!"[77] Of course, the man who Bremer had previously told us was behind the deadly terrorist network called al Qaeda, and the crimes of 9/11, was never captured. Instead, OBL was allegedly killed seven and a half years later by the JSOC, which quickly dumped his remains in the sea.

Bremer and Jenkins have gone on to lend their voices in support of the never-ending War on Terror. In fact, Jenkins' assessment today is that, "We are not going to end terrorism, not in any future I see."[78] That prediction undoubtedly inspires the national security bureaucracies that Larry Johnson had mentioned, which were desperately seeking to justify their existence. However, considering what we know about these men, their strong links to terror propaganda, and their extraordinary roles with respect to 9/11, it seems an end to terrorism might begin simply through a closer examination of L. Paul Bremer and Brian Michael Jenkins.

Chapter 12

Wirt Walker and KuwAm

On September 21, 2001, the U.S. Securities and Exchange Commission (SEC) referred specific transactions to the FBI for criminal investigation as potential insider trades related to 9/11. One of those trades was a September 6, 2001 purchase of 56,000 shares of a company called Stratesec, which was a security contractor for several of the facilities that were compromised on 9/11. Those facilities included the WTC complex, Dulles Airport, where American Airlines Flight 77 took off, and also United Airlines, which owned two of the other three ill-fated planes.

The Stratesec stock was purchased by a director of the company, Wirt D. Walker III, and his wife Sally Walker.[1] This is clear from the memorandum generated to record the FBI summary of the suspicious trades.[2] The Stratesec stock that the Walkers purchased doubled in value in the one trading day between September 11th and when the stock market reopened on September 17th. Unfortunately, the FBI did not interview either of the Walkers and they were both cleared of any wrongdoing because they were assumed to have "no ties to terrorism or other negative information."[3]

However, Wirt Walker was connected to people who had connections to al Qaeda. For example, Stratesec director James Abrahamson was the business partner of Mansoor Ijaz, a Pakistani businessman who claimed on several occasions to be able to contact Osama bin Laden.[4] Additionally, Walker hired a number of Stratesec employees away from a subsidiary of The Carlyle Group called BDM International, which ran secret (black) projects for government agencies. The Carlyle Group was partly financed by members of the Bin Laden family.[5]

The insider trading evidence indicates that Wirt Walker could be brought up on charges today, for crimes related to 9/11. But there are many other reasons why Walker should be investigated. The work that Stratesec did at the WTC and at the other 9/11-impacted facilities is of considerable interest and, although only briefly covered in this chapter, those activities will be examined more closely in the next. One thing that will be important to consider is that Stratesec's role in managing the security systems for the WTC and Dulles Airport suggests that the company could have had backdoor access to those systems.

Apart from the access and the insider trading suspicions, reasons to investigate Walker include the following.

- From the early 1980s, Walker ran what would be Stratesec's parent company, the Kuwait-American Corporation (KuwAm), which was linked through its directors to the terrorist financing network BCCI.

- Walker's activities with regard to Kuwait ran parallel to those of two men who were known to be CIA operatives.

- KuwAm had a number of subsidiaries that went bankrupt shortly after 9/11 and there are reasons to believe that some of those subsidiaries, including Stratesec, were fronts for covert operations.

- Walker was always able to maintain strong cash flow despite dismal business performance.

- After 9/11, the people who had become Stratesec's majority stockholders were convicted of conspiracy.

- And several of Walker's companies were located in the same offices that were later occupied by Zacarias Moussaoui's flight trainer.

It is informative to begin a review of Walker's possible role with an examination of his history, as well as the background of Stratesec and KuwAm.

The History of Wirt Walker

Wirt Walker, CEO of Stratesec and managing director at KuwAm, was the son of a career U.S. intelligence officer who had worked for both the CIA and, later, the Defense Intelligence Agency (DIA).[6] Walker was also a descendant of James Monroe Walker, who ran the businesses of the U.S. deep state organization called Russell & Company that had used profits from the Opium Wars to purchase much of the infrastructure of the United States.[7] Coincidentally, the son-in-law of James Monroe Walker, John Wellborn Root, was the first employer and guardian of Emery Roth, whose company was the architect of record for both the WTC towers and building 7.[8]

Today Wirt Walker lives in McLean, Virginia, home of the CIA. He graduated from Lafayette College in 1968 and in 1971 he married Sally Gregg White, a Washington DC debutante. Sally is a descendant of architectural ironwork magnate George White, whose son "Doc" White was a World Series winning pitcher for the Chicago White Sox. "Doc" was actually a dentist but his brother, Charles Stanley White, was a famous Washington DC surgeon and grandfather to Sally. Charles Stanley White Jr., Sally's father, was a surgeon too and, like Walker's father, he was an officer in the Army Air Corps during World War II.[9]

Walker was fortunate to land a position, right out of college, as a broker for an investment firm called Glore Forgan.[10] Originally a company called Field Glore, financed by Marshall Field III; Glore Forgan was renamed in 1937 for its new partner, James "Russ" Forgan. Russ was one of the most influential men in the history of U.S. intelligence, having led the European division of the CIA's predecessor organization, the Office of Strategic Services (OSS).[11] In the OSS, Forgan focused on infiltrating the German intelligence apparatus with the help of William Casey. Before going back to work in the investment business, Forgan helped to write the documents that created the CIA. Later chairman of the SEC under Nixon, Casey was to become the long-term director of the CIA under Reagan.

While Walker worked there, William Casey was house counsel for Glore Forgan. It was at this time that the firm was at the center of a near collapse of Wall Street. In 1970, it began to be clear that Glore Forgan had somehow sold many millions of dollars more in securities than what were actually available to sell. As a result, the company was expected to fail and, due to a cascading effect, its failure was projected to take down dozens of other firms causing a panic and huge losses on Wall Street.[12] These projections compelled President Nixon to ask Ross Perot, through Treasury Secretary John Connally, to intervene and save Glore Forgan. Perot suffered dramatic losses in an attempt to save the company (the only business loss of his career) and Glore Forgan went bankrupt anyway. The U.S. government created the Securities Investor Protection Corporation in response.[13]

Walker left Glore Forgan to become a young vice president at the investment firm of Johnston & Lemon in Washington, DC. As of 1980, he worked in the corporate finance department at Johnston & Lemon with several others including Stephen Hartwell, a fellow alumnus of Lafayette College.[14] Hartwell went on to become an advisor at First American Bank of Virginia, a subsidiary of the BCCI-owned First American Bank.

Shortly thereafter, Walker went from being an investment broker to running an assortment of small companies that tended to go bankrupt. Yet somehow, he always had funding. That could have been due to the fact that Walker was a close associate of members of the Kuwaiti royal family and, by 1982, he was a director of KuwAm.

KuwAm owned a company called Aviation General, for which Walker was CEO, and like Stratesec this company and its subsidiaries went broke shortly after 9/11. Furthermore, a company called Hanifen Imhoff was the underwriter for one of those subsidiaries.[15] A division of a company led by George W. Bush's first cousin, George Herbert Walker III, Hanifen Imhoff was "nailed for Correspondent's fraud" in December 2000.[16]

Stratesec and the KuwAm Corporation

Twenty-one year old Mish'al Yusuf Saud Al-Sabah, the majority owner of KuwAm Corporation, became the company's first chairman in 1982. Wirt Walker was named managing director. The two men already had a close history, because Al-Sabah had actually lived with Walker and his family for six months in 1976, when Al-Sabah was only 15 years of age.[17] That was when George H.W. Bush was CIA director and Ted Shackley was one of his assistant directors.

As a great-grandson of Kuwaiti's historic ruler Muhammad I, Mish'al Al-Sabah is very well connected to the Kuwaiti royal family and, therefore, to the Kuwaiti government. Through his relations, Al-Sabah brought Walker and KuwAm "many rich, limited partnership investors from Kuwait, Europe and the U.S."[18] And Walker brought the Kuwaiti royal family into a position of implementing security systems for facilities that were central to the events of 9/11.

A November 1990 article in *The Boston Globe* reported that Mish'al was not the only member of the Kuwaiti royal family that was a director at KuwAm. Also on the board was a partner in a prominent U.S. law and lobbying firm.

> "A Securities and Exchange Commission filing shows another member of the Al-Sabah family on the KuwAm board, alongside a partner of the politically well-connected Washington law firm of Patton, Boggs & Blow. According to the Dow Jones News Retrieval Service, tiny KuwAm (estimated assets: $20 million) also owns significant portions of Los Angeles-based videocassette distributor Prism Entertainment Corp., where Walker sits on the board, and a Sunnyvale, Calif.-based light-sensor equipment distributor called ILC Technology Inc., where Walker is chairman of the board."

The first Gulf War was started on the basis of blatant lies, at least one of which involved a relative of Mish'al Al-Sabah. This was a 15-year old girl named Nayirah, who was the daughter of Mish'al's first cousin, Saud Nasser Al-Saud Al-Sabah, the Kuwaiti ambassador to the United States.[19] The girl lied about having witnessed Iraqi soldiers taking babies out of incubators and leaving them on the "cold floor to die." It was later learned that she had been coached to tell the lies by the public relations firm Hill & Knowlton.[20]

Hill & Knowlton chairman Robert Gray had previously been a director of First American Bank, BCCI's Washington subsidiary, along with Dick Cheney's Halliburton colleague Charles DiBona. Gray had been on the Reagan-Bush election team and was known for being open about his companies doing work for the CIA. A good review of the Nayirah story that covers Gray and his close relationship with William Casey can be found in Susan Trento's book *The Power House*.[21]

Stratesec started off in 1987 as Burns & Roe Securacom, founded by Sebastian Cassetta, an assistant to Nelson Rockefeller. During the first Bush presidency, in 1991, Securacom (from here on called Stratesec) was hired by the Port Authority of New York and New Jersey to provide a review of security risks at the WTC. Stratesec's report warned of "international activities" arising from recent "Mideast events," hinting at the possibility of Arab terrorism at the WTC. The report called for the adoption of "a master plan approach to the development of security systems."[22]

KuwAm took over Stratesec the next year, in 1992, at which time Walker became CEO. Walker was among the new shareholders of Stratesec and, along with Al-Sabah, he joined the Stratesec board. Throughout the next decade, Stratesec stock would be held by shell companies, controlled by Walker and Al-Sabah, called Fifth Floor Company for General Trading and Contracting, and Special Situation Investment Holdings.

When Walker was sued by the president of an existing company with an identical name (Securacom at the time), Wirt became abusive and told the other businessman that he "would bury him financially and take everything he had" by "filing a barrage of frivolous arguments in multiple jurisdictions."[23] Walker lost the case and had to change his company's name to Stratesec. While this incident suggested that Walker was abusive, it also indicated that he had the kind of deep pockets that allowed for frivolous lawsuits.

Marvin Bush, son of George H.W. Bush, joined the board of Stratesec after meeting members of the royal family of Kuwait on a trip to that country with his father in April 1993. During that trip, the Kuwaiti royals displayed enormous gratitude to the elder Bush for having saved their country from Saddam Hussein only two years earlier.

But the Bush-Kuwaiti connection went back much farther, to 1959, when the Kuwaitis helped to fund Bush's start-up company, Zapata Off-Shore.[24] As a CIA business asset during this time, Bush and his company worked directly with anti-Castro Cuban groups in Miami before and after the Bay of Pigs invasion.[25]

During the 1993 trip, the royals in the United Arab Emirates (UAE) showed similar gratitude to the Bush family by putting Marvin on the board at Fresh Del Monte, which was purchased by the UAE-owned company IAT in 1994. The alleged 9/11 hijackers had many connections to the UAE, and much of the funding for the attacks came through that country.

As mentioned in the chapter on Richard Clarke, the Joint Congressional Inquiry into 9/11 stated that the UAE was one of three countries where the operational planning for 9/11 took place. For some reason, although the Joint Inquiry went into detail on the other two countries, it seemed to make a point of avoiding further comment about the role of the UAE.[26] The UAE was also behind the creation of BCCI and, after the alleged dissolution of that terrorist network, had purchased its assets entirely.

In 1996, Al-Sabah announced that KuwAm's subsidiary Aviation General was selling aircraft to the National Civil Aviation Training Organization (NCATO) in Giza, Egypt.[27] NCATO was in a partnership with Embry-Riddle University where two of the alleged 9/11 hijackers, Saeed Alghamdi and Waleed Al-Shehri, were said to have gone to flight school.[28] Ten days after the attacks, Embry-Riddle was relieved by reports that Al-Shehri was alive.[29] Unfortunately, the reports that some of the alleged hijackers had turned up alive were never investigated by the FBI or the 9/11 Commission.[30]

Like Stratesec, all three of KuwAm's aircraft companies went bankrupt within three years after 9/11. The company blamed terrorism and the war in Iraq for a reduced demand for its products.[31] Despite the losses, the Kuwaiti royal family can be said to have benefited from 9/11 due to the War on Terror that removed Saddam Hussein from power. Of course, that was the second consecutive U.S. war that Kuwait benefited from, the first being the 1991 Gulf War led by President George H.W. Bush.

Other KuwAm Directors and Investors

As stated before, *The Boston Globe* reported that KuwAm's directors included a partner of the law firm Patton, Boggs & Blow.[32] This is the firm that took over representation of BCCI after Clark Clifford's demise in the late 1980s. Patton Boggs & Blow also represented BCCI's owners – the royal family of the United Arab Emirates.

KuwAm had other principals and partners over the years, including Pamela S. Singleton, who was associated with Winston Partners, another company run by Marvin Bush. Richard J. Cordsen was another director of KuwAm and its subsidiary Commander Aircraft. Cordsen was primarily associated with United Gulf Group, a Saudi Arabian company. However, it was KuwAm director Robert D. van Roijen who was said to be the man responsible for getting Walker involved in the aircraft business.

Like Walker, van Roijen was the son of a CIA officer. His father was born a Dutch citizen in England, had immigrated to the U.S. in the 1930s, and was an intelligence officer in the Army Air Corps, just like Walker's father was before he joined the CIA. The senior van Roijen later became the owner of Robert B. Luce, Inc., a Washington-based company that published *The New Republic*.

Van Roijen's grandfather was the Dutch ambassador to the United States in the 1920s, and his uncle, Jan H. van Roijen, had the same appointment from 1950 to 1964. Uncle Jan was also a member of the Bilderberg Group. During the 1973 Oil Crisis (when Rumsfeld was at NATO headquarters), the Dutch government sent Jan H. van Roijen to Saudi Arabia in an unsuccessful attempt to patch things up diplomatically.

Unlike Walker, KuwAm's van Roijen admits that he was an intelligence officer too, with the U.S. Marines from 1961 to 1963. It is interesting to note that the CIA-trained anti-Castro Cubans that Marvin Bush's father was helping, during this same time, thought that the U.S. Marines would be right behind them as they stormed the shores at the Bay of Pigs.

KuwAm's Van Roijen had once been Tricia Nixon's White House party escort during the Nixon Administration. Van Roijen's sister was working in the White House communications office, and he used those connections to his advantage as a lobbyist for IBM, obtaining strategic information from government offices such as the White House Office of Management and Budget (OMB).[33] At the time, future Carlyle Group CEO Frank Carlucci was Deputy Director of the OMB.

Another interesting connection between KuwAm, the Nixon years, and Saudi Arabia was that KuwAm's offices were in the Watergate Hotel, the same building that was burglarized in the 1972 scandal that led to Nixon's resignation. In the years leading up to 9/11, both Stratesec and Aviation General convened their annual shareholders' meetings in KuwAm's Watergate office, in Suite 900.[34] As of 1998, the building was owned by The Blackstone Group and the offices that KuwAm occupied were leased by the Royal Embassy of Saudi Arabia which occupied the suite just below KuwAm. The Kuwait embassy also had offices in the building.

The directors and shareholders of Stratesec formed a notable group, as will be discussed in the next chapter. Even more interesting are the links between KuwAm and BCCI.

Were Walker and KuwAm Working for an Intelligence Network?

There are a number of reasons to suspect that Wirt Walker and the KuwAm Corporation were working either for the CIA or for a private intelligence network. These reasons include that Walker became close to the Kuwaiti royals at the same time as they were working closely with two other Americans who were involved in deep state operations. Moreover, the people pulling the strings from the Kuwaiti side in these endeavors were close relatives of KuwAm chairman Mish'al Al-Sabah.

The first of the two deep state operatives was the famous CIA man who led the private network, Ted Shackley. Having worked in the CIA for decades, Shackley was the agency's Associate Deputy Director of Operations from 1976 to 1977. He was described by former CIA director Richard Helms as "a quadruple threat - Drugs, Arms, Money and Murder."[35] Walker has a number of things in common with Shackley. In the 1980s, both men were strongly linked to the Bush family network, to Kuwait, and to aviation. They both ran security companies as well.

As stated in Chapter 3, Shackley was a close friend of Frank Carlucci. While Carlucci was functioning as an operative in the "foreign service" and then the Nixon Administration, Shackley was leading many CIA operations around the world including the anti-Castro plan Operation Mongoose, the secret U.S. war in Laos, and the overthrow of Salvadore Allende in Chile.

After leaving the CIA in 1979, Shackley formed his own company, TGS Associates, which appeared to be focused on obtaining access to places like Kuwait and Iran. TGS functioned as a broker for Boeing 747 aircraft, attempted to sell food and medical supplies to Iran, and did construction work in Kuwait.

At the same time, Shackley took part in the Reagan campaign operation which resulted in the American hostages in Iran being held until Reagan was inaugurated in 1981. Over a period of years following this, Shackley and some of his former CIA friends, Thomas Clines and Richard Secord, became involved in the Iran-Contra affair.[36]

When Walker's KuwAm was just getting off the ground, Shackley was beginning to secure contracts with the Kuwaiti government. George H.W. Bush had helped Shackley get started in Kuwait around that time. Bush's contacts there went back to the days when Kuwait and other oil-rich royals in the region helped fund his Zapata Off-Shore operation.[37]

In his biography of the man, author David Corn wrote that "Shackley viewed Kuwait as a tremendous source of profits." Those profits appeared to be tied to the Kuwaiti royal family's interests. In 1982, the year that KuwAm was incorporated in Washington, the Kuwaiti government specifically requested that the U.S. Navy award Shackley's firm a $1.2 million contract to rehabilitate a warehouse for the Kuwaiti Air Force, although Shackley had "little experience in this area."[38]

By the end of 1983, "TGS had before the Kuwaiti Air Force several proposals that could bring it up to $200 million. What Shackley received was more modest, but nevertheless much money. Toward the end of 1983, TGS International signed a $6.3 million deal with the Navy to perform construction at the Ali Al-Salem Air Base, forty miles outside of Kuwait City."[39]

But TGS did not serve the Navy well, falling behind schedule and failing to complete the contract. The result was a lawsuit between TGS and its sub-contractor, RJS Construction, and another between TGS and the U.S. government. TGS prevailed in the latter, claiming that its suppliers and employees could not function well in a war environment (the Iran-Iraq War was ongoing). Several of TGS' shareholders were Iranian exiles, including former SAVAK agent Novzar Razmara.[40]

TGS was also involved in dealings on the other side of the world. In October 1984, when Congress had cut off funding to the Contras, John Ellis Bush (brother of Stratesec director Marvin Bush) put the Guatemalan politician Dr. Mario Castejon in touch with Oliver North. This led to Castejon proposing that the U.S. State Department supply miscellaneous, ostensibly non-military assistance to the Contras. The proposal was passed to the CIA through TGS International, the firm owned by Shackley.[41]

Shackley continued working in Kuwait by way of another of his ventures called Research Associates International (RAI), which specialized in "risk analysis" by providing intelligence to business interests. Shackley also testified that RAI was a security company. "We design security systems," he said, confirming yet another similarity between his business activities and those of Walker.[42]

RAI's primary customer was Trans-World Oil, run by a Dutch citizen named John Deuss. The work involved smuggling oil into South Africa in violation of an embargo.[43]

Another CIA operative was working with the Kuwaiti royals at the same time as Walker and Shackley. In the case of Robert M. Sensi, CIA connections to the Kuwaiti royal family, at the same time that Walker became a close colleague of Mish'al Al-Sabah, were confirmed. While working for the Washington office of Kuwait Airways, which was owned by the Kuwaiti government, Sensi operated covertly as a CIA asset. He organized the 1980 flights for William Casey to Europe for meetings on the deal to hold the hostages. In the mid-1980s, he helped set up CIA fronts in Iran along with Iranian exile Habib Moallem.

Sensi's work for the Kuwaitis and the CIA came to light in a late 1980s series of articles in the *Washington Post* that covered legal proceedings in which Sensi had been accused of embezzling funds from Kuwait Airways. During the proceedings, the CIA admitted that Sensi had worked for the agency for years and Sensi's supervisor at the company, Inder Sehti, admitted that Sensi had been allowed by the Kuwaiti government to use a slush fund for CIA purposes.[44] Apparently, these purposes included managing the U.S. visits of Kuwaiti royal family members. Presumably, this would have included the travel arrangements for young Mish'al Al-Sabah when he came to live with Walker's family.

Sensi claimed that he was nominally working for Kuwait Airways and the Kuwaiti royal family was funding his activities. He also claimed to be acting under the direction of the Kuwait ambassador to the United States.[45] When Sensi signed on to the job, in 1977, the Kuwait ambassador to the U.S. was Khalid Muhammad Jaffar. In January 1981, while Sensi was still using the Kuwaiti funds for CIA work, Jaffar was succeeded by Nayirah's father, the first cousin of KuwAm's Mish'al Al-Sabah.

Sensi also clarified that, as a CIA asset, he was "being run directly by CIA director William Casey, in close concert with Vice President Bush."[46] This is yet another interesting connection between Walker and Sensi, in that Walker worked with Casey at Glore Forgan a decade earlier and with Bush's son at Stratesec.

The Kuwaiti royal who approved the use of this CIA slush fund for Sensi was Jabir Adbhi Al-Sabah, the vice chairman of Kuwait Airways and Kuwait's chief of civil aviation.[47] Like Nayirah, Jabir Adbhi Al-Sabah was closely related to KuwAm's Mish'al Al-Sabah, as a first cousin once removed. What's more, Jabir's colleague, the chairman of Kuwaiti Airways, was none other than Faisal al-Fulaij, BCCI's nominee from Kuwait. Al-Fulaij was deeply involved in the operations of BCCI and its U.S. subsidiaries.[48]

The U.S. Senate investigation into BCCI, led by John Kerry, stated that "Some funds were borrowed by one 'investor,' Fulaij, from the Kuwait International Finance Company (KIFCO), which BCCI purportedly had a 49 percent interest in, but actually owned and controlled through its nominee, Faisal al-Fulaij." The man who was both Finance and Oil minister in Kuwait was Abdul Rahman Al-Atiqi, a major investor in BCCI and later a director of a related company called InvestCorp.

This BCCI connection leads to a discussion of Hamzah M. Behbehani, who was a director and partner at KuwAm from 1995 to 1997, and was named as a principal, along with Walker and Al-Sabah, in lawsuits in which KuwAm engaged. Behbehani had come to KuwAm after spending three years with investment companies in London. Prior to that, from 1986 to 1992, Behbehani had worked for the British branch of the Banque Arabe et Internationale d'Investissments (BAII), one of the Arab-Western partnership banks started in the 1970s.

BAII was "heavily involved in the oil trade" and it financed "oil imports and the export of capital goods and equipment for the refining and petrochemical industries."[49] But as authors Peter Truell and Larry Gurwin noted, BAII was also intimately associated with the CIA-linked network BCCI.

"Run by a board member of BCCI, Yves Lamarche, BAII had played a critical role in some of BCCI's dubious schemes, lending $50 million to help finance the takeover of First American and also providing funds to allow [Ghaith] Pharaon to buy Independence Bank in Los Angeles."[50] KuwAm director Behbehani worked for BCCI's partner BAII from the time Pharaon purchased Independence Bank and throughout the time that the financial crimes, in which these banks engaged, were revealed.

BCCI was known for funding terrorism and was also closely linked to Pakistan's ISI. These facts, and the UAE links to al Qaeda, have led many to suspect that BCCI was behind al Qaeda. The connections between the KuwAm Corporation and BCCI are therefore of great interest given Stratesec's security contracts at the facilities that were affected by the 9/11 attacks.

In 2005, a different Mish'al Al-Sabah, who was another first cousin of KuwAm's Mish'al, provided yet more evidence that Kuwait had al Qaeda ties. This Al-Sabah was brought to trial in Kuwait for certain inflammatory claims he had made. Mish'al Al-Jarrah Al-Sabah, Kuwait's Assistant Undersecretary for State Security Affairs at the time of the 9/11 attacks, made these claims in an interview on a U.S.-funded Kuwaiti television program called *Al Hurra*. Al-Sabah was charged with claiming that "that there is an old base for the al-Qaeda organization in Kuwait." He also accused two Kuwaiti government MPs "of belonging to al-Qaeda." During a five and a half hour closed-door inquisition, he recanted the claims.[51] Despite this retraction, other evidence exists that links KuwAm and al Qaeda.

Wiley Post Airport

KuwAm's Aviation General was the parent of two wholly-owned subsidiaries: Commander Aircraft Company, which manufactured Commander-brand aircraft, and Strategic Jet Services, which provided aircraft brokerage and refurbishment services. Aviation General, Commander Aircraft, and Strategic Jet Services were all located in Hangar 8 of Wiley Post Airport in Bethany, OK, near Oklahoma City.

In another apparent coincidence, CIA asset Robert Sensi had listed an Oklahoma City address as his residence for a period of time.[52] The address Sensi gave was for the Oklahoma City Halfway House, a drug and alcohol rehabilitation center located 11 miles from Wiley Post Airport.

As reviewed in Chapter 5, a motel not far from Wiley Post was frequented by alleged 9/11 pilots Mohamed Atta and Marwan Al-Shehhi, and their alleged accomplice Zacarias Moussaoui. Curiously, just a few years before, convicted OKC bombers Timothy McVeigh and Terry Nichols stayed at the same motel, "interacting with a group of Iraqis during the weeks before the bombing."[53] Louis Freeh's FBI didn't seem to want this information even though it was repeatedly provided by the motel owner. In August 2001, the motel owner testified that he saw Moussaoui, Atta, and Al-Shehhi at his motel when they came late one night to ask for a room.

Between February and August of 2001, Moussaoui lived twenty miles away in Norman where he attended a flight school run by David Boren's university. According to Moussaoui's indictment, Atta and Al-Shehhi had visited the same flight school in July 2000, but did not take classes there.

FBI summary documents prepared for the 9/11 investigations state that Mohamed Atta was also spotted at Wiley Post Airport within six months of the 9/11 attacks. Atta was witnessed flying at Wiley Post along with two other alleged 9/11 hijackers, Marwan Al-Shehhi and Waleed Al-Shehri.[54] Other FBI summary documents indicate that Saeed Al-Ghamdi was also seen flying in to Wiley Post Airport on an unspecified date and that Hani Hanjour had made inquiries to a flight school there.[55]

Therefore it is a remarkable fact that Wirt Walker and his companies were located at this same airport. But the surprises don't stop there. Wiley Post has approximately 24 hangars and Hangar 8 is set off away from the rest.[56] Although Aviation General and its subsidiaries all went bankrupt or were sold off in the few years after 9/11, Hangar 8 still houses three businesses. These are Jim Clark & Associates, Valair Aviation, and Oklahoma Aviation.

At first glance, the most interesting of these new Hangar 8 companies is the flight school called Oklahoma Aviation. This is due to an incredible coincidence regarding the young man who heads the company, Shohaib Nazir Kassam.

In March 2006, Kassam was a government witness against Zacarias Moussaoui. He was, in fact, Moussaoui's flight instructor. To emphasize, the guy who now occupies Wirt Walker's offices in Hangar 8 at Wiley Post Airport not only knew Zacarias Moussaoui, he was

Moussaoui's primary flight instructor at Airman Flight School in Norman, OK.

Kassam moved to Norman in 1998, at the age of 18, coming from Mombassa, Kenya. He was originally from Pakistan. Two years after he arrived in Norman, he completed his training to become a flight instructor. He was only 21 years of age when he spent 57 hours (unsuccessfully) trying to train Zacarias Moussaoui to fly.

Oklahoma Aviation was a flight school that was just getting off the ground in 2005. Yet as it took over Hangar 8 from Aviation General, shortly after the company formed, it soon boasted of having the best planes around. This was the opposite of the apparent financial fortunes of the Aviation General companies that all went belly up that year. And it was also unlike Airman Flight School which, although it was in the same area and same business as Oklahoma Aviation, shut down in 2005 because it could not pay the rent.

It seems there is more to the story of KuwAm's aviation companies, and those related to Hangar 8. If nothing else, an investigation must consider that it is not simply a coincidence that Zacarias Moussaoui's primary trainer is now occupying the offices of Wirt Walker's former businesses at Wiley Post Airport. And although the three KuwAm companies operated out of Wiley Post, they were all officially headquartered at the famous Watergate Hotel in Washington DC, in office space leased by the Saudi and Kuwaiti governments.

In the few years leading up to this change in tenancy at Wiley Post Airport, other interesting things were happening with KuwAm's aviation companies. In September 2000, John DeHavilland of British Aerocraft joined as CEO of Strategic Jet Services. Three months later, and on the same day that a young man named Kamran Hashemi joined Stratesec, Walker's president at Commander Aircraft, Dean N. Thomas, died suddenly at a young age.[57]

Aviation General continued to be, like Stratesec and the other companies that Wirt Walker ran, a rare example of well-financed business failure. As of 1998, Aviation General was losing millions of dollars every year. The year 2000 performance was the best in the company's history, according to Walker, although it represented only humble positive returns. But by August 2001, the company was reporting million-dollar losses again and it began to miss lease payments at Wiley Post Airport. Despite the problems, Walker said the company would survive because "we've got pretty deep pockets."[58]

In late 2002, Strategic Jet Services "discontinued its operations and began the process of dissolving the company."[59] Commander Aircraft filed for Chapter 11 bankruptcy at the same time and that status was changed to Chapter 7 in January 2005. Commander Aircraft left Oklahoma in September 2005 to move to an "undisclosed location." And Aviation General was sold to Tiger Aircraft, a small company with Taiwanese investors that went bankrupt in 2006.

Incredibly, after 9/11 Walker showed up the next time an airplane crashed into a tall building. The first such occurrence after the attacks, in an incident in Italy, led to Walker being interviewed because the plane that crashed was related to his company, Aviation General.[60]

He Just Owned Some Stock

After the 9/11 attacks, Walker was interviewed by phone about his company's work at the WTC. When asked whether FBI or other agents had questioned him or others at Stratesec or KuwAm about the security work the company did related to 9/11, Walker declined to comment. Disclaiming any responsibility, he simply said, "I'm an investment banker. We just owned some stock." Walker went on to say that his investment company (KuwAm) "was not involved in any way in the work or day-to-day operations" of the security company.

Of course, these answers were diversionary and untrue because Walker had served as Stratesec's CEO. Furthermore, his activities with regard to Kuwait ran parallel to those of two known CIA operatives, and Walker would soon thereafter be suspected of engaging in insider trading related to 9/11.

KuwAm was owned by people who stood to gain much from the response to 9/11. This was highlighted by the fact that KuwAm held its meetings in space leased by the Saudi Arabian and Kuwaiti embassies. Marvin Bush was reelected to his annual board position in Saudi and Kuwaiti-leased meeting rooms at the Watergate.

Additionally, the CIA-linked Riggs Bank, for which Marvin's uncle was a board member, also had a large office at the Watergate. Saudi Princess Haifa bint Faisal, the wife of Prince Bandar, used her checking account at Riggs to send money to Omar Al-Bayoumi, the man who first sponsored Al-Mihdhar and Al-Hazmi in San Diego. Other Saudi accounts at Riggs were also linked by investigators to some of the 9/11 hijackers.[61]

In September 2003, both Hamzah Behbehani and Mish'al Al-Sabah had U.S. warrants issued for their arrest for contempt of court (failure to appear). This was a result of a lawsuit involving KuwAm's subsidiary Advanced Laser Graphics.[62]

By this time, KuwAm had already divested from Stratesec and Walker had turned to financing from another dubious operation. A company called ES Bankest became Stratesec's majority shareholder, owning about 47% of the company's stock. According to SEC documents, Stratesec reached a "verbal agreement" with the financier in October 2000 in which accounts receivable were sold at a discounted price to provide cash flow.[63] Walker transferred millions of dollars in shares of Stratesec stock to ES Bankest as a way to reduce debt.[64]

By the time Stratesec "abruptly shut its doors," in September 2003, it had become entirely dependent on ES Bankest.[65] The owners of ES Bankest, brothers Eduardo and Hector Orlansky, were convicted only months later of conspiracy and bank fraud when $185 million went missing due to "huge overadvances."[66] Apparently, $2 billion was "flowed through the Orlansky's two businesses from 1998 to 2003 to create the appearance they were healthy and growing."[67]

Walker now runs his own private investment company called Eigerhawk, and he is a director at Vortex Asset Assessment. He also works with Arthur Barchenko at Electronic Control Security. Barchenko was a member of several committees addressing FAA regulations related to "access control and perimeter intrusion devices" and was a member of the special access control security task force for the FAA.

To reiterate some of the reasons that Walker should be investigated for 9/11:

- From the early 1980s, Walker managed KuwAm, which was linked through its directors to the terrorist financing network BCCI.

- KuwAm's subsidiaries went bankrupt shortly after 9/11 and there are reasons to believe that some of those subsidiaries, including Stratesec, were fronts for covert operations.

- Through its security contracts, Stratesec had unparalleled access to several of the facilities which were central to the events of 9/11.

- Stratesec held its company meetings in space leased by the governments of Kuwait and Saudi Arabia, both of which benefited from the response to 9/11.

- Walker's activities with regard to Kuwait ran parallel to those of two men who were known to be CIA operatives.

- Shortly after 9/11, Stratesec's primary stockholders were convicted of conspiracy.

- A stock purchase made by Walker and his wife, the week of 9/11, was flagged by the SEC as possible 9/11 insider trading.

- And several of Walker's companies were located in the same offices that were later occupied by Zacarias Moussaoui's flight trainer.

The next chapter, focused on Stratesec's chief operating officer, will give more detail on the company's 9/11-related contracts and opportunities.

Chapter 13

✈

Barry McDaniel and Stratesec

At the WTC, Barry McDaniel was in charge of the security operation in terms of what he called a "completion contract," to provide services "up to the day the buildings fell down."[1] McDaniel came to Stratesec directly from BDM International, where he had been vice president for seven years. BDM was a major subsidiary of The Carlyle Group during that time.

In the decade prior to 9/11, KuwAm held a controlling interest in Stratesec. The previous chapter reviewed links between KuwAm's leadership and the first Gulf War, BCCI, and other deep state entities. Also reviewed were Stratesec's business dealings with people that were convicted of conspiracy.

Unfortunately, there has not yet been any government investigation into this company or its leaders. After 9/11, journalist Margie Burns asked Barry McDaniel in a brief telephone interview whether the FBI or other agents had questioned anyone at Stratesec about the company's 9/11-related security work. McDaniel answered simply, "No."[2]

Regardless of the FBI's lack of interest, however, the public deserves to know whether Stratesec's access to the WTC and other 9/11-impacted facilities might have contributed to the events of that day. That access was controlled and utilized by the company's COO, Barry McDaniel, who should be scrutinized.

Iran-Contra, Carlucci and Saudi Arabia

During the years when Frank Carlucci was running the "spook central" company called Sears World Trade (SWT), McDaniel was the Deputy Director for Readiness at the U.S. Army Materiel Command (AMC). In this role, McDaniel was responsible for selling Army materiel and services to allies. The weapons sales to Iran (via Israel and otherwise) as part of the Iran-Contra crimes were managed by the AMC when it was led by McDaniel. The U.S. arming of Iraq, referred to as Iraqgate, also occurred during McDaniel's tenure.

In an interview as he was leaving the AMC job in 1988, McDaniel recalled his supervision of acquisition officers worldwide.[3] He made mention of the importance of the Southwest Asia Petroleum Distribution Project during his tenure. Apparently, pipelines and petroleum in that area of the world, which includes Afghanistan, Iran, Iraq and Pakistan, had something to do with the deployment of U.S. Army materiel during the mid 1980s. What McDaniel's exact role in that deployment was, and what it might have had to do with arming the Mujahideen, needs to be further investigated.

McDaniel's choice to leave his long career in military logistics to go into industry was understandable, despite the fact that he was on track to become an Assistant Secretary of Defense by his own assessment. Although BDM was mired in the Operation Ill Wind scandal after Carlucci's tenure as secretary of defense, it was a lucrative company to hire onto considering the extensive contracts it continued to secure. When McDaniel started at BDM the company began getting a large amount of government business 'in an area the Navy called Black Projects,"or budgets that were kept secret.[4]

Philip Odeen, the former assistant to Henry Kissinger, was president and CEO of BDM Holdings, the holding company for both BDM International and its subsidiary, the Vinnell Corporation. At the time McDaniel joined the company, Odeen was bullish on the company's growth prospects, saying "Defense and national security remain areas of major emphasis."[5] A year later a special task force of the Defense Science Board, led by Odeen, recommended a vast increase in the outsourcing of intelligence.

BDM was a prominent contractor in areas like missile defense and advanced weapons research. However, in the early 1990s the company was beginning to branch out into work on "air traffic control and airspace management" and "space sciences and applications."[6] In 1993,

BDM won a huge contract to consolidate the U.S. Air Force computer systems.

In the three years before McDaniel left BDM for a relatively minor position at Stratesec, BDM contracts with Saudi Arabia grew exponentially. The company received over a trillion dollars in work from Saudi Arabia, for things like training the Saudi National Guard and building the Saudi Air Force.[7] Throughout this period, McDaniel was BDM's vice president of Material Distribution and Management Systems.

Just before McDaniel left BDM, the company's Vinnell subsidiary was the target of one of the earliest terrorist attacks attributed to Saudi Arabian extremists.[8] At the time, Richard Secord was working for Vinnell, which was considered another "spook outfit."[9] Having been a major contractor in Vietnam during the war, Vinnell was saved from impending bankruptcy in 1975, receiving a large contract to train the Saudi Arabian National Guard.[10] Vinnell has since been seen as a private mercenary army that props up the Saudi monarchy using U.S. arms distributed by people like Barry McDaniel.

After McDaniel joined Stratesec the company secured at least one contract in the Saudi kingdom. This was "a joint venture agreement with Ahmad N. AlBinali & Sons Co., a large Saudi Arabian engineering and construction company, to develop and conduct business in the Kingdom of Saudi Arabia."[11]

Although McDaniel's career change from government to BDM was predictable, his choice to leave BDM for Stratesec was not. He gave up a lucrative career as a vice president with a major defense contractor to become COO of Stratesec, a relatively small operation that was just getting by. When McDaniel took the job, the majority of Stratesec's revenue was coming from its WTC and Dulles Airport contracts.

There might have been undisclosed reasons why McDaniel's expertise in military logistics was the right fit for running that airport and WTC security outfit. That is, McDaniel's move would make sense if he came to Stratesec to manage an important project involving the distribution of military ordnance (i.e. explosives). In any case, like Carlucci's inexplicable decision to quit his powerful position at the department of defense to join SWT, McDaniel's move to Stratesec indicates something more than a typical career development.

Stratesec Operations and Contracts

McDaniel joined Stratesec at the exact time that the company started to get more extensive work at the World Trade Center. Although Stratesec had completed a security evaluation at the WTC as early as 1991, and had worked with Kroll Associates to develop the security system after the 1993 bombing, its WTC work increased dramatically upon McDaniel's arrival.

Stratesec secured an $8.3 million WTC contract in October 1996. That year, KuwAm owned 90% of the company, either directly or through holding companies that it owned. Although this contract was nothing compared to the work BDM was getting, Stratesec's new project generated 28% of overall revenues for the company that same year. In the first full year of McDaniel's tenure as COO, the WTC and Dulles Airport contracts accounted for 75% of the company's revenues.

Stratesec went public in 1997, raising more than $16 million from the stockholders mentioned below. A prospectus summary for the company listed some of the company's other clients at this time. These included United Airlines, Washington National Airport (now called Reagan National) and several facilities of the U.S. Department of Energy including Los Alamos National Laboratories (LANL).[12]

McDaniel stated that Stratesec's work for United Airlines was focused on one site, in Indianapolis.[13] McDaniel said that work was completed before he joined the board, which was in 1999.

In any case, it was unprecedented for a foreign-owned company to obtain the contract for any international airport, and certainly Dulles Airport. Dulles was "absolutely a sensitive airport," according to security consultant Wayne Black, head of a Florida-based security firm.[14]

Aviation experts considered Dulles a very high profile target for terrorism because it was the primary international airport near the nation's capital.[15] Serving as port of entry to fifteen international airlines, Dulles also hosted eight of the top eleven U.S. commercial airlines.

With regard to KuwAm's ownership of Stratesec, Black said "Somebody knew somebody," or the contract would have been scrutinized more closely. One reason for the concern was that such a security contract allowed access to all client information. Because KuwAm owned Stratesec, the two companies shared computer systems and together had access to the most sensitive information and systems at the WTC and Dulles Airport.

At the WTC, Stratesec focused on electronic badging, security gates, and the closed circuit video systems (CCTV). These security controls could therefore have been set-up to be bypassed as needed. Former FAA special agent Brian F. Sullivan commented, "If they knew about the security system, they knew how to bypass it."[16]

Examples can be found of other security lapses at the sites where Stratesec worked. For example, in 1999 a major security breach at LANL, involving the release of nuclear secrets to China, became big news.[17] The U.S. government made a weak case against an employee named Wen Ho Lee, but the charges were later dropped and Lee won a substantial settlement for damages. A federal judge had to apologize to Lee for the government's misconduct.[18] The security breach itself was never solved and whether security systems were bypassed is a possibility that remained unaddressed.

Stratesec Investors and Directors

In June 2000, there was a mass sell-off of Stratesec stock.[19] Marvin Bush had apparently sold his stock in the company already, but the investors who remained formed a most surprising group.

- Baria Salim Al-Sabah was a Stratesec shareholder. She was the exiled Kuwaiti royal who had called for the ouster of Saddam, in a televised 1990 plea.[20] She was also the daughter of the former ruler of Kuwait (from 1965 to 1977), Sabah III. Two days after Baria's plea, on September 11, 1990, President Bush addressed a joint session of Congress and the American people and called for an intervention (and a New World Order).

- Journalist Arnaud de Borchgrave was an investor in Stratesec. De Borchgrave was editor-at-large of both *The Washington Times* and United Press International. He was also a director at CSIS, where 9/11 suspect John Hamre worked. Additional Stratesec stock was held by a trust in the name of De Borchgrave's wife, Alexandra, who was the granddaughter of American journalist and financier Henry Villard. Alexandra's father and grandfather both owned the left-leaning magazine *The Nation*.

- Another prominent Kuwaiti family, represented by Adel & Anwar Mustafah T. Alghanim, was a large volume stockholder in Stratesec. The family runs Anwar Alghanim Engineering in Kuwait.

- A man named Manuchehr Riah was a Stratesec stockholder. This appears to be the same person as Manouchehr (or Manoutchehr) Riahi, who worked for the Shah of Iran. It was said that Mr. Riahi's family had "devoted itself to the service of the Persian royal families since the 1500s." Riahi's wife was the sister of the woman married to the Shah's half-brother, Prince Abdul Reza-Pahlavi. Riahi fled to the United States when the Shah fell from power.

- A businessman of Iranian descent named Kamran Hashemi was both a director and large volume stockholder at Stratesec. Hashemi had worked many years for a U.S. defense contractor called Radian Inc., which was a subsidiary of Engineered Support Systems where William H.T. Bush (the younger brother of George H.W. Bush) became a director in 2000. Hashemi came to Stratesec when the company bought a firm called Security Systems Integration in December 2000.[21] The two companies de-merged eighteen months later.[22]

- Additional Stratesec stock was held by the company's director Harrison Augur, an attorney and financier. Augur was the sole business partner of Robert D. Van Roijen in a private investment firm called Patience Partners. He was also a fellow director with Wirt Walker at ILC Technologies, a maker of electrical arc devices. Throughout the 1980s, Augur was an executive vice president at the French firm Banque Worms, reported to be aligned with the Cercle Pinay network.[23]

Add to this interesting list of Stratesec stockholders an equally interesting list of board directors. There was Wirt Walker, Mish'al Al-Sabah, and, as of 1999, Barry McDaniel. But, additionally, there were a number of other directors who had remarkable connections to 9/11-related agencies and people.

- Marvin Bush, the president's brother, was reelected annually to Stratesec's board of directors from 1993 through 1999. Bush was also a shareholder.

- Charles W. Archer became a director in March 1998. He had recently retired from his position as the FBI's Assistant Director in charge of the Criminal Justice Information Services Division, under Louis Freeh. In that role he was responsible for the National Crime Information Center (NCIC), which provided the nation's authoritative database on terrorism.

- Robert B. Smith, Jr. became a director in 1995. He was formerly Chief Counsel and Staff Director of the Senate Government Operations Committee, which today is called the Committee on Homeland Security and Governmental Affairs.

- Lt. General James A. Abrahamson, the former head of the Strategic Defense Initiative and head of Hughes Aircraft Company, became a director in December 1997. As noted before, he was business partners with a Pakistani man who claimed to be able to contact Osama bin Laden.

- Ronald C. Thomas was Stratesec's President and Chief Executive Officer from 1992 to 1998. He was a member of the National Fire Protection Association (NFPA) and was on that organization's Fire Systems Subcommittee.

These directors appeared to have significant influence as Stratesec soon listed the U.S. Army, Navy, Air Force, and Department of Justice as clients. The associated projects were said to "often require state-of-the-art security solutions for classified or high-risk government sites."[24] By the year 2000, the U.S. Army accounted for 29% of the company's earned revenues.

After George W. Bush's election had been determined by the U.S. Supreme Court, in December 2000, Stratesec added a government division. As a result, the company secured "an open-ended contract with the General Services Administration (GSA) and a Blanket Purchase Agreement (BPA) with the agency that allows the government to purchase materials and services from the Company without having to go through a full competition."[25]

As of 9/11, Stratesec director Marvin Bush had three relatives working for companies located in the impact zones of the Twin Towers. This included his uncle, Prescott Bush Jr. a semi-retired consultant at the Marsh & McLennan subsidiary Johnson & Higgins, his cousin's husband Craig Stapleton, who also worked for Marsh & McLennan, and his cousin Jim Pierce, who worked for the impact zone tenant AON Corporation. Of these, Pierce had the most impressive 9/11 story because a meeting he had organized for that morning was moved from the south tower to the Millennium Hotel across the street, from where he watched the attacks unfold.[26]

McDaniel became the CEO of Stratesec in January 2002. When questioned, he declined on security grounds to give specific details about work the company did at the WTC. According to McDaniel, the contract was ongoing and "not quite completed when the Center went down." Echoing the developing official account for the destruction of the WTC, he added that the contract "didn't have anything to do with planes flying into buildings."[27]

Stratesec and the World Trade Center

In terms of the WTC, the primary issue to be considered is the destruction of three tall buildings and how the possible bypassing of the security system could have contributed to that destruction. That is, how were explosives placed in those highly-secure buildings without that fact being noticed?

As stated in the introduction, this book is not meant to revisit the overwhelming evidence for explosives at the WTC. It will be sufficient to say here that no tall building has ever suffered global collapse, either before or after 9/11, for any reason other than demolition. On 9/11, the official account says that there were three such instances—all on the same day and in the same place.

Unfortunately, the NIST WTC reports are based on computer modeling which is not available for public inspection. The few actual physical tests that were completed failed to support the fire-based models, and the remaining steel evidence was destroyed.[28]

The evidence that is available, including eyewitness testimony, videos and photographs, and independent scientific studies, strongly supports the theory that the buildings were intentionally demolished.[29] Readers interested in that detailed evidence can find more information in the bibliography.

For the purposes of this discussion, it is useful to remember that McDaniel had worked for the U.S. government managing the distribution of military armaments. During that time, he was the main logistics administrator responsible for procuring and fielding all of the weapons systems for the U.S. Army. Therefore, in terms of logistics and ordnance experience, McDaniel's background prior to joining BDM and Stratesec made him well suited to the job of acquiring and distributing explosive materials.

In his role as COO for Stratesec, McDaniel had unparalleled access to the entire WTC complex. Because his company implemented the electronic security systems, McDaniel was in a position to grant the access needed to place the explosives.

The timing of McDaniel's arrival at Stratesec, which coincided with the company's new contract for extensive work at the WTC, also matched the start of a project to install new fireproofing in the towers.

There is a remarkable correlation between the floors that were upgraded for fireproofing during this time, and the floors of impact, fire, and failure on 9/11.[30] This relationship is unmistakable for WTC 1, the north tower, in that Flight 11 struck the exact eight floors, out of

110, that had been fully upgraded. On 9/11, these upgraded floors failed simultaneously, in accordion-like fashion, before the rest of the building fell.[31]

The fireproofing upgrade project began in 1996, when McDaniel arrived, and was ongoing at the time of the 9/11 attacks. The floors of impact and failure had just been completed shortly before the attacks.[32]

The upgrades called for shutdown of the affected floors and the exposure of the floor assemblies and columns while the new fireproofing was being applied. Other companies that were involved in the fireproofing upgrades, as indicated by documents released via the Freedom of Information Act, included Turner Construction and Phoenix Fireproofing.[33] The former was a well-established company tied to the Bush family and the latter was a little known contractor.[34]

It should be of interest to investigators that Stratesec's client LANL was among the few laboratories in the world at the cutting edge of research on thermitic materials.[35] Prior to 9/11, LANL had a program for the development of nanothermite, similar to that which has been found in WTC dust.[36] Overall, the evidence for the use of thermite in the demolition of the WTC buildings is substantial.[37]

Contrary to the common misperception, the fireproofing at the WTC was not insufficient. In fact, the upgrades resulted in extraordinarily thick fireproofing where it counted—on the floors of impact and failure. This thickness was reported to be on the order of 3.25 inches, more than twice what was needed.[38]

One possibility to explain the extra-thick fireproofing was that electrical components for explosives, or incendiary materials like nanothermite, might have been applied beneath the fireproofing. The presence of such materials could explain some of the otherwise inexplicable dynamics of the towers' destruction, including the unusual fire dynamics on the floors of impact and in the debris pile afterward. Use of thermitic materials would also explain the environmental data obtained at Ground Zero over a period of months after 9/11 and, perhaps, some of the unusual illnesses suffered by first responders.[39]

A close inspection of the upgraded fireproofing might have revealed such a deception. Unfortunately, although Rudy Giuliani's Department of Buildings (DOB) was supposed to inspect the upgrades, it never did. In fact, Giuliani's DOB took steps to weaken the City's oversight of WTC fire code compliance which allowed tenants to make modifications without the intrusion of government.[40] Tenants like Marsh & McLennan and Joseph Kasptuys' Baseline Financial, located in the impact zones of the two towers, made unsupervised modifications in the exact areas that were impacted.[41]

The fireproofing upgrade project would have allowed for the placement of whatever explosives or incendiary materials were used. One hypothesis to consider is that the buildings might have been preliminarily rigged with the necessary electrical systems and devices during these upgrades, so that the actual charges could be easily placed within those systems at a time closer to the event.

The fireproofing upgrade project was not the only opportunity for contractors to place explosives or related equipment at the WTC. In 1994, a company called ACE Elevator won the contract to service the WTC elevators, over the more established Otis Elevator Company. In the year prior to 9/11, ACE worked on an extensive project to upgrade the WTC elevator system.[42]

The elevator system in the WTC towers was located in the core of the building, which was supported by an inner and an outer framework. As with the fireproofing upgrades, those working on the elevator project had direct access to structural steel.

Engineer Gordon Ross pointed out that the behavior of the towers as they fell indicated that elevator access was emphasized in the demolition plan. Ross reported that "columns which were situated adjacent to and accessible from inside the elevator shafts failed at an early stage of the collapse. Those columns which were remote from the elevator shafts, and not accessible from the elevator shafts, survived the early stages of the collapse."[43] In fact, the outer framework of the core, which was less accessible via the elevators, was left standing after the inner framework had completely collapsed.

It was not just the behavior of the falling structure that indicated explosives had been placed in the elevator shafts. ACE Elevator's mechanics were widely reported to have fled the scene unexpectedly, before the towers fell. In such crises elevator mechanics are expected to stay and help rescue people trapped in the elevators.[44] Why the ACE mechanics did not help was a mystery, but foreknowledge that something was wrong with the elevator shafts might have been the cause. And like Stratesec and the other KuwAm companies, ACE Elevator went bankrupt shortly after the attacks.

What role McDaniel might have played with regard to the fireproofing and elevator upgrades is not publicly known. As COO of Stratesec, however, he was in the position to offer access to the related areas of the towers while those areas were otherwise off-limits. He was also in the position to deny access to ensure that secret activities would not be inadvertently revealed.

Other Interesting Leads

Many people are still not aware of the third skyscraper that fell on 9/11. This was World Trade Center Building 7, or the Salomon Brothers building. This building was 47 stories tall, making it taller than any building in 33 U.S. states. It was not hit by a plane and yet, at 5:20 in the afternoon on 9/11, it fell through the path of what should have been the most resistance. It kinked in the middle and collapsed inward, falling vertically and symmetrically in 6.5 seconds.

Salomon Smith Barney (SSB) was the company that occupied all but ten of the 47 floors in WTC building 7.[45] SSB even shared the much-discussed 23rd floor with the New York City OEM. More striking is the fact that Donald Rumsfeld was the chairman of the SSB advisory board, and Dick Cheney was a board member as well. Rumsfeld served as chairman of the SSB advisory board since its inception in 1999, but had to resign in 2001 when he was confirmed as George W. Bush's defense secretary. And Cheney resigned at the same time when he became vice president.

Cheney and McDaniel had a close colleague in common as will be reviewed below. In any case, covert access to WTC 7 was likely not a problem, considering the other tenants in the building.

Carl Truscott knew WTC 7 because he had worked at the Secret Service's New York field office, the largest of its kind, which was located in that building. Also located in WTC 7 was the largest field office of George Tenet's CIA, as well as offices for Rumsfeld's department of defense and the Securities and Exchange Commission (SEC). The SEC lost many important documents on 9/11 when WTC 7 was destroyed, including much of what was needed to effectively prosecute Enron and WorldCom, the two largest securities scandals of the time.

It is interesting that there was a meeting scheduled at WTC 7 the morning of 9/11 that included explosive disposal units from the U.S. military. The Demolition-Ordnance Disposal Team from the Army's Fort Monmouth happened to have a meeting in WTC 7 that very morning with the building's owner, Larry Silverstein.

Silverstein "was reportedly planning to hold a meeting at 7 World Trade Center to discuss terrorism prevention efforts. The meeting, which was set for 8:00 a.m. [on 9/11], was canceled when one of his executives could not make it, said one market player who has spoken with Silverstein."[46]

Richard Spanard, an Army captain and commander of Fort Monmouth's explosive disposal unit was there to attend the meeting. "On the morning of September 11, he was enjoying breakfast at a deli 50 feet from the World Trade Center twin towers when the first plane hit. General hysteria inundated the deli. Spanard decided that he and the three soldiers with him should move to number 7 World Trade Center, where they had a scheduled meeting."[47]

"The building was full of people in the midst of evacuating. A second explosion was heard, and people began mobbing the three escalators in a state of panic. Spanard and the now five soldiers with him began yelling for everyone to remain calm and walk to the elevators in an orderly fashion."[48]

In yet another "eerie quirk of fate," on 9/11 Fort Monmouth personnel were preparing for an exercise called Timely Alert II.[49] This was a disaster drill focused on response to a terrorist attack, and included law enforcement agencies and emergency personnel. The drill simply changed to an actual response as the attacks began.

Fort Monmouth was home to several units of the Army's AMC, which McDaniel had led years before. The commander of Fort Monmouth at the time was Lt. Col. Stephen N. Wood, a U.S. Army intelligence officer. After 9/11, Wood was promoted to Colonel and assigned to a Joint Command at the National Security Agency. He went on to work in intelligence at the Transportation Security Administration and today is a federal officer in charge of security for three airports.[50]

Fort Monmouth's response included the explosives unit and the Army's Communications-Electronics Command (CECOM). As the drill was converted to an actual response, teams of CECOM experts were deployed to locate cell phone transmissions in the pile at Ground Zero. The remainder of the base's explosive ordnance company was there by the afternoon of 9/11 and stayed for three days in order to help the Secret Service look for possible explosives in the debris.[51]

It appears that the explosive disposal/terrorism meeting was not entirely a request of Larry Silverstein, but was organized by the U.S. Secret Service field office. The U.S. Navy's explosive ordnance disposal (EOD) Mobile Unit 6 had also been invited to WTC 7 that morning, again at the request of the Secret Service. As they arrived, the planes began to strike the towers.[52]

Dulles Airport and Related Topics

Stratesec had worked at Dulles Airport since 1995. The project accounted for 22% of the company's revenues in 1996 and in 1998. The issues of concern when investigating Stratesec's ties to Dulles include not only access, but the evidence produced to implicate the alleged hijackers.

The company was not hired to manage the screening of passengers at Dulles. Instead, its contract was for maintenance of the airfield access system, the CCTV (closed circuit television) system, and the electronic badging system.[53] Each of these three systems would be of interest to any honest 9/11 investigation.

Airfield access and electronic badging concerns were certainly raised after 9/11. As *TIME* magazine reported, investigators were originally of the opinion that weapons had been pre-positioned within some of the aircraft on 9/11, and it was suspected that the alleged hijackers "may have had accomplices deep within the 'secure' areas of airports."[54] As the investigation proceeded, the evidence led officials "to broaden their investigative and security efforts to encompass not only the carry-on bag screening system but the entire aviation security apparatus."[55]

Stratesec and KuwAm's role in managing the airfield access and electronic badging systems at Dulles should have led investigators to immediately investigate the company. Even a cursory review of Stratesec's ownership and management would have revealed cause to investigate further. The same was true for the companies that handled passenger screening in the 9/11-impacted facilities, which should be briefly mentioned.

A company called Argenbright managed passenger screening at Dulles and at Newark Airport, where Flight 93 took off that day. Argenbright also managed some security checkpoints at Logan Airport in Boston, where the two other 9/11 planes took off. Argenbright had been purchased in December 2000 by a British firm called Securicor. As discussed below, one of McDaniel's colleagues today is an associate of the Lord Paul Condon of Securicor.

The year before 9/11, Securicor was employing criminals in similar security functions, and three of its executives pled guilty to conspiracy.[56] Argenbright had pled guilty to falsifying employee records so that it could hire those convicted of drug possession and assault.[57]

After 9/11, Securicor faced about 30 lawsuits from victim's families. Another director that Condon supervised at Securicor, Trevor Dighton, said of the company's liability – "I'm not worried about it (the litigation) one little bit. The two planes involved weren't those that crashed into the towers – that's the first thing." Dighton's confidence might have had something to do with his opinion of Condon, whom Dighton said was "brilliant and knows what he's doing."[58]

Frank Argenbright Jr., the founder of Argenbright Security, went on to start another company called SecurAmerica LLC. One of the directors there was a senior advisor to Ronald Reagan and CEO of the Hill & Knowlton sister company, Burson-Marsteller.[59] When BCCI was facing criminal charges in the late 1980s, Henry Kissinger suggested the firm hire Burson-Marsteller to control its publicity.[60]

American Airlines contractor Globe Aviation Services of Irving, Texas managed the passenger screening at Logan Airport in Boston as it related to Flight 11. Globe Aviation was owned by Pinkerton-Burns, which had been acquired by Securitas Group of Sweden in 1999.

United Airlines contractor Huntleigh USA Corporation performed the screening of passengers related to Flight 175. Huntleigh was bought out in 1999 by the Israeli company ICTS International.

In early 1998, the FAA introduced a new process of selecting passengers for increased scrutiny at U.S. airports. Called the Computer Assisted Passenger Prescreening System (CAPPS), it was a computer-based formula that assessed the likelihood of a "selectee" causing a problem during flight. In practice, the result was a much less effective screening process.[61]

The use of the new CAPPS process was cited as a potential root cause for the success of the hijackers in boarding the planes. However, the official account says that many of the alleged hijackers were identified by the system as selectees. When the FAA later investigated, however, the screeners "could not recall that any of the passengers they screened had been selected by CAPPS."[62]

The alleged hijackers were not only selected for extra inspection in the screening process, some of them failed to pass the metal detector screening. In two cases they failed twice.[63]

Overall, the *9/11 Commission Report* cited little evidence for its account of how the alleged hijackers boarded the planes. The most substantial evidence that was produced came from the security video system at Dulles Airport. The report referenced the security videotapes from Dulles as sources in footnotes 11, 14 and 15 to Chapter 1. The videotapes provided critical evidence implicating all of the accused Flight 77 hijackers. The men are shown in the tapes moving through the screening checkpoints and being checked with hand-held metal detectors in a process that was later criticized by a screening expert.[64]

This critical evidence is interesting in that, shortly before 9/11, Stratesec was responsible for the closed circuit videotape processes that produced it. This certainly calls for further investigation. The Commission stated that neither Logan nor Newark had such security videotape evidence to provide and therefore Stratesec's role was unique in terms of the 9/11 historical record.[65]

With regard to security at airports, and at Dulles in particular, there is another company that should be examined. That is Security Storage of Washington (SSW), a storage and logistics company that worked for U.S. government agencies. KuwAm's Robert Van Roijen was the chairman of the board. SSW provided high-tech storage containers and video surveillance for Dulles Airport. The company also performed background checks and drug screenings on potential airport security employees.[66]

McDaniel's Current Colleagues

As mentioned earlier, McDaniel is currently business partners with one of Dick Cheney's closest former colleagues, Bruce Bradley. Bradley was one of the founders of Bradley Woods & Company, where Cheney worked in between assignments for Nixon and Ford. Bradley's business partner Alan Woods worked closely with Rumsfeld in the Ford DOD and also with Frank Carlucci at the "spook central" firm Sears World Trade.

The company that McDaniel now leads is called Lancaster Systems & Solutions (LS2). As CEO at LS2, McDaniel has a board of directors which is led by Bradley.[67] Shortly after independent investigators began to discuss this coincidence, the company removed its website from the internet.[68]

LS2 is a company that is highly focused on the military-industrial-counterterrorism complex's response to 9/11. In fact, few companies are more focused on the 9/11 aftermath than LS2, whose mission is to "deliver a diversified suite of responsive defense solutions to government organizations and multinational corporations who provide military, law enforcement, security, peacekeeping, and emergency response operations across the globe.'[69] The company's subsidiary, Global Service and Trade, provides equipment for police state operations around the world.

The board of directors which Bradley leads for McDaniel at LS2 includes Larry Johnson, the former CIA employee and State department official mentioned in the discussion of L. Paul Bremer. Johnson was a paramilitary CIA officer from 1985 to 1989, but he also directed crisis management for hijackings and helped investigate the Lockerbie Bombing (Pan Am 103).

In 1994, Johnson started scripting special operations exercises for the State Department. From 1996 to 2006, as Deputy Director of Counterterrorism within the State Department, he led terrorism training for senior-level government officials and served as an expert witness in cases against al Qaeda suspects.[70]

Another director working with Bradley and McDaniel at LS2 is David Pillor, the former director and Executive VP of InVision Technologies. As the leading provider of bomb detecting equipment for airports, InVision had an interesting history which included installation of its equipment at most major airports prior to 9/11, including those from which the hijacked planes took off.

Sergio Magistri was the CEO of InVision from 1992 through 2004. In a court case related to this period, InVision was charged "with authorizing improper payments to foreign government officials in violation of the Foreign Corrupt Practices Act (FCPA)."[71] The case represented the first, and perhaps only, time that the U.S. Department of Justice decided to not prosecute a company that had violated the FCPA.

Magistri and LS2's Pillor are now both board members at Vidient Systems, a video surveillance company that serves the "homeland security" industry. Vidient is in strategic partnership with Autonomy Corp, where we find the "Prince of Darkness," Richard Perle. Fellow directors at Vidient include several people who played critical roles related to the events of September 11.

One director at Vidient is Richard Clarke, the former "Counterterrorism Czar," whose job for nine years prior to 9/11 was to protect the United States from a terrorist attack.[72] At Vidient we also find The Lord Paul Condon, who was previously mentioned.

Working with Pillor, Clarke and Condon is Michael Sheehan, the former U.S. State Department Ambassador at Large for Counterterrorism. Sheehan was a long time member of the U.S. Army Special Forces. He also served on the National Security Council for two presidents, George H.W. Bush (with Wayne Downing, who is discussed in Chapter 15), and Bill Clinton.

After the bombing of the *USS Cole*, Sheehan asked Richard Clarke: 'What's it going to take to get them to hit al-Qaeda in Afghanistan? Does al-Qaeda have to hit the Pentagon?"[73] That certainly seems like a prescient statement considering that, less than one year later, that was exactly what happened.

In summary, Stratesec and Barry McDaniel call out for investigation for the following reasons.

- Explosives were used to bring down the WTC.

- Stratesec's security contracts allowed it unparalleled access to the WTC, Dulles Airport, and other related facilities.

- McDaniel had expertise in the acquisition and distribution of military ordnance.

- The timing of McDaniel's unusual career move to become COO at Stratesec matched the timing of work at the WTC that provided opportunities to plant explosives.

- Official investigators suspected that the alleged hijackers may have had accomplices in the secure areas of the airports.

- Stratesec managed the airfield access and electronic badging for Dulles Airport. It had also managed the security video system that provided some of the rare and critical evidence implicating the alleged hijackers.

- The company was led by directors and investors who were linked to deep state entities and who benefited from the response to the 9/11 crimes.

- Barry McDaniel had links to the Iran-Contra crimes and to "spook" companies like SWT and Vinnell.

- After 9/11, McDaniel started a company that profited from the 9/11 Wars, with Dick Cheney's old partner Bruce Bradley.

In the next chapter, a man who used 9/11 for his own political benefit is considered. As might be expected, a number of the same themes seen in previous chapters will be revealed again in a discussion of New York City's 9/11 mayor.

Chapter 14

Rudy Giuliani and the World Trade Center

As mayor of New York City on 9/11, Rudy Giuliani was in a unique position to benefit from the attacks. That's because he gained national notoriety for his presumed valiant response that day, and he received the kind of publicity that every ambitious politician desires. Immediately after 9/11, Giuliani's approval rating rocketed to 79% among New York City voters, a dramatic increase over the 36% rating he had received a year earlier. He was called "America's Mayor" by Oprah Winfrey at a 9/11 memorial service. And on December 24, 2001, *TIME* magazine named Giuliani its Person of the Year for 2001.

In the years since 9/11, Giuliani's public persona has unraveled. It has been revealed that he did more damage than good during his tenure as mayor and there are many reasons to suspect him with regard to the events of 9/11. These reasons include the following.

- He led enforcement actions against the terrorist financing network BCCI and then joined a law firm that represented that terrorist network.

- In the years between the first WTC bombing and 9/11, Giuliani's administration ignored problems with the NYC fire department radios. Those faulty radios contributed to the deaths on 9/11.[1]

- He and his staff had foreknowledge that the WTC towers would fall when no one could have predicted such a thing.

- He was primarily responsible for the destruction of critical WTC evidence.

- He told people in the Ground Zero area that the air was safe to breathe, when it was not, in order to speed the removal of evidence at Ground Zero.

- Several members of Giuliani's family have been involved with organized crime, and Rudy hired companies linked to organized crime to remove and dispose of the WTC debris.

Considering these things it is worthwhile to look at Giuliani's past before looking closely at his actions and decisions with respect to 9/11.

The History of Rudy

Rudolph W. Giuliani was born an only child in 1944. Rudy's father, Harold Giuliani (alias Joseph Starrett), was a convicted hold-up man who served time in Sing Sing prison, and was later employed as an enforcer for a mafia loan shark operation. Rudy's uncle (his mother's brother), Leo D'Avanzo, ran a loan-sharking and gambling operation with Jimmy Dano, "who was a made man."[2] Additionally, Rudy's cousin Lewis D'Avanzo "was a stone cold gangster who was shot to death in 1977 by FBI agents when he tried to run them down with his car."[3]

Of course, the sins of his father, and his uncle, and his cousin, should not be used to judge Rudy himself. Although Rudy was close to his family (he was actually married to one of his second cousins for 14 years) that doesn't mean he inherited the family penchant for mafia associations. These connections to the mob are worth considering, however, in that Rudy hired mafia–connected companies to cleanup Ground Zero after the attacks. Additionally, Rudy's friend and close colleague Bernard Kerik, whose police department provided crucial 9/11 evidence, was also linked to organized crime.[4] Also worth considering is that, as mentioned in the introduction, deep events often involve cooperation between government leaders and organized crime.

Despite (or perhaps due to) his family's background, Giuliani's career soared from the start as if he had friends in high places. At the age of 29, after graduating from law school and working briefly for a judge in NYC, Giuliani was appointed as the attorney in charge of the cases resulting from the Knapp Commission's investigation of police corruption. The indictments and convictions of NYC police officers that followed did not end the corruption however and, in particular, drug-related corruption continued unabated.[5]

Two years later, in 1975, Giuliani was named Associate Deputy Attorney General and chief of staff to Deputy Attorney General Harold Tyler. A former judge from the Southern District of New York (SDNY), Tyler was the original choice to be the Watergate special prosecutor but he rejected the position. He was then brought into the Ford Administration, along with his young chief of staff Giuliani, specifically to restore the public trust after Watergate. Giuliani worked with Ford Administration officials, including Ford's chief of staff Dick Cheney, during this time. As early as May 1976, Rudy was warning about domestic terrorism and recommending that intelligence collection policies be relaxed.[6]

In 1981, at the age of 37, Reagan appointed Giuliani to be Associate Attorney General, the third-highest position in the Department of Justice. In this position he supervised several law enforcement agencies including the Department of Corrections and the Drug Enforcement Administration (DEA). Journalist Gary Webb reported that the DEA protected Norwin Meneses during this time while Meneses ran cocaine into the United States to fund the Nicaraguan Contras.[7]

Rudy's mentor, Harold Tyler, became the chief author of a report that exonerated the Reagan Administration of any wrongdoing related to the 1980 killings of four American nuns in El Salvador.[8] At the time, L. Paul Bremer was effectively running the State Department that had commissioned the report and Brian Michael Jenkins was reportedly running a "war of terror" against the citizens of Nicaragua.[9]

While Giuliani was in the Justice department, he chaired a committee that provided oversight to the government's use of the software called PROMIS. A database integration program, PROMIS was used by Oliver North to track terrorist threats and may have evolved into a tool for deep state uses.[10] Reportedly the software was also used by the Continuity of Government group led by Dick Cheney, Donald Rumsfeld, and Richard Clarke.[11] An enhanced version of PROMIS was said to be capable of functioning as a tool for espionage, collecting and relaying information from the systems on which it was installed without the knowledge of the system owner.

One of Giuliani's colleagues in the department, Peter Videnieks, was involved with illegally distributing the enhanced PROMIS software to foreign governments with the approval of "high level Justice Department officials."[12] Journalist Daniel Casolaro found that Videnieks and Earl Brian were involved in a wide-ranging criminal conspiracy involving PROMIS, BCCI, organized crime, the "October Surprise" holding of the hostages, and the Iran-Contra affair. Brian was a CIA and Reagan associate who had previously been part of the Phoenix Program in Vietnam and went on to run United Press International (with Stratesec investor Arnaud de Borchgrave). Casolaro was apparently murdered as a result of his investigation.[13]

Giuliani was appointed U.S. Attorney for SDNY in 1983. It was in this position that he first gained national prominence by prosecuting high-profile cases, including those of Wall Street figures Ivan Boesky and Michael Milken. As the U.S. attorney for the SDNY, from 1983 to 1989, Giuliani was not only handling drug and organized crime cases, he was also in charge of representing the Federal Reserve Bank in its enforcement actions against Bank of Credit and Commerce International (BCCI). These actions led to a RICO plea agreement and forfeiture of BCCI's United States assets, valued at $550 million.[14] It was reported that during this time Giuliani received documents about secret bank accounts related to terrorist financing that were held by companies like Citibank, Barclays, Credit Lyonnais, and the Japanese company Nomura.[15]

During Giuliani's tenure at the Department of Justice in the 1980s, Kamal Adham and other high-level Saudis behind BCCI were allowed to gain control of several American financial institutions. BCCI was subsequently allowed to continue funding terrorism, without being prosecuted, for many years.[16]

Giuliani remained in the U.S. attorney position until January 1989, resigning at the end of the Reagan Administration. He then joined the law firm White & Case in NYC as a partner.

While working at White & Case, Giuliani ran for mayor of NYC in the 1989 election. In that failed campaign, it was revealed that Giuliani's firm represented the Panamanian dictator, and colleague of President George H.W. Bush, Manuel Noriega. Author Russ Baker wrote that Bush, "as Ford's CIA director and then as Reagan's vice president, had fostered a relationship with the notorious drug trafficker [Noriega] during the seventies and eighties, even keeping him on the payroll at more than a hundred thousand dollars a year."[17]

Giuliani's reaction to the revelation that his firm represented Noriega was to claim ignorance of the fact, which brought derision down upon him. Incumbent mayor Ed Koch remarked, "Obviously, you're vulnerable when you are receiving income from a firm that's lobbying for a company that's perceived as damaging our civilization. You can get rich, or you can get elected." Harrison Goldin, former city treasurer, added, "If Rudy Giuliani doesn't know his law firm is representing Noriega, a notorious drug dealer and dictator, how is he going to manage a city with nearly a quarter of a million employees?"[18]

At the time, White & Case also had an office in Saudi Arabia. What is less well reported is that Giuliani's firm represented not only Noriega but also BCCI, which was funded by powerful royals in Saudi Arabia and the United Arab Emirates.[19] This should be of concern considering that "BCCI was the mother and father of terrorist financing operations."[20]

Another fact of concern is that Giuliani's reputation for being tough on crime was a false front. He actually did such a poor job in his prosecutions that many of his major convictions were later overturned.[21] The question of whether he was purposely placed in that position to undermine such cases, and thereby provide a door out for some of the accused, must be considered. His primary activities at the time included "publicly handcuffing mob bosses and business leaders on trumped up charges only to quietly drop the charges later," demonstrating that, for his own part, Rudy was in it for the publicity.[22]

Nonetheless, with detailed knowledge of the terrorist funding bank BCCI, it is remarkable that Giuliani never mentioned terrorism as an issue in his second campaign for NYC mayor in 1993. In fact, he barely mentioned the 1993 WTC bombing that had occurred earlier that year, referring to it only once publicly. What's more, when he won the election, and began looking for his first police commissioner, he never questioned the candidates about terrorism. For someone who had made a career both before 1993, and after 9/11, as a terrorist fighter, it was inexplicable that Giuliani would never talk about terrorism when running for his first elected office. Some have said that it was his relationship with BCCI, and questions that might arise about it, that kept him quiet.[23]

Considering that al Qaeda and 9/11 are commonly seen as a direct outgrowth and evolution of BCCI intelligence operations,[24] Giuliani's link to that network is enough to justify investigating his possible role in the attacks. There are a number of other compelling reasons to do so, however.

Foreknowledge

In a televised interview with ABC News immediately after the 9/11 attacks, Rudy Giuliani stated that he was told that the World Trade Center towers were going to collapse before they actually did. This is what he said of the warning, which occurred shortly before the first tower fell.

> "I .. I went down to the scene and we set up a headquarters at 75 Barkley Street, which was right there with the Police Commissioner, the Fire Commissioner, the Head of Emergency Management, and we were operating out of there when we were told that the World Trade Center was gonna' collapse. And it did collapse before we could actually get out of the building, so we were trapped in the building for 10, 15 minutes, and finally found an exit, got out, walked north, and took a lot of people with us." [25]

Problems with this remark include that, at the time, no one familiar with structural fires or tall building construction expected anything of the kind.[26] That is because no tall building had ever suffered global collapse from fire before and, moreover, none have experienced such a failure since that day. In fact, many architects and engineers still consider it impossible.[27]

In this same interview Giuliani claimed that no one had ever predicted airliner crashes into the WTC, saying, "Oh there's no question we were all caught totally off balance. No one, no one, no one could possibly expect, uh, large airplanes to crash into the, you know, the World Trade Center, uh, the way this happened."[28] This stammering statement was not just unconvincing, it was patently false. Those in charge of securing the WTC in the decade before 9/11, specifically Brian Michael Jenkins of Kroll Associates, had considered exactly that scenario.[29] Another person who worked with Jenkins at Kroll Associates was James R. Bucknam. Once a senior adviser to Louis Freeh, Bucknam had worked with Giuliani and Freeh in the offices of the SDNY during the time that Giuliani was investigating BCCI.[30]

On 9/11, staff at Giuliani's Office of Emergency Management (OEM) also had foreknowledge about the collapse of the buildings, and they warned some people. This was reported by Richard Zarrillo, an Emergency Medical Technician at the scene, when he said: "OEM says the buildings are going to collapse; we need to get out," and "I was just at OEM. The message I was given was that the buildings are going to collapse; we need to get our people out."[31]

Fire department Captain Abdo Nahmod was with Zarrillo, just before they were warned, and both had been told to make the OEM functional in WTC Building 7. But, Nahmod reported: "Moments thereafter we were advised by the staff at OEM that we were to vacate the building [and] that they believed there was another possible plane on its way and [we] proceeded down the stairwell of World Trade [7] all the way down to the ground floor."[32]

In the lobby of Building 7, Zarrillo and Nahmod apparently met with Division Chief John Peruggia, OEM Deputy Director Richard Rotanz and an unidentified representative from the City's Department of Buildings. Peruggia later said "it was brought to my attention, it was believed that the structural damage that was suffered to the towers was quite significant and they were very confident that the building's stability was compromised and they felt that the north tower was in danger of a near imminent collapse."[33]

Richard Rotanz was later said to be the one behind the claim that a third plane was heading toward New York. Rotanz reportedly got that information from a Secret Service agent who was with him in WTC 7 at the time, and spread the information to OEM leadership.[34] Therefore Rotanz was actually behind two important claims that morning, the first was that there was a third hijacked plane headed for the area, which was presumably the reason why the OEM emergency center was closed down before either tower fell (before 9:44 AM), and the second claim was that the towers were in danger of imminent collapse.

In any case, this is an incredible statement—that "they felt that the north tower was in danger of a near imminent collapse"—considering that no building had ever suffered global collapse from fire. Zarrillo learned just how incredible this information was when he tried to spread the word to the fire chiefs in other areas, none of whom had predicted any such danger. When Zarrillo told Chief Peter Ganci about Peruggia's startling news, Ganci's response was, "who the fuck told you that?"[35]

Rudy's Posse

While Zarrillo was trying to warn people, Giuliani and his police commissioner Bernard Kerik were wandering around the WTC site after the planes had hit the towers. Fire Marshal Steven Mosiello stated, "At that point the Mayor shows up. I was standing away from the command post, and the Mayor showed up... I remember the Mayor being with Commissioner Kerik and himself and a lot of their aides and escorts or whatever."[36]

By the time the south tower did fall, Giuliani and Kerik had already moved away from immediate danger. As they were walking, they coincidentally happened upon a TV reporter who had, just the year before, published a flattering biography of Giuliani called "Rudy Giuliani: Emperor of the City." This supposedly coincidental meeting is what led to Giuliani being portrayed as the heroic leader of the response to 9/11, through a series of "walking press conferences" on that day.[37]

Fire Chief Joseph Pfeifer, who was at the command post in the lobby of the North Tower, testified that, "Right before the South Tower collapsed, I noticed a lot of people just left the lobby, and I heard we had a crew of all different people, high-level people in government, everybody was gone, almost like they had information that we didn't have."[38]

Who were these high-level people in government gathering in the lobby of the North Tower that had information others did not have? This group reportedly included Richard Sheirer, the director of the OEM. It was said that, "He's the guy Giuliani calls the man behind the curtain."[39] Others suggested: "Since September 11, Sheirer has taken charge of the biggest cleanup effort in American history." Whether or not he helped with the cleanup, Sheirer did have significant responsibility in his role as director of the OEM, having at various times "briefed President Bush, Tony Blair, and Henry Kissinger".[40]

The group of high-level government officials congregating in the north tower lobby also included John Odematt, the First Deputy Director of the OEM and former Executive Officer of the NYC Police Department's Intelligence Division. Odematt left the OEM in 2003 to work for Citigroup, the parent company for WTC 7 tenant Salomon Smith Barney.

It was reported that Sheirer and others spent a full hour in the north tower lobby, while the towers were burning. But no one knows what they were doing there. As stated before, the OEM center in WTC 7 was shut down early, and Sheirer himself never went there. Instead, he and his staff went to the north tower lobby and apparently did nothing but waited. Although Sheirer later claimed to have made some calls, "no steps to coordinate the response were ever discovered."[41]

To some degree, Sheirer was officially portrayed as incompetent. John Farmer, a 9/11 Commission staff member, said of Sheirer:

"We [the 9/11 Commission] tried to get a sense of what Sheirer was really doing. We tried to figure it out from the videos. We couldn't tell. Everybody from OEM was with him, virtually the whole chain of command. Some of them should have been at the command center."

Fire Captain Kevin Culley, who worked for the OEM, was later asked why most of the OEM's top brass were with him at the scene of the incident, and he said: "I don't know what they were doing. It was Sheirer's decision to go there on his own. The command center would normally be the focus of a major event and that would be where I would expect the director to be."[42]

After 9/11, Sheirer joined Giuliani's new consulting firm, Giuliani Partners, along with Pasquale J. (Pat) D'Amuro, the FBI agent who ran the PENTTBOM investigation and stole evidence from Ground Zero (see below). Also at Giuliani Partners was Michael Hess, who was present in WTC 7 when explosives were going off in the building, along with witness Barry Jennings.[43]

Bernard Kerik worked at Giuliani Partners as well, from the time he left his police commissioner post in December 2001 until resigning from the firm in December 2004. While he worked at Giuliani's firm, Kerik took a short leave when he was appointed by George W. Bush to be Minister of the Interior for Iraq and Senior Policy Advisor to L. Paul Bremer, then the Iraq Occupation Governor. In Iraq, Kerik was assigned to oversee the training of the Iraqi Police by contractor Dyncorp.

It was claimed that "Mr. Kerik brings a wide array of experience to the new job, and a familiarity with the culture and political realities of the Middle East. Beginning in the 1970's, he worked in the region as a security expert, including four years in the employ of the Saudi royal family."[44] During Kerik's first experience in Saudi Arabia, starting in 1978, he worked in security at a construction site in the desert and learned from a "squad of mercenaries and disillusioned Vietnam War veterans how to carry himself." He also developed "a taste for the spoils of mercenary pay: Gucci shoes, Rolex watches, European suits, according to his memoir."[45]

Kerik's later work in Iraq was widely recognized as a dismal failure. By the time his remarkably short assignment was over, he had offended the U.S. military and left the newly forming Iraqi police force in shambles. General Ricardo Sanchez, the top military leader in Iraq during that time said that Kerik focused more on "conducting raids and liberating prostitutes" than training the Iraqis.[46]

It seemed that only one person was impressed with "The Baghdad Terminator," as Kerik was called during his three months in Iraq, and that one supporter was Donald Rumsfeld. For some reason, Rumsfeld's perspective on Kerik's performance seemed biased. "Since Bernie Kerik left," Rumsfeld complained, "I understand things have slowed down on police training."[47]

After returning from Iraq, Kerik went back to Giuliani Partners and remained there until President Bush nominated him to replace Tom Ridge as Secretary of the Department of Homeland Security. That nomination was shot down quickly, as the public began to understand more about Kerik's background.

Giuliani had appointed Kerik as NYC Police Commissioner in August 2000, despite the fact that "More than half of Giuliani's cabinet opposed Kerik's appointment."[48] Giuliani later remembered having been briefed "on some aspects of Bernard B. Kerik's relationship with a company suspected of ties to organized crime before Mr. Kerik's appointment as New York City police commissioner". It seemed odd that Giuliani would need such a briefing, however, considering that Kerik had worked for Giuliani as a campaign bodyguard and chauffeur as early as 1993.[49]

Kerik's connections to the mob were not a surprise to many people, because he was regularly embroiled in scandal. Bribery, tax fraud and document falsification are only some of the crimes for which Kerik was accused.[50] Finally, in October 2009, Kerik was sent to federal prison after a judge revoked his $500,000 bail and berated him publicly from the bench. The judge described Kerik as a "toxic combination of self-minded focus and arrogance."[51]

What is known about Kerik today should make people wonder about the leadership he provided while he was still a public figure. For example, Kerik was the first person to tell the public that explosives were not likely to have been used to bring down the WTC buildings. When asked this question in their first press conference on the afternoon of 9/11, Giuliani turned to Kerik for the answer and Kerik responded in the negative.[52]

An Unprecedented Destruction of Evidence

Regardless of who had foreknowledge or what the imminent danger was, in the weeks and months after 9/11 there were heroic efforts made to rescue survivors. But those efforts were hampered by Giuliani's drive to clean up the site rapidly. The commonly held story was that the government wanted to re-open Wall Street, and for that reason didn't care about the health of New Yorkers and first responders or about facilitating the most careful rescue operations.[53] But the facts also align with the hypothesis that authorities were actually in a hurry to remove evidence that pointed to the use of explosives.

The U.S. House Committee on Science reported, in March 2002:

> "In the month that lapsed between the terrorist attacks and the deployment of the [FEMA] BPAT team, a significant amount of steel debris — including most of the steel from the upper floors — was removed from the rubble pile, cut into smaller sections, and either melted at the recycling plant or shipped out of the U.S.. Some of the critical pieces of steel — including the suspension trusses from the top of the towers and the internal support columns — were gone before the first BPAT team member ever reached the site."[54]

The steel evidence, "a significant amount" of which was quickly removed before investigators arrived, might have shown evidence of explosive damage, like metal "pedaling." But the steel was not the only evidence that was removed. For example, the black boxes that contain the flight data recorders and cockpit data recorders on every airliner were officially never found for either American Airlines Flight 11 or

251

United Airlines Flight 175. This claim came from the FBI and was supported by the *9/11 Commission Report*, but was contradicted by a number of people who worked at the site. Two Ground Zero workers claimed that they helped authorities find three of the four black boxes in October of 2001. One of them, New York City firefighter Nicholas DeMasi, described the recovery of the devices in a book.[55] Additionally, a source from the National Transportation Safety Board (NTSB) said, "Off the record, we had the boxes. You'd have to get the official word from the FBI as to where they are, but we worked on them here."[56]

The idea that the indestructible black boxes could not be found also appears to be in contradiction to the official claim that a passport of one of the alleged hijackers was found. On September 12th, 2001, it was reported that the passport of Satam al Suqami, who was said to be aboard American Airlines Flight 11, was recovered.[57] Because Flight 11 crashed directly into the middle of the north face of the north tower, and was buried within the building, this passport would have had to stay intact throughout the crash event and then withstand the blast from the fuel fire and the ensuing fires fed by office furnishings (and thermitic materials). The rest of the spectacularly improbable path of the passport is not entirely clear, as the first reports said that it was found "in the rubble" but, later, 9/11 Commission staff member Susan Ginsberg testified that "A passerby picked it up and gave it to a NYPD detective shortly before the World Trade Center towers collapsed."[58] In other words, the passport was delivered through Bernard Kerik's department.

During the five-month cleanup effort, there were unprecedented measures taken to control access to the site. The site was restricted, and photographs were banned, by order of Rudy Giuliani.[59] Anthony Mann of E.J. Electric, one of the contractors for the WTC towers, said that "Security is unbelievable. It's really on a need-to-be-down-there basis."[60]

Several people were reported to be in charge of the cleanup operation at Ground Zero. It was said that OEM was in charge, and that Richard Sheirer was the point person for the cleanup efforts. Others believed that Mike Burton, the executive deputy commissioner of the New York City Department of Design and Construction (DDC), was in charge.

Although Burton managed some of the demolition and cleanup operations, he later testified that "Everything was coordinated through his boss Holden, deputy mayors and the mayor."[61]

After his WTC work was done, DDC's Burton was hired as Senior Vice President of URS Corporation. URS is the same company that bought The Washington Group (i.e. Morrison-Knudsen), the south tower tenant that, in the preceding years, had been hired by the Army Corps of Engineers to demolish over 200 buildings.[62]

At Ground Zero, DDC handed over the most important of its decision-making responsibility to LZA/Thornton-Tomasetti, whose leaders were Charles Thornton, later a member of the advisory board for the NIST WTC investigation, and Richard Tomasetti. The importance of LZA/Thornton-Tomasetti became clear when someone needed to take responsibility for the decision to recycle all the steel evidence. It was finally said that Richard Tomasetti made that decision, despite the outrage from the public, fire engineering experts and the victim's family members. When asked why he did it, Tomasetti claimed that, "had he known the direction that investigations into the collapses would take, he would have taken a different stand."[63]

The recycling of the most important steel evidence was done in a hurry, as indicated by the U.S. House Committee on Science report mentioned earlier. It was done so fast, in fact, that the City took much less than market value for the scrap metal. At the time, steel scrap was selling for $150 per ton, but those in charge of the WTC cleanup took just $120 per ton for the WTC steel.[64] It's not difficult to see that the $9 million lost in that transaction would have been useful to the many 9/11 first responders who became gravely ill from their exposure to toxins at Ground Zero.

Tomasetti's extremely unpopular, and possibly criminal, decision was supported by the new mayor of NYC, Michael Bloomberg. Using a strange, diversionary excuse, Bloomberg said: "If you want to take a look at the construction methods and the design, that's in this day and age what computers do. Just looking at a piece of metal generally doesn't tell you anything." Bloomberg's claim was not at all true, as forensic investigators will confirm.

Other than the supervisory firm LZA/Thornton-Tomasetti, the City also hired five construction companies to handle the majority of the debris removal, and the site was divided up among them. These five companies were AMEC Construction Management, Bovis Lend Lease, Turner Construction, Tully Construction and Tishman Construction. Charlie Vitchers, who worked for Bovis, said the site was then broken up "into basically five segments. Building 7 debris was given to Tishman. The northwest corner of the site was given to AMEC. The northeast section of the site was given to Tully. And the southwest corner of the site and Tower 2 debris removal was given to Bovis."[65] Turner Construction was assigned to a central location between building 5 and building 6.

Other sub-contractors were hired to complete most of the actual debris removal. Most of those companies were suspected of being associated with organized crime. Some sub-contractors were reportedly linked to the Colombo crime family, including Civetta Cousins and Yonkers Contracting. Others were associated with the Luchese crime family.

A contractor with a big presence at Ground Zero was Seasons Contracting, owned by Salvatore Carucci, a reputed Luchese associate. "We were called in by AMEC, one of the team of general contractors managing the cleanup," said Bill Singley, a Seasons project manager. AMEC also hired Big Apple Wrecking, owned by Harold Greenberg, a reputed mob associate whose firm was barred from government work because of his convictions in bid-rigging and bribery conspiracies. Another firm allegedly controlled by Greenberg, Safeway Environmental, was also hired to work at Ground Zero.

One of the first debris removal companies on the scene was Mazzocchi Wrecking, brought in by the New York City Housing Preservation Department, but then hired by AMEC. A few months after 9/11, the N.J. Division of Gaming Enforcement "charged that three members of the DeCavalcante crime family worked for Mazzocchi."[66] Another member of the DeCavalcante family, Thomas Vastola, was known to be an associate of a BCCI-backed arms dealer.[67]

Other AMEC contractors that were linked to the mob were Peter Scalamandre & Sons, and Breeze National, both linked to the Luchese crime family. AMEC's lead person on the ground was Vice President Leo DiRubbo, a reputed associate of the Luchese crime family. Another company that was "all over ground zero" was Laquila Construction, run by mob boss Dino Tomassetti.[68]

These companies all made a lot of money at the WTC site. Of the $458 million in federal 9/11 aid spent on debris removal, AMEC took $65.8 million, Bovis hauled in $277.2 million, Tully got $76 million and Turner got $39 million. Subcontractors Breeze National, Peter Scalamandre & Sons, Civetta Cousins, Safeway Environmental and Yonkers Contracting made millions of dollars from their work at the site. Subcontractors Mazzocchi Wrecking and Seasons Contracting made tens of millions of dollars.

Turner Construction, one of the primary contractors at Ground Zero, occupied the 38th floor of the north tower, and was involved in performing the fireproofing upgrades in the towers. It has been noted that these upgrades were completed, in the three years before 9/11, on floors that match up almost identically to the floors of impact and failure on 9/11.[69] In any case, since 1999 Turner has been a wholly owned subsidiary of Hochtief AG, and its CEO is Thomas Leppert, who later became mayor of Dallas. President George W. Bush appointed Mayor Leppert to the President's Commission on White House Fellows, and Bush now lives in Dallas, about a mile away from Leppert.[70]

Of the other primary contractors, Tishman Construction oversaw the construction of the new WTC 7, as well as the "Freedom Tower," designed to replace the north tower. Tully Construction retained Controlled Demolition Inc. (CDI), a company that had been involved in the demolition of the bombed Murrah Building in Oklahoma in 1995. CDI was led by Mark Loizeaux, who later became a major defender of the government's story about 9/11. Like some other experts with large government contracts, Loizeaux was at first uncertain about what had happened at the WTC, then he changed his opinion, apparently in order to harmonize with the official story.[71]

Once the cleanup was fully coordinated, the operations were consolidated under the control of two of the five primary contractors: AMEC Construction Management and Bovis Lend Lease. These are the two companies that were originally assigned the areas of Ground Zero that included the north tower (AMEC) and the south tower (Bovis).

At Ground Zero AMEC was led by its Vice Chairman, John Cavanagh, who had previously been the President and COO of Morse Diesel International, the predecessor to AMEC. Morse Diesel had also retrofitted WTC building 7 for Salomon Brothers in 1989. But at the time of the 9/11 attacks, Cavanagh reported to Peter Janson, the CEO of AMEC Construction and long-time business associate of Donald Rumsfeld. Under Janson's leadership, AMEC had just completed a $258 million refurbishment of Wedge 1 of the Pentagon, exactly where American Airlines Flight 77 impacted the building.[72]

Bovis Lend Lease was another British construction giant founded by Sir Frank Lampl, a Czech holocaust survivor who worked in the Middle East in the 1970s.[73] The company built the Abu Dhabi Chamber of Commerce and the Riyadh Olympic stadium in Saudi Arabia.

Years later, Bovis project leader Jim Abadie was also in charge of the Deutsche Bank demolition and the September 11th memorial. This was before he resigned in the midst of an investigation into billing and payroll practices at five Bovis projects in New York, including the memorial and Deutsche Bank.[74] For the Deutsche Bank demolition, in 2004, Abadie hired a previously non-existent company called John Galt Construction.[75] After the deaths of two firefighters during the demolition project, John Galt was found to be in the middle of a multi-million dollar "check-cashing" scandal led by two characters named Riad Khalil and Neil Goldstein.[76]

Also involved in the Deutsche Bank demolition was Charles Schwab, an associate of Harold Greenberg who "once controlled seven banks, a casino in Reno and a big chunk of Hilton Head Island [and] the largest demolition company in the country."[77] Schwab was also associated with Phoenix Wrecking, a demolition and abatement company. It's not clear if this is the same company as the Phoenix Fireproofing listed in FOIA-obtained documents related to the WTC fireproofing upgrades.[78] But it is clear that mayor Bloomberg's office and the Lower Manhattan Development Corporation (LMDC) were aware of the suspicious companies involved in the Deutsche Bank fiasco.[79]

LMDC was mandated to "alleviate existing conditions that pose a serious and immediate threat to the health or welfare of New York City or meet community development needs resulting from Sept. 11, 2001." In practice, this meant that LMDC made a lot of the decisions about what happened at Ground Zero after the cleanup and perhaps even before it was completed. LMDC was created by Governor Pataki and Mayor Giuliani without approval from the state legislature, in November 2001.[80]

The federal government promised $21.4 billion in aid in order to rebuild Manhattan, and LMDC was in charge of spending a great deal of that money. Unfortunately, much of it was doled out in pork projects that benefited friends of LMDC.

A good friend of George W. Bush was a director of LMDC. This was Roland Betts, who once owned the Texas Rangers with Bush and Bush's relative, Marsh & McClennan's Craig Stapleton. Betts was also a "heavy contributor to the Bush election campaign in 2000."[81] Another LMDC director was Frank Zarb, who was one of the first U.S. Energy Czars, appointed by President Ford.[82]

Debris Removal and Theft

The debris removed from Ground Zero was either hauled away on trucks or shipped away on barges. Despite the effort to rapidly dispose of the steel and sell it a bargain price, the WTC debris was considered highly sensitive. At first the trucks were tracked using a paper-based system, and later GPS devices were fixed to each truck with "antennas to monitor location, cellular wireless antennas to communicate, and multiple I/Os to track vehicle signals from engine systems."[83] Apparently it was important for officials to know not only where the trucks were at any given time, but also the status of the engine. As for

257

the barges, the process was setup "in record time," in order to "transport debris to the city's Fresh Kills landfill and to recycling sites, all scrutinized by the Corps of Engineers."[84]

As the debris was received at Fresh Kills landfill, it was sorted carefully. This sorting process was supervised by federal agents, and described in this way: "Teams of officers and agents watch as the rubble is sifted down to a fine ashy silt that they then rake through by hand."[85]

More than a year later, honest FBI agents reported the theft of some of this debris at the Fresh Kills site. It was then discovered that Evidence Recovery Teams (ERTs) involved in the sorting process stole pieces of debris, and kept or disposed of them. This removal of debris was condoned and encouraged by the FBI agents in charge.

The final report on the debris theft concluded that "many FBI agents took rubble as souvenirs from Fresh Kills." An example given was that one Oklahoma City Emergency Response Team member took 80 pounds of various debris materials, including things like an "electrical outlet." More commonly, building pieces were taken, including "red granite building façade." The claim that these were merely souvenirs seemed unlikely considering the volume of materials stolen, and considering that WTC building 7 was the focus of much of the theft. In fact, pieces of the building "were stacked in a designated location of the Building 7 inspection area" in order for Secret Service agents to retrieve.[86]

Pat D'Amuro, who was mentioned earlier as an employee of Giuliani Partners, was involved in the theft of WTC debris materials from the Fresh Kills site. D'Amuro had specifically requested that certain kinds of items be kept for his retrieval, ostensibly so that he could give them away as mementos to various dignitaries. What is odd about that is that D'Amuro was not in charge of the Fresh Kills operation, but he had been the counterterrorism chief in the FBI's New York City office since 1997, which meant that his responsibilities included oversight of the Joint Terrorism Task Force.

As the FBI's lead person in terms of investigating and preventing terrorist acts before 9/11, D'Amuro had also been appointed to lead the investigations of the 1993 WTC bombing and other al Qaeda-attributed crimes. The 1993 bombing plot had been infiltrated by the FBI, which played a role in either trying to prevent that operation or allowing it to go forward, as described in Chapter 4. It was later claimed that the investigation of the bombing, led by D'Amuro, was fraudulent. Frederick Whitehurst, of the FBI crime laboratory, said that "attempts had been made to alter his lab reports to exclude scientific interpretations other than" the official explanation. Whitehurst went on to claim that FBI leadership had been altering evidence and test results for a number of years, in order to support pre-determined conclusions.[87]

Despite failing to follow-up on any of the leads that could have prevented the attacks of 9/11, D'Amuro was placed in charge of the PENTTBOM investigation immediately after the attacks.[88] PENTTBOM stood for Pentagon/Twin Towers Bombing and was notable for how quickly the case was solved. U.S. authorities claimed to have had little knowledge of or ability to stop the 9/11 attacks in advance yet, within 72 hours after the attacks, the FBI was able to identify all nineteen alleged hijackers.[89]

Giuliani's Public Image Faded as Facts Became Clearer

In the days following 9/11, Giuliani downplayed the health effects of the air in the areas surrounding Ground Zero. He said, in the first month after the attacks, "The air quality is safe and acceptable."[90] However, that was not the case and thousands of first responders have paid dearly for such false claims with their health and their lives.

Firefighter and police unions have since criticized Giuliani over the issue of protective equipment and illnesses after the attacks.[91] An October 2001 study by the National Institute of Environmental Safety and Health confirmed that workers in the cleanup operations lacked adequate protective equipment.[92] A letter from the International Association of Fire Fighters in 2007 suggested that Giuliani rushed to end the victim recovery effort after gold and silver had been recovered from World Trade Center (WTC) vaults. The letter stated that "Mayor Giuliani's actions meant that fire fighters and citizens who perished would either remain buried at Ground Zero forever, with no closure for families, or be removed like garbage and deposited at the Fresh Kills Landfill."[93]

During 9/11 Commission hearings, victims' family members interrupted to demand answers on another Giuliani-related scandal. They wanted an explanation from Giuliani for the first responders' lack of working radios. The radios used by firefighters in the WTC were a concern, and were actually known by NYC officials to be faulty as early as 1993.[94]

By April 2007, Giuliani had been forced to limit his appearances in New York City due to the increasing protests by family members of 9/11 victims, particularly police, fire and other emergency workers.[95] A general campaign sponsored by The International Association of Firefighters followed, aimed at exposing Giuliani as a fraud with respect to his 9/11 activities.[96]

All of these facts point to the need to investigate Rudy Giuliani with respect to the environmental crimes of 9/11. However, his actions and decisions related to the work at Ground Zero imply that he was hiding something greater. What needed to be hidden was evidence of the demolition of the WTC buildings.

During the cleanup of Ground Zero there were many indications that the public was being deceived. These included the discovery of foreknowledge about the destruction that originated with Rudy Giuliani, his OEM staff, and perhaps the U.S. Secret Service. Additionally, the steel was destroyed in an unprecedented manner and the black boxes were officially reported as not being found when it was clear that they had been. The restrictions on FEMA investigators and photographers and the extensive site security are all indications that something was being hidden.

These facts give us additional reasons to suspect that explosive materials were being hidden or destroyed during the cleanup. Those who were in control of Ground Zero certainly had the means and opportunity to dispose of any evidence of explosives. The opportunity came in the form of access to the highly secure site, as well as the authority to hire suspected crime syndicate companies to perform the actual cleanup. Theft of evidence by FBI agents at Fresh Kills landfill provides yet more suspicion that remnants of explosive devices were being removed.

As for motive, those who were involved in activities at the WTC site appear to have gone on to profitable partnerships with each other, with WTC tenant company representatives, and in the Middle East. Examples included Giuliani Partners like Bernard Kerik, who was promoted to work with L. Paul Bremer in Iraq, and also Mike Burton, who was hired as a Vice President at URS (Washington Group). URS and its Washington Group division are among the companies that were awarded major contracts in Iraq and that depend largely on military contracts in general.[97]

Perhaps not surprisingly, those involved with the cleanup had strong links to Saudi Arabia. This included Giuliani, whose law firm represented BCCI shortly after Giuliani led enforcement actions against that terrorist network. It also included Kerik and the British construction companies AMEC and Bovis. Kerik worked for the Saudi royal family for years and AMEC and Bovis had done significant work for the Kingdom. AMEC also went on to win enormous contracts in Iraq to renovate buildings, rebuild water and sewage networks, restore power, "and improve operations and security at military bases for the new Iraqi Armed Forces."[98]

Another company that was connected to both the cleanup of Ground Zero and the cover-up of the crimes of 9/11 was Science Applications International Corporation (SAIC). The next chapter will cover the man in charge of SAIC at the time.

Rudy Giuliani can be brought up on charges today for his participation in the deception and negligence that led to the deaths and illness of so many workers at Ground Zero. However, his actions in that regard, and his personal history, point to the possibility that he was engaged in greater crimes related to 9/11. There is no question that 9/11 provided this publicity-greedy man the ideal opportunity to grow a legend around his perceived response to those crimes. That legend has now faded into something which points toward a need to look more closely at Rudy Giuliani.

Chapter 15

Duane Andrews and SAIC

"There isn't a politically correct way to put it, but this is what needs to be said: 9/11 was a personal tragedy for thousands of families and a national tragedy for all of America, but it was very, very good for SAIC." – journalists Donald Barlett and James Steele[1]

Both before and after 9/11, one private company had a greater impact on counterterrorism programs in the Unites States than any other. That same company, Science Applications International Corporation (SAIC), also profited more from the events of 9/11 than any other. Its chief operating officer (COO), Duane Andrews, had expert-level knowledge of the vulnerabilities that were exploited on 9/11. He also happened to be a long-time, close colleague of Dick Cheney and Donald Rumsfeld.

SAIC feeds on terrorism, having won many of its record number of government contracts through the national security state that has arisen via the War on Terror. From building primary software systems for the FBI and NSA to providing the evidence for the capture of vital suspects, SAIC first helps define the problem of terrorism and then profits from that problem through contracts worth tens of billions of dollars.

As a leader in the outsourcing of U.S. military and intelligence work, SAIC exemplifies the loss of democracy inherent in the revolving door of the military-industrial-counterterrorism complex. And through its numerous contracts and employee security clearances, it has become a private business that cannot be distinguished from a permanent form of government. In short, SAIC is "the fraternal twin of the intelligence establishment."[2]

With regard to 9/11, SAIC's impact cannot be overstated as the company:

- created the national databases that tracked and identified the alleged terrorists

- supplied U.S. airports with terrorism screening equipment

- predicted and investigated terrorist attacks against U.S. infrastructure including national defense networks and the World Trade Center

- helped create the official account for what happened at the WTC both in 1993 and after 9/11

- was a leader in research on thermitic materials like those found in the WTC dust[3]

- provided the information used to capture the alleged mastermind of the attacks, Khalid Sheikh Mohammed

Furthermore, Dick Cheney's long-time protégé Duane P. Andrews ran SAIC's government business for thirteen years, from 1993 to 2006, and was therefore a principal character in these activities. During this time, Andrews was also a leading corporate representative on government commissions and task forces that evaluated threats to U.S. defense and information systems. In order to better understand Andrews' role in the failures experienced on 9/11, and to consider the need to investigate his activities further, review of his background is instructive.

From Vietnam to Cheney's Protégé

Andrews began his career like some of the other suspects, as a soldier in the last war in which the U.S. was defeated. After being commissioned in the U.S. Air Force in 1967, Andrews began "analyzing aerial image intelligence for special operations missions over Vietnam."[4] Andrews recalled that he "went to Intelligence School because I thought I was going to be in bacteriological warfare." Instead, he went into imagery analysis and "ended up in Da Nang, seeing plenty of combat."[5]

After returning from Vietnam, Andrews remained an intelligence officer in the Air Force until 1977. He then got a position as a staff member for the U.S. House Intelligence Committee. This was the congressional body assigned to oversee the secretive work of the CIA and other intelligence agencies after the scandals of the 1970s showed that those agencies could not be trusted to uphold U.S. laws. Andrews remained in this role for eleven years, rising to chief of staff for the committee.

During this time, which spanned the entirety of the Reagan Administration, Dick Cheney was a prominent member of the House Intelligence Committee along with Lee Hamilton, the future 9/11 Commission Vice-Chairman. Therefore Andrews, Cheney and Hamilton were together informed of details about the illegal Iran-Contra activities, allegations of U.S. government involvement in drug trafficking, the U.S. training and funding of the Mujahedeen in Afghanistan, and the CIA's collaboration with the terrorist network known as BCCI.[6] Andrews' role was reported to be in "cryptology, tactical intelligence and agency budgets" but, as chief of staff for the committee, he was almost certainly engaged in policy discussions.[7]

George H.W. Bush must have been impressed with his work because he nominated Andrews for the post of Assistant Secretary of Defense for Command, Control, Communications, and Intelligence (ASD/C3I). Shortly thereafter, Andrews was personally giving Secretary of Defense Dick Cheney his daily intelligence briefs. During the Gulf War, Andrews' primary role was to manage intelligence surveillance and reconnaissance operations.

Although today Andrews publicly calls for increased information security and warns about information warfare, he and Cheney used false information to start the Gulf War. This included satellite photos allegedly showing a build-up of Iraqi troops on the Saudi Arabian border, which were later proved false by St. Petersburg Times reporter Jean Heller.[8] The satellite photos, provided by the Defense Intelligence Agency (DIA), which reported through Andrews, are still classified. The false information also included the testimony of the 15-year old Kuwaiti royal, Nayirah, a cousin to Wirt Walker's colleague Mish'al Al-Sabah.

In March 1991, Andrews gained Cheney's approval to dramatically increase the powers of the DIA, in part as a way to "fend off congressionally directed change."[9] The new powers included consolidation of the review of all intelligence production and redirection of covert operations from a Soviet to a "worldwide" focus based on experiences in the Persian Gulf.[10] The DIA was later involved in tracking the alleged 9/11 hijackers through an operation called Able Danger.[11] As early as 1991, however, DCI Robert Gates began to feel threatened by the power Andrews was gaining and as a result invited him to work more closely with the CIA.[12]

In his new role as assistant secretary of defense, Andrews also oversaw CIA budgets. While he worked for Cheney, Andrews supervised Stephen Cambone, who went on to become Donald Rumsfeld's right-hand man in the George W. Bush administration.

Andrews left the Pentagon in 1993 to join SAIC as the President and COO of its Federal Business Division, which accounts for a majority of SAIC's revenues. In this role, he supervised "much of the company's work on secret projects with defense and national security agencies."[13] He was quickly asked to become a board director and was ultimately promoted to COO for the entire company.

Andrews' fellow board members during his tenure included CIA leaders like former deputy director Bobby Ray Inman, former directors Robert Gates and John Deutch, and Donald Kerr, Deputy Director of the Science and Technology Division in 2001. Other SAIC bigwigs included Admiral William Owens, who became an influential member of Rumsfeld's Defense Policy Board, and Christopher Henry, who became a key aide to Under Secretary of Defense for Policy Douglas Feith. SAIC employees included former New York City OEM director Jerome Hauer and anthrax attack suspect Stephen Hatfill.

Also having worked for SAIC was Cathal "Irish" Flynn, who until the year 2000 was Michael Canavan's predecessor in the FAA's hijack coordinator position.[14] It was Flynn who made the decision to allow passengers to carry 4-inch blades onto commercial aircraft. People who worked with Flynn said he made the exception so that passengers could "while away the time on long flights."[15] Despite his own lax approach, after the "underwear bomber" struck in late 2009, Flynn joined Brian Michael Jenkins in co-authoring a letter to the *Washington Post* that chastised U.S. leaders about airline security.[16]

Andrews described the need for the secret defense and national security projects that he managed by saying "One of the things we spotted 10 to 12 years ago [in 1990] was that we needed to deal with information security or we, as a superpower, would be put at a great disadvantage by an enemy that could attack systems effectively."[17] As a result, Andrews personally managed SAIC's programs for the National Security Agency (NSA), and other agencies within the U.S. intelligence community, in the years leading up to 9/11 and afterward.

As the man hired to defend the U.S. against attacks on its defense information systems, Andrews became a critical part of the national security apparatus. He was, more than anyone else, "the invisible hand behind a huge portion of the national security state – the one sector of the government whose funds are limitless and whose continued growth is assured every time a politician utters the word 'terrorism.'" Under Andrews, SAIC began to epitomize the essence of the "military industrial counterterrorism complex."[18] All the while, he considered Dick Cheney his personal, lifelong hero.[19]

SAIC and the Road to 9/11

SAIC also worked for many years in close partnership with oil-rich royals in the Middle East, particularly those which have become suspect with regard to 9/11. The first international contract that the company won was for training the Kuwaiti Defense Forces, starting in 1976. That was the year that the fifteen-year-old Kuwaiti royal, Mish'al Al Sabah, came to live with Wirt Walker in Washington DC. Three years later, SAIC secured its biggest and longest-lasting international contract, training the Saudi Arabian Navy. SAIC founder Robert Beyster, a former scientist from Los Alamos National Laboratory, described his pleasure at these deals in his book on the history of the company.[20]

Other high-profile projects that SAIC worked on included the cleanups after the Three Mile Island nuclear disaster and the Exxon Valdez oil spill in Alaska. The company seemed to thrive on profiting from disasters. It also built the architecture for the U.S. Strategic Air Command and Army Missile Command systems, engaged in C3I activities during the first Gulf War (when Andrews was ASD/C3I).[21]

In 1986, SAIC was hired by the Port Authority of New York and New Jersey (PANYNJ) "to conduct a general security review of the WTC" with respect to terrorism. SAIC's report rated the public areas of the WTC as very attractive targets for terrorism, emphasizing especially the basement levels.[22] Securacom, later called Stratesec, was coincidentally hired by the PANYNJ in 1991 to provide a similar review and report.

After Andrews joined the company, SAIC was hired to investigate the 1993 bombing of the WTC, an event remarkably like the one which it had foreseen.[23] Moreover, SAIC ultimately provided input that led to the official account of what happened. The company boasted that "After the 1993 World Trade Center bombing, our blast analyses produced tangible results that helped identify those responsible."[24]

In the early 1990s, SAIC was also a leader in developing technology for aviation security. At the time, SAIC had been contracted by a congressional advisory panel, led by L. Paul Bremer and Brian Michael Jenkins among others, to evaluate terrorist threats with regard to airport security.[25] By 1994, the company's explosives detection equipment was installed in major airports around the country, including in New York City, Miami, and Washington, DC.[26]

While SAIC continued training the Saudi Navy during this time, it was also bringing Saudi military personnel to company headquarters in San Diego. Meanwhile the Carlyle Group subsidiary Vinnell Corporation was training the Saudi Arabian National Guard and Booz Allen Hamilton was managing the Saudi Marine Corps and running the Saudi Armed Forces Staff College.[27] All things considered, the Saudi military was essentially a U.S. corporate-built institution and SAIC was a major contributor.

Under Andrews, SAIC was heavily focused on analyzing risks to U.S. defense information systems and led the partnership between the U.S. government and industry in that area. As the chairman of a Defense

Science Board task force on information warfare, Andrews learned about the specific vulnerabilities of U.S. national defense systems. In early 1997, he reported to Congress that U.S. defense systems were a "target-rich environment" and that attacks on certain facilities and information systems "would seriously affect the ability of the Department of Defense to carry out its assigned missions and functions."[28] Andrews went on to build and secure the Defense Information System Network (DISN). The secret component of the DISN, which was called SIPRnet, linked command and control systems throughout the United States.

As of March 2001, SAIC was also part of the National Coordinating Center for telecommunications (NCC). NCC provided oversight to the agency which, on the morning of 9/11 but before the attacks began, implemented a secret communications system called the Special Routing Arrangement Service (SRAS) for the first time. That system had been developed in conjunction with the Continuity of Government (COG) plans that Dick Cheney had worked on for nearly twenty years along with Richard Clarke, who implemented COG for the first time as the events of 9/11 proceeded.[29]

The fact that Andrews was the most knowledgeable person in terms of the vulnerabilities of information and communications networks for U.S. national security calls for further consideration. That's because so many inexplicable problems occurred with defense communications networks on 9/11, including the following.

- There were serious problems with the National Military Command Center's conference calls that morning. Important participants could not be connected or were repeatedly dropped from the calls, including the FAA.[30]

- U.S. national security facilities were in an information void on 9/11. Agencies that should have known the most about a terrorist event were blind to the ongoing attacks.[31]

- The DISN's SIPRnet did not have any information about the attacks even as late as the afternoon of 9/11[32]

- President Bush complained of poor communications in that he "could not reach key officials, including Rumsfeld" and "The line to the White House shelter conference room—and the Vice-President—kept cutting off."[33]

In addition to being a leader in identifying and mitigating risks to national security information systems, SAIC was also a pioneer in the intelligence contracting business. In 1979, as a founding member of the Security Affairs Support Association along with companies like Booz Allen Hamilton, Lockheed, and Hughes Aircraft, SAIC helped define the outsourcing policies. Yet another special task force of the Defense Science Board, led in 1993 by BDM's Philip Odeen, recommended a vast increase in the outsourcing of intelligence, which all these companies ended up benefiting from greatly.

In the mid-1990s, SAIC created the U.S. systems for tracking terrorist suspects. For the FBI, SAIC developed CODIS, the national DNA database, and NCIC, the national criminal background check system.[34] To clarify, when in August 2001 Robert Fuller of the FBI went to search for Khalid Al-Mihdhar and Nawaf Al-Hazmi's presence in the U.S. via the NCIC system, he was checking a database built by SAIC. Although Fuller claimed to have found nothing, the *9/11 Commission Report* said that such checks should have unearthed driver's licenses, car registrations, and telephone listings for Al-Mihdhar and Al Hazmi, all of which were in their names.[35] This fact alone is enough to call for the investigation of SAIC with regard to 9/11.

SAIC purchased Boeing Information Services (BIS) in 1999. BIS specialized in information systems integration, logistics, networking, and outsourcing, and dealt with management of data communications to Boeing aircraft. Its work in progress included "a five-year Defense Information Systems Network contract with the Defense Information Systems Agency," and "the Army's Reserve Component Automation System, a 12-year contract worth $1.6 billion that the company won in 1991."[36]

In 2001, Andrews was involved in several sensitive government commissions with interesting members. He was a member of the Global Organized Crime Steering Committee, with soon-to-be U.S.

Customs Commissioner Robert Bonner (who helped identify the alleged 9/11 hijackers), former Stratesec stockholder Arnaud de Borchgrave, neocon guru Fred Ikle, and former CIA directors William Webster, Robert Gates and James Woolsey.[37]

Andrews was also a member of Donald Rumsfeld's Commission to Assess National Security Space Management and Organization. This commission argued that the U.S. should avoid international agreements that limit the deployment of weapons in space, and that, in order to avoid a "Space Pearl Harbor," the U.S. needed to "develop the capability for power projection in, from, and through space."[38] As a result, SAIC's missile defense contracts tripled between 2001 and 2004, going from $47 million to $169 million in value.

Working with Andrews on the Rumsfeld Space Commission was Stephen Cambone, the Commission's staff director. Cambone had spent three years in the Cheney DOD working under Duane Andrews as director for strategic defense policy, advocating for the satellite-based missile defense system known as "Star Wars." During the years of the Clinton Administration, Cambone worked for the conservative think tank the Center for Strategic and International Studies (CSIS), where he wrote a book proposing a new structure for national security planning and another on how to avoid the impending "train wreck" in U.S. military affairs.

In January 2001, Cambone returned to the Pentagon, reporting directly to Defense Secretary Donald Rumsfeld as "Special Assistant to the Secretary and Deputy Secretary (Wolfowitz)." Reportedly, Cambone was not well-liked by the military staff. But when Rumsfeld presented the work of the Space Commission in a press conference on May 8, 2001, he brought Andrews along with him and acknowledged Cambone. Later, Cambone was confirmed as the first ever Under Secretary of Defense for Intelligence, a role in which he coordinated 85% of the U.S. intelligence budget despite having no previous intelligence experience.[39] When the 9/11 Commission requested documents from the psychological operations office of the Pentagon (SO/LIC), when that office was officially unoccupied, the requests went through Cambone.[40]

Another SAIC leader who had strong links to the events of 9/11 and the actions that followed was the company's director Wayne Downing. A member of the SAIC board from 1996 to 2001, Downing was Chairman of the Special Projects Committee, which reviewed classified programs involving special operational risks.

Like Brian Michael Jenkins, Downing was also a member of the Bremer Commission, which had defined the latest terrorism risks in June 2000. Prior to that, Downing had been the commander of U.S. Special Operations (SOCOM) during the first Gulf War and a member of the National Security Council (NSC) for George H.W. Bush. Downing rejoined the NSC immediately after the 9/11 attacks, replacing Richard Clarke.

Clarke was actually an old friend and office mate of SAIC director Downing. In his book *Against All Enemies*, Clarke wrote, "Replacing me as the senior NSC counterterrorism official was Wayne Downing, the retired four-star Army general who had led Special Operations Command. Wayne and I had first met twenty-eight years earlier when he was a young Major and I was an even younger Pentagon analyst, thrown together to share a windowless office in the bowels of the Pentagon."[41]

According to Jeff Griffith, FAA Assistant Director of Air Traffic Control, immediately following the 9/11 attacks Downing had meetings by secure video teleconference with the FAA and the White House. Those meetings covered a "lot of intelligence issues—any issues regarding the AT [air traffic] system."[42] Agencies that participated in the secure teleconferences with Downing included the Secret Service, the Joint Chiefs of Staff, the FBI, and the CIA.

During the early months after 9/11, Downing accompanied Andrews' hero Dick Cheney on "visits to the CIA to discuss U.S. intelligence on Iraq."[43] Downing then served as an unpaid adviser to Iraqi exile Ahmed Chalabi and he was an early advocate of war against Iraq.

SAIC and the WTC After 9/11

Perhaps not surprisingly, SAIC was one of the first organizations to show up at Ground Zero. The company claimed in its 2004 shareholder report that "Following the September 11, 2001, terrorist attacks, we responded rapidly to assist a number of customers near ground zero in New York City and in Washington, D.C."[44] In one of these instances, "SAIC technicians raced to Ground Zero within hours to install an *ad hoc* communications network for first responders and local financial companies."[45] Therefore, SAIC was in control of at least some of the communications at Ground Zero.

Perhaps the most interesting SAIC connection to the cleanup was John Blitch, a Lieutenant Colonel (LTC) in the U.S. Army's Special Forces, who retired from the Army just the day before 9/11. It was reported that Blitch was "filling out the paperwork in an out-processing office of the Pentagon on the morning of September 10, 2001," and that after "three years at the helm of the Defense Department's Tactical Mobile Robots Program," he was "leaving to direct the Center for Intelligent Robotics and Unmanned Systems at the Science Applications International Corporation."[46]

However, instead of traveling to his SAIC office in Colorado on 9/11 as he had planned, "Blitch scrapped the trip and headed for New York. On the road, Blitch donned his fatigues, dug out his military ID, and worked his cell phone, summoning colleagues from Florida to Boston to pack up their finest tactical robots and rendezvous at Ground Zero." And "Over the next 11 days, the group's 17 robots squeezed into spaces too narrow for humans, dug through heaps of scalding rubble, and found seven bodies trapped beneath the mountains of twisted steel and shattered concrete."[47]

An award presentation for Blitch stated that, "Within 15 minutes of the second plane crash into the WTC, Blitch called roboticists and manufacturers with field-ready robots to supplement robots donated by the federal government's Defense Applied Research Projects Agency (DARPA). He drove to New York from Washington, DC, and within six hours was met by teams from nearby companies. Eighteen hours after the attacks, robots were on the rubble pile."[48] How Blitch might have predicted, within 15 minutes of the second plane crash, that the towers would completely collapse (a process that did not begin for another 40 minutes) and generate a rubble pile to clean up, is not evident.

LTC Blitch was experienced at such search missions, having done "ground-breaking research in robot assisted search and rescue conducted during the Oklahoma City Bombing response."[49] Blitch was the former chief of unmanned systems for SOCOM during the period when Wayne Downing was SOCOM commander. Therefore Downing and Blitch had worked together before coming to SAIC.

An expert on unmanned aircraft, including Predator 2 and other drones, Blitch developed his knowledge when he led the DARPA Tactical Mobile Robots program from 1998 to 2001. [50] During this time, Blitch worked with NIST, the Commerce Department agency that wrote the final report on what happened at the WTC.[51]

In 1999, a report submitted to Blitch described laser technology being developed by the Army in partnership with Lawrence Livermore National Laboratory, where nanothermite was being developed.[52] By May 2001, laser technology was being used by Blitch's robot program. It was reported that "Robots are performing quite successfully in the field of explosive ordnance disposal (EOD)" and "EOD units [include] a laser weapon for ordnance neutralization [used to] burn unexploded ordnance."[53]

Therefore, LTC Blitch of SOCOM and SAIC had the means and opportunity to neutralize any unwanted explosives that might have been buried in the pile at Ground Zero. Environmental data generated by U.S. Environmental Protection Agency (EPA) and the University of California, Davis are supportive of the hypothesis that unexplained explosive or incendiary events were occurring at the site during the cleanup efforts. The fires in the debris pile, which were violent and long-lasting, could not be extinguished even through extreme firefighting efforts and indicted the presence of energetic materials.[54]

Could it be that SAIC, a company that benefited tremendously from the attacks and had worked on development of related explosive and incendiary materials was working to eliminate un-ignited energetic materials at Ground Zero?

SAIC has extensive links to nanothermite development and had judged related research proposals for the military and its contractors. SAIC had also been involved in developing and formulating nanothermite directly. What's more, SAIC's subsidiary Applied Ordnance Technology did research on the ignition of nanothermite with lasers.[55] Therefore the finding that thermitic materials were present in the WTC dust leads to questions about the company's involvement.

SAIC supplied the largest contingent of non-governmental investigators to the NIST WTC investigation. The SAIC employees involved in the investigation included computer programmers, project managers, public outreach personnel, graphics and writing personnel, and administrative staff. SAIC was thanked specifically for having helped with NCSTAR 1-5 and its sub-reports, which focused on the computer modeling that predicted the intensity of the fires and the structural responses to those fires.

Manufacturing and Then Profiting From War

Since 9/11, a majority of government intelligence work has been outsourced, and SAIC is the leader in that arena. SAIC sells expertise about weapons, homeland security, surveillance, computer systems, and information warfare, and it has been awarded more individual government contracts than any other private company in America.[56]

For many years, SAIC was a pioneer in the intelligence contracting business. Through September 11th, however, SAIC's power grew exponentially and it is now integral to the operations of all the major intelligence collection agencies, particularly the NSA, the National Geospatial-Intelligence Agency, and the CIA. As an example of how powerful the company has become, the CIA relies on SAIC to spy in its own workforce.[57]

SAIC has also played an integral role in the War on Terror and was even responsible for capturing Khalid Sheikh Mohammed. It was SAIC staff and technology that "tease[ed] out crucial clues about Mohammed's activities from intercepted text messages that he sent to his al Qaeda operatives using as many as 20 different cell phones."[58]

After 9/11, SAIC was hired to fix the problems it had created with terrorist tracking systems. Duane Andrews was personally in charge of the project called Trailblazer, which was originally launched in 1999 but ostensibly was not tested for operational use by the U.S. government until six years later. The system was meant to translate all NSA intercepts, including telephone, email and other electronic information, into actionable intelligence.

An oft-cited example of the failures that Trailblazer was meant to avoid was the reported incident in which messages stating "tomorrow is zero hour" and "the match begins tomorrow" were intercepted by the NSA on September 10, 2001 but not translated until September 12th. The Trailblazer system was not the answer to those problems, however, and was ultimately a total failure. After six years and $1.2 billion spent, the NSA cancelled the project in 2005.

Another huge failure led by SAIC was with the FBI system called Virtual Case File (VCF), which was intended to solve the supposed information sharing problem that prevented the FBI from tracking terrorists like Al-Mihdhar and Al-Hazmi (who lived with an FBI informant). VCF was meant to provide a centralized database of terrorism related information that all FBI agents could utilize. However, after three years and hundreds of millions in costs, VCF was written off as "the most highly publicized software failure in history."[59]

SAIC's 9/11 profiteering didn't stop there. While helping NIST to determine the causes of the WTC destruction, "SAIC personnel were instrumental in pressing the case that weapons of mass destruction existed in Iraq under Saddam Hussein, and that war was the only way to get rid of them."[60] The company helped supply the faulty intelligence claiming that Saddam had WMDs; then it profited from the invasion by generating Iraq contracts worth billions of dollars. In 2003 alone, SAIC pulled in $5.4 billion in government revenue.

But Wayne Downing was not the only SAIC representative pushing for war in Iraq. In 1998, the former United Nations weapons inspector David Kay had become director of SAIC's Center for Counterterrorism Technology and Analysis. At the time, Kay testified to Congress that Saddam Hussein "remains in power with weapons of mass destruction." For the next four years, Kay joined with Downing in leading the claims that Iraq had WMDs and was a threat to world security. Incredibly, after the U.S. invasion in 2003 found no such weapons, Kay left SAIC to head the CIA's Iraq Survey Group, which was used to officially discredit the sources of the warmongering claims that he and Downing had so eagerly promoted.[61]

Shortly after the invasion, SAIC hired Paul Wolfowitz's extra-marital girlfriend, Shaha Riza, to go to Iraq as a subject matter expert to help set-up an interim government.[62] Through unidentified channels of authority, deputy secretary Wolfowtiz had "directed SAIC to hire Riza" and had gotten her a security clearance despite the fact that she was a foreign national.[63]

In the lead-up to the U.S. invasion, SAIC was awarded a contract to help establish the Iraqi Reconstruction and Development Council. The Council was a group of Iraqi-born U.S. citizens who came to Baghdad to serve as the "Iraqi face" of the occupation authority. There they were trained for key leadership positions in Iraqi ministries.[64] At the same time, SAIC went on to work with Vinnell Corporation to train the Iraqi military.[65] The company worked there with L. Paul Bremer and, very likely, Bernard Kerik.

In 2003, SAIC was awarded a no-bid contract from the Pentagon's Joint Psychological Operations Support group to run the Iraqi Free Media Program. It was reported that SAIC was hand-picked for this program by L. Paul Bremer, despite the fact that the company had no news operations experience. The propaganda program that SAIC created was later said to be the only functioning weapon of mass destruction in Iraq. Swelling to a 5-year, $300 million contract to boost the United States' image, it called for developing slogans, advertisements, newspaper articles, radio spots, and TV programs to build support for U.S. policies in the occupied country.

With the help of SAIC, John Poindexter of Iran-Contra fame was able to convince the U.S. government to hire him to ensure "Total Information Awareness" as a result of the 9/11 attacks. Through related programs, SAIC won major contracts for management of huge IT systems that involved spying on Americans and running the Joint Intelligence Operations Centers (JIOCs).[66]

Moving Toward Knowledge and Justice

In 2006, Andrews quit SAIC to join a company called QinetiQ, which had evolved from a British Ministry of Defence program. Through its subsidiaries Apogen, Westar, Foster & Miller, and Planning Systems Inc., QinetiQ provided services in psychological warfare, information security, and electronic warfare. The company became the largest supplier of unmanned vehicles, including robots and drones, to the U.S. military and intelligence community.[67]

QinetiQ also acquired a company called Analex, which was previously called Hadron. As an employee of Hadron, which was principally owned by Earl Brian, Rudy Giuliani's Justice Department colleague Peter Videnieks had, years before, illegally transferred PROMIS software to foreign governments. According to journalist Daniel Casolaro, Earl and Videnieks were involved in a criminal conspiracy related to PROMIS, BCCI, and several deep state operations. That criminal conspiracy allegedly also involved the Wackenhut Corporation, whose director Frank Carlucci later ran the Carlyle Group.[68]

In 2003, The Carlyle Group took over control of QinetiQ as the company's new, primary shareholder. Andrews joined three years later as head of the North American division. Shortly after Andrews was hired, former CIA Director George Tenet was elected to QinetiQ's board of directors and Stephen Cambone left the Pentagon to sign on as Vice President for Strategy. Under Andrews, Cambone began to secure huge government contracts to support programs that he had set up when he was Under Secretary of Defense for Intelligence.

Recently, Andrews' division of QinetiQ was hired to provide engineering services and products to NASA's Kennedy Space Center. The contract, worth billions, calls for the development of ground systems and equipment for the processing of launch vehicles, spacecraft, and payloads; as well as flight systems support in terms of both hardware and software.[69]

Stratesec director James Abrahamson's company GeoEye worked in partnership with QinetiQ to secure oil fields in Nigeria.[70] GeoEye is a satellite-based company, providing services that increased intelligence gathering capabilities as well as enabled spying on citizens from above. Coincidentally, Abrahamson added Andrews' former DIA director (and future Director of National Intelligence) James Clapper to his board. Hopefully, these companies are not making preparations for a "Space Pearl Harbor."

Considering the incredible growth in contracts that SAIC realized from the events of 9/11, any independent investigation into those events should carefully consider the role played by that company and its leadership. Andrews and his company were integral to U.S. counterterrorism programs in the years prior to 9/11. The company's role included creating the national databases that tracked and identified terrorists, supplying airport screening equipment, predicting and investigating terrorist attacks against the WTC, helping to create the official account for what happened at the WTC after 9/11, and providing the information to capture KSM. Undoubtedly, SAIC's impact on counterterrorism programs prior to 9/11 was unique and pervasive.

Combined with the company's huge profits as a result of the attacks, a solid case can be made for the need to investigate SAIC and its leaders for conflicts of interest if not for fraud due to the failed systems that SAIC created.

Duane Andrews should be a person of interest because he had expert knowledge of the vulnerabilities of the U.S. defense and information systems at a time when many of those systems failed catastrophically. If anyone knew how to exploit weaknesses in these telecommunications and electronic systems, it was Cheney's protégé Andrews.

Chapter 16

Porter Goss and the Cover-up

Evidence has not been presented to demonstrate how the nineteen accused hijackers could have accomplished the crimes of 9/11. However, there are remarkable links between the alleged hijackers and some of the people reviewed in this book. Wirt Walker, for example, had his offices at Wiley Post Airport in OKC where some of the suspects were seen. Richard Clarke represented the UAE, the country from which the accused men traveled and their funding came. Louis Freeh and George Tenet had close relationships with Saudi Prince Bandar, whose wife was implicated in financing two of the suspects. Another example is that the Joint Congressional Inquiry into 9/11 was led by Porter Goss, the former CIA operative who represented Florida districts where many of the alleged hijackers had lived and trained.

In his book *At the Center of the Storm*, George Tenet wrote about how Pakistani ISI General Mahmud Ahmed was meeting with Congressman Goss as the first plane struck the WTC. Thirty minutes after the second plane hit, Ahmed was being chauffeured along Constitution Avenue in Washington when smoke from the Pentagon became visible.[1] Then, astonishingly, Goss showed up at the Pentagon too, and he spoke to reporters only minutes after a plane reportedly hit that building.[2]

The Goss-Ahmed meeting is interesting due to the Pakistani ISI's history with the CIA in funding and arming the "Afghan Arabs" from which al Qaeda evolved. The meeting even included discussion of Osama bin Laden, who was allegedly striking at the heart of the very capital where the attendees met.

Ahmed has been linked to accused 9/11 paymaster Omar Saeed Sheikh, and has been suspected of ordering Sheikh to wire money to Mohamed Atta before the attacks.[3] Although the latter accusation has been challenged, it seems to be an unusual coincidence that the leader of the Pakistani ISI would be present as al Qaeda's historic attack was taking place. Ahmed's meeting with Goss is also remarkable in light of Goss' history as a CIA operative.

Goss was a ten-year veteran of the CIA's clandestine operations. Later, as chairman of the House Intelligence Committee, he was responsible for most of the intelligence abuses that were identified by the 9/11 Commission investigation. Regardless of this fact, it was Goss who replaced George Tenet as DCI after Tenet resigned. As DCI, Goss continued the obstruction of the 9/11 investigations and facilitated the crimes that were committed in the name of 9/11.

Because he led the first investigation into 9/11, Goss should have been above reproach, but he was far from it. In fact, his history as a deep state operative, his proximity to the alleged hijackers, and his behavior during the investigations suggest that he might have had a role in the attacks.

The History of Porter

Goss attended Yale University, where he was a member of the secret society Book and Snake. He was also a member of the Psi Upsilon fraternity with William H.T. Bush, the brother of George H.W. Bush.[4] At Yale, Goss joined the Army Reserve Officers Training (ROTC) program and, during his junior year in 1961, was recruited by the CIA.

Over the next few years he was based at JM/WAVE, the CIA station in Miami where he worked with famous deep state operatives such as Ted Shackley. In a 2002 interview with *The Washington Post*, Goss stated that he performed "small-boat handling," leading to "some very interesting moments in the Florida Straits."[5]

It has been reported that Goss was one of the hundreds of CIA officers employed in Operation Mongoose, the covert U.S. project to displace Cuban leader Fidel Castro.[6] Vince Cannistraro, who was a CIA agent at JM/WAVE, claimed that Goss "was involved in the Bay of Pigs operation, he worked out of Miami with Cuban exiles... and took part in... attempts to overthrow Castro."[7]

Goss later acknowledged that he had recruited and run foreign agents and he said that he would be uncomfortable traveling to Cuba.[8] *Reuters* called him a "mystery man," and said that he had been "close-mouthed about his past."[9]

In an interview Goss claimed that during the 1962 Cuban missile crisis he worked for the CIA as a photo interpreter.[10] Wirt Walker's father did the same kind of work for the CIA's National Photographic Interpretation Center at the same time.[11]

Over the next decade, Goss worked for the CIA's Directorate of Operations as a covert operative in Haiti, the Dominican Republic, Mexico, and Western Europe. His primary role was to infiltrate trade unions in the fight against the perceived threat of communism.[12]

In his book, *Barry and the Boys*, journalist Daniel Hopsicker published a photograph that he had received from the wife of CIA operative and drug-trafficker Barry Seal. Hopsicker claimed that the picture "was taken at a night-club in Mexico City on January 22, 1963" and included members of a team called Operation 40. One of these men, according to Hopsicker, was Porter Goss.[13]

Operation 40 was a CIA-sponsored team of operatives accused of conducting assassinations. According to a senior member of the Cuban security apparatus, it was funded by an "important group of businessmen headed by George Bush (Snr.) and Jack Crichton, both Texas oilmen."[14] Operation 40 would assassinate military or political members of a target foreign country, as well as those suspected of being agents of those foreign countries.[15] There have even been suspicions that the group was involved in the assassination of President Kennedy.[16]

Frank Sturgis, one of the "plumbers" who broke into the Democratic National Committee headquarters at the Watergate hotel in 1972, later admitted to having been part of Operation 40.[17] Other infamous CIA operatives who belonged to the group were Thomas Clines and Ted Shackley.

In 1970, Goss came down with a bacteriological infection that nearly killed him. The following year he left the CIA and purchased a home on Sanibel Island in Florida. Starting in 1974 he spent eight years in Sanibel City government. Then, in an unusual move by then Governor Bob Graham, Republican Goss was appointed to fill a Democrat vacancy as commissioner of Lee County.

Later, in 1988, Goss was elected to the U.S. Congress as a Republican representative from the 13th district. The 13th district included Venice, where Huffman Aviation was located. After the district was re-zoned, Goss became the representative from district 14, where he was re-elected four times. In the few years prior to 9/11, the alleged terrorists used Goss' district, in Charlotte County, as one of their main bases of operations.[18]

The area that Goss represented was known for a long history of CIA-linked drug running. In fact, the man who ran Huffman Aviation, the flight school where Mohamed Atta and friends trained, was arrested for drug trafficking in 2012.[19] That was not surprising given that "three weeks after Atta showed up at Huffman Aviation, the flight school's owner, Wally Hilliard, had his Learjet (N351WB) seized on a runway at Orlando Executive Airport. It was carrying 43 lbs of heroin."[20]

The drug-trafficking in Goss' district went on while he was the congressional representative there, and while the brother of Stratesec's Marvin Bush, Jeb Bush, was governor. What's more, Jeb Bush was noted arriving at Huffman Aviation, within a day after the 9/11 attacks, to recover and escort documents from Huffman Aviation back to Washington.[21]

The history of covert drug operations in that area went back at least 60 years. The tiny Venice Airport, where the alleged hijackers trained, originated as the Venice Army Airfield and was the home of the operatives who worked for General Claire Chennault.[22] Civil Air Transport, the successor to Chennault's Flying Tigers and the world's largest heroin-trafficking operation at the time, transported the drugs that funded the early covert operations of the CIA, and those airmen worked closely with organized crime while doing so.[23]

In *American War Machine*, Peter Dale Scott described how many covert U.S. operations since World War II have been intimately connected with, even dependent on, illicit drug trafficking. From Mexico to Laos and Vietnam, and more recently in Afghanistan, a "shadow CIA" has worked with organized crime figures and banking networks like BCCI to use drug money to undermine democracy.[24] Such deep state operations have been overlooked by those responsible for oversight of related U.S. intelligence and military operations.

In 1996, Goss became chairman of the House Permanent Select Committee on Intelligence. That same year, Goss made a concerted effort to support Newt Gingrich during a House Ethics Committee tax fraud investigation. As a member of the committee, Goss refused to remove himself from the process despite his financial support for Gingrich's political action group. Goss then wrote a letter urging Republican representatives to support Gingrich for the Speaker of the House.

Later, Goss oversaw the House Intelligence Committee's inquiry into the drug and gun trafficking that supported the Nicaraguan Contras. This scandal had been exposed a decade earlier by Senator John Kerry's Senate investigation.[25] The Goss inquiry covered-up the CIA's involvement and ignored the evidence that Vice President Bush was involved.[26]

In the years just after 9/11, Goss continued to be a stalwart defender of the new Bush Administration's policies and plans. He supported the deceptions used to terrify Americans about Iraq's nonexistent weapons of mass destruction. He repeated false claims that Iraq and Saddam Hussein were behind the 9/11 attacks.[27] He promoted the idea that Syria and Iran needed to be attacked to defend American interests.[28] And he covered-up the use of White House-approved torture.[29]

Goss made a statement regarding U.S. intelligence activity on terrorism in the summer of 2001, saying that the "chatter level [went] way off the charts" around this time and continued until 9/11.[30] Due to Goss' role as chairman of the House Intelligence Committee, he would have been expected to know such things.

However, between January 1998 and the attacks, Goss's House Intelligence Committee held just two hearings on terrorism.[31] Despite his own lax approach to the subject, after the 1998 bombings of the U.S. embassies in Africa, Goss declared that the CIA had become too "gun-shy."[32]

In August 2001, Goss traveled, along with Senators Jon Kyl and Bob Graham, to Pakistan to meet with President Pervez Musharraf. Perhaps coincidentally, Senator Kyl's state of Arizona was another major base of operations for the alleged 9/11 hijackers, as described in part by FBI agent Ken Williams' famous Phoenix Memo.

Taliban leaders were involved in Goss' Pakistan meeting, which included discussions about extraditing Bin Laden. But apparently no agreements were made and Pakistan opted to stay neutral. George Tenet didn't get what he wanted from General Ahmed either, having made a trip to Pakistan only three months earlier to meet with the ISI director. As with Goss' August meeting, Ahmed was reportedly not willing to cooperate with Tenet on issues related to Bin Laden.[33]

According to Graham, in the September 11 meeting with Ahmed they "were talking about terrorism, specifically terrorism generated from Afghanistan" and how the U.S. wanted more support from Pakistan in the hunt for Bin Laden.[34] Reportedly, Ahmed said Pakistan would not help unless the U.S. lifted economic sanctions against Pakistan.[35]

Just two years earlier, FBI informant Randy Glass had gained some interesting information from Pakistani ISI agent Rajaa Gulum Abbas. As Glass, Abbas and two others were having dinner in a New York City restaurant surrounded by undercover FBI agents, Abbas pointed to the WTC and said, "Those towers are coming down."[36] Abbas later made two other references to an attack on the WTC. Glass sent this information to Senator Graham in August 2001, yet it is not clear whether Graham and Goss brought this foreknowledge up at either their meeting in Pakistan or with ISI chief Ahmed on the morning of 9/11.[37]

The attacks of 9/11 certainly changed Pakistan's tune. Shortly after 9/11, under pressure from Washington, President Musharraf fired Ahmed and announced sweeping changes within the country. He outlawed several Islamic groups and instituted laws preventing the building of any new mosques in the country without government permission.[38] Within days of the attacks, Bush responded by lifting the economic sanctions against Pakistan.[39]

At the same time, people were beginning to question what the Bush Administration might have known about a potential al Qaeda hijacking plot. As a member of Congress presumed to be independent of the Administration despite his history of supporting the Bush clan, Goss shouted down the accusations: "The only thing that this uproar does is give aid and comfort to the enemy and I don't think there's anybody who wants to give aid and comfort to the terrorists," said Goss.[40] By that time, he was leading the first official inquiry into the attacks.

The Joint Congressional Inquiry

In the months following 9/11, both Goss and Senator Graham rejected calls for an investigation.[41] However, in December the Senate voted for one anyway, which led both Bush and Cheney to attempt to stop it or limit its scope. After consultations with Cheney, Senate leader Tom Daschle agreed to an inquiry that would be restricted to intelligence issues only. Moreover, it would be conducted by the House and Senate committees which had overseen the related intelligence work. The Inquiry was announced on Valentine's Day, 2002, more than five months after the attacks.

Goss immediately made it clear that the Inquiry would not be looking for guilt or accountability with regard to 9/11. Saying he was "looking for solutions, not scapegoats," Goss continued to defend the White House with regard to warnings the president had received about an impending attack, saying it was "a lot of nonsense."[42] Throughout the inquiry, the approach taken by Goss and Graham was one of uncritical deference to the Bush Administration and the intelligence community.

As discussed in Chapter 4, the FBI refused to cooperate. One glaring example of this was that the Bureau would not allow Inquiry staff to interview Abdussattar Shaikh, the FBI informant that two of the alleged hijackers had lived with in San Diego. The FBI also refused to serve a deposition notice and subpoena on the informant, despite knowing where he was.[43]

Not only that, although the Joint Inquiry agreed to serve only written interrogatories on the informant, and the FBI had agreed to that plan, Shaikh's lawyer later said that his client would not respond to the interrogatories. The attorney also warned that, if subpoenaed, Shaikh would be unwilling to testify unless he was granted immunity.

According to the final report from the Joint Inquiry, when interviewed by the FBI Shaikh gave inaccurate information and had an "inconclusive" polygraph examination about his foreknowledge of the 9/11 attacks. Apparently, some FBI agents believed that Shaikh had knowledge not only of the two alleged hijackers with whom he lived, but also of alleged pilot Hani Hanjour.[44]

The Joint Inquiry's passive response to Shaikh's lack of cooperation was astonishing. It cannot be reconciled with the approach that Goss and the intelligence agencies took with other persons of interest. This informant clearly had more information and stronger links to the alleged hijackers than almost anyone. Yet the FBI was intent on protecting him and the Joint Inquiry, led by Porter Goss, allowed that protection.

Although torture should never be condoned, the public must wonder why authorities did not simply arrest and torture this man as they did so many others. How can this preferential treatment of Shaikh, someone who obviously knew something about al Qaeda operatives, be reconciled with the treatment of other "persons of interest"? Shaikh was handled as if he was too important to be troubled, whereas people like Abu Zubaydah, who turned out to not have any connection to al Qaeda, were treated horrendously. This difference might have had something to do with Shaikh's ties to Saudi Arabia.

As reviewed in Chapters 4 and 6, the Saudi who brought Al-Mihdhar and Al-Hazmi to San Diego to live with Shaikh was Omar Al-Bayoumi. Previously the subject of an FBI investigation, Al-Bayoumi appeared to be a Saudi intelligence agent. He was associated with the Saudi Civilian Aviation Administration and Dallah AVCO Trans Arabia Company.[45] Dallah was owned by Sheikh Saleh Abdullah Kamel, a member of the Golden Chain who was suspected of having provided financial backing for al Qaeda.[46]

In November 2002, an FBI official sent a letter to Graham and Goss saying, "the Administration would not sanction a staff interview with [Abdussattar Shaikh], nor did the Administration agree to allow the FBI to serve a subpoena or a notice of deposition on [him]." The letter caused Graham to comment, "We were seeing in writing what we had suspected for some time: the White House was directing the cover-up."[47]

However, the Joint Inquiry rolled over on other important issues. As stated in Chapter 5, the Inquiry could not convince DCI Tenet to be interviewed, and operational cables and certain other documents could not be viewed other than at CIA headquarters. Further restrictions included that no copies could be made. Clearly, protecting the CIA's secrets was more important than the safety of potential victims of terrorism.

As with the CIA, the FBI would not allow the Joint Inquiry to take notes on or make copies of documents deemed sensitive by the Bureau. This restricted the Inquiry's ability to complete its charter, which was very limited to begin with. Yet Goss did not complain.

The FBI took the same approach with the 9/11 Commission. According to author Philip Shenon, the FBI was "as uncooperative with the 9/11 Commission as it had been in the Congressional investigation" and was "painfully slow to meet the Commission's initial request for documents and interviews."[48]

It was claimed by insiders that Goss and Graham exercised "near total control over the panel, forbidding the inquiry's staff to speak to other lawmakers."[49] Other members of the Inquiry complained that the two co-chairmen withheld information and controlled the process. One way in which Graham and Goss controlled the investigation was to ask the FBI to look into panel members who might have leaked information.[50] This resulted in the FBI investigating the Inquiry as the Inquiry was investigating the FBI.

Goss and Graham, who represented the areas where CIA operations and drug-running had become common and terrorist training had occurred, wanted to keep the facts about 9/11 under wraps. They were, however, curiously coy about one major U.S. ally: Saudi Arabia.

The report from the Joint Inquiry, which was partially released in December 2002 and then finalized in July 2003, appeared to imply Saudi government involvement in the 9/11 attacks. A significant section of the report, 28-pages in length, was never released but hints were made that it contained evidence implicating the Saudis.[51] The report, however, said nothing about the probable links between the Pakistani government, including General Ahmed's ISI, and al Qaeda.

Senator Graham continued for the next decade to suggest that Saudi Arabia may have played a role in the 9/11 attacks.[52] Others like Richard Clarke joined Graham in making these suggestions, yet they always seemed to ignore the many interesting connections between U.S. leaders and Saudi Arabian royals.[53]

Shortly after the public release of the Inquiry's final report, the *Los Angeles Times* claimed that "for all that it answers about the attacks, the nearly 900-page report is stocked with reminders of the many questions that remain—about other puzzling aspects of the plot, the possible role of foreign governments, and even such politically charged matters as what Presidents Clinton and Bush had been told about al-Qaeda."[54]

Goss replied, "I can tell you right now that I don't know exactly how the plot was hatched. I don't know the where, the when and the why and the who in every instance. That's after two years of trying. And we will someday have the documents to exploit, we will have the people to interrogate, we will have ways to get more information to put the rest of the pieces of this puzzle on the table. But right now, we don't have it."[55]

Years later, Graham claimed that the White House had disrupted the Inquiry's work. He said, "Looking back at it, I think we were clearly set up by Dick Cheney and the White House. They wanted to shut us down. And they wanted to shut down a legitimate Congressional inquiry that might raise questions in part about whether their own people had aggressively pursued al-Qaeda in the days prior to the September 11 attacks. The vice president attempted to manipulate the situation, and he attempted to manipulate us. But if his goal was to get us to back off, he was unsuccessful." According to Graham, Goss was of the same opinion.[56]

Goss agreed that he and Graham were of like mind, even to the point of saying they were "like Frick and Frack" at the time of the inquiry.[57] But the idea that Goss felt obstructed by the White House does not make sense in view of Goss' own actions.

For one thing, as a congressman Goss had been, and would continue to be, essentially a Bush Administration cheerleader. Additionally, there was no evidence that Goss was in any way interested in achieving truth or justice with regard to the crimes of 9/11.

An example, as stated in Chapter 5, was that the CIA's IG report on 9/11 originally called for accountability with respect to certain individuals including DCI Tenet. In 2004, DCI Goss changed that wording to call for "accountability boards" to be formed at a later date. Then in 2005, when the revised report came out, Goss removed the accountability boards altogether.

The Inquiry protected not only the CIA and FBI, however. The Inquiry's report also concealed the possible involvement of the United Arab Emirates. The report noted the FBI claim that "[t]he operational planning for the September 11th attacks took place in overseas locations, most notably Germany, Malaysia and the United Arab Emirates." This is remarkable in that the report went on to make detailed comments in subsequent sections on Malaysia and Germany, but, tellingly, ignored the UAE entirely.[58]

A similar example was the Joint Inquiry's treatment of the ease with which the alleged hijackers received their travel visas. After noting that special treatment was given to visa applicants from two countries, the report asked why, considering that the "pervasiveness in Saudi Arabia of Wahhabism, a radical, anti-American variant of Islam, was well-known before 9/11."[59] Saudi Arabia was singled out, but the same tough questions were not asked of the second country, the UAE. Neither Richard Armitage nor his subordinate, former Sears World Trade executive Grant Green, were examined at all—despite having overseen the Bureau of Consular Affairs which issued the visas.

Was the preferential treatment of the UAE a result of the close relationship that Richard Clarke had with its leaders? More specifically, was Clarke's relationship merely a result of the fact that the UAE owned BCCI and therefore was able to finance and conduct CIA-like covert operations as part of a private or officially-sanctioned network? In other words, was 9/11 a CIA-like operation conducted with the help of countries that the Joint Inquiry failed to criticize – Pakistan and the UAE?

Considering these shortcomings should lead investigators to review where the evidence against the accused terrorists originated. Some of it, as with the magic passport found at the WTC, was provided by organizations like the NYC Police Department, which were controlled by suspects such as Rudy Giuliani. Most of the remaining evidence came from the FBI and the CIA but often originated in the UAE and in Florida.

As discussed earlier, the UAE was the source of the much of the alleged funding of the alleged hijackers. And evidence concerning the travel of the accused was traced back to the UAE, as all but three of the nineteen alleged hijackers traveled through the UAE on their way to the United States.

Porter Goss' home district was the primary base for Atta and Al-Shehhi, two of the alleged pilots. Many of the alleged hijackers stayed in Florida, however, and some were said to have trained at the Pensacola Air Base. In fact, much of the evidence that established the official account about the accused men came from Florida.[60] Twelve of the young men were said to have opened bank accounts in Florida, primarily through one institution – SunTrust Bank. Deposits made to these accounts often came from the United Arab Emirates.[61]

Like Khalid Sheikh Mohammed, many of the alleged hijackers seemed to live more like playboys than devout Muslims. Their behavior, associations, and dress habits indicated that they might be members of an organized crime syndicate, or a covert network of operatives.[62] That makes some sense, considering that the old covert operative Porter Goss, who represented the areas where the accused lived and trained, did not seem to want to find the truth about the crimes for which they were accused.

290

The 9/11 Commission

Taking off from where the Joint Inquiry had left off, the 9/11 Commission accepted the Inquiry's findings uncritically and staffed its investigation with many of the same people.

The Commission's stated charter was to "provide the fullest possible account of the events surrounding 9/11."[63] The Commission's leaders, Thomas Kean and Lee Hamilton, claimed their investigation would be much broader than that of the Inquiry. Kean suggested the Inquiry's mandate covered only "one-seventh or one-eighth" of what the Commission's investigation would cover.[64]

In the end, however, the 9/11 Commission addressed less than one third of the questions posed by the 9/11 victims' family members.[65] It seemed that, as late as fourteen months after the attacks, the U.S. government had by its own admission examined only a small fraction of the facts surrounding 9/11. After the Commission's report was issued, it was clear that not much more had been done.

Like the Joint Inquiry, the Commission did not seem to have any intention of revealing the facts about 9/11. This was evident from the start in that the Commission's executive director, Philip Zelikow, had prepared a full outline of the final report, complete with headings and sub-headings, *before* any investigation had occurred. This pre-conceived outline was shared with Kean and Hamilton but kept secret from the staff throughout the investigation.[66]

Throughout the investigation, each of the commissioners was invited to have private meetings with Donald Rumsfeld. These meetings often "took the form of breakfasts or lunches in a room next to Rumsfeld's office at the Pentagon."[67] Rumsfeld gave the commissioners advice, for instance urging them to not issue interim reports.[68] This was despite the fact that, with only a few months to go, Rumsfeld's DOD had failed to provide many of the documents that had been requested and Commission staffers were recommending the issuance of subpoenas.

The Joint Inquiry treated the 9/11 Commission with the same uncooperative attitude that it had accepted from the CIA and FBI. Kean and Hamilton wrote that they had to personally reach out to

Goss six months after their investigation first began to request access to Inquiry documents. Although they were allowed to review the declassified parts of the Inquiry's report, only at Joint Inquiry's offices, they were not allowed access to the supporting materials.[69]

The Commission found creative ways to get around its challenges though. One way was a tried-and-true method of claiming that no evidence could be found. That was the method used by the Warren Commission, recalled by President Ford. Ford said his Commission was "very careful to say we 'found' no evidence."[70]

As mentioned in Chapter 1, the phrase "we found no evidence" appears in the *9/11 Commission Report* three dozen times. This seems to be an unusually high number of instances begging ignorance, given that the Commission claims to have done "exacting research" in the production of a report that was the "fullest possible accounting of the events of September 11, 2001."[71]

The number of times these "we found no evidence" disclaimers appear in the report is doubly amazing considering how infrequently some of the most critical witnesses and evidence are referenced. For example, the FAA's national operations manager, Benedict Sliney, who was coordinating the FAA's response that day, appears only once in the narrative (and twice in the notes). And the FAA's hijack coordinator, Michael Canavan, appears only twice in the narrative, with neither of those citations having anything to do with his assigned role as the key link between the military and the FAA. This is stunning given that it was Canavan's failure which allowed the attacks to succeed, according to the Commission.

Some of the instances in which the Commission claimed to have "found no evidence" were used to conceal the fact that it has never been explained how the alleged hijackers entered the cockpits of any of the hijacked planes. As discussed in Chapter 10, this might not have been an issue with respect to the actual operation if the perpetrators had utilized existing technology to remotely control the aircraft.

Insider trading was another area of the investigation for which the Commission claims to have found no evidence. The Commission reported that "Exhaustive investigations by the Securities and Exchange Commission, FBI, and other agencies have *uncovered no evidence* that anyone with advance knowledge of the attacks profited through securities transactions."[72]

However, the "exhaustive investigations" conducted by the FBI, on which the *9/11 Commission Report* was based, were clearly bogus. The FBI did not interview the suspects and did not appear to compare notes with the 9/11 Commission to help make a determination if any of the people being investigated had ties to al Qaeda. The Commission's memorandum summary on the subject suggests that the FBI simply made decisions on its own regarding the possible connections of the suspects and the alleged terrorist organizations. Those unilateral decisions were not appropriate, as at least three of the trades involved suspicious links to Osama bin Laden or his family. Another suspect was a soon-to-be convicted criminal who had direct links to FBI employees who were later arrested for securities-related crimes.[73]

The FBI also claimed in August 2003 that it had no knowledge of hard drives recovered from the WTC, which were publicly reported in 2001. According to the people who retrieved the associated data, the hard drives gave evidence for "dirty doomsday dealings."[74]

The evidence for informed trading on 9/11 includes many financial vehicles, from stock options to Treasury bonds to credit card transactions made at the WTC just before it was destroyed. Financial experts from around the world have since provided strong evidence, through established and reliable statistical techniques, that the early suspicions were correct and 9/11 informed (possibly insider) trading did occur.[75]

Another area where the Commission could not seem to find evidence was in the false claims about the air quality at Ground Zero. These false claims, made by Rudy Giuliani and Christine Todd Whitman (previously of Rumsfeld's Office of Economic Opportunity), contributed to the deaths of thousands of first responders. The Commission wrote that "Although Whitman told us she spoke with White House senior economic advisor Lawrence Lindsay regarding the need to get the markets open quickly" – *"We found no evidence* of pressure on EPA to say the air was safe in order to permit the markets to open.*"76*

Like other carefully worded claims in the *9/11 Commission Report*, this might be technically true but the premise is probably false. Whitman, who was director of the U.S. Environmental Protection Agency just after 9/11, did claim that the air in lower Manhattan was safe to breathe when it was known that was not the case. This was probably not done solely for the purpose of re-opening the stock market, however. It is more likely that these false claims were made in order to expedite the removal of evidence at the WTC site.

Findings No Longer Supported

Today, one forgotten prisoner provides a startling contradiction to the official account and the myth of al Qaeda. This is Abu Zubaydah, a man once called al-Qaeda's "chief of operations."

As discussed in Chapter 5, information allegedly obtained from Zubaydah's torture played a large part in the creation of the official account of 9/11 and in the justification for the continued use of torture. Yet in September, 2009, the U.S. government admitted that Zubaydah was never a member or associate of al Qaeda at all. These facts raise an alarming number of questions about the veracity of our knowledge about al Qaeda, and the true identity of the people who are said to be behind the 9/11 attacks.

The 9/11 Commission called Zubaydah an "Al Qaeda associate," a "long-time ally of Bin Ladin," a "Bin Ladin lieutenant," and an "al Qaeda lieutenant."77

Other claims made by the 9/11 Commission were that "KSM and Zubaydah each played key roles in facilitating travel for al Qaeda operatives," and that "Zubaydah had been a major figure in the millennium plots." These claims were said to be supported primarily by the torture testimony of Zubaydah and others, and by Zubaydah's diary.

In an amazing turnabout in 2009, an attorney for Zubaydah wrote in *The Guardian* that the majority of the accusations against Zubaydah were understood by all parties to be false. In fact, he wrote, they "were known to be false when uttered."[78] Attorney Brent Mickum said that his client, said to be the "number three man in al Qaeda," was never a member or associate of al Qaeda and that "These facts really are no longer contested: [Zubaydah] was not, and never had been, a member of either the Taliban or al-Qaida. The CIA determined this after torturing him extensively." In fact, he "was never a member or a supporter of any armed forces that were allied against the United States," and he was never the "head of a military camp that trained terrorists. That allegation is false at all levels."[79]

As of September 2009, the U.S. government agreed that Zubaydah was never an al Qaeda operative. In response to Zubaydah's *habeas corpus* petition, the government indicated that Abu Zubaydah had never been a member of al-Qaeda, nor was he involved in the attacks on the African embassies in 1998, or the attacks on the United States on September 11, 2001.[80]

In order to better understand just how much Zubaydah meant as a primary source for the official account of 9/11, one must review the extensive claims made about Zubaydah by the U.S. government and mainstream media over the years. The 9/11 Commission called Zubaydah an "al Qaeda lieutenant." The Joint Congressional Inquiry did the same, calling him "al-Qa'ida leader Abu Zubaydah," and the "Bin Ladin lieutenant captured in March 2002." As late as 2006, the 9/11 report from the Justice Department's Inspector General called Zubaydah a "Bin Laden lieutenant."

Because Zubaydah was never an al Qaeda operative, or even an al Qaeda associate, the public is now forced to realize that all of these claims were false. The questions that should arise from that realization include: How much of the commonly held myth about al Qaeda, and how much of the War on Terror, was built on the torture testimony of a man who clearly could not have known anything about al Qaeda?

Originally, it was said that it was Zubaydah who first identified KSM as the Bin Laden associate called "Mukhtar." This was according to Ali

Soufan, the FBI official who first interrogated him at a secret CIA site in Thailand. Soufan also claimed that Zubaydah said KSM was the "mastermind" behind the 9/11 attacks. In his 2007 book, CIA director Tenet went further, claiming that "interrogating Abu Zubaydah led to Ramsi bin al Shibh."[81]

But the CIA reportedly told Abu Zubaydah during his interrogation that they had discovered he was not an al-Qaeda fighter, partner, or even a member.[82] Still, KSM and Bin Al-Shibh were caught and tortured too.

The official account of 9/11 was largely based on third-hand accounts of what these tortured detainees had allegedly said, with "two of the three parties in the communication being government employees."[83] The Commission itself indicated that "Chapters 5 and 7 rely heavily on information obtained from captured al Qaeda members."[84]

The truth is, however, that more than half of the *9/11 Commission Report* is based on completely unreliable torture testimony to which the Commission had absolutely no access – not even through interviews with the interrogators. KSM's torture testimony is referred to 221 times in the report, and that of Bin Al-Shibh is referred to 73 times. The Commission used one or more of these "interrogations" as its source a total of 441 times in its report footnotes.

These facts call for a complete re-evaluation of the official myth of al Qaeda and the findings of the 9/11 Commission.

The WTC Cover-up

One of the many aspects of 9/11 that was never mentioned by the 9/11 Commission was WTC Building 7.

This could be due to the fact that most people who view the video of that 47-story building, which fell into its own footprint at 5:20 in the afternoon on 9/11, immediately recognize it as a demolition event. It could also be that the Commission realized there was no other way to explain it.

Attempts to explain the destruction of the three WTC buildings began when four engineers showed up within a few days of the attacks. These were Gene Corley, who led the cover-up investigation of the OKC bombing event, and the three people who helped him in that endeavor: Charles Thornton, Mete Sozen, and Paul Mlakar. As leader of the Pentagon engineering assessment, Mlakar was reviewed in Chapter 10.

For the WTC, Corley and company came up with a series of failed explanations, including what was called the Pancake Theory.[85] But it is the falsity of the official reports later produced by the National Institute of Standards and Technology (NIST), for which Corley played only supporting roles, that is of interest today. See the bibliography for more information.

WTC Building 7 gives investigators a simple starting point to reconsider the events in New York City. Apart from the sudden onset, the completely symmetrical fall in a matter of seconds, and the small rubble pile, many people were told that WTC 7 would come down before it actually did. In fact, over 60 firefighters and 25 emergency medical staff were told to leave the area and they testified to a count-down and/or explosions going off.[86] Additionally, both the CNN and BBC networks reported that this building had already collapsed 25 minutes before it actually did.[87]

That's incredible not simply because news people apparently predicted which one of the many other buildings in the area would fall. It is even more remarkable because no one could have predicted the sequence of events that led to this building falling, at least the sequence given by the official NIST report.

In 2008, after seven years of waiting, NIST finally put out its official report on WTC 7. That report said that normal office fires caused fully fireproofed steel beams to fail in one area of the building, and that's what led to this entire structure falling uniformly into a neat rubble pile. To reiterate, the official story of the "collapse" of WTC 7 is that a typical office fire caused this 47-story building to fall in a matter of seconds.

Therefore, accepting the NIST WTC 7 report would require concluding that no tall buildings are safe from the possibility of total unexpected collapse due to the smallest of office fires. All tall buildings experience office fires at some point; therefore it must be assumed that what happened to WTC 7 can happen again at any time.

There are many reasons to suspect that we are safe from such disasters, however. The obviously false nature of the NIST WTC reports is one reason. The fact that building professionals around the world have not taken those reports seriously is another. That is, building codes have not been updated to address the root causes given by the NIST WTC reports, and therefore there is no reason to consider those root causes as valid.[88]

Additionally, NIST now agrees that WTC 7 experienced free-fall over a vertical distance of at least 8 floors.[89] That is physically impossible without the instantaneous removal of the associated 8-story structure, and instantaneous removal can only be accomplished through demolition.

Who was involved in producing false reports for the WTC? At the time of the WTC investigation, NIST reported to George W. Bush's old friend, oil industry executive Donald Evans. In the 2000 presidential election, Evans was Bush's campaign chairman. As Secretary of Commerce in 2001, Evans led NIST and was also a member of the National Security Council Principals Committee.

Working for Evans at NIST was the agency's director, Arden Bement, who had been appointed by George W. Bush within weeks after 9/11. Like many of the NIST investigators, Bement had an interesting background including that he was a director at Battelle Memorial Institute which managed U.S. national laboratories. Battelle had oversight for both the U.S. Army's Fort Detrick facility, to which the anthrax attacks were traced, as well as the U.S. Department of Energy laboratories where nanothermite was developed.[90]

In November 2004, Bement was replaced by Hratch Semerjian, who took over the WTC investigation until the completion of the WTC

298

reports. Semerjian had co-authored ten academic papers with the world's leading expert on nanothermite, Michael Zachariah.[91]

Support for the NIST WTC reports came from a few questionable sources. For example, the companies that worked with NIST on the reports provided supportive comments.[92] And as discussed in Chapter 1, certain media sources were enlisted to boost public perception of the process with each politically-convenient issuance of a NIST report or update.[93]

A Job Well Done

In sum, Porter Goss was certainly not responsible for all the deception behind the official account of 9/11. But he led the way. At the very least, as a long-time deep state operative he knew what not to ask questions about and when to attack those who did.

A month after the *9/11 Commission Report* was issued, George W. Bush announced that Goss was his nominee to become the next Director of the CIA. The appointment was pushed by Dick Cheney.

At the time, former CIA analyst Ray McGovern reported that Goss "has long shown himself to be under the spell of Vice President Dick Cheney."[94] Democrats who had been involved in intelligence matters said of the nomination that "Goss was unwilling to pursue matters that could cause him problems with the vice-president's office."[95]

After becoming DCI in September 2004, Goss filled that promise by telling CIA staff that their job was "to support the Bush administration and its policies in our work."[96] Some senior CIA officers who had opposed the Iraq War resigned. This included Michael Scheuer, the former head of Alec Station (the Bin Laden-focused station). The former head of the CIA's CTC, Vince Cannistraro, said of Goss' approach that "It can only be interpreted one way – there will be no more dissenting opinions."[97]

As DCI, Goss was known for blocking investigations. He blocked house investigations into the Abu Ghraib prisoner abuse scandal and the Bush Administration's links with its Iraqi ally Ahmad Chalabi.[98] He denounced the Abu Ghraib revelations as a political "circus." In the case of the leak of CIA covert agent Valerie Plame's identity, Goss denounced her complaint as mere "partisan politics," not a "worry about national security." And he later supported the destruction of the CIA's torture tapes that had formed the basis of the *9/11 Commission Report.*[99]

Goss resigned as DCI in May 2006 under uncertain circumstances. The *Los Angeles Times* reported that he "was pushed out by [Director of National Intelligence John] Negroponte after clashes between them over Goss' management style, as well as his reluctance to surrender CIA personnel and resources to new organizations set up to combat terrorism and weapons proliferation." Others said Goss resigned as a result of the investigation of CIA official Kyle Foggo, who had been accused of improperly coordinating a $2.4 million contract for a close college friend.

In the end, however, it just seemed that the job Goss came to do was done. He had successfully helped the Bush Administration ride out the storm of initial 9/11 questions and helped to cover-up the war-mongering lies that were born from 9/11. Despite having been a long-time covert operative himself, he never once questioned if 9/11 had been an operation influenced or facilitated by U.S. or other government operatives.

Chapter 17

Conclusions and Next Steps

This book has shown that there are powerful people who had the means, motive and opportunity to accomplish the crimes of 9/11. Nineteen suspects were reviewed and reasons to investigate or bring charges against them were emphasized in each case. All of these men were linked in one way or another to Dick Cheney and Donald Rumsfeld, who were in perfect position on 9/11 to coordinate the attacks.

Cheney led the campaign of lies behind the first Gulf War and twelve years later he and Rumsfeld led a more intensive campaign of lies to start the disastrous Iraq War. In between these deceptions were the crimes of 9/11, in which Cheney and Rumsfeld were found to be central characters in a series of inexplicable failures to defend the nation. Therefore, this discussion of alternate 9/11 suspects began with a review of the histories of an "alternate OBL and KSM"—Dick and Don—in order to set the stage.

Frank Carlucci and Richard Armitage, deep state operatives who were old colleagues of Cheney and Rumsfeld, were examined. It was shown that both of these men had links to 9/11 and both were in positions to continue the illegal activities for which they had become known. Carlucci was meeting with a member of the Bin Laden family on 9/11, and had been the employer of Stratesec COO Barry McDaniel. Armitage was among those in the secure video teleconference who failed to defend the nation that morning, and his State Department had issued visas to the alleged hijackers.

The first of the major aspects of 9/11 that was left unaddressed by the official investigations was the failure of U.S. authorities to stop the attacks. Recalling those unexplained aspects as given in Chapter 1:

1. The many opportunities for U.S. intelligence agencies to track down and capture the alleged hijackers should have resulted in the attacks being stopped before they happened.

In Chapters 4 and 5, two U.S. intelligence community leaders were reviewed with regard to the lack of action taken in response to terrorism. That discussion began with Louis Freeh, who was Director of the FBI from 1993 to June 2001.

Under Freeh, the FBI failed miserably at preventing terrorism when preventing terrorism was the Bureau's primary goal. The actions of FBI management suggest that it was facilitating and covering-up acts of terrorism throughout the time that Freeh was the Bureau's director. Additionally, the FBI took extraordinary measures to hide evidence related to the 9/11 attacks and was remarkably uncooperative with the investigations.

CIA Director George Tenet was responsible for an agency that hyped the threat of terrorism yet failed to perform its duties related to counterterrorism. Overall the evidence suggests that, as with Louis Freeh and the FBI, some of those failures were intentional. Concerns that have never been addressed include that Tenet and Freeh had developed secret paths of communication with certain Saudi authorities and that the two men appeared to have disrupted plans to capture and investigate al Qaeda suspects. Ten specific areas of inquiry for an ongoing investigation into George Tenet's 9/11-related activities were given.

In Chapter 6, "Counterterrorism Czar" Richard Clarke was shown to be a close associate of the owners of the old terrorism funding network BCCI. As a good friend of the United Arab Emirates, Clarke personally thwarted at least two U.S. plans to capture or kill Osama bin Laden in the years just before 9/11. Moreover, he was a member of the secret Continuity of Government (COG) planning group, which implemented its plans on 9/11. Along with Clarke, the members of the COG group included Dick Cheney, Donald Rumsfeld, George H.W. Bush, Boeing director Kenneth Duberstein, and former CIA director James Woolsey.

Additionally, Clarke appears to have been deceptive with regard to a number of issues before and after 9/11. He was responsible for a May 2001 email alleging that Abu Zubaydah, whom Clarke called one of "Al Qaeda's top operational managers," was planning major terrorist plots.[1] It was later learned that none of this could have been true because Zubaydah was never associated with al Qaeda in any way.

In his book, Clarke attempted to give an alibi for the mysterious absence of Donald Rumsfeld on the morning of 9/11. Suggesting that Rumsfeld was present in the secure video teleconference during and after the Pentagon attack, Clarke gave the impression that Rumsfeld only left to move from one conference room to another.[2] The truth, however, was that Rumsfeld went directly out to the crash site and could not be contacted for approximately 30 minutes.[3]

Chapter 7 began considering the unanswered questions related to the U.S. national air defenses including the hijacking prevention systems. That is,

2. The four planes should not have been hijacked because the systems in place to prevent hijackings should have been effective.

Problems that contributed to the failure of the hijacking prevention systems centered on the FAA's hijack coordinator, Michael Canavan. Just months before 9/11, Canavan had written an internal FAA memorandum that initiated a new policy of more lax fines for airlines and airports that had security problems. The memo suggested that, if the airlines or airports had a written plan to fix the problem, fines were not needed. This memo was repeatedly cited as a cause of failure to fix security problems in the months leading up to 9/11.

Additionally, according to Canavan's Red Team leader Bogdan Dzakovic, in 2001 the FAA was grossly negligent with regard to the inspections being done. As discussed in Chapter 7, Dzakovic said that FAA officials knew something like 9/11 was going to happen and they covered-up the related evidence.

Features of airport security were discussed in Chapter 13 as well, concerning Barry McDaniel and Stratesec. With regard to Washington's Dulles Airport, Stratesec not only had access to sensitive areas, but also worked on the video system that produced the evidence to implicate the alleged hijackers. As *TIME* magazine reported, early investigators suspected that the alleged hijackers may have had accomplices in the secure areas of airports. Apart from Stratesec, other companies like Securicor (Argenbright Security), Globe Aviation Services, and ICTS International (Huntleigh USA), all of which provided passenger screening services at the airports, were touched on as well.

Two policy changes enacted by the U.S. defense department also impacted the ability of the air defenses to respond. The first was a July 1997 order that requests for assistance with hijackings be approved by the Secretary of Defense.[4] A June 2001 update to this order included an exception for emergencies but still left the power in Rumsfeld's hands with regard to "potentially lethal assistance."[5] That is, to shoot down a commercial airliner, orders had to come through the secretary of defense (or the president). Therefore, the fact that both Bush and Rumsfeld were out of the loop in the critical moments meant that the normal hijacking response procedures could not be completed.

Once it was known that multiple hijackings were in progress, the response from the nation's leadership should have been swift. In other words,

3. The U.S. chain of command should have responded to the attacks immediately but it did not.

As seen in Chapter 8, Cheney now says that he was in charge on 9/11, and that he basically told the president to stay away from Washington. Cheney's former protégé, Duane Andrews, was the country's top expert on the defense communications systems that failed that day. One such failed system ensured that the president had difficulty reaching Rumsfeld and others for most of the morning on 9/11.

The U.S. Secret Service's failures to protect the president were also relevant to the failed chain of command. Instead of simply being failures, the related anomalies could alternatively be explained as the intentional removal of the president from the scenarios in which he could have done something in response or been criticized for not doing so.

The other half of the national command authority, DOD secretary Donald Rumsfeld, was also missing in action. Instead of rushing to defend the United States as would be expected of the secretary of defense, Rumsfeld remained in meetings with the CIA and others and made several startling predictions that reflected what was happening. He then wandered out to the lawn and parking lot and was out of reach for approximately 30 minutes at the height of the attacks. The evidence suggests that Rumsfeld was aware of the attack plan and was removing himself from the situations in which he would be expected to lead the response.

4. The U.S. national air defenses should have responded effectively and some, if not all, of the hijacked aircraft should have been intercepted by military jets.

The failure of the U.S. air defenses on 9/11 can be traced to several people, three of whom were closely examined in this book. These people were the leaders of the FAA and NORAD.

Despite being given plenty of notice about the four planes hijacked on 9/11, FAA headquarters did not request military assistance to ensure the planes were intercepted before they crashed. The 9/11 Commission attributes this to a string of gross failures in communication between the FAA and the military on 9/11. However, the report places no blame on any of the people who were involved and doesn't even mention the one person who was most important to this chain of communications.

That one person was the FAA's hijack coordinator, Michael Canavan. A career special operations commander, Canavan had come to the civilian FAA job only nine months before 9/11 and would leave only one month after the attacks. One of the first things Canavan did in that job was lead and participate in exercises that, according to the FAA officer involved, were "pretty damn close to the 9/11 plot."[6]

With regard to the communication failures, Canavan offered the unsolicited excuse that he was absent during the morning hours of 9/11, in Puerto Rico. The 9/11 Commission did not pursue this excuse nor did it ask who was filling the critical hijack coordinator role in Canavan's absence.

Another of the most important people involved was Benedict Sliney, who had, just before 9/11, left a lucrative law career defending Wall Street financiers to return to work as a specialist at the FAA. As the FAA's national operations manager, 9/11 was his first day on the job.

Investigation of NORAD Commander Ralph Eberhart would almost certainly reveal more of what the public needs to know. As stated in Chapter 8, military exercises were occurring on 9/11 under Eberhart's command. Those exercises mimicked the attacks and caused confusion among the responders. Additionally, the apparent failures to follow air defense procedures were followed by a string of lies about those failures. NORAD officials, including Eberhart, covered up the facts about the lack of air defense on 9/11 by lying to the American people and by failure to cooperate with the 9/11 investigations.

5. The three WTC buildings should not have fallen through what should have been the path of most resistance.

The evidence indicates that the WTC buildings were brought down through a deceptive form of demolition. This means that a program for procuring and installing explosives throughout the WTC complex was needed. Frank Carlucci's former colleague Barry McDaniel was well-qualified for the job. He and Wirt Walker should be prime suspects due to their access as leaders of Stratesec, which had a suspicious history.

Terrorism propagandists L. Paul Bremer and Brian Michael Jenkins also had strong connections to the World Trade Center. One was an employee of a WTC tower impact zone company who spent the day giving the public the official story before anyone knew what had happened. The other was the man who led the design of the WTC security program after the 1993 bombing.

Many reasons can be found to investigate New York City mayor Rudy Giuliani. His foreknowledge of the inexplicable demise of the towers and his destruction of the remaining evidence are important areas that require inquiry. Giuliani's associations with organized crime as well as his early knowledge of the terrorism network BCCI provide further leads. His failure to replace the first responder radios that failed that day and his role in communicating the false notion that the air was safe to breathe at Ground Zero are other areas to study.

The fact that Donald Rumsfeld and Dick Cheney were board members for the company that occupied all but ten of the 47 floors in WTC building 7 might be important. They both resigned from that board only eight months before 9/11. As the attacks began, WTC 7 was the scheduled site of a terrorism-related meeting planned by Larry Silverstein and the Secret Service. Military explosive disposal units were invited to this meeting while the leaders of the Secret Service were simultaneously huddled with Cheney in the White House bunker.

Duane Andrews and his company SAIC played a wide-ranging role relative to 9/11. This included creating the national databases that tracked and identified terrorists. SAIC also supplied U.S. airports with terrorism screening equipment, and predicted and then investigated terrorist attacks against U.S. infrastructure including the national defense networks and the World Trade Center.

SAIC helped to create the official account for what happened at the WTC both in 1993 and after 9/11. The company also provided the information to capture the alleged architect of the attacks, Khalid Sheikh Mohammed. SAIC's extensive involvement in the facilities and systems that were affected on 9/11, as well as its involvement in providing the official account for what happened, calls out for close examination.

SAIC was also a leader in research on thermitic materials like those found in the WTC dust. What's more, a new employee of the company, John Blitch, was in charge of the teams operating the robotic equipment used to search the pile at Ground Zero. That equipment had been designed for use in explosive ordnance disposal, giving reason to suspect that Blitch was looking for, and disposing of, explosive remnants.

Chapter 10 provided a realistic alternative to the official account for the attack on the Pentagon. This alternative centered on the Pentagon renovation project. It presented an evidence-based hypothesis that explains everything the official account does while also giving explanations for six major, previously unexplained, questions related to that event. This hypothesis implicates SECDEFs Paul Wolfowitiz, John Hamre, and John Deutch as managers of the renovation project, as well as Donald Rumsfeld's long-time business colleague Peter Janson, whose company performed the work.

What Should be Examined More Closely

Some of the suspects reviewed in this book could be brought up on charges today. This includes George Tenet and Ralph Eberhart, both of whom lied to the U.S. Congress during the investigations. Wirt Walker can be charged with 9/11-related insider trading; Richard Clarke appears to be guilty of treason; and Rudy Giuliani should be tried for his role in deceiving first responders about the air quality at Ground Zero.

More detailed investigation will be required in order to evaluate the best path to justice with respect to other suspects. But there are good leads to follow. As discussed throughout this review, there are significant links between the suspects and deep state entities that were known for secretive plans. For example, the terrorist financing network BCCI was cited in the following ways.

- The network was created with the blessing of then-DCI George H.W. Bush, father of Stratesec's Marvin Bush and President George W. Bush.

- The UAE helped start the BCCI network and then bought up the remnants as Richard Clarke began working with the country's leaders.

- BCCI was linked to George W. Bush's former company, Harken Energy, through several investors.[7]

- Duane Andrews and Dick Cheney worked together on the House Intelligence Committee as the CIA was working with BCCI. George Tenet worked for the Senate intelligence committee at the same time. Presumably, these men were informed of the CIA's involvement with the terrorist financing bank.

- Kissinger Associates, then led by L. Paul Bremer, had a number of meetings with BCCI representatives but refused to release its documents related to BCCI during the related Senate investigation.

- Rudy Giuliani led the enforcement actions against BCCI and his associate Louis Freeh may also have been involved. Giuliani also worked for White & Case, which represented BCCI.

- Wirt Walker's KuwAm Corporation was linked to BCCI through its director Hamzah Behbehani as well as an unnamed director from Patton, Boggs, & Blow. KuwAm's Mish'al Al-Sabah was the cousin of Jabir Adbhi Al-Sabah who worked closely with BCCI nominee Faisal Al-Fulaij.

- BCCI was inseparable from the Pakistani ISI, which on 9/11 was led by a man who was meeting in Washington with suspects Richard Armitage, Porter Goss, and Paul Wolfowitz.

Knowledge of past crimes against democracy, including the Phoenix Program in Vietnam, Operation Gladio, the "October Surprise," Iran-Contra, and the deceptions behind the first Gulf War, call for a comparative analysis with regard to 9/11. Such an investigation should carefully consider these suspects and review the potentially related activities of private network leader Ted Shackley. There are good reasons to suspect that both Barry McDaniel and Frank Carlucci were involved in the Iran-Contra crimes, and at least five of the suspects reviewed were connected in one way or another to Shackley.

- Shackley was "very close friends" with Frank Carlucci.

- Richard Armitage had a long, close relationship with Shackley as well.

- Michael Canavan's JSOC, perhaps the most secretive U.S. agency, was started by Shackley's OPC colleague Richard

Stillwell. An assassination squad of the JSOC was placed under Cheney's command after 9/11.

- Shackley's activities in Kuwait paralleled those of KuwAm director Wirt Walker.

- Porter Goss worked with Shackley at the CIA station JM/WAVE and also in Operation 40.

Solving the case of 9/11 is not a question of whether the crimes were perpetrated by "the terrorists" or "the government." In fact, many U.S. government officials tried to get to some aspect of the truth and retaliation was their reward. These included congressional representatives Cynthia McKinney, Curt Weldon and Dennis Kucinich, along with Senators Max Cleland and Mark Dayton.

What's more, half of the suspects in this book were not in government positions on 9/11. It does seem clear, however, that the U.S. could not have been attacked so easily, with the national defenses being so handily defeated, without the involvement of some members of the U.S. government and military. Apart from the nineteen suspects named, former Senator David Boren stands out as someone who should be examined more closely.

Further investigation must prioritize the activities and people involved in the Continuity of Government (COG) program. Some of the reasons that COG is so important to understanding 9/11 include the following.

- At least three of the suspects reviewed here, Cheney, Rumsfeld, and Clarke, were among a select few involved in COG planning over a period of 20 years.

- Clarke revised the COG plan in 1998 to make it a response to an act of terrorism like 9/11. This happened at the same time as there was a concerted effort to hype the threat of terrorism from al Qaeda.

- Richard Clarke implemented the secretive COG plan for the first time on 9/11, thereby effectively installing a "shadow government." That shadow government was still in effect in 2002 and may still be today.

- A secret communications system developed for COG implementation, called SRAS, was activated on 9/11 before the attacks began. Duane Andrews' company provided oversight to the agency which activated the system.

- Since 9/11, requests from U.S. congressional representatives to review COG documentation have been refused by the White House.[8]

Throughout the book, evidence was presented that implicates certain oil-rich royals in non-democratic kingdoms of the Middle East. The possibility that the government of Saudi Arabia might have been involved in the 9/11 plot appeared to have been intentionally emphasized by the Joint Congressional Inquiry, through redaction of the report and through hints made by Bob Graham afterward. However, Graham and others failed to emphasize the strong Saudi relationships with Western governments. Instead, the evidence implicating Saudi leaders seems to be used as a political tool more than a vehicle for justice.

The 9/11 Commission made a point of covering for the Saudis in several of its "we found no evidence" claims. However, the world's leading insurance provider, Lloyd's of London, filed a lawsuit alleging that the Kingdom of Saudi Arabia was a major sponsor of al Qaeda and a "knowing and material participant in al Qaeda's conspiracy to wage jihad against the United States." The suit claimed that without the Saudi sponsorship, "al Qaeda would not have possessed the capacity to conceive, plan and execute the September 11th Attacks."[9] Although Lloyd's dropped the lawsuit just days later without explanation, the 154-page legal filing described a good deal of evidence for Saudi backing of al Qaeda.

Lloyd's was not the first to contradict the Commission on this topic, as many of the 9/11 victims' relatives joined together to file a multi-trillion dollar lawsuit against the Saudis. That lawsuit was thrown out on a technicality related to the ability to sue a foreign government and, later, the Obama Administration backed the Saudis during the appeal. What's important to realize, however, is that it was only the 9/11 Commission that claimed that no evidence for Saudi financing could be found. Obviously, such evidence could be found, it just could not be used to prosecute the Saudi government in the United States.

The governments of two other foreign countries that benefited should be at the top of the list to be examined. These are Kuwait, whose royal family included the owners of KuwAm Corporation; and the United Arab Emirates, the country with so many links to the alleged hijackers and whose leaders bought up the remnants of BCCI. Like Saudi Arabia, these countries are non-democratic monarchies and therefore calling for investigation of prominent members of the royal families (for example Freeh and Tenet's confidant Prince Bandar) is analogous to calling for investigation of the governments.

Also of great interest are a number of British companies. This includes AMEC, which did the construction and cleanup at the Pentagon impact zone and also led the cleanup of the WTC site. The British firms Bovis Lend Lease, the other major contractor that cleaned up Ground Zero; and Securicor, which managed airport screening, are also of interest. Furthermore, a number of the suspects later went to work at the British defense firm purchased by the Carlyle Group—QinetiQ.

Israel has also been discussed in terms of the possibility that elements of its government were involved. Unfortunately, such claims are often made without supporting evidence and coherent reasoning. Although there is evidence that Israeli intelligence knew details about the attacks in advance—the story of the "Dancing Israelis" verified this foreknowledge[10]—many governments had advanced knowledge of the attacks as indicated by the warnings issued.

If there was an Israeli operative in this group of suspects, Carl Truscott might be a candidate in that he went on to work with a leading official from the Israeli Security Agency. Paul Wolfowitz and his advisor Douglas Feith would also be candidates as they were both strong supporters of Israel.[11] On the other hand, Wolfowtiz's history suggests that his connections to a deeper, non-national state, as indicated by the training that he and Richard Perle received from Dean Acheson, might be more important.

Considering 9/11 as a product of a deeper, non-national (or trans-national) state brings to mind the Safari Club and Cercle Pinay, which preceded and drove organizations like BCCI, as well as the "CIA within the CIA" private intelligence network. Further investigation might focus on the Iranian exiles working with Shackley, Sensi, and Walker to determine if they were linked to the Safari Club network. How these groups related to COG and CSIS, and to certain people who seemed to be behind the scenes with respect to 9/11, would also be useful avenues of further inquiry.

It was known that Rumsfeld deferred to Richard Perle on many issues in 2001, sometimes in an obsequious manner.[12] Additionally, PNAC members Rumsfeld, Cheney, Wolfowitz and Armitage were all known to be followers of Andrew Marshall, the man behind the calls for a revolution in military affairs. People like Arnaud de Borchgrave, Henry Kissinger, Fred Ikle, and James Woolsey also turned up repeatedly throughout this discussion of suspects.

Another point to consider is that the events of 9/11 appear to have revealed a few well-tested mechanisms by which societies are deceived en masse. One such mechanism is something called controlled opposition. That is, pitting two opponents against each other, while backing or manipulating both, can be an effective means by which a more powerful group can direct aggression away from itself while profiting immensely from the process. This worked with the eight-year long Iran-Iraq War, for example, and with similar conflicts that led to massive gains for the military-industrial complex. The concept is also reflected in the superficial left-right paradigm of U.S. politics, in which national discussions are often framed around relatively meaningless issues while the facts about things like 9/11, or the vulnerabilities of electronic voting machines, are largely ignored.

Controlled opposition is the basic concept behind the idea that al Qaeda works for an international intelligence network to induce public support for policy when needed. Might the Arab-Israeli conflict be partly co-opted and aggravated in such ways as well, by those representing a deeper state? It seems possible. If true, then a continued exacerbation of both sides in the conflict would serve the purposes of the deep state, perhaps by keeping the resource-rich region unstable and in need of continued intervention.

In any case, an honest investigation into the events of 9/11 must proceed from the evidence regarding what happened and who was in a position to make it happen, no matter where that evidence leads. Considering the knowledge and access to the facilities and systems needed to accomplish the attacks, the evidence suggests that the 19 people reviewed in this book should be examined first.

Other Motivations

The people who committed the crimes of 9/11 probably thought that they were doing the right thing. Whether they were Arab extremists who were fighting a jihad, or people posing as Arab extremists in covert operations, they undoubtedly believed their actions were part of a difficult but necessary good. Similarly, any U.S. players involved in promoting an "Islamic" terrorist threat, disabling the air defenses, demolishing the WTC, or accomplishing the other necessary activities, most likely thought they were acting in the nation's best interest. In fact, that Machiavellian concept has been attributed to Bush Administration officials many times.[13]

Actions taken since 9/11 indicate that the crimes of that day were part of a power play coordinated by powerful, trans-national interests. The events provided the pretext for implementation of pre-existing plans to seize critical resources and implement more government control over citizenry. The seizure of resources like oil and natural gas is necessary in order for Western economies to continue functioning without major upheaval.[14] And more protection for the most wealthy and powerful will likely be necessary as the gap between the demand and availability of energy resources continues to widen, causing economic hardship. Since 9/11, the actions taken to protect the public from terrorism cannot be distinguished from actions that would be taken to protect governments, and the wealthiest of their sponsors, from the public.

U.S. government leaders have known about the risks of energy resource depletion for some time and Cheney's secret energy task force of early 2001 appears to have been a confirmation of that knowledge. It would therefore not be surprising that a secretive group of deep state operatives embedded within the U.S. government might have taken action to secure the nation's interests for the long term.

It appears that production of illicit drugs might have also played a part. As discussed earlier, many U.S. covert operations have been dependent on drug trafficking. Richard Armitage was involved with such activities in Southeast Asia, Porter Goss' district in Florida was a center for drug trafficking (including Huffman Aviation, where the alleged hijackers trained), and the Iran-Contra crimes depended on drug funding. Therefore it is relevant that, less than two years after 9/11, occupied Afghanistan became the world's largest heroin producer.[15] Afghani opium production continued to rise through 2012.[16]

Most of the suspects reviewed here were shown to have benefited from the 9/11 attacks through promotions, or political or business gains. However, there is an intangible benefit to consider as well. Many of them were players in the last war in which the United States was defeated.

For example, Ralph Eberhart began his military career as a forward air controller stationed out of Pleiku Air Base in South Vietnam. Benedict Sliney, who was in charge of FAA operations on 9/11, was an air traffic controller stationed in Pleiku at about the same time. Duane Andrews was also an Air Force Special Operations soldier in Vietnam.

Fighting in related operations was Michael Canavan; the FAA's missing hijack coordinator on 9/11, who was in the 5th Special Forces Group (SFG). Also in the 5th SFG were Brian Michael Jenkins, who as Deputy Chairman of Kroll designed the WTC security systems; and CJCS Hugh Shelton, who was yet another high-level leader missing on 9/11. Special Forces soldier Richard Armitage was active in Vietnam as well.

Along with Donald Rumsfeld and Dick Cheney, all these men were undoubtedly devastated by the defeat in Vietnam. Author Kevin Phillips noted that memories of the loss in Vietnam "became an important seedbed for aggressiveness with respect to Iraq" and that Rumsfeld, Cheney, Shackley and George H.W. Bush were all "embarrassed or embittered" by the setback.[17]

Cheney and Rumsfeld experienced their only other significant career loss when President Ford was defeated in the 1976 election a year later. Other people who played critical roles on 9/11 and also worked in the Ford Administration included L. Paul Bremer, Frank Carlucci, Rudy Giuliani, and DOD employees Richard Clarke, Paul Wolfowitz, and Richard Armitage.

The defeats in Vietnam and the 1976 presidential election made their marks on these men. Years later, the attacks of 9/11 brought all of them a late chance for redemption and victory. And it made them all heroes.

Using 9/11 for the purposes realized required identification of an enemy that could be pursued throughout all of the most strategically important lands. That pursuit of al Qaeda in the "War on Terror" has led to the oppression of more countries than Afghanistan and Iraq. The West has pursued "regime change" in Libya, Syria and other countries of the Middle East as well.

What goes little noticed in all of this is that al Qaeda was an ally of the U.S. in the recent efforts to effect regime change in Libya, and was apparently working on the same side as the U.S. in Syria as well.[18] None of that is surprising given that al Qaeda was born of the CIA-funded Afghan Mujahideen in the 1980s.

Unfortunately, these facts are missed as mainstream media and government leaders continue to use threats about al Qaeda for political purposes. This might be surprising to some but others have realized that the "media serve, and propagandize on behalf of, the powerful societal interests that control and finance them."[19] As a result, the evidence that al Qaeda is a controlled opponent, making political hay for its supposed enemies at every opportunity, goes largely unnoticed.[20]

Adding to the suspicion that U.S. authorities continue to be behind terrorist acts are the reports that the FBI has planned terrorism and has engaged in entrapment of the related "terrorists" since 9/11. Journalist

Glenn Greenwald wrote that, in the decade after 9/11, the FBI's actions included "purposely seeking out Muslims (typically young and impressionable ones) whom they think harbor animosity toward the U.S. and who therefore can be induced to launch an attack despite having *never taken even a single step toward doing so before the FBI targeted them.* Each time the FBI announces it has disrupted its own plot, press coverage is predictably hysterical (new Homegrown Terrorist caught!), fear levels predictably rise, and new security measures are often implemented in response." [21]

It appears that the CIA has been caught in the same kind of trickery. In the case of a would-be "underwear bomber," it was later revealed that the suspect was working for the CIA and Saudi intelligence.[22] These kinds of manipulations, and related questions about 9/11, continue to go unreported by the U.S. media, despite the historical revelations of Operation Gladio, Operations Northwoods, and the Gulf of Tonkin non-event.

There is no longer any question that the official reports for 9/11 failed to address a majority of the evidence and left most of the critical questions unanswered. This was due in part to the fact that the related investigations, completed when Cheney and Rumsfeld were still leading the country, were produced through a process that suffered from uncooperative, deceptive maneuvers among the agencies involved.

The U.S. government will not conduct an honest investigation into the events of 9/11. That much is clear. But there are many other countries that were impacted and many whose citizens were killed that day. People from 59 different countries perished in the 9/11 attacks.[23] Eight were Pakistanis, ten from Italy, eleven from Germany, an amazing 47 from the Dominican Republic, and 14 from Trinidad and Tobago. These 59 countries have the right, and the responsibility, to open their own investigations into the deaths of their citizens. An effort to bring about one or more such investigations could do much for the cause of truth and justice. The work of independent investigators and activists is the key to further progress today.

The attacks of 9/11 were crimes that have never been appropriately investigated. This is despite the fact that the citizens of the world have invested their futures in the myth surrounding those events. As of June 2011, a conservative estimate of the cost of the wars resulting from 9/11 was approximately $4 trillion.[24] A more recent estimate puts the financial cost at $6 trillion.[25] As this financial disaster continues, the expected fate of the U.S. economy will resound throughout the world.

Civilian deaths resulting from the Iraq War alone have been estimated to be over one million.[26] The U.S. soldiers who have died in Iraq and Afghanistan number more than double the victims from the 9/11 attacks. The wounded go uncounted. And according to the United Nations refugee agency, Afghanistan and Iraq continue to lead the world in generation of refugees, millions of them, primarily due to the wars of aggression being conducted in those countries.

A critical obligation to future generations becomes obvious when, to all of this, we add the loss of civil rights reflected in police-state legislation, the moral losses involved in torture, and the near total loss of public trust in government. These facts should help us focus on the common root cause of these tragedies—the origin of the War on Terror.

Although the response to public skepticism has been to ignore or belittle those questioning the events of 9/11, this book provides a next step for those wanting to know the truth. People around the world know what is needed to make corrections to the destructive path that we have taken since September 11, 2001, and start moving toward peace, justice, and lasting positive change. We need to know what happened on 9/11.

Index

Al-Bayoumi, Omar, 57, 64, 99, 218, 286
Albright, Madeline, 194
Alec Station, 61, 194
Al-Faisal, Prince Turki, 91, 99
Al-Fulaij, Faisal, 213, 309
Al-Ghamdi, Saeed, 69, 207, 215
Alghanim, Anwar Mustafah T., 225
Al-Hada, Ahmed, 60
Al-Hawsawi, Mustafa Ahmed, 77, 92
Al-Hazmi, Nawaf, 57, 61, 63, 72, 77, 78, 86, 94, 98, 218, 269, 275
Ali Abdul Aziz Ali, 95
Ali Al-Salem Air Base, 211
Al-Kifah, 188
Alleged hijackers and takeover of planes, 292
Allende, Salvadore, 210
Al-Maktoum, Mohammed bin Rashid, 91, 92, 93, 99, 101
Al-Mihdhar, Khalid, 57, 60, 63, 72, 77, 78, 86, 94, 96, 98, 218, 269, 275
Al-Nayan, Sheikh Zayed bin Sultan, 90, 91
Al-Qadi, Yassin, 59
Al-Qahtani, Mohammed, 12
Al-Sabah, Baria Salim, 224
Al-Sabah, Jabir Adbhi, 212, 309
Al-Sabah, Mish'al Al-Jarrah, 214
Al-Sabah, Mish'al Yusuf Saud, 204, 206, 207, 209, 212, 213, 218, 226, 266
Al-Sabah, Nayirah, 31, 205, 264
Al-Sabah, Saud Nasser Al-Saud, 205, 212
Al-Shehhi, Marwan, 69, 71, 76, 80, 99, 214, 290
Al-Shehri, Waleed, 69, 207, 215

Al-Shibh, Ramsi bin, 71, 82, 83, 296
Alwaleed, Prince of Saudi Arabia, 154
Al-Zawahiri, Ayman, 12, 55, 74
Amalgam Virgo, 126, 127, 128
Amalgam Warrior, 127
Ambassador-at-Large for Counterterrorism, 192
AMEC, 161, 173, 174, 261, 312
AMEC Construction Management, 159, 160, 161, 163, 166, 176
at the WTC, 254
John Cavanagh, 256t
Leo DiRubbio, 255
American Airlines Arena, 161
American Enterprise Institute, 25
American Society of Civil Engineers (ASCE), 163, 164, 172
Amraams, 131
Analex, 277
Anderson, George, 182
Andrews, Duane, 25, 31, 36, 83, 89, 262-278, 304, 307, 308, 311, 315
USAF, 263
Andrews AFB, 121, 136, 137, 149, 150, 151
Anteon, 116
Anteon Corporation, 76
Anteon International Corporation, 115
AON Corporation, 20, 227
Apogen, 277
Apollo Guardian, 127
Applied Ordnance Technology, 274
Arab oil embargo, 22, 23
Arab-Israeli conflict, 313

Notes to Chapter 1

[1] Family Steering Committee for the 9/11 Independent Commission, Unanswered Questions, http://www.911independentcommission.org/questions.html

[2] David Ray Griffin, The 9/11 Commission Report: Omissions and Distortions, Olive Branch Press, 2005

[3] Thomas H. Kean and Lee H. Hamilton with Benjamin Rhodes, Without Precedent: The Inside Story of the 9/11 Commission, First Vintage Books, 2006

[4] Private meeting with Lee Hamilton, May 2007

[5] Dana Bash, Jon Karl and John King, Bush asks Daschle to limit Sept. 11 probes, CNN, January 29, 2002

[6] Kristen Breitweiser, Wake-Up Call: The Political Education of a 9/11 Widow, Warner Books, 2006

[7] Philip Shenon, 9/11 Commission Could Subpoena Oval Office Files, New York Times, October 26, 2003

[8] Ron Nessen, It Sure Looks Different From the Inside, Playboy Press, 1978, p 59

[9] Kevin R. Ryan, The 9/11 Commission claims that "We found no evidence," DigWithin.net, October 30, 2011

[10] National Commission on Terrorist Attacks Upon the United States, The 9/11 Commission Report, p 172

[11] Kevin R. Ryan, Why the NIST WTC 7 Report is False, http://www.youtube.com/watch?v=ArnYryJqCwU

[12] Thomas Hargrove, Third of Americans suspect 9-11 government conspiracy, Scripps News, August 1, 2006

[13] History Commons, Complete 9/11 Timeline

[14] In August 2011 I appeared as a guest on NPR, along with James Meigs of *Popular Mechanics*. As the only 9/11 skeptic in a show about 9/11 skeptics, I was given 5 minutes to respond to various leading questions. Meigs and the host used the remainder of the 42-minute program to belittle anyone questioning the official account. They used some form of the phrase "conspiracy theorist" every 30 seconds throughout the show. Similarly, I debated *Skeptic* Magazine's Michael

Shermer in 2007, on Air America radio. Shermer used the same techniques in response to pointed questions.

[15] CIA Document #1035-960

[16] David E. Scheim, Trust or Hustle: The Bush Record, CampaignWatch.org

[17] James Bamford, Body of secrets: anatomy of the ultra-secret National Security Agency, Random House, 2002

[18] U.S. Joint Chiefs of Staff, "Justification for US Military Intervention in Cuba (TS)", U.S. Department of Defense, March 1962. For online pdf file, see the National Security Archive at the George Washington University Gelman Library, Washington, DC

[19] Kevin R. Ryan, Muslims did not attack the U.S. on 9/11, DigWithin.net, March 17, 2012

[20] Peter Dale Scott, American War Machine: Deep Politics, the CIA Global Drug Connection, and the Road to Afghanistan, Rowman & Littlefield Publishers, 2010

[21] Readers interested in the propaganda model of the mainstream media should see Edward S. Herman and Noam Chomsky, Manufacturing Consent: The Political Economy of the Mass Media, Random House, 1988 and 2002

[22] Peter Dale Scott, American War Machine

Notes to Chapter 2

[1] Vernon Loeb and Greg Schneider, Colorful Outsider Is Named No. 3 At the CIA, The Washington Post, March 17, 2001

[2] Ken Ringle, Lenzner: Private Eye Or Public Enemy?, The Washington Post, March 2, 1998

[3] Rowan Scarborough, Rumsfeld's War: The Untold Story of America's Anti-terrorist Commander, Regnery Publishing, 2004

[4] The U.S. Department of State, Office of the Historian, Milestones: 1969-1976, OPEC Oil Embargo, 1973-1974

[5] Kathryn S. Olmsted, Challenging the Secret Government: The Post-Watergate Investigations of the CIA and FBI, University of North Carolina Press, 1996, pp 131-135

[6] Joseph J. Trento, Prelude to Terror: The Rogue CIA And The Legacy Of America's Private Intelligence Network, Basic Books, March 2006

7 Kevin R. Ryan, Demolition Access to the WTC Towers: Part One, 911Review.com, August 9, 2009.

8 Joseph J. Trento, Prelude to Terror: Edwin P. Wilson and the Legacy of America's Private Intelligence Network, Carroll & Graf, 2005

9 Dana Priest, Rumsfeld's '84 Visit was to Reassure Iraqis: Trip Followed Criticism Of Chemical Arms' Use, The Seattle Times, December 19, 2003

10 Matthew Everett, Before 9/11, Donald Rumsfeld Was Preoccupied With Pearl Harbor and Other Military Surprises, Shoestring 9/11, July 16, 2007

11 Paul Koring, Going Backwards: U.S. to Militarize Space, Toronto Globe & Mail, May 9, 2001

12 Ron Suskind, The Price of Loyalty: George W. Bush, the White House, and the Education of Paul O'Neill, Simon and Schuster, 2004

13 Russ Baker, Family of Secrets: The Bush Dynasty, America's Invisible Government, and the Hidden History of the Last Fifty Years, Bloomsbury Publishing, 2010

14 Lou Dubose and Jake Bernstein, Vice: Dick Cheney and the Hijacking of the American Presidency, Random House, 2006, p 27

15 Michael Parenti, "State vs. Government," in Contrary Notions: The Michael Parenti Reader [San Francisco: City Lights, 2007], p. 203.

16 Congressional Research Service, Memorandum to House Government Reform Committee on Terrorist Attacks by al Qaeda, March 31, 2004, accessed at: http://www.fas.org/irp/crs/033104.pdf

17 The Fifth Estate, The Unauthorized Biography of Dick Cheney, CBC News, aired October 6, 2004

18 Russ Baker, Family of Secrets

19 In July 1996, Komatsu-Dresser patented a thermite demolition device that could "demolish a concrete structure at a high efficiency, while preventing a secondary problem due to noise, flying dust and chips, and the like." Taku Murakami, US Patent 5532449 - Using plasma ARC and thermite to demolish concrete.

20 The Fifth Estate, The Unauthorized Biography of Dick Cheney

21 Lou Dubose and Jake Bernstein, Vice

22 Ibid

23 White House press release, May 8, 2001

[24] Lou Dubose and Jake Bernstein, Vice
[25] The Fifth Estate, The Unauthorized Biography of Dick Cheney
[26] Stephen F. Hayes, Cheney: The Untold Story of America's Most Powerful and Controversial Vice President, HarperCollins, 2009
[27] Gregor Holland, The Mineta Testimony: 9/11 Commission Exposed, 911Truth.org, July 22, 2005
[28] Transcript of Rumsfeld Interview with Larry King, CNN, December 5, 2001, http://www.defense.gov/transcripts/transcript.aspx?transcriptid=2603
[29] PBS Frontline, Interview: Condoleezza Rice, http://www.pbs.org/wgbh/pages/frontline/shows/campaign/intervie ws/rice.html
[30] William Langley, Revealed: what really went on during Bush's 'missing hours', The Telegraph, December 16, 2001
[31] Secretary Rumsfeld Interview with Larry King, CNN, U.S. Department of Defense, Office of the Assistant Secretary of Defense (Public Affairs), Dec. 5, 2001
[32] Kevin R. Ryan, An 8-year war built on lies: But when did the lying begin?, Foreign Policy Journal, February 28, 2011
[33] Michael Ratner and the Center for Constitutional Rights, The trial of Donald Rumsfeld: a prosecution by book, New Press, 2008

Notes to Chapter 3

[1] Greg Schneider, Connections And Then Some: David Rubenstein Has Made Millions Pairing the Powerful With the Rich, The Washington Post, March 16, 2003
[2] Kevin R. Ryan, The Small World of 9/11 Players: LS2, Vidient and AMEC, DigWithin.net, Jan 1, 2012
[3] Manoj Joshi, India helped FBI trace ISI-terrorist links, The Times of India, October 9, 2001
[4] Michel Chossudovsky, Political Deception: The Missing Link behind 9-11, Centre for Research on Globalisation (CRG), Globalresearch.ca , 20 June 2002 (revised 27 June)
[5] Edward T. Pound, The easy path to the United States for three of the 9/11 hijackers, US News and World Report, 12/12/01

[6] Craig Unger, House of Bush, House of Saud: The Secret Relationship Between the World's Two Most Powerful Dynasties, Scribner, 2004, p161

[7] Dan Briody, The Iron Triangle: Inside the Secret World of the Carlyle Group, John Wiley & Sons, 2003

[8] Joseph Trento, Prelude to Terror: Edwin P. Wilson and the Legacy of America's Private Intelligence Network, Carroll & Graf, 2005, p 124

[9] Ibid

[10] Spartacus International, Profile for Richard V. Secord

[11] Dan Briody, The Iron Triangle

[12] James Mann, Rise Of The Vulcans: The History of Bush's War Cabinet, Viking Press, 2004

[13] Joseph Trento and Susan Trento, The United States and Iran: The Secret History Part One: Carter and the Shah, National Security News Service, July 27, 2009

[14] Wikipedia page for Operation Cyclone

[15] James Mann, Rise of the Vulcans

[16] Dan Briody, The Iron Triangle, p 4

[17] Pierre Tristam, What Was Operation Eagle Claw, the Failed Rescue of American Hostages in Iran?, About.com

[18] Ibid

[19] Kevin R. Ryan, KuwAm and Stratesec: Directors and investors that link 9/11 to a private intelligence network, DigWithin.net, February 24, 2012

[20] Joseph J. Trento, Prelude to Terror, p 283

[21] Lawrence E. Walsh, Final Report of the Independent Counsel For Iran-Contra Matters, August 4, 1993

[22] Joseph J. Trento, Prelude to Terror, p 283

[23] The Traffail Group, profile page for Ambassador S. Linn Williams

[24] For the report of Ismay's information on the Kennedy assassination, see the Mary Ferrell Foundation

[25] For Ismay not being questioned see William E. Kelly, JFK Countercoup. For Ismay burning the logbook see Patrick Gavin, Politico Click, November 23, 2010

[26] Rockwell International history, Commander History, http://rockwell-commander.tripod.com/history.htm

[27] Reagan Presidential Library, Appointment of Eight Special Assistants

to the President for National Security Affairs, February 11, 1987
[28] Commission on Wartime Contracting, resume for Grant S. Green
[29] NewsMeat, Political contributions of Grant S. Green Jr.
[30] Dan Briody, The Iron Triangle
[31] Alice-Leone Moats, Weapons' Consultants . . . And You Could Get It Through Sears, Philadelphia Inquirer, December 16, 1986
[32] Wikipedia page for Lee W. Hamilton
[33] U.S. Army Materiel Command, Reflections of senior AMC officials, 1990, http://cgsc.cdmhost.com/cdm/compoundobject/collection/p4013col 111/id/863/rec/2214
[34] Tom Redburn and James Gerstenzang, Reagan Picks Carlucci as New Security Adviser : Says His Many Years of Service 'Uniquely Qualify' Him for Job, The Los Angeles Times, December 3, 1986
[35] Jonathan Marshall, Peter Dale Scott and Jane Hunter, The Iran Contra Connection: Secret Teams and Covert Operations in the Reagan Era, South End Press, 1987

Notes to Chapter 4

[1] Wikipedia page for Robert Wright Jr.
[2] Statement of Louis J. Freeh, Former FBI Director, before the Joint Intelligence Committees, October 8, 2002
[3] News Release, Judicial Watch Rejoices At Resignation Of FBI Director Louis Freeh, May 3, 2001
[4] Ibid
[5] Judicial Watch press release, U.S. Supremes Rule in Favor of JW
[6] Joseph J. Trento, Prelude to Terror: Edwin P. Wilson and the Legacy of America's Private Intelligence Network, Carroll & Graf, 2005, p 351
[7] Ralph Blumenthal, "Tapes Depict Proposal to Thwart Bomb Used in Trade Center Blast," New York Times, October 28, 1993
[8] Pierre Thomas and Mike Mills, FBI Crime Laboratory Being Probed, The Washington Post, September 14, 1995
[9] See the film A Noble Lie: Oklahoma City 1995
[10] Stephen Labaton, Man in the Background at the F.B.I. Now Draws Some Unwelcome Attention, The New York Times, May 28, 1995
[11] Geoffrey Fattah, Nichols says bombing was FBI op, Deseret News,

February 22, 2007

12 Peter Dale Scott, Systemic Destabilization in Recent American History: 9/11, the JFK Assassination, and the Oklahoma City Bombing as a Strategy of Tension, The Asia-Pacific Journal: Japan Focus, September, 2012

13 Alasdair Scott Roberts, The Collapse of Fortress Bush: The Crisis of Authority in American Government, NYU Press, 2008, p 35

14 April 1995 memo from Jamie Gorelick outlining the "Wall" procedures, http://old.nationalreview.com/document/document_1995_gorelick_memo.pdf

15 Louis J. Freeh, My FBI: Bringing Down the Mafia, Investigating Bill Clinton, and Fighting the War on Terror, MacMillan, 2006

16 James T. McKenna, Report Cites Obstacles To Witness Interview, Aviation Week and Space Technology, December 15, 1997

17 Don Van Natta Jr, Prime Evidence Found That Device Exploded in Cabin of Flight 800, The New York Times, August 23, 1996

18 CNN, FBI: No criminal evidence behind TWA 800 crash, November 18, 1997

19 Peter Lance, Triple Cross: How bin Laden's Master Spy Penetrated the CIA, the Green Berets, and the FBI – and Why Patrick Fitzgerald Failed to Stop Him, HarperCollins Publishers, 2006

20 Peter Lance, Triple Cross

21 Patrick Fitzgerald, Testimony before 9/11 Commission, June 16, 2004

22 Peter Dale Scott, The Road to 9/11: Wealth, Empire, and the Future of America, University of California Press, 2007, p 152-160

23 Peter Lance, 1000 Years for Revenge: International Terrorism and the FBI--the Untold Story, HarperCollins, 2003

24 Peter Lance, 1000 Years for Revenge

25 Peter Lance, Greg Scarpa Jr. A Mafia wiseguy uncovers a treasure trove of al Qaeda intel, http://peterlance.com/wordpress/?p=682

26 Greg B. Smith, Panel told bureau rejected flight school warnings, new York Daily News, September 25, 2002

27 See FBI summary of information from the UAE with regard to KSM, document obtained by Internlink.com,

http://intelfiles.egoplex.com/1999-07-08-FBI-summary-KSM.pdf
[28] The 9/11 Commission Report, p 138
[29] Henry Pierson Curtis, Orlando's link to the hunt for Osama bin Laden, The Orlando Sentinel, May 2, 2011
[30] The Washington Post, FBI's Uneasy Role: Work In Lands With Brutal Police, October 29, 2000
[31] Tony Karon, The Curious Case of Hani al-Sayegh, TIME, Oct. 05, 1999
[32] Wikipedia page for Hani El-Sayegh
[33] Transcript of Hardball Special Edition, MSNBC, July 24, 2004
[34] History Commons Complete 9/11 Timeline, Profile for Omar Al-Bayoumi
[35] U.S. Justice Department office of Inspector General's Inquiry into 9/11, http://www.justice.gov/oig/special/s0606/final.pdf
[36] Lawrence Wright, The Looming Tower: Al-Qaeda and the Road to 9/11, Alfred A. Knopf, 2006, p 296
[37] FBI website, Veteran FBI Agent Arrested and Charged with Espionage, February 21, 2001
[38] Jerry Seper, Osama access to state secrets helped 9/11, Computer Crime Research Center
[39] Jerry Seper, Osama access to state secrets helped 9/11
[40] Pierre-Henri Bunel, Al Qaeda: The Database, Centre for Research on Globalization, May 12, 2011
[41] Jamey Hecht, PTech, 9/11, and USA-Saudi Terror - Part I, From The Wilderness Publications, 2005
[42] History Commons Complete 9/11 Timeline, Profile for PTech Inc.
[43] United States v. Usama bin Laden et al., transcript of day 14, March 7, 2001, accessed at Cryptome, http://cryptome.org/usa-v-ubl-14.htm
[44] Kevin Fenton, Disconnecting the Dots: How CIA and FBI officials helped enable 9/11 and evaded government investigations, Trine Day, 2011, p 220
[45] Transcript of Hardball Special Edition, MSNBC, July 24, 2004
[46] Brian Ross and Vic Walter, FBI Informant Says Agents Missed Chance to Stop 9/11 Ringleader Mohammed Atta, ABC News, September 10, 2009
[47] Kevin Fenton, Disconnecting the Dots
[48] Transcript of Hardball Special Edition, MSNBC, July 24, 2004

[49] The Associated Press, FBI official made pre-9/11 comment linking Moussaoui, World Trade Center, 2005, accessed at: http://usatoday30.usatoday.com/news/nation/2002-09-24-moussaoui_x.htm

[50] Coleen Rowley's Memo to FBI Director Robert Mueller, May 21, 2002

[51] U.S. Justice Department office of Inspector General's Inquiry into 9/11

[52] National Commission on Terrorist Attacks Upon the United States, The 9/11 Commission Report, 2004, p 539

[53] Transcript of Hardball Special Edition, MSNBC, July 24, 2004

[54] Ibid

[55] Julian Borger, Mystery men link Saudi intelligence to Sept 11 hijackers, The Guardian, November 24, 2002

[56] CNN, Text of Freeh's statement, May 1, 2001

[57] CNN, Text of Freeh's statement

[58] David Johnston, Senators Angered After F.B.I. Says Weapons Are Missing The New York Times, July 18, 2001

[59] Ibid

[60] Ronald Kessler, The Bureau: The Secret History of the FBI, St. Martin's Press, July 2002

[61] Statement of Louis J. Freeh, Former FBI Director, before the Joint Intelligence Committees, October 8, 2002,

[62] Brian Ross and Vic Walter, Called Off the Trail?: FBI Agents Probing Terror Links Say They Were Told, 'Let Sleeping Dogs Lie', ABC News, December 19, 2002

[63] 911Research.wtc7.net, Pentagon Attack Footage

[64] Daniel Hopsicker, Welcome to Terrorland: Mohamed Atta & the 9-11 Cover-up in Florida, MadCow Press, 2004

[65] History Commons Complete 9/11 Timeline, 11:30 p.m. September 11, 2001: FBI Uninterested in Flight 93 Witness's Evidence

[66] Kevin R. Ryan, Demolition Access to the WTC Towers: Part Four – Cleanup, February 11, 2010, 911Review.com

[67] James Risen, THREATS AND RESPONSES: THE INQUIRY; Congress Seeks F.B.I. Data On Informer; F.B.I. Resists, The New York Times, October 06, 2002

[68] Kevin R. Ryan, Abu Zubaydah Poses a Real Threat to Al Qaeda, DigWithin.net, October 15, 2012

[69] Philip Shenon, The Commission: The Uncensored History of the 9/11 Investigation, Hachette Book Group, 2008

[70] Kevin R. Ryan, Evidence for Informed Trading on the Attacks of September 11, Foreign Policy Journal, November 18, 2010

Notes to Chapter 5

[1] PBS Frontline, Interview: Condoleezza Rice, http://www.pbs.org/wgbh/pages/frontline/shows/campaign/intervie ws/rice.html

[2] George Tenet with Bill Harlow, At the Center of the Storm: The CIA During America's Time of Crisis, Harper Perennial, 2007

[3] Jim Crogan, The Terrorist Motel: The I-40 connection between Zacarias Moussaoui and Mohamed Atta, LA Weekly, July 24, 2002

[4] See FBI summary document for Marwan Al-Shehhi, accessed at Sribd, 911DocumentArchive, http://tinyurl.com/bnp7vrr

[5] See FBI summary documents for Saeed Al-Ghamdi and Hani Hanjour found in 911 archives at Scribd.com: http://www.scribd.com/911DocumentArchive

[6] Kevin R. Ryan, Two Oklahoma Airports: David Boren, KuwAm, and 9/11, DigWithin.net, October 28,2012

[7] Message sent to the 9/11 Commission from Michael P. Wright, entitled Al Qaeda and CIA Activities in Oklahoma, dated Thu, 25 Sep 2003, accessed at http://bellaciao.org/en/spip.php?article7465

[8] Kelli Arena, Berg's encounter with 'terrorist' revealed, CNN, May 14, 2004

[9] Transcript of PBS NewsHour show, Intelligence Investigation, September 11, 2001, PBS.org

[10] Peter Finn, Hamburg's Cauldron of Terror, Washington Post Foreign Service, Washington Post Foreign Service

[11] George Tenet with Bill Harlow, At the Center of the Storm

[12] Pakistani General Mahmud Ahmed met with Goss and Graham, along with Wolfowitz and several others. The itinerary was released via FOAI request: http://911blogger.com/node/21978.

[13] Interview with Kirk S. Lippold, Q&A (C-SPAN series), July 8, 2012,

http://www.q-and-a.org/Transcript/?ProgramID=1399

[14] James Risen, State of War: The Secret History of the CIA and the Bush Administration, Free Press, 2006

[15] James Risen, State of War

[16] Peter Dale Scott, The Road to 9/11, University of California Press, 2007, pp 82-84

[17] Joseph J. Trento, Prelude to Terror: Edwin P. Wilson and the Legacy of America's Private Intelligence Network, Basic Books, 2006

[18] Robin Cook, The struggle against terrorism cannot be won by military means, The Guardian, July 8, 2005

[19] PBS NewsHour, Al Qaeda's Second Fatwa, February. 23, 1998

[20] The Atlantic Monthly, How Not to Catch a Terrorist (reprinted letter from Michael Scheuer), December 2004

[21] James Risen, State of War

[22] Ned Zeman, David Wise, David Rose, and Bryan Burrough, The Path to 9/11: Lost Warnings and Fatal Errors, Vanity Fair, November 2004

[23] Wikipedia page for 1998 United States embassy bombings

[24] John J. Miller, The Cell: Inside the 9/11 Plot, and Why the FBI and CIA Failed to Stop It, Hyperion, 2010

[25] Ibid

[26] Michael Moran, Bin Laden comes home to roost: His CIA ties are only the beginning of a woeful story, MCNBC, August 28, 1998

[27] George Tenet, memorandum to his staff entitled "Usama Bin Ladin," December 4, 1998, accessed at Scribd

[28] OIG Report on CIA Accountability With Respect to the 9/11 Attacks, page viii

[29] Frank Carlucci, Robert Hunter, and Zalmay Khalilzad, A Global Agenda for the U.S. President, RAND Corporation, March 2001

[30] Colum Lynch; Vernon Loeb, Bin Laden's Network: Terror Conspiracy or Loose Alliance?, The Washington Post, August 1, 1999

[31] Terry McDermott, Perfect Soldiers, HarperCollins, 2009, p 73

[32] Ibid pp 278-279

[33] James Risen and Benjamin Weiser, U.S. Officials Say Aid for Terrorists Came Through Two Persian Gulf Nations, The New York Times, July 8, 1999

[34] Paul Thompson, The Terror Timeline: Year by Year, Day by Day,

Minute by Minute: A Comprehensive Chronicle of the Road to 9/11--
and America's Response, HarperCollins, 2004

[35] Kevin Fenton, Disconnecting the Dots: How CIA and FBI officials helped enable 9/11 and evaded government investigations, TrineDay, 2011, p 104

[36] Ibid pp 121-125

[37] Ibid p 376

[38] Ibid pp 115-119

[39] Senate Select Committee on Intelligence, Statement by Director of Central Intelligence George J. Tenet Before the SSCI on the Worldwide Threat in 2000: Global Realities of Our National Security, 106th Congress, 2nd Session

[40] 9/11 Commission Report, pp 342-344

[41] Greg Palast and David Pallister, FBI claims Bin Laden inquiry was frustrated. The Guardian, November 7, 2001

[42] Greg Palast, The Best Democracy Money Can Buy, Penguin, 2003

[43] Wikipedia page for George Tenet

[44] Senate, Select Committee on Intelligence, and House, Permanent Select Committee on Intelligence, United States Congressional Serial Set, Serial No. 14750: Joint Inquiry Into Intelligence Community Activity Before and After Terrorists Attacks of September 11, 2001 With Errata, Government Printing Office

[45] Ibid

[46] Terry McDermott, Early Scheme to Turn Jets Into Weapons, The Los Angeles Times, June 24, 2002

[47] Daniel Hopsicker, Mad Cow Morning News, http://www.madcowprod.com/

[48] Kevin R. Ryan, Muslims did not attack the U.S. on 9/11, DigWithin.net, March 17, 2012

[49] Senate, Select Committee on Intelligence, and House, Permanent Select Committee on Intelligence, p 135

[50] Ibid

[51] Paul Thompson, The Terror Timeline: Year by Year, Day by Day, Minute by Minute: A Comprehensive Chronicle of the Road to 9/11--and America's Response, HarperCollins, 2004, p 520

[52] Wikipedia page for Richard Shelby

[53] Ibid

54 Gregory C. McCarthy, Congressional Oversight of Intelligence: 9/11 and the Iraq War, ProQuest, 2009, p 170

55 Kevin Fenton, Those 9/11 Commission Minders Again, History Commons Groups, May 27, 2009. See also another post from Kevin Fenton in the same venue entitled "Newly Released Memo: Government 'Minders' at 9/11 Commission Interviews 'Intimidated' Witnesses," dated April 27, 2009

56 Peter Finn and Julie Tate, CIA Says It Misjudged Role of High-Value Detainee Abu Zubaida, Transcript Shows, The Washington Post, June 16, 2009

57 Kevin R. Ryan, Abu Zubaydah Poses a Real Threat to Al Qaeda, DigWithin.net, October 15, 2012

58 George Tenet, At the Center of the Storm: The CIA During America's Time of Crisis, Harper Perennial, 2007

59 Thomas H. Kean and Lee H. Hamilton, Stonewalled by the C.I.A., The New York Times, January 2, 2008

60 USA Today, Reactions to the Tenet's resignation, June 3, 2004

61 Kevin R. Ryan, Evidence for Informed Trading on the Attacks of September 11, Foreign Policy Journal, November 18, 2010

62 Business Wire, Former Federal Bureau of Investigations Director Louis Freeh Joins the Viisage Board of Directors; Freeh Brings 26 Years of Experience in Federal Law Enforcement to Viisage, July 24, 2006

63 Reuters, Ex-CIA chief Tenet joins 'James Bond' firm, October 24, 2006

Notes to Chapter 6

1 For a description and link to the 2011 interview with Richard Clarke, see Jason Leopold, Former Counterterrorism Czar Accuses Tenet, Other CIA Officials of Cover-Up, Truth-out.org, August 11, 2011

2 NYPD Confidential, Charm school for top cops, May 6, 1996

3 Grossman is a 9/11 person of interest according to FBI whistleblower Sibel Edmonds. See Philip Giraldi, Who's Afraid of Sibel Edmonds?, The American Conservative, November 1, 2009. Also note that Grossman was reportedly one of the people who met with Pakistani ISI General Mahmud Ahmed the week of 9/11. See Michel

Chossudovsky, Political Deception: The Missing Link behind 9-11, Centre for Research on Globalisation, June 20, 2002

[4] Peter Dale Scott, Continuity of Government: Is the State of Emergency Superseding our Constitution?, GlobalResearch.ca, November 24, 2010

[5] James Mann, The Armageddon Plan, The Atlantic, March 2004

[6] Howard Kurtz, 'Armageddon' Plan Was Put Into Action on 9/11, Clarke Says , The Washington Post, April 7, 2004

[7] Barton Gellman and Susan Schmidt, Shadow Government Is at Work in Secret, The Washington Post, March 1, 2002

[8] Peter Dale Scott, 'Continuity of Government' Planning: War, Terror and the Supplanting of the U.S. Constitution, Japan Focus

[9] Leslie Filson, Air war over America: Sept. 11 alters face of air defense , mission, Headquarters 1st Air Force, Public Affairs Office, 2003

[10] History Commons 9/11 Timeline, Profile: Zayed bin Sultan Al Nahyan

[11] Nafeez M. Ahmed, The War on Truth: 9/11, Disinformation And The Anatomy Of Terrorism, Olive Branch Press, 2005. See also, History Commons Complete 9/11 Timeline, Context of 'July 1993: Ramzi Yousef and KSM Attempt to Assassinate Pakistani Prime Minister'.

[12] Jonathan Beaty and S.C. Gwynne, Scandals: Not Just a Bank, TIME, September 2, 1991

[13] Peter Truell and Larry Gurwin, False Profits: The Inside Story of BCCI, The World's Most Corrupt Financial Empire, Houghton Mifflin, 1992

[14] The BCCI Affair: A Report to the Committee on Foreign Relations United States Senate, December 1992, Abu DhabiI: BCCI'S founding and majority shareholders, http://www.fas.org/irp/congress/1992_rpt/bcci/14abudhabi.htm

[15] Ibid

[16] Congressional Research Service, Terrorist Attacks by Al Qaeda, March 31, 2004, http://www.fas.org/irp/crs/033104.pdf

[17] Matthew Everett, 9/11 Counterterrorism Chief Richard Clarke and the Rwandan Genocide, Shoestring 911 blog, February 23, 2010

[18] Ibid

[19] History Commons 9/11 Timeline, Profile: United Arab Emirates (UAE)

[20] The story of Berger's inexplicable attempts to steal 9/11-related documents from the National Archives is told in Philip Shenon's book, The Commission: The Uncensored History of the 9/11 Investigation, Hachette Book Group, 2008

[21] James Risen and Benjamin Weiser, U.S. Officials Say Aid for Terrorists Came Through Two Persian Gulf Nations, The New York Times, July 8, 1999

[22] Paul Thompson, The Terror Timeline: Year by Year, Day by Day, Minute by Minute: A Comprehensive Chronicle of the Road to 9/11-- and America's Response, HarperCollins, 2004

[23] Ibid

[24] Wikipedia page for Dubai Ports World controversy

[25] PBS News Hour, Bin Laden's Fatwa, August, 1996

[26] PBS News Hour, Al Qaeda's Fatwa, February 23, 1998

[27] Steve Coll, Ghost Wars: The Secret History of the CIA, Afghanistan, and Bin Laden, from the Soviet Invasion to September 10, 2001, Penguin Books, 2004, pp 447-450

[28] The 9/11 Commission Report, 2004, p 138

[29] Richard Clarke's June 2002 "briefing" testimony to the Joint Congressional Inquiry was classified for years and was only released after significant effort. It can be accessed at the website of the Federation of American Scientists, http://www.fas.org/irp/congress/2002_hr/061102clarke.pdf

[30] History Commons 9/11 Timeline, Profile: United Arab Emirates (UAE), Context of 'August 2001: Six 9/11 Hijackers Live Near Entrance to NSA'

[31] History Commons 9/11 Timeline, Profile: Rick Garza

[32] Paul Thompson, Alhazmi and Almihdhar: The 9/11 Hijackers Who Should Have Been Caught, HisotryCommons.org

[33] The Middle East Media Research Institute, Al-Ahram Al-Arabi: A High-Ranking Yemenite Intelligence Official Blames the US for the Cole Bombing, July 17, 2001

[34] Kevin R. Ryan, The USS Cole: Twelve years later, no justice or understanding, DigWithin.net, October 7, 2012

[35] Richard Miniter, Losing Bin Laden: How Bill Clinton's Failures

Unleashed Global Terror, Regnery Publishers, 2003
[36] 9/11 Commission Report, footnote 11 to Chapter 8
[37] 9/11 Commission Report, p 256
[38] Richard A. Clarke, Against All Enemies: Inside America's War on Terror, Simon & Schuster, 2004
[39] Kevin R. Ryan, Abu Zubaydah Poses a Real Threat to Al Qaeda, DigWithin.net, October 2012
[40] History Commons 9/11 Timeline, Alhazmi and Almihdhar: The 9/11 Hijackers Who Should Have Been Caught
[41] See 2011 interview with Richard Clarke
[42] Paul Thompson, They Tried to Warn Us: Foreign Intelligence Warnings Before 9/11, History Commons Complete 9/11 Timeline
[43] Khalifa University website, http://www.kustar.ac.ae/aboutus/bot/
[44] Intelligence Online, Richard Clarke's Big Footprint in United Arab Emirates

Notes to Chapter 7

[1] The 9/11 Commission Report, page 14
[2] The 9/11 Commission Report, pages 17 to 18
[3] The 9/11 Commission Report, page 34
[4] Ibid
[5] Matthew Goldstein, When Bad Scams Go Good, The Wall Street Journal, May 21, 2001
[6] NASD Regulation, Inc. Office of Dispute Resolution, Arbitration No. 9644952
[7] Westlaw citation WL 31426028, United States District Court, S.D. New York, No. 00 CR 91-11 RWS, Oct. 28, 2002
[8] United States District Court, E.D. New York, 103 F.Supp.2d 579, Downes v. O'Connell, 103 F.Supp.2d 579 (2000)
[9] Lynn Spencer, Touching History: The Untold Story of the Drama That Unfolded in the Skies Over America on 9/11, Free Press, 2008, page 2
[10] 9/11 Commission memorandum for the record, Interview with Benedict Sliney, May 21, 2004
[11] Notes from interview of ATSC officers, T8 B18 HQ FAA 1 of 3 Fdr- Air Traffic Services Cell (ATSC) Events Summary 074, access at

911DocumentArchive, Scribd, http://tinyurl.com/d6s68bf

[12] Matthew Everett, The Repeatedly Delayed Responses of the Pentagon Command Center on 9/11, Shoestring 9/11 Blog, November 7, 2010

[13] National Commission on Terrorist Attacks upon the United States, Twelfth Public Hearing, June 17, 2004

[14] 9/11 Commission memorandum for the record, Interview with Benedict Sliney, May 21, 2004

[15] Canadian Broadcasting Corporation, The Secret History Of 9/11: United flight 93

[16] The 9/11 Commission report, page 113

[17] Peter Dale Scott, American War Machine, Rowan & Littlefield, 2010, p 115

[18] Harvey M. Sapolsky, Benjamin H. Friedman, Brendan Rittenhouse Green, US military innovation since the Cold War: creation without destruction, Taylor & Francis Publishers, 2009

[19] History Commons Complete 9/11 Timeline, Profile for William S. Cohen

[20] Kevin R. Ryan, Gofer and Trout: Questions on Two Flights Out of Andrews AFB on 9/11, DigWithin.net, December 4, 2011

[21] 9/11 Commission Memorandum for the Record (MFR) on John Hawley interview, October 8, 2003

[22] Transcript of 9/11 Commission public hearing of May 23, 2003, 9/11 Commission Archive

[23] Andrew R. Thomas, Aviation Security Management: Volume 1, Greenwood Publishing Group, page 78

[24] Ricardo Alonso-Zaldivar, FAA Culture of Bureaucracy Stymies Security Reform Efforts, Critics Say, Los Angeles

[25] Catherine Rampell, Ex-employee says FAA warned before 9/11, USA Today, November 24, 2006

[26] National Commission on Terrorist Attacks upon the United States, Public Hearing, May 23, 2003

[27] Interview of Michael Canavan, 9/11 Commission Public Hearing, May 23, 2003

[28] See "Lee Longmire 4/30/04 Background See Team 7 Interview", accessed at the 911Archive at Scribed.

See also the 9/11 Commission Memorandum for the Record:

Interview with Lee Longmire, Prepared by Bill Johnstone, dated
October 28, 2003.
[29] 9/11 Commission Memorandum for the Record (MFR) on John
Hawley interview, October 8, 2003
[30] 9/11 Commission Report, footnote 36 to Chapter 10
[31] White House press briefing by Leon Panetta, January 10, 1996
[32] Gordon Thomas, Gideon's Spies: The Secret History of the Mossad,
Thomas Dunne Books, 1995, pp 309-310
[33] John T. Carney, Benjamin F. Schemmer, No Room for Error: The
Story Behind the USAF Special Tactics Unit, Presido Press, 2002, p
232
[34] Graeme C. S. Steven, Rohan Gunaratna, Counterterrorism: a
reference handbook, ABC-CLIO, 2004, p 230
[35] Abbas Al Lawati, 'You can't authorise murder': Hersh, Gulf News,
May 12, 2009
[36] Blake Hounshell, Seymour Hersh unleashed, Foreign Policy, January
18, 2011
[37] Matthew Phelan, Pulitzer Prize Winner Seymour Hersh And The
Men Who Want Him Committed, WhoWhatWhy.com, Feb 23, 2011
[38] Summary of 9/11 Commission interview with John Flaherty, Chief
of Staff for Secretary of Transportation, Norman Mineta, April 2004
[39] Spartacus Educational webpage for Richard Armitage
[40] CNN Politics, Armitage admits leaking Plame's identity, September
08, 2006
[41] Kevin R. Ryan, Demolition Access To The WTC Towers: Part Two
– Security, 911Review.com, August 22, 2009

Notes to Chapter 8

[1] Nicholas Levis, Senator Dayton: NORAD Lied About 9/11,
911Truth.org, August 1, 2004,
[2] Bob Arnot, What Was Needed to Halt the Attacks?: Cockpit security,
quick response not in evidence Tuesday, MSNBC, September 12, 2001
[3] North American Aerospace Defense Command, NORAD Regulation
55-7, Peterson Air Force Base, Colorado, July 6, 1990,
http://www.fas.org/spp/military/docops/norad/reg55007.htm. Also

see Chairman of the Joint Chiefs of Staff Instruction, Aircraft Piracy (Hijacking) And Destruction Of Derelict
Airborne Objects, June 1, 2001, http://tinyurl.com/brmjd2p
4 United States General Accounting Office, Continental Air Defense: A Dedicated Force Is No Longer Needed, May 3, 1994
5 Nicholas Levis, Senator Dayton: NORAD Lied About 9/11
6 Senate Armed Services Committee, General Myers Confirmation Hearing, September 13, 2001
7 Transcript of Hearing Before the Committee on Armed Services, United States Senate, October 25, 2001, U.S. Government Printing Office
8 Transcript of Hearing Before the Committee on Armed Services, United States Senate, October 25, 2001, U.S. Government Printing Office
9 See memo from Dan Marcus to the Inspector General of both the DOD and Department of Transportation, dated July 29, 2004. See also email response from John Farmer to 9/11 Commission staff (dated 1/19/2004) and associated messages. See also memorandum from John Farmer and Philip Zelikow to the 9/11 Commissioners in which they state that "Team 8 has unearthed evidence strongly suggesting the possibility that a USAF officer, and possibly others at the USAF and FAA, must have known that the official story was false, yet persisted in telling it or did not correct the record."
10 United States Code, 18 USC § 1001, This law is otherwise known as "making false statements"
11 The NORAD notification of Flight 175's hijacking at 8:42 am was listed in an email from NORADJ3 to Eberhart. It was also listed in the NORAD timeline given by Eberhart to the Senate Armed Services Committee in October 2001.
12 National Commission on Terrorist Attacks upon the United States, Thomas H. Kean, Lee Hamilton, 9/11 Commission Report, p 31
13 David Ray Griffin, The 9/11 Commission's Incredible Tales, first published at 911Truth.org, December 13, 2005
14 Michael Bronner, "9/11 Live: The NORAD Tapes", Vanity Fair, September 2006, 262-285
15 Kyle F. Hence, UQ Wire: Statement from FAA Contradicts 911 Report, Unanswered Questions Wire, August 2, 2004

[16] Kevin R. Ryan, FAA Failures on 9/11: The Wall Street Lawyer and the Special Ops Hijack Coordinator, DgWithin.net, April 2011

[17] Matthew L. Wald, F.A.A. Official Scrapped Tape of 9/11 Controllers' Statements, The New York Times, May 6, 2004

[18] National Commission on Terrorist Attacks upon the United States, Transcript of twelfth public hearing, June 17,2004

[19] On 1 October 1999, the Commander, USSPACECOM (USCINCSPACE), assumed command of a brand new mission area, DoD-Computer Network Defense (CND). Also effective the same date, the Secretary of Defense (SECDEF) delegated to USCINCSPACE the authority to declare DOD Infocon levels.

[20] 1st Fighter Wing History Excerpt, July through December 2001, p 61, accessed at 911Document Archive, Scribd, http://tinyurl.com/cnzmhyz. The Infocon level was raised again during the morning of September 11, immediately after the second attack on the World Trade Center.

[21] The Infocon alert system was developed in response to a coordinated hacking called Solar Sunrise that occurred in 1998 and started at Andrews Air Force Base. For more on Solar Sunrise, see Kevin Poulsen, Video: Solar Sunrise, the Best FBI-Produced Hacker Flick Ever, Wired, September 23, 2008

[22] 9/11 Commission, Memorandum for the Record: Interview with CINCNORAD Eberhart, prepared by Geoffrey Brown, March 1, 2004

[23] Transcript: 9/11 Commission Hearings for June 17, 2004, published at The Washington Post, June 17, 2004

[24] 9/11 Commission, Memorandum for the Record: Interview with CINCNORAD Eberhart

[25] 9/11 Commission, Memorandum for the Record: Interview with CINCNORAD Eberhart

[26] National Commission on Terrorist Attacks upon the United States, Thomas H. Kean, Lee Hamilton, 9/11 Commission Report, p 38

[27] 9/11 Commission, Memorandum for the Record: Interview with CINCNORAD Eberhart

[28] Eberhart told the Commission that the "newest NORAD time line [delivered to Commission staff on February 23, 2004] was likely the result of his 'standing order' to correct the record of events whenever possible." 9/11 Commission, Memorandum for the Record: Interview

with CINCNORAD Eberhart
[29] Matthew Everett, The Actions and Inactions of the Commander in Charge of the U.S. Air Defense Failure on 9/11, Shoestring 911, June 18, 2010
[30] See memorandum from 9/11 Commission Team 8 re: DOD Document Production, dated October 29, 2003
[31] National Commission on Terrorist Attacks upon the United States, Transcript of twelfth public hearing, June 17,2004
[32] Transcript of Hearing Before the Senate Armed Services Committee, August 16 and 17, 2004, http://www.gpo.gov/fdsys/pkg/CHRG-108shrg24495/html/CHRG-108shrg24495.htm
[33] A NORAD Exercises Hijack Summary, released by the 9/11 Commission, lists 28 exercise events involving hijackings between October 1998 and September 10, 2001. This does not include the Amalgam Virgo exercises, http://www.scribd.com/doc/16411947/NORAD-Exercises-Hijack-Summary
[34] Matthew Everett, NORAD Exercise a Year Before 9/11 Simulated a Pilot Trying to Crash a Plane into a New York Skyscraper--The UN Headquarters, Shoestring 911, July 27, 2010
[35] SEADS Concept Proposal: Amalgam Virgo 01, accessed at www.ratical.org/ratville/CAH/linkscopy/AmalgumVirgo.pdf
[36] 9/11 Commission, Memorandum for the Record: Interview with Colonel Robert Marr, prepared by Geoffrey Brown, January 23, 2004
[37] SEADS Concept Proposal: Amalgam Virgo 01
[38] Daniel Hopsicker, Will secret deal bring old management back to Venice Airport FBO?, Mad Cow Morning News, January 5, 2010
[39] 9/11 Commission, Memorandum for the Record: Interview with Ken Merchant and Paul Goddard, Prepared by: Geoffrey Brown, March 4, 2004
[40] 9/11 Commission, Memorandum for the Record: Interview with Ken Merchant and Paul Goddard
[41] 9/11 Commission, Memorandum for the Record: Interview with Ken Merchant and Paul Goddard
[42] History Commons Complete 9/11 Timeline, Context of '9:05 am (and After) September 11, 2001: Flight 77 Reappears on Radar, but Flight Controllers Do Not Notice'

43 9/11 Commission, Memorandum for the Record: Interview with Ken Merchant and Paul Goddard

44 History Commons Complete 9/11 Timeline, Profile: Twin Star

45 For example, see 9/11 Commission "DOD Document Request No. 18."

46 Transcript of 9/11 Commission Hearing of May 23, 2003

47 Joe Dejka, Inside StratCom on September 11 Offutt exercise took real-life twist, The Omaha World-Herald, February 27, 2002

48 Mark H. Gaffney, Why Did the World's Most Advanced Electronics Warfare Plane Circle Over The White House on 9/11?, The Journal of 9/11 Studies, July 2007. See also the update several months later at same source.

49 National Commission on Terrorist Attacks upon the United States, Thomas H. Kean, Lee Hamilton, 9/11 Commission Report, Notes to Chapter 1, footnote 116

50 Vigilant Guardian 01-02 planning document, Accessed at 911Document Archive, Scribd, http://tinyurl.com/cn52tpf

51 Vigilant Guardian 01-02 planning document

52 Matthew Everett, 'Real-World or Exercise': Did the U.S. Military Mistake the 9/11 Attacks for a Training Scenario?, Shoestring 911, March 22, 2012

53 Matthew Everett, 'Real-World or Exercise'

54 Matthew Everett, 'Real-World or Exercise'

55 Vigilant Guardian 01-02 planning document

56 Matthew Everett, 'Let's Get Rid of This Goddamn Sim': How NORAD Radar Screens Displayed False Tracks All Through the 9/11 Attacks, Shoestring 911, August 12, 2010

57 Matthew Everett, On 9/11, the U.S. Military Was Preparing for a Simulated Nuclear War, Shoestring 911, November 23, 2011

58 Matthew Everett, The Repeatedly Delayed Responses of the Pentagon Command Center on 9/11, Shoestring 911, November 7, 2010

59 Matthew Everett, 'Let's Get Rid of This Goddamn Sim'

60 Matthew Everett, On 9/11, the U.S. Military Was Preparing for a Simulated Nuclear War

61 Email timeline provided to General Eberhart by "NORAD J3", September 14, 2001, available at Scribd, 911Document Archive

[62] 9/11 Commission, Memorandum for the Record: Interview with Colonel Robert Marr

[63] Paul Schreyer, Anomalies of the Air Defense on 9/11, Journal of 9/11 Studies, Volume 33, October 2012

[64] Ibid

[65] Transcript of 9/11 Commission Hearing of May 23, 2003

[66] Memoranda dated July 29, 2004 from 9/11 Commission counsel Dan Marcus, and emails between 9/11 Commission staff members

[67] 9/11 Commission, Memorandum for the Record: Interview with Colonel Robert Marr

[68] Transcript of 9/11 Commission Hearing of May 23, 2003

[69] 9/11 Commission, Memorandum for the Record: Interview with CINCNORAD Eberhart

[70] Excerpts from May 22 and May 23, 2003 9/11 Commission Hearings, with Richard Ben Veniste questioning Jane Garvey and the military, 911Workin Group, http://tinyurl.com/c75t89h

[71] National Commission on Terrorist Attacks upon the United States, Public Hearing, Friday, May 23, 2003

[72] Interview of Craig Borgstrom by Leslie Filson

[73] 9/11 Commission, Memorandum for the Record: Interview with Craig Borgstrom, Prepared by Miles Kara, December 1, 2003

[74] Transcript of interview with Craig Borgstrom and David E. Somdahl, Conducted Thursday, 25 October 2001 at Langley AFB, VA

[75] 9/11 Commission, Memorandum for the Record: Interview with John Harter, Operations Supervisor, prepared by Miles Kara, December 1, 2003

[76] Interview of Craig Borgstrom by Leslie Filson

[77] 9/11 Commission, Memoranda for the Record:, GIANT KILLER visit, December 3, 2003

[78] 9/11 NEADS Tape Transcription, DRM DAT2, CHANNEL 3 WD1-3 TK. WAV, Transcribed by Judy Zenge, Seak Professional Services accessed at 911Depsoitory.info

[79] North American Aerospace Defense Command, NORAD Regulation 55-7

[80] David Ray Griffin, Flights 11, 175, 77, and 93: The 9/11 Commission's Incredible Tales, 911Truth.org, December 4, 2005

[81] Paul Thompson, The Failure to Defend the Skies on 9/11,

HistoryCommons.org

[82] National Commission on Terrorist Attacks upon the United States, Public Hearing, Friday, May 23, 2003, http://www.9-11commission.gov

[83] National Commission on Terrorist Attacks upon the United States, Thomas H. Kean, Lee Hamilton, 9/11 Commission Report, p 44

[84] 9/11 Commission, Memorandum for the Record: Interview with General David Wherley, Prepared by: Philip Zelikow, August 28, 2003

[85] Christopher Conkey, Retired Major General Wherley Died in Crash, Wall Street Journal, June 24, 2009

[86] 9/11 Commission, Memorandum for the Record: Interview with Lt Col Mark E. Stuart, Prepared by Miles Kara, October 30, 2003

[87] The handwritten notes and personal statements of ATCs and air traffic managers can be found at the website of the 9/11 Working Group of Bloomington, http://www.911workinggroup.org/p/foia-research.html. See, for example, "5 AWA 204."

[88] National Commission on Terrorist Attacks upon the United States, Public Hearing, Friday, May 23, 2003

[89] See documents obtained by the 9/11 Working Group of Bloomington, 5AWA323 and 5AWA342, at http://www.911workinggroup.org/p/foia-research.html.

[90] 9/11 Commission, Memorandum for the Record: Interview with CINCNORAD Eberhart

[91] Matthew Everett, Was Delta 1989 Part of a Live-Fly Hijacking Exercise on 9/11?, Shoestring 9/11, July 22, 2009

[92] Transcript of Leslie Filson interview with Craig Borgstrom

[93] 9/11 Commission, Memorandum for the Record: Interview with CINCNORAD Eberhart

[94] National Commission on Terrorist Attacks upon the United States, Thomas H. Kean, Lee Hamilton, 9/11 Commission Report, p 41

[95] Lynn Spencer, Touching History, Pp 225-226

[96] Transcript: 9/11 Commission Hearings for June 17, 2004

[97] Ibid

[98] Jim Hoffman, The Crash of Flight 93: Evidence Indicates Flight 93 Was Shot Down, 911Research.wtc7.net

[99] Mark H. Gaffney, Black 9/11: Money, Motive & Technology, Trine Day, 2012

[100] Maureen Dowd, Vice comes clean: He was the real president, and he stands by all of his mistakes, The Pittsburgh Post-Gazette, March 7, 2013

[101] NORAD and USNORTHCOM Public Affairs, NORAD and USNORTHCOM honour 9/11 heroes, October. 15, 2012

[102] See Bloomberg Businessweek profile for Ralph Eberhart. He has been a director at Triumph Group (military aviation), Jacobs Engineering (Oil & gas services), VSE Corp. (DOD equipment support), Rockwell Collins (military aviation), The Spectrum Group (Homeland security), Eid Passport (Homeland security), Standard Aero Holdings (military aviation), ObjectVideo (Homeland Security), and ICx Technologies (Homeland security).

Notes to Chapter 9

[1] Allan Wood and Paul Thompson, An Interesting Day: President Bush's Movements and Actions on 9/11, History Commons Complete 9/11 Timeline

[2] Matthew Everett, The 90-Minute Stand Down on 9/11: Why Was the Secret Service's Early Request for Fighter Jets Ignored?, Shoestring 9/11 Blog, December 20, 2009

[3] Tom Bayles, The Day Before Everything Changed, President Bush Touched Locals' Lives, The Sarasota Herald-Tribune, September 10, 2002

[4] Allan Wood and Paul Thompson

[5] Philip H. Melanson, Secret Service: The Hidden History of an Enigmatic Agency, Carroll & Graf, 2002

[6] Command Consulting, Bio for Edward Marrnizel, http://www.commandcg.com/en/edward-marinzel

[7] For references to the 2004 Edward Marinzel interview, see The 9/11 Commission Report, footnotes 204 and 207 from Chapter 1, and footnotes 1 to 3 from Chapter 10

[8] 911Research.wtc7.net, George W. Bush: Cover Stories of the People in Charge

[9] See the 9/11 Commission Report, p 325. The footnote referenced says that Cheney had reported the anonymous threat and that the director of the White House Situation Room later disputed the story.

[10] Command Consulting, Bio for Edward Marrnizel

[11] Command Consulting, Bio for Joseph Hagin,
http://www.commandcg.com/en/joseph-w-hagin

[12] The 9/11 Commission Report, page 36

[13] FOIA documents released by the U.S. Secret Service to Aidan
Monaghan on April 23,
2010,.http://www.mediafire.com/?vydb4nxdmyy

[14] Washington's Blog, Mineta's testimony CONFIRMED, March 04,
2007

[15] Michael C. Ruppert, Crossing the Rubicon (Chapter 24), New
Society Publishers, 2004

[16] Richard A. Clarke, Against All Enemies: Inside America's War on
Terror, Simon & Schuster, 2004, p 7

[17] FOIA documents released by the U.S. Secret Service

[18] 9/11 Commission summary of "USSS Statement and interview
reports," dated July 28, 2003, accessed at Scribd,
http://tinyurl.com/cs8dhho

[19] Lynn Spencer, Touching History: The untold story of the drama that
unfolded in the skies over America on 9/11, Free Press, 2008

[20] Christopher Conkey, Retired Major General Wherley Died in Crash,
Wall Street Journal, June 24, 2009

[21] Matthew Everett, The 90-Minute Stand Down on 9/11: Why Was
the Secret Service's Early Request for Fighter Jets Ignored?, Shoestring
9/11 Blog, December 20, 2009

[22] History Commons Complete 9/11 Timeline, Profile: Daniel Caine

[23] Empty Wheel, Who Is Carl Truscott and Why Did Bush's DOJ
Protect Him?, March 5, 2008

[24] Bloomberg Businessweek profile for ASERO Worldwide

Notes to Chapter 10

[1] Kevin R. Ryan, Two dozen questions about Flight 77 and the
Pentagon that might lead to justice, DigWithin.net, July 9, 2011,

[2] For more information on Hani Hanjour and his poor piloting skills,
see Clueless Super-pilot: Jetliner Aerobatics by Flight School Dropout
Who Never Flew a Jet, 911Research.wtc7.net

[3] Rebecca Sheir, Rebuilding the World's Largest Office Building,

WAMU Metro Connection, September 9, 2011
[4] David S. Chartock, Industry Rallies To Cleanup WTC Aftermath, Special Report! (9/12/01 -- noon), New York Construction News, http://newyork.construction.com/news/WTC/0109_rallies.asp
[5] National Priorities Project, U.S. Security Spending Since 9/11, May 26, 2011
[6] Jamey Hecht, PTech, 9/11, and USA-Saudi Terror, From The Wilderness Publications, 2005, For more on PTech, see National Corruption Index profile for Felix Rausch, October 14, 2008
[7] Jamey Hecht, PTECH, 9/11, and USA-SAUDI TERROR - Part I: PROMIS Connections to Cheney Control of 9/11 Attacks Confirmed, From the Wilderness Publications, 2005,
[8] Kevin R. Ryan, Carlyle, Kissinger, SAIC and Halliburton, 911Blogger.com, December 12, 2009,
[9] Dan Briody, The Iron Triangle: Inside the Secret World of The Carlyle Group, Wiley publishers, 2003
[10] Brian Friel, CIA suspends former director's security clearances, Government Executive, August 24, 1999
[11] NNDB page for John P. White, http://www.nndb.com/people/086/000170573/
[12] Sourcewatch page for Global Technology Partners, http://www.sourcewatch.org/index.php?title=Global_Technology_Partners,_LLC
[13] 911research.wtc7.com, Pentagon Renovation
[14] Rebecca Leung, Cashing In For Profit?, CBS News 60 Minutes, February 11, 2009,
[15] Steve Vogel, The Pentagon: a history : the untold story of the wartime race to build the Pentagon – and to restore it sixty years later, Random House, 2008
[16] Boeing Defense, Space and Security, Boeing Satellites, Milstar II, http://www.boeing.com/defense-space/space/bss/factsheets/government/milstar_ii/milstar_ii.html
[17] SpaceToday.org, The Satellite Wars, http://www.spacetoday.org/Satellites/YugoWarSats.html
[18] Air Force National Symposia, comments by Darleen Druyun, Los Angeles - October 27, 1995, http://afa.org/aef/pub/la2.asp

[19] Steve Vogel, The Pentagon: a history : the untold story of the wartime race to build the Pentagon – and to restore it sixty years later, Random House, 2008

[20] Project for a NEW American Century, Statement of Principles, June 3, 1997

[21] Ken Silverstein, The Man from ONA, The Nation, October 7, 1999

[22] Douglas McGray, The Marshall Plan, Wired, February 2003

[23] See, for example, Jennifer Morrison Taw, Paul A. McCarthy, and Kevin Jack Riley, The American Armies: 1993, RAND Corporation, 1994

[24] Michael Russell Rip and James M. Hasik, The precision revolution: GPS and the future of aerial warfare, Naval Institute Press, 2002

[25] Project for a New American Century, Rebuilding America's Defenses, September 2000

[26] Andrew Cockburn, Rumsfeld: His Rise, Fall, and Catastrophic Legacy, Scribner, 2007

[27] Lyndon Larouche reported that Telos' board of directors was a "who's who" of Richard Perle associates, http://www.larouchepub.com/other/2002/2931murawiec_doss.html

[28] Andrew Cockburn

[29] Washington's Blog, Continuity of Government Measures WERE Implemented on 9/11 . . . Were They EVER Revoked?, February 10, 2008

[30] John Parkinson, Special Report: Lee Evey: The Man And His Mission, Today's Facility Manager, September 2002

[31] Website for AMEC, http://www.amec.com/

[32] Nicholas A. Vardy, The World's Most Valuable Companies, The Global Guru, December 2009

[33] C.L. Taylor, Rebuilding The Pentagon, Capstone Communications, http://www.capstonestrategy.com/PopHTML/Pentagon.html

[34] Alexander's Oil and Gas Connections, AGRA officially changes its name to AMEC, May 15, 2000

[35] ABB website, ABB announces proposed Board, share split, February 19, 2001

[36] Randeep Ramesh, "The two faces of Rumsfeld," The Guardian, May 9, 2003.

37 Benjamin Weinthal, 'Nazi-era corporate behavior repeated', Jerusalem Post, January 21, 2010
38 Businessweek profile for Peter Janson,
39 Steve Vogel
40 Concrete Pumping, Pumping at the Pentagon Puts Reconstruction Months Ahead of Schedule, Cached/copied 09-13-08, http://tinyurl.com/cvq7sfo
41 Website for Facchina Global Services (FGS), Secure networks and VTC, http://facchinaglobal.com/networks.aspx
42 History Commons 9/11 Timeline, Events related to SVTC problems
43 William Viner interview by OSD, October 12, 2001, accessed at Scribd, http://tinyurl.com/bvvatsb
44 Register of graduates and former cadets of the United States Military Academy, 1991
45 GlobalSecurity.org, Military Communications webpage, http://www.globalsecurity.org/space/systems/com-overview.htm
46 Donald H. Martin, A History of U.S. Military Satellite Communication Systems, The Aerospace Corporation, http://www.aero.org/publications/crosslink/winter2002/01.html
47 Steve Vogel
48 Jean-Pierre Desmoulins, The damage before impact, http://jpdesm.pagesperso-orange.fr/pentagon/pages-en/trj-before.html
49 ASCE and SCI, The Pentagon Building Performance Report, January 2003, http://fire.nist.gov/bfrlpubs/build03/PDF/b03017.pdf
50 Steve Vogel
51 Eric Bart's Pentagon Attack Eyewitness Account Compilation, 911research.wtc7.net
52 ASCE and SCI, The Pentagon Building Performance Report, January 2003
53 Andrew S. Carten, Jr., Aircraft Wake Turbulence: An Interesting Phenomenon Turned Killer, Air University Review, July-August 1971
54 U.S. Department of Justice, Criminal Division, written non-disclosure agreement between DOJ attorney Daniel Levin and Philip Zelikow, July 11, 2003, found at 9/11Document Archive (Scribd), under the title SK B9 Tier a-B Interviews 1 of 2 Fdr- Letters Re

Minders- Interviews- Recording- Etc170

[55] Eric Bart's Pentagon Attack Eyewitness Account Compilation
[56] Steve Vogel
[57] See diagram of the impact scene, with Flight 77 drawn to scale. http://www.engr.psu.edu/ae/WTC/pentagon_092301.gif
[58] 911Research.com, Pentagon Attack Footage: The Suppression of Video Footage of the Pentagon Attack
[59] The Smithsonian Institution, Archive of September 11 photos, image of FBI laboratory personnel collecting debris from Pentagon attack site, http://tinyurl.com/cozoyma
[60] David Ray Griffin, 9/11 Ten Years Later: When State Crimes Against Democracy Succeed, Olive Brach Press, 2011
[61] Secretary Rumsfeld Interview with Larry King, CNN, U.S. Department of Defense, Office of the Assistant Secretary of Defense (Public Affairs), Dec. 5, 2001
[62] 911Research.wtc7.net, Pentagon Victims
[63] George Cahlink, Restoring Hope, Government Executive, May 1, 2002
[64] Esther Schrader, Pentagon, a Vulnerable Building, Was Hit in Least Vulnerable Spot, Los Angeles Times, September 16, 2001
[65] Aidan Monaghan, Plausibility Of 9/11 Aircraft Attacks Generated By GPS-Guided Aircraft Autopilot Systems, Journal of 9/11 Studies, October, 2008
[66] David Jensen, WAAS: Back in Step, Avionics Magazine, February 1, 2002
[67] Aidan Monaghan
[68] NTSB, Office of Research and Engineering, Flight path study – American Airlines Flight 77, February 19, 2002
[69] Matthew Everett, The 9/11 Hijackers: Amateur Aviators Who Became Super-Pilots on September 11, Shoestring's Blog, July 11, 2011
[70] Raytheon company news release, Raytheon and the U.S. Air Force demonstrate new technology aircraft precision approach and landing system, September 6, 2001
[71] Space Daily, GPS Alert: Civil-Military Interoperability For GPS Assisted Aircraft Landings Demonstrated, October 1, 2001
[72] Wikipedia, Joint Precision Approach and Landing System

[73] Michael Russell Rip and James M. Hasik

[74] See FAA report, "Report of Aircraft Accident," Nov. 13, 2001; John Hendershot interview (Dec. 22, 2003); FAA report, "Summary of Air Traffic Hijack Events: September 11, 2001," Sept. 17, 2001; NTSB report, "Flight Path Study-American Airlines Flight 77," Commission analysis of radar data.

[75] The 9/11 Commission Report

[76] Instrument Approach, Answers.com, http://www.answers.com/topic/precision-approach

[77] George Washington's Blog, Mineta's testimony CONFIRMED, March 04, 2007

[78] History Commons Complete 9/11 Timeline, Dick Cheney's Actions on 9/11

[79] See diagram of impact zone at 911Research.wtc7.net, http://911research.wtc7.net/essays/pentagon/docs/impact757.gif

[80] Pentagon OSD Historical Office interview with Georgine K, Glatz, December 7, 2001, accessed at 911DocumentArchive (Scribd), http://tinyurl.com/caqhjde

[81] 911Research.wtc7.net, Pentagon Explosion

[82] History Commons 9/11 Timeline, Context of '(9:45 a.m.-10:45 a.m.) September 11, 2001: Secondary Explosions Heard inside Pentagon

[83] Bomb Goes Off At Pentagon During Porter Goss Q&A, YouTube, http://www.youtube.com/watch?v=q44verk-cwM

[84] Eric Bart's Pentagon Attack Eyewitness Account Compilation

[85] J. Robert Beyster and Peter Economy, The SAIC solution: how we built an $8 billion employee-owned technology company, John Wiley & Sons, 2007

[86] PatentMaps, Patent applications made by Paul Mlakar, http://www.patentmaps.com/inventor/Mlakar_Paul_F_1.html

[87] Steve Vogel, p417

[88] ASCE and SCI, The Pentagon Building Performance Report, January 2003

[89] The Oklahoma Bombing Investigation Committee, Final Report on the Bombing of the Alfred P. Murrah Federal Building, 2001

[90] Kevin R. Ryan, Pentagon investigation leader, Paul Mlakar, obstructed investigation in New Orleans, according to UC Berkeley professor, 911Blogger.com, October 15, 2010

[91] C.L. Taylor

[92] Sarah Krouse, D.C. engineer helps bring structure to chaos, Washington Business Journal, August 26, 2011

[93] Washington Business Journal, D.C. engineer helps bring structure to chaos, August 26, 2011

[94] Pentagon OSD Historical Office interview with Georgine K, Glatz

[95] William Viner interview

[96] United States Department of Defense News Transcript, Thursday, March 7, 2002, http://tinyurl.com/c84zbsu

[97] Patrick Creed and Rick Newman, Firefight: Inside the Battle to Save the Pentagon on 9/11, Ballantine Books, 2008

Notes to Chapter 11

[1] John Glaser, CIA Documents: US Drastically Overestimated Soviet Capabilities, AntiWar.com, September 28, 2011

[2] Burton Hersh, The Old Boys, Tree Farm Books, 1992, p 271

[3] Right Web, Committee on the Present Danger, updated November 24, 2009, http://tinyurl.com/cqoq2c9

[4] Peter Dale Scott, The Road to 9/11: Wealth, Empire, and the Future of America, University of California Press, 2007, p 59

[5] Department of the Navy – Navy Historical Center, The Gulf of Tonkin, The 1964 Incidents, Hearing Before the Committee on Foreign Relations, February 20, 1968, http://www.ibiblio.org/hyperwar/NHC/tonkin1.htm

[6] Douglas Frantz and David McKean, Friends in high places: the rise and fall of Clark Clifford, Little, Brown, 1995

[7] The Liberty Incident, The Clark Clifford Report, http://www.thelibertyincident.com/clifford.html

[8] John Crewdson, New revelations in attack on American spy ship, Chicago Tribune, October 2, 2007

[9] Joseph J. Trento, Prelude to Terror: Edwin P. Wilson and the Legacy of America's Private Intelligence Network, Basic Books, 2006, p 101

[10] James Mann, Rise Of The Vulcans: The History of Bush's War Cabinet, Viking Press, 2004

[11] James Bamford, Body of secrets: anatomy of the ultra-secret National Security Agency. Random House. 2002

[12] U.S. Joint Chiefs of Staff, "Justification for US Military Intervention in Cuba (TS)", U.S. Department of Defense, March 1962. For online pdf file, see the National Security Archive at the George Washington University Gelman Library, Washington, D.C., http://www.gwu.edu/~nsarchiv/news/20010430/northwoods.pdf

[13] Daniele Ganser, NATO's Secret Armies: Operation Gladio and Terrorism in Western Europe, Frank Cass, 2005

[14] Ibid, page 29

[15] David Teacher, Rogue Agents: Habsburg, Pinay and the Private Cold War 1951 – 1991

[16] Kevin R. Ryan, KuwAm and Stratesec: Directors and investors that link 9/11 to a private intelligence network, DigWithin.net, February 24, 2012

[17] Statement by Karpiloff, http://securitysolutions.com/mag/security_world_trade_center/

[18] Brian Michael Jenkins and Frances Edwards-Winslow, Saving City Lifelines: Lessons Learned in the 9-11 Terrorist Attacks, Mineta Transportation Institute, September 2003

[19] Greg Krikorian, Calmly taking terror's measure, Los Angeles Times, January 31, 2008

[20] Gerry O'Sullivan, Boom! – World Trade Center bombing – Column, Humanist, May-June, 1993 issue, http://findarticles.com/p/articles/mi_m1374/is_n3_v53/ai_13818521/

[21] Wikipedia page for Guatemalan Civil War

[22] Wikipedia page for United States occupation of the Dominican Republic (1965–1966)

[23] Greg Krikorian, Calmly taking terror's measure

[24] Brian Michael Jenkins, The Unchangeable War, re-published November 1970 by the RAND Corporation for the Advanced Research Projects Agency, http://www.rand.org/pubs/research_memoranda/2006/RM6278-2.pdf

[25] Douglas Valentine, The Phoenix Program, iUniverse, 2000

[26] In an email communication, Douglas Valentine told the author that he had heard Jenkins' name mentioned with regard to Phoenix and that another journalist was writing about it but he could not recall the

details.

27 Brian M. Jenkins, A People's Army for South Vietnam: A Vietnamese Solution, RAND Corporation, November 1971, http://www.prgs.edu/content/dam/rand/pubs/reports/2008/R897.pdf

28 Greg Krikorian, Calmly taking terror's measure

29 Brian Michael Jenkins, Terrorism Works – Sometimes, RAND Corporation, April, 1974, http://www.rand.org/pubs/papers/2006/P5217.pdf

30 Brian M. Jenkins, International Terrorism: A New Kind of Warfare, RAND Corporation, June 1974, http://www.rand.org/pubs/papers/2008/P5261.pdf

31 Ibid

32 Brian Jenkins, George Tanham, Eleanor Wainstein and Gerald Sullivan, Report of a Discussion, October 19-20, 1976 at the RAND Corporation, Washington, DC, July 1977, http://www.rand.org/pubs/papers/2008/P5830.pdf

33 Brian Michael Jenkins. The Psychological Implications of Media-Covered Terrorism, RAND Corporation, June 1981, http://www.rand.org/content/dam/rand/pubs/papers/2005/P6627.pdf

34 Powerbase page for Brian Jenkins, http://www.powerbase.info/index.php/Brian_Jenkins

35 Greg Krikorian, Calmly taking terror's measure

36 James Mann, Rise Of The Vulcans

37 Peter Dale Scott, The Road to 9/11, pp 111-116

38 Peter Dale Scott, The Road to 9/11

39 White House Commission on Aviation Safety and Security, Final Report To President Clinton, February 12, 1997, http://www.fas.org/irp/threat/212fin~1.html

40 Paul Wilkinson and Brian Michael Jenkins, Aviation Terrorism and Security, Frank Cass, Mar 1, 1999

41 David Teacher, Rogue Agents

42 Nafeez Ahmed, The War on Truth (Northampton, MA: Olive Branch Press, 2005), p. 3

43 James Fallows, Gary Hart, Lynne Cheney, and War with China, The Atlantic, July 5, 2007

[44] U.S. Commission on National Security/21st Century (Hart-Rudman), Road Map for National Security: Imperative for Change, January 31, 2001, http://www.fas.org/irp/threat/nssg.pdf
[45] Lewis Paul Bremer III on Washington, DC, NBC4 TV, 11 September 2001, Vehmgericht http://vehme.blogspot.com/2007/08/lewis-paul-bremer-iii-on-washington-dc.html
[46] Craig Eisendrath and Tom Harkin, National Insecurity: U.S. Intelligence After the Cold War, Temple University Press, 2000
[47] Tanzania Expels 2 U.S. Diplomats. AP. The New York Times, Jan 16, 1965
[48] Letter to Paul Bremer from Victor Tomseth, September 2, 1979, accessed at Wikisource, http://tinyurl.com/d7s4twu
[49] Phil Gailey and Warren Weaver Jr. Briefing, New York Times, July 10, 1982
[50] Daniele Ganser, NATO's Secret Armies
[51] Stephen Engelberg, The World: Washington's War on Terrorism Captures Few Soldiers, The New York Times, March 5, 1989
[52] Jonathan Beaty and S.C. Gwynne, Scandals: Not Just a Bank, TIME, September 2, 1991
[53] John Kerry and Hank Brown, The BCCI Affair: A Report to the Committee on Foreign Relations United States Senate, December 1992, Senate Print 102-140, http://www.fas.org/irp/congress/1992_rpt/bcci/
[54] Catherine S. Manegold, Explosion at the Twin Towers: The Precautions; With Talk of a Bomb, Security Tightens, The New York Times, February 28, 1993
[55] L. Paul Bremer, Terrorists' Friends Must Pay a Price, The Wall street Journal, August 5, 1996
[56] In July 1996, Komatsu-Dresser patented a thermite demolition device that could "demolish a concrete structure at a high efficiency, while preventing a secondary problem due to noise, flying dust and chips, and the like." Taku Murakami, US Patent 5532449 - Using plasma ARC and thermite to demolish concrete, http://www.patentstorm.us/patents/5532449/description.html
[57] Congressional Research Service, Memorandum to House Government Reform Committee on Terrorist Attacks by al Qaeda,

March 31, 2004, http://www.fas.org/irp/crs/033104.pdf

[58] Tim Weiner, After The Attacks: The Outlook; Raids Are Seen As One Battle In a Long Fight, The New York Times, August 23, 1998

[59] Colum Lynch; Vernon Loeb, Bin Laden's Network: Terror Conspiracy or Loose Alliance?, The Washington Post, August 1, 1999

[60] Tim Weiner, After The Attacks

[61] RAND National Security Research Division, Gilmore Commission – Panel Chair and Members, http://www.rand.org/nsrd/terrpanel/panel.html

[62] Congressional Record Volume 153, Number 161 (Tuesday, October 23, 2007), Statements by Representative Bennie Thompson (D, MS), http://www.gpo.gov/fdsys/pkg/CREC-2007-10-23/html/CREC-2007-10-23-pt1-PgH11854-3.htm

[63] First Annual Report to The President and The Congress of the Advisory Panel To Assess the Domestic Response Capabilities For Terrorism Involving Weapons Of Mass Destruction (Gilmore Commission), RAND Corporation website, http://www.rand.org/content/dam/rand/www/external/nsrd/terrpanel/terror.pdf

[64] Laurie Goodstein, Gephardt Bows To Jews' Anger Over a Nominee, The New York Times, July 09, 1999

[65] Kevin Fenton, Disconnecting the Dots: How 9/11 Was Allowed to Happen, Trine Day, 2011

[66] Pranay Gupte, Maurice Sonnenberg: A Concerned Optimist, The New York Sun, March 23, 2005

[67] Sourcewatch page for Bear, Stearns & Co

[68] James Risen, Terrorism Panel Faults U.S. Effort on Iran and 1996 Bombing, The New York Times, June 4, 2000

[69] Defending America in the 21st Century: New Challenges, New Organizations, and New Policies, Center for Strategic and International Studies, 2000, http://csis.org/files/media/csis/pubs/defendamer21stexecsumm.pdf

[70] PBS Online Newshour, Global Threat, June 6, 2000

[71] Wikipedia pager for Larry C. Johnson

[72] Ibid

[73] Kevin R. Ryan, The small world of 9/11 players: LS2, Vidient and AMEC, DigWihtin.net, January 1, 2012

[74] Sourcewatch page for Crisis Consulting Practice of Marsh, Inc.

[75] David Teacher, Rogue Agents

[76] Sourcewatch page for L. Paul Bremer III

[77] Max Brockbank, 'Ladies and Gentlemen — We Got Him!', TIME, December 14, 2003

[78] Greg Krikorian, Calmly taking terror's measure

Notes to Chapter 12

[1] Kevin R. Ryan, Evidence for Informed Trading on the Attacks of September 11, Foreign Policy Journal, November 18, 2010

[2] 9/11 Commission memorandum entitled "FBI Briefing on Trading", prepared by Doug Greenburg, 18 August 2003, http://media.nara.gov/9-11/MFR/t-0148-911MFR-00269.pdf This memorandum refers to the traders involved in the Stratesec purchase. From the references in the document, we can make out that the two people had the same last name and were related. This fits the description of Wirt and Sally Walker, who are known to be stock holders in Stratesec. Additionally, one (Wirt) was a director at the company, a director at a publicly traded company in Oklahoma (Aviation General), and chairman of an investment firm in Washington, DC (KuwAm Corp).

[3] Ibid

[4] Sourcewatch.org, Profile for Mansoor Ijaz/Sudan

[5] Dan Briody, The Iron Triangle: Inside the Secret World of The Carlyle Group, Wiley publishers, 2003

[6] The Washington Post, obituary for WIRT D. WALKER - Intelligence Analyst, June 15, 1997

[7] Kevin R. Ryan, The History of Wirt Dexter Walker: Russell & Co, the CIA and 9/11, 911blogger.com, 3 September 2010

[8] Wikipedia page for Emery Roth

[9] The Washington Post, Times Herald, Dr. C.S. White Jr., 48, Surgeon, Chief of Staff, April 13, 1964

[10] The Washington Post, Times Herald, White-Walker wedding announcement, April 29, 1971

[11] Richard Harris Smith, OSS: The Secret History Of America's First Central Intelligence Agency, Globe Pequot, 2005
[12] Alec Benn, The Unseen Wall Street, of 1969 to 1975: And Its Significance for Today, Quorum Books, 2000
[13] Donald Morrison, Ambush on Wall Street, Texas Monthly, April 1974
[14] Standard & Poor's Security Dealers of North America, Volumes 109-120
[15] SEC News Digest, Issue 93-47, March 12, 1993
[16] Bloomberg Businessweek, Stifel Nicolaus & Company, Incorporated Hanifen Imhoff Division
[17] Bertie Charles Forbes, Forbes, Volume 153, Issues 8-13, 1994
[18] Ibid
[19] Although there is considerable variation in the English spellings of Kuwaiti names, Mish'al Yusuf Saud Al Sabah and Saud Nasir Saud Al Sabah (along with Saud Nasir's daughter, Neira) are listed in Al-Sabah: history & genealogy of Kuwait's ruling family, 1752-1987, by Alan Rush. See pp 132 and 133
[20] Mitchel Cohen, How the War Party Sold the 1991 Bombing of Iraq to US, AntiWar.com, December 30, 2002
[21] Susan Trento, The Power House: Robert Keith Gray and the Selling of Access and Influence in Washington, St. Martin's Press, 1992 pp 93-96, 258, and 379-383
[22] New York County Supreme Court, Matter of World Trade Ctr. Bombing Litig, 2004 NY Slip Op 24030 [3 Misc 3d 440], January 20, 2004
[23] Securacomm Consulting Inc. v. Securacom Incorporated, United States Court of Appeals for the Third Circuit, January 20, 1999, 49 U.S.P.Q.2d 1444; 166 F.3d 182
[24] Kevin Phillips, American Dynasty, Viking Penguin,2004, p 279
[25] Joseph Trento, Prelude to terror: the rogue CIA and the legacy of America's private intelligence network, Carroll & Graf, 2005
[26] Report from the Joint Congressional Inquiry into 9/11
[27] Margie Burns, The Best Unregulated Families, The Progressive Populist, 2003
[28] The Washington Post, Four Planes, Four Coordinated Teams, 2001, http://www.washingtonpost.com/wp-

srv/nation/graphics/attack/hijackers.html
[29] Embry-Riddle University media, Embry-Riddle Alumnus Cleared of Reported Hijacker Link, September 21, 2001
[30] In the weeks after 9/11, many mainstream news sources reported that the accused hijackers were still alive. These claims were reported by major media sources like The Independent, the London Telegraph and the British Broadcasting Corporation. Although BBC attempted to retract the claims later, the Telegraph reported that it had interviewed some of these men, who the newspaper said had the same names, same dates of birth, same places of birth, and same occupations as the accused. See David Harrison, Revealed: the men with stolen identities, The Telegraph, 23 Sep 2001
[31] Securities and Exchange Commission, Form 8-K for Aviation General, Incorporated, March 26, 2004
[32] Alex Beam, He's Back, The Boston Globe, November 19, 1990
[33] Catherine Hinman, A Joint Venture Of Business, Philosophy Secor Group Partner Has Will To 'Win Or Lose It All', The Orlando Sentinel, February 01, 1988
[34] Margie Burns, Trimming the Bushes: Family Business at the Watergate, Washington Spectator, February 15, 2005
[35] Spartacus Educational, Profile for Theodore (Ted) Shackley, http://www.spartacus.schoolnet.co.uk/JFKshackley.htm
[36] Spartacus Educational, webpage for Theodore (Ted) Shackley
[37] Joseph Trent, Prelude to Terror
[38] David Corn, Blond Ghost: Ted Shackley and the CIA's Crusades, Simon & Schuster, 1994
[39] David Corn, Blond Ghost
[40] U.S. Senate Report, Deposition of Ted Shackley in the Iran-Contra Investigation, United States Congressional Serial Set Serial Number 13766, United States Government Printing Office Washington: 1989. See Joseph Trento, Prelude to Terror, for reference to Razmara as a SAVAK agent.
[41] Spectrezine, Bush-Law in the Land of Mannon, http://www.spectrezine.org/resist/bush.htm
[42] U.S. Senate Report, Deposition of Ted Shackley in the Iran-Contra Investigation
[43] Suzan Mazur: John Deuss - The Manhattan projects, Scoop News,

September 22, 2004

[44] Nancy Lewis, Defendant Backed in Kuwaiti Case; Royalty Allegedly Allowed Use of Fund, The Washington Post, May 31, 1988

[45] Larry J. Kolb, America at Night: The True Story of Two Rogue CIA Operatives, Penguin, 2008

[46] Larry J. Kolb, America at Night

[47] Nancy Lewis, Ex-Kuwait Airways Official Testifies of CIA Ties, The Washington Post, October 21, 1987

[48] Peter Truell and Larry Gurwin, False Profits: The Inside Story of BCCI, The World's Most Corrupt Financial Empire, Houghton Mifflin, 1992

[49] Traute Wohlers-Scharf, Arab and Islamic banks: new business partners for developing countries, OCDE Paris, 1983

[50] Peter Truell and Larry Gurwin, False Profits, p 297

[51] Wikileaks document 05KUWAIT4792, Public Prosecution Questions Ruling Family Member About His Public Criticism Of GOK, dated November 16, 2005, http://www.cablegatesearch.net/cable.php?id=05KUWAIT4792

[52] Larry J. Kolb, America at Night, Riverhead Books, 2007

[53] Jim Crogan, The Terrorist Motel: The I-40 connection between Zacarias Moussaoui and Mohamed Atta, LA Weekly, July 24, 2002

[54] See FBI summary document for Marwan Al-Shehhi, accessed at Sribd, 911DocumentArchive, http://tinyurl.com/bnp7vrr

[55] See FBI summary documents for Saeed Al-Ghamdi and Hani Hanjour found in 911 archives at Scribd.com: http://www.scribd.com/911DocumentArchive

[56] Wiley Post Airport website, Airport Guide

[57] NewsOK, Dean N. Thomas obituary, December 7, 2000

[58] Rick Robinson, Aircraft Manufacturer to Keep Lease at Oklahoma City-Area Airport, Daily Oklahoman, December 29, 2001

[59] Aviation General Inc, Form 8-K, March 26, 2004

[60] UK Mail Online, Plane crashes into Milan tower, http://www.dailymail.co.uk/news/article-110475/Plane-crashes-Milan-tower.html

[61] Margie Burns, Bush-Linked Company Handled Security for the WTC, Dulles and United, Prince George's Journal, February 4, 2003

[62] Legal Metric, WALKER, et al v. MONES, et al, District of Columbia

District Court,
[63] Washington Business Journal, Chantilly Firm Folds Under Factoring, September 29, 2003
[64] SEC filing for Bankest Capital, SC 13D, March 13, 2003
[65] Ibid
[66] Reuters, Former exec to pay $165 million in fraud case, Aug 28, 2007
[67] Peter Zalewski, The Accounting: Indictments, receiver's report on Bankest Capital present picture of a $170 million mystery, Daily Business Review, November 22, 2004

Notes to Chapter 13

[1] Margie Burns, Bush-Linked Company Handled Security for the WTC, Dulles and United, Prince George's Journal, February 4, 2003
[2] Ibid
[3] U.S. Army Materiel Command, Reflections of senior AMC officials, 1990
[4] Dan Briody, The Iron Triangle: Inside the Secret World of The Carlyle Group, Wiley publishers, 2003, p35
[5] PRNewswire, BDM Anticipates Strong Year Marked By Continued Diversification, May 14, 1992
[6] BDM Year End Financials, PRNewswire, March 5, 1992
[7] Craig Unger, House of Bush, House of Saud: The Secret Relationship Between the World's Two Most Powerful Dynasties, Simon and Schuster, 2004, pp 296-297
[8] William D. Hartung, Mercenaries Inc.: How a U.S. Company Props Up the House of Saud, The Progressive, April, 1996
[9] Ibid
[10] Ian Urbina, Saudi Arabia: Vinnell and the House of Saud, Asia Times, May 17, 2003
[11] SEC filing for Stratesec, May 2, 1997, http://www.secinfo.com/dS7kv.82.htm
[12] Securacom S-1A Securities Registration Statement filed with the U.S. Securities and Exchange Commission, 1997
[13] Margie Burns, Security, Secrecy and a Bush Brother, The Progressive Populist, 2003
[14] Ibid

[15] Ibid

[16] Ibid

[17] James Risen and Jeff Gerth, Breach at Los Alamos: A special report.; China Stole Nuclear Secrets For Bombs, U.S. Aides Say, The New York Times, March 6, 1999

[18] Wikipedia page for Wen Ho Lee

[19] S-3 SEC Filing, filed by STRATESEC INC on 6/12/2000

[20] News Film Online, Gulf Crisis: Exiled Kuwaiti Family, September 9, 1990

[21] Comtex, STRATESEC Incorporated Acquires Security Systems Integration, December 4, 2000, http://www.siliconinvestor.com/readmsg.aspx?msgid=14940791

[22] Morningstar.com, Exhibit 10.2 Demerger Agreement, May 29, 2002, http://globaldocuments.morningstar.com/DocumentLibrary/Document/8a9e95dbff8fd9a2.msdoc/original/ex102.txt

[23] Institute for the Study of Globalization and Covert Politics, Le Cercle and the struggle for the European continent, https://wikispooks.com/ISGP/organisations/Le_Cercle.htm

[24] Ibid

[25] Margie Burns, Security, Secrecy and a Bush Brother

[26] Kevin R. Ryan, Demolition Access to the WTC Towers: Part One, Tenants, UnansweredQuestions.org, July 9, 2009

[27] Margie Burns, Security, Secrecy and a Bush Brother

[28] See the Journal of 9/11 Studies for details.

[29] For example, see Graeme MacQueen, 118 Witnesses: The Firefighter's Testimony to Explosions in the Twin Towers, Journal of 9/11 Studies, August 2006

[30] Kevin R. Ryan, Another amazing coincidence related to the WTC, 911Blogger.com, January 6, 2008

[31] Ibid

[32] See NIST WTC Report NCSTAR 1-6A page 45

[33] See WTC Fireproofing Documents obtained by James Gourley via FOIA, 911blogger.com, February 2, 2009, http://www.911blogger.com/node/19271, and Aidan Monaghan, Port Authority of NY/NJ: Records For Reported WTC Renovation Work Destroyed On 9/11, 911Blogger.com, April 21, 2009

[34] Kevin R. Ryan, Demolition Access to the WTC Towers: Part Four – Cleanup, 911review.com, February 11, 2010

[35] Danen, W.C., Jorgensen, B.S., Busse, J.R., Ferris, M.J. and Smith, B.L. "Los Alamos Nanoenergetic Metastable Intermolecular Composite (Super Thermite) Program," 221st ACS National Meeting, San Diego, CA, 1-5 April 2001

[36] Niels H. Harrit, et al, Active thermitic material discovered in dust from the 9/11 World Trade Center catastrophe, The Open Chemical Physics Journal, Vol 2, 2009

[37] For example, see Steven E. Jones et. al, Extremely high temperatures during the World Trade Center destruction, Journal of 9/11 Studies, January 2008.

[38] The National Institute of Standards and Technology (NIST), WTC Report NCSTAR 1-6A, figure A-60

[39] The fire dynamics in the impact zones of the WTC towers were unusual in that the fires died down after the initial explosive effects of impact, and then began to rage again much later. The behavior of the fires within the pile and the related environmental data can be reviewed in Kevin R. Ryan, et al, Environmental anomalies at the World Trade Center: evidence for energetic materials, The Environmentalist, Volume 29, Number 1, 2009. For discussion of the illnesses suffered by first responders and how they might be attributed to thermitic materials, see Kevin R. Ryan, Energetic Materials as a Potential Cause of the 9/11 First Responder Illnesses, Foreign Policy Journal, February, 2010

[40] Wayne Barrett and Dan Collins, Grand Illusion: The Untold Story of Rudy Giuliani and 9/11, HarperCollins, 2006, pp 125-134

[41] Kevin R. Ryan, Demolition Access to the WTC Towers: Part One, 911Review.com, August 9, 2009

[42] Robert Baamonde Jr., Drive to the Top, Elevator World, March 2001. The elevator upgrade project was also described by the firm Merritt and Harris, which provided a report to the Port Authority of New York and New Jersey in December 2000.

[43] Gordon Ross, How the Towers Were Demolished, http://gordonssite.tripod.com/id2.html

[44] Dennis Cauchon and Martha T. Moore, Elevators were disaster within disaster, USA Today, September 4, 2002

[45] List of tenants in Seven World Trade Center, Wikipedia, http://en.wikipedia.org/wiki/List_of_tenants_in_Seven_World_Trade_Center

[46] Real Estate Finance & Investment, Silverstein Vows To Help Rebuild WTC Complex, September 17, 2001,

[47] SAGA, the newsletter of the Sigma Tau Gamma society, A Brotherhood United: Sig Taus share their personal accounts of September 11, 2001, Issue 2, Winter 2002

[48] Ibid

[49] Sherry Conohan, Training exercise quickly became reality, The Hub, September 21, 2001

[50] Transportation Security Administration, TSA Names Stephen Wood Federal Security Director for Three Tennessee Airports, TSA Press Office, November 19, 2009

[51] Debbie Sheehan, Force protection plan a 'timely alert', Fort Monmouth Public Affairs Office, September 21, 2001. Also see Sherry Conohan, Fort personnel fill many roles in tragedy's aftermath From locating cell phones to dealing with explosives, CECOM experts are on call, The Hub, September 21, 2001

[52] U.S. Navy Press Release, Ground Zero Chief Receives Navy and Marine Corps Medal for Heroism, Navy.mil website, December 4, 2002

[53] Margie Burns, Security, Secrecy and a Bush Brother

[54] Sally Donnelly, TIME Exclusive: An Inside Job? TIME, September. 22, 2001

[55] Ibid

[56] Audrey Gillan and Stuart Millar, "Securicor could face legal claims over hijack airports," The Guardian, September 13, 2001

[57] Michele Orlecklin, "Airlines: Why Argenbright Sets Off Alarms," Time, November 19, 2001

[58] Tom Berry, "The Financial Director interview – Making crime pay," Financial Director, December 8, 2003

[59] SecurAmerica profile for Thomas D. Bell,

http://www.securamericallc.com/about-us/executive-biographies/thomas-bell.php
[60] Peter Truell and Larry Gurwin, False Profits, p 256
[61] Arnold Barnett, The Worst Day Ever: The Sept. 11 catastrophe raises many troubling questions, OR/MS Today - December 2001
[62] The 9/11 Commission Report, p 3
[63] CBS News, A Hard Look At 9/11 Errors, February 11, 2009
[64] The 9/11 Commission Report, p 3
[65] The only other videotape evidence of the alleged hijackers moving through the airports was from Atta and Al-Shehhi's oddly timed trip to Portland. There were some unexplained problems with that video, however. For example, when they checked in Atta and Al-Omari were observed wearing ties and jackets but in the security video footage taken minutes later, the jackets or ties were gone.
[66] Kathleen Hickey, One of a kind: Security Storage lives up to its name with state-of-the-art, automated warehouse near Dulles international airport, Traffic World, February 24, 2003, http://www.accessmylibrary.com/article-1G1-98465543/one-kind-security-storage.html
[67] Website for LS2, http://www.ls2global.com/team.html
[68] Investigator Jeremy Rys noted that the LS2 website was taken down after he posted images related to the research provided in this book at other high traffic web pages.
[69] Website for LS2
[70] Website for Berg Associates, profile for Larry C. Johnson, http://www.berg-associates.com/
[71] U.S. Securities and Exchange Commission, Litigation Release No. 19078, February 14, 2005
[72] Kevin R. Ryan, Questions for Richard Clarke on COG, the UAE, and BCCI, DigWithin.net, August 20, 2011
[73] Richard Miniter, Losing Bin Laden: How Bill Clinton's Failures Unleashed Global Terror, Regnery Publishers, 2003

Notes to Chapter 14

[1] Wayne Barrett, "Rudy Giuliani's 5 Big Lies About 9/11: On the Stump, Rudy Can't Help Spreading Smoke and Ashes About His

Dubious Record," Village Voice, August 8–14, 2007, p. 35-36

[2] Wayne Barrett, Thug Life: The Shocking Secret History of Harold Giuliani, the Mayor's Ex-Convict Dad, The Village Voice, July 4th 2000

[3] The Smoking Gun, Giuliani: The Hits Keep on Comin', April 06, 2007

[4] William K. Rashbaum, .Kerik Is Accused of Abusing Post as City Official, The New York Times, November 16, 2005

[5] Dean J. Champion, Police Misconduct in America: A Reference Handbook, ABC-CLIO, 2001, p 15

[6] Timothy Naftali, "There's Very Little We Can Do:" Gerald Ford and Counterterrorism, Version 1.3, Draft Section for Study of US Counterterrorism Strategy, 1968 – 1993, Washington Decoded, http://www.washingtondecoded.com/files/tngrf.pdf

[7] Gary Webb, Dark Alliance, Seven Stories press, 1998

[8] Wolfgang Saxon, Harold Tyler, 83, Lawyer and Former Federal Judge, Dies, The New York Times, May 27, 2005

[9] Gerry O'Sullivan, Boom! – World Trade Center bombing – Column, Humanist, May-June, 1993 issue

[10] Christopher Ketcham, The Last Roundup, Radar Magazine, May 5, 2008

[11] Ibid

[12] The Inslaw Affair, Investigative Report By the Committee On The Judiciary, U.S. Government Printing Office, 1992

[13] Casolaro's death was ruled a suicide despite many suspicious facts that indicated he was murdered. His family and associates contend to this day that he was murdered due to his PROMIS-centered investigation. For details, see Kenn Thomas and Jim Keith's book "The Octopus: Secret Government and the Death of Danny Casolaro," Feral House, 1996.

[14] Beth Kaswan describes her role as a Giuliani assistant managing the BCCI case in her bio at Scott & Scott, http://www.scott-scott.com/attorney-beth-kaswan.html

[15] Lucy Komisar, Tracking Terrorist Money -- Too Hot For U.S. to Handle?, Pacific News Service, October 4, 2001, http://130.94.183.89/magazine/money.html

[16] Rachel Ehrenfeld, Evil Money: Encounters Along the Money Trail,

HarperCollins Publishers, 1992, pp 177-178

[17] Russ Baker, Family of Secrets, Bloomsbury Press, 2009, p 430

[18] New York Magazine, Is Giuliani Running Like It's 1989?, March 19, 2007

[19] One case in which White & Case represented BCCI is listed here: http://tinyurl.com/c6mn3xd

[20] David Sirota and Jonathan Baskin, Follow the Money: How John Kerry busted the terrorists' favorite bank, Washington Monthly, September 2004

[21] James Traub, Rudy's reversals: Giuliani's lost convictions, The New Republic, September 9, 1991

[22] Biography.com, Rudy Giuliani, http://www.biography.com/people/rudolph-giuliani-9312674?page=2

[23] Wayne Barrett and Dan Collins, Grand Illusion: The Untold Story of Rudy Giuliani and 9/11, HarperCollins, 2006, pp 94-101

[24] David DeGraw, The Financial Puzzle Behind 9/11, Consortium News, October 22, 2010

[25] Peter Jennings of ABC interview with Rudy Giuliani, 9/11/01 Rudy Giuliani warned of WTC collapse beforehand - Interview with Peter Jennings, accessed on YouTube, http://www.youtube.com/watch?v=Ou4MakVHCYc

[26] Jim Hoffman, Giuliani Warned: Mayor Giuliani Had Privileged Warning of Unprecedented Collapse, 911Research.WTC7.net

[27] See Architects and Engineers for 9/11 Truth, http://www.ae911truth.org/

[28] Peter Jennings of ABC interview with Rudy Giuliani

[29] In 1993 Kroll Associates, an investigative and security consulting firm headquartered in New York, was asked by the Port Authority of New York and New Jersey, the owner and manager of the World Trade Center at the time, to assist it in dealing with the aftermath of the terrorist bombing that took place in February of that year and to help design new security measures. This report's Principal Investigator, Brian Michael Jenkins, was then Deputy Chairman of Kroll and led the analysis of future terrorist threats and how they might be addressed. The report specifically considered the possibility of "terrorists

deliberately crashing a plane into the towers."
http://transweb.sjsu.edu/MTIportal/research/publications/document
s/Sept11.book.htm#pgfId-1010258

[30] Windfalls of War: Kroll Inc. The Center for Public Integrity,
http://projects.publicintegrity.org/wow/bio.aspx?act=pro&ddlC=32

[31] World Trade Center Task Force Interview, EMT Richard Zarrillo,
October 25, 2001, http://tinyurl.com/clrdagc

[32] World Trade Center Task Force Interview, Abdo Nahmod, October
11, 2001, http://tinyurl.com/btz5ng9

[33] Graeme MacQueen, Waiting for Seven: WTC 7 Collapse Warnings
in the FDNY Oral Histories, Journal of 9/11 Studies, January 11, 2008

[34] History Commons Complete 9/11 Timeline: Profile for Richard
Rotanz

[35] Graeme MacQueen, Waiting for Seven

[36] World Trade Center Task Force Interview, Fire Marshal Steven
Mosiello, October 23, 2001, http://tinyurl.com/ccoa23g

[37] Wayne Barrett and Dan Collins, Grand Illusion: The Untold Story of
Rudy Giuliani and 9/11, HarperCollins, 2006, p12

[38] World Trade Center Task Force Interview, Chief Joseph Pfeifer,
October 23, 2001, http://tinyurl.com/bmzybnp

[39] Testimony of Richard Sheirer to the 9/11 Commission, May 18,
2004

[40] History Commons Complete 9/11 Timeline: Profile for John
Odermatt

[41] Wayne Barrett and Dan Collins, Grand Illusion, p 33-35

[42] History Commons profile for John Odermatt

[43] Dennis P. McMahon, Barry Jennings Revisited, Ae911truth.org, May
31, 2012

[44] Christopher Marquis, Ex-Top Cop Gets Iraq Post, The New York
Times, May 16, 2003

[45] Russ Buettner, Tough Guy With Charm, Often Living on the Edge,
November 10, 2007, The New York Times

[46] Stephanie Gaskell, Former Iraq Commander: Bernard Kerik was 'a
waste of time' in Iraq, New York Daily News, May 5th 2008

[47] Memo from Donald Rumsfeld to Jerry Bremer and Gen. John

Abizaid, CC: Gen. Dick Myers, Paul Wolfowitz, and Doug Feith, "Subject: Training Iraqi Police," September 29, 2003. See also Memo from Donald Rumsfeld to Jerry Bremer, CC: Paul Wolfowitz, October 2, 2003.
http://www.rand.org/pubs/monographs/2009/RAND_MG847.pdf
[48] Wikipedia page for Bernard Kerik
[49] William K. Rashbaum, Giuliani Testified He Was Briefed on Kerik in '00, The New York Times, March 30, 2007
[50] Paul Kiel, TPM's Ultimate Kerik Scandal List!, TPM Muckraker, November 9, 2007
[51] The New York Times, Times Topics – People, Bernard B. Kerik, Nov. 5, 2009
[52] See video of the 2:30 pm press conference which was televised by ABC and can be found at YouTube.
http://www.youtube.com/watch?v=Epqoa6TJZWI
[53] Suzanne Mattei, Pollution and Deception at Ground Zero: How the Bush Administration's Reckless Disregard of 9/11 Toxic Hazards Poses Long-Term Threats for New York City and the Nation, Sierra Club,
http://www.gothamgazette.com/rebuilding_nyc/sierraclub_report.pdf
[54] Report from the Committee on Science, US House of Representatives, March 6,2002
[55] Gail Swanson, Behind-the-Scenes: Ground Zero, A Collection of Personal Accounts, available at this link:
http://www.summeroftruth.org/groundzero.html
[56] Jim Hoffman, Black Boxes: Contents of Flight Data and Cockpit Voice Recorders Are Missing, 911Research.wtc7.net
[57] ABC News, Terrorist Hunt: Suspects ID'd; Rescue Efforts Go On; White House Originally Targeted, September 12, 2001,
http://911research.wtc7.net/cache/disinfo/deceptions/abc_hunt.html
[58] Susan Ginsberg testimony to National Commission on Terrorist Attacks Upon the United States, Public Hearing, Monday, January 26, 2004
[59] Jim Hoffman, Access Restrictions: The Closure of Ground Zero to Investigators, 911Research.WTC7.net
[60] Amy Florence Fischbach, CEE News, September 20, 2001
[61] Wayne Barrett and Dan Collins, Grand Illusion, p 257

[62] Mark MacIntyre, Bunker Hill: light at the end of the tunnel, The Seattle Daily Journal of Commerce, August 20, 1998

[63] History Commons Complete 9/11 Timeline: Profile for Richard Tomasetti

[64] China.org.cn, Baosteel Will Recycle World Trade Center Debris, http://china.org.cn/english/2002/Jan/25776.htm

[65] PBS, Interview with Charlie Vitchers for the film "America Rebuilds: A Year at Ground Zero", http://www.pbs.org/americarebuilds/profiles/profiles_vitchers_t.html

[66] New York Daily News, Exposed: Map of Ground Zero spoils: Where the money went to clear Trade Center debris, cached at AsthmaMoms 9/11 WTC Environmental Health News, http://www.asthmamoms.com/worldtradecenter2005.htm

[67] Peter Truell and Larry Gurwin, False Profits: The Inside Story of BCCI, The World's Most Corrupt Financial Empire, Houghton Mifflin, 1992, p 181

[68] Charles V. Bagli, US: At Ground Zero, Builder Is Barred but Not His Kin, The New York Times, July 21st, 2006, accessed at CorpWatch, http://www.corpwatch.org/article.php?id=13922

[69] Kevin R. Ryan, Another amazing coincidence related to the WTC, 911Blogger, January 6, 2008

[70] Aidan Monaghan, Pre-9/11 WTC Steel Fireproofing/Post-9/11 Ground Zero Clean-Up Contractor, Planned 2000 Seattle Kingdome Demolition, 911Blogger.com, March 4, 2009

[71] Jim Hoffman, Notable Retractions: Experts Change Their Tune to Harmonize with the Official Story, 911Research.WTC7.net

[72] U.S. Department of Defense, News Transcript, Mr. Lee Evey, Pentagon Renovation Manager, September 15, 2001, http://www.defenselink.mil/transcripts/transcript.aspx?transcriptid=1636

[73] Wikipedia page for Frank Lampl

[74] Douglas Feiden and Greg B. Smith, James Abadie, executive at Bovis Lend Lease in charge of Sept. 11 Memorial, resigns amid probe, New York Daily News, June 15th 2009

[75] Charles V. Bagli, David W. Dunlap and William K. Rashbaum, Obscure Company Is Behind 9/11 Demolition Work, The New York Times, August 23, 2007

[76] Colin Moynihan, 2 Charged in Check Scheme Uncovered After Bank Fire, The New York Times, July 28, 2009

[77] William K. Rashbaum and Charles V. Bagli, Demolition Man, The New York Times, July 31, 2009

[78]See WTC Fireproofing Documents obtained by James Gourley via FOIA, 911blogger.com, February 2, 2009

[79] Charles V. Bagli and William K. Rashbaum, Questions on City's Role in Demolition Near 9/11 Site, The New York Times, August 29, 2007

[80] The New York Daily News Investigative Team: Russ Buettner, Heidi Evans, Robert Gearty, Brian Kates, Greg B. Smith and Assistant Managing Editor Richard T. Pienciak, Ground Zero: $2.7B money pot, December 6, 2005, http://listserv.fsl.com/pipermail/wtcrc/2005-December/000032.html

[81] Wikipedia page for Roland Betts

[82] The initial directors of LMDC are listed in documents obtained via FOAI request by Cryptome, http://cryptome.org/wtc-foia.htm

[83] Jacqueline Emigh, GPS on the Job in Massive World Trade Center Clean-up, Access Control & Security Systems, Jul 1, 2002

[84] Debra K. Rubin, Creating order from chaos in leading the public-private construction team that responded to the Sept. 11 devastation at Ground Zero, Engineering News-Record, April 22, 2002

[85] NPR News, Sifting Through the WTC Rubble: 'Ground Zero' Effort Nears End, Search Continues at Fresh Kills, May 30, 2002

[86] Ibid

[87] John Kelly and Phillip Wearne, Tainting Evidence: Inside The Scandals At The FBI Crime Lab, The Free Press, 1998, pp 162-167

[88] Federal Bureau of Investigation, Bios of James T. Caruso and Pasquale J. D'Amuro, January 31, 2002, http://www.fbi.gov/pressrel/pressrel02/mueller013102.htm

[89] Federal Bureau of Investigation, FBI Announces List of 19 Hijackers, September 14, 2001, http://www.fbi.gov/pressrel/pressrel01/091401hj.htm

[90] Anita Gates, "Buildings Rise from Rubble while Health Crumbles," "New York Times," September 11, 2006, reporting on the documentary, "Dust to Dust: The Health Effects of 9/11"

[91] Ben Smith, "Rudy's Black Cloud", New York Daily News, September 18, 2006, p. 14

[92] Wayne Barrett, "Rudy Giuliani's 5 Big Lies About 9/11
[93] Fletcher Smith, Giuliani Criticized by Firefighters in Letter, Yahoo News Network, May 9, 2007
[94] Wayne Barrett, Rudy Giuliani's Five Big Lies About 9/11
[95] David Saltonstall, "Rudy gets earful at stop here: Some FDNY survivors rally against him". Daily News (New York). April 24, 2007
[96] See the website Rudy Giuliani, Urban Legend, http://www.rudy-urbanlegend.com/
[97] David R. Baker, US: SF Firm Awarded Contract in Iraq, San Francisco Chronicle, March 12th, 2004
[98] See AMEC website, Iraq webpage, http://tinyurl.com/bwgp8b8 and see AMEC description of just one of these contracts, worth $500 million, http://tinyurl.com/bszmdlu

Notes to Chapter 15

[1] Donald L. Barlett and James B. Steele, Washington's $8 Billion Shadow, Vanity Fair, March 2007
[2] Ibid
[3] Kevin R. Ryan, The Top Ten Connections Between NIST and Nanothermites, Journal of 9/11 Studies, July 2008
[4] Gerry Simone, Getting the Big Picture, GovConExec, December 7th, 2011
[5] Ibid
[6] At the CIA's website, Andrews is listed as one of the HPSCI staff members who were briefed on Oliver North's Nicaraguan Contra program and the associated drug trafficking allegations.
[7] Patricia Daukantas, Information security is too often MIA, GCN, Aug 14, 2002, http://gcn.com/articles/2002/08/14/information-security-is-too-often-mia.aspx
[8] Morris Berman, Dark Ages America: The Final Phase of Empire, W. W. Norton & Company, 2011
[9] Douglas F. Garthoff, Directors of Central Intelligence as Leaders of the U.S. Intelligence Community, 1946-2005, Potomac Books, Inc., Oct 31, 2007, p 187
[10] UPI, Cheney Overhauls Intelligence Structure, March 21, 1991
[11] Able Danger was an electronic search and linking project that

identified Mohamed Atta and three other of the alleged hijackers before the 9/11 attacks. In early 2001, the program was shut down and all records were ordered to be destroyed. Congressman Curt Weldon made considerable efforts to expose the program after 9/11

[12] Douglas F. Garthoff, Directors of Central Intelligence as Leaders of the U.S. Intelligence Community, p 213

[13] Bruce V. Bigelow, No. 2 executive at SAIC resigns after 13 years, The San Diego Union-Tribune, February 2, 2006

[14] Fifties Frogs Magazine, Biographies of Navy Frogmen, Vol. 4, RADM Cathal L. Flynn,
http://www.navyfrogmen.com/fiftiesfrogs/vol4/vol4kbio.htm

[15] Bill Salisbury, Ex-Navy SEALS Wage War Over Airport Security, San Diego Reader, September 27, 2001, accessed at:
http://cursor.org/venturawatch/fight_flight.htm

[16] Brian Michael Jenkins, Bruce Butterworth and Cathal Flynn, What we can learn from the Christmas Day bombing attempt, The Washington Post, March 26, 2010

[17] Patricia Daukantas, Information security is too often MIA

[18] Donald L. Barlett and James B. Steele, Washington's $8 Billion Shadow

[19] Laura Rozen, The First Contract, The American Prospect, March 30, 2007

[20] J. Robert Beyster, The SAIC Solution: How We Built an $8 Billion Employee-Owned Technology Company, John Wiley & Sons, Mar 31, 2007

[21] The Center for Public Integrity, Winning Contractors: U.S. Contractors Reap the Windfalls of Post-war Reconstruction, October 30, 2003. See also J. Robert Beyster, The SAIC Solution.

[22] New York County Supreme Court, Matter of World Trade Ctr. Bombing Litig, 2004 NY Slip Op 24030 [3 Misc 3d 440], January 20, 2004

[23] New York State Law Reporting Bureau, In The Matter of World Trade Center Bombing Litigation, 2004 NY Slip Op 24030 [3 Misc 3d 440], January 20, 2004

[24] Science Applications International Corporation, Annual Report 2004
http://www.saic.com/news/pdf/Annual-Report2004.pdf

[25] U.S. Congress, Office of Technology Assessment, Technology

Against Terrorism: The Federal Effort, OTA-ISC-481, Washington, DC: U.S. Government Printing Office, July 1991.

[26] A. Maureen Rouhi, Government, Industry Efforts Yield Array Of Tools To Combat Terrorism, Chemical & Engineering News, July 24, 1995

[27] Tim Shorrock, Spies for Hire, Simon and Schuster, 2008

[28] Statement by Duane P. Andrews, Chairman, Defense Science Board Task Force on Information Warfare & Defense, accessed at: https://www.fas.org/irp/congress/1997_hr/h970320a.htm

[29] Matthew Everett, Backup Communications System Was 'Miraculously' Switched on for 'Exercise Mode' and Ready for Use on 9/11, Shoestring 9/11, January 10, 2011

[30] Matthew Everett, The Repeatedly Delayed Responses of the Pentagon Command Center on 9/11, Shoestring 9/11, November 7, 2010

[31] Matthew Everett, Why Were U.S. Intelligence Facilities in an 'Information Void' During the 9/11 Attacks?, Shoestring 9/11, August 19, 2012

[32] Ibid

[33] The 9/11 Commission Report, p 40. Note that these communication failures helped ensure that the President was out of the loop for a longer period of time.

[34] Science Applications International Corporation, Press Release, August 24, 1994

[35] National Commission on Terrorist Attacks Upon the United States, The 9/11 Commission Report, 2004, p 539

[36] Nick Wakeman, Boeing Information Services Sale Has Industry Abuzz, Washington Technology, Jan 21, 1999

[37] James A. Leach, Russian Money Laundering: Congressional Hearing, DIANE Publishing, 2001

[38] Report of the Commission to Assess United States National Security Space Management and Organization

[39] Peter Ogden, Who is Stephen Cambone, Center for American Progress, July 20, 2004

[40] See the "9/11 Document & Briefing Requests" summary of August 22, 2003, and the October 29, 2003 Memorandum from the 9/11 Commission's Team 8, describing the DOD's non-compliance. These

documents are available at Scribd, via the 911DocumentArchive.

[41] Richard Clarke, Against All Enemies: Inside America's War on Terror, Simon and Schuster, 2004

[42] 9/11 Commission Memorandum for the Record, Interview of Jeff Griffith, prepared by Lisa Sullivan, March 31,2004

[43] Jane Mayer, What Did the Vice-President Do for Halliburton?, The New Yorker, February 16 & 23, 2004 issue

[44] SAIC shareholder report, 2004, http://tinyurl.com/bwslby7

[45] William Launder, Homeland Security Goes Public, Forbes.com, August 3.2006

[46] Michael Behar, The New Mobile Infantry: Battle-ready robots are rolling out of the research lab and into harm's way, Wired, Issue 10.05, May 2002

[47] Ibid

[48] Developer of Robots Used in World Trade Center Rescue Efforts Honored by ACM, March 11, 2002, http://www.acm.org/announcements/lawler_2001.html

[49] American Android Corp webpage, About Us, http://www.americanandroid.com/about.jb.html

[50] Del Quentin Wilber, Drones Raise Safety Issues as Service Roles Multiply, Washington Post, July 20, 2007

[51] Sylvia Pagán Westphal, Robots join search and rescue teams, The New Scientist, 19 September 2001

[52] Elli Angelopoulou and John R. Wright Jr., Laser Scanner Technology, University of Pennsylvania Department of Computer & Information Science Technical Reports (CIS), 1999

[53] Sandra I. Erwin, Battlefield Robots: Not Just 'Entertainment', National Defense, May 2001

[54] Kevin R. Ryan, et al, Environmental anomalies at the World Trade Center

[55] Kevin R. Ryan, The Top Ten Connections Between NIST and Nanothermites

[56] Donald L. Barlett and James B. Steele, Washington's $8 Billion Shadow

[57] Tim Shorrock, Spies for Hire, Simon and Schuster, 2008

[58] Paul Kaihla, US: In The Company Of Spies, CorpWatch, May 1st, 2003

[59] Harry Goldstein, Who Killed the Virtual Case File?: How the FBI blew more than $100 million on case-management software it will never use, IEEE Spectrum, September 2005

[60] Charlie Cray, "Science Applications International Corporation," CorpWatch, http://www.corpwatch.org/section.php?id=17 ; cf. Barlett and Steele, "Washington's $8 Billion Shadow."

[61] Frida Berrigan, Merchant of Death of the Month: Science Applications International, Non-Violent Activist, Jan.-Feb. 2006

[62] Steven R. Weisman and David E. Sanger, Unusual Trip to Iraq in '03 for Wolfowitz Companion, The New York Times, April 17, 2007

[63] Government Accountability Project, Paul Wolfowitz Scandal, Background – 2006

[64] Frida Berrigan, Merchant of Death of the Month

[65] The Center for Public Integrity, Winning Contractors: U.S. Contractors Reap the Windfalls of Post-war Reconstruction, October 30, 2003

[66] Tim Shorrock, QinetiQ Goes Kinetic: Top Rumsfeld Aide Wins Contracts from Spy Office He Set Up, CorpWatch, January 15, 2008

[67] Tim Shorrock, QinetiQ Goes Kinetic

[68] For references to the Wacknehut connection to the Casolaro investigation, see Kenn Thomas and Jim Keith's book "The Octopus: Secret Government and the Death of Danny Casolaro," Feral House, 1996.

[69] Lisa Singh, The Top 20 People to Watch in 2011, EcecutiveBiz, December 14, 2010

[70] See the website for GeoQinetiQ, http://www.geoqinetiq.com/

Notes to Chapter 16

[1] George Tenet with Bill Harlow, At the Center of the Storm: The CIA During America's Time of Crisis, Harper Perennial, 2007

[2] Goss was interviewed on the morning of 9/11 at the Pentagon. During that interview, blast sounds could be heard, which were apparently the secondary explosions discussed in Chapter 10. Goss also remarked about the possibility of the use of planes as missiles. The interview can be found on YouTube. See "Bomb Goes Off At

Pentagon During Porter Goss Q&A."

[3] Michael Meacher, The Pakistan connection, The Guardian, July 21, 2004. Also note that Pakistan President Pervez Musharraf wrote in his book that Sheikh, who was involved in the kidnapping and murder of Daniel Pearl have been recruited by British intelligence (MI6) in the 1990s.

[4] Violet Jones, W's "Uncle Bucky" (Secret Society Pal of John Negroponte and Porter Goss) Makes a Killing off Iraq War, InfoWars.com, February 25. 2005

[5] Richard Leiby, A Cloak But No Dagger: An Ex-Spy Says He Seeks Solutions, Not Scapegoats for 9/11, The Washington Post, May 18, 2002

[6] Spartacus Educational, Porter Goss: Biography, http://www.spartacus.schoolnet.co.uk/JFKgoss.htm

[7] Ibid

[8] Richard Leiby, A Cloak But No Dagger

[9] Daniel Hopsicker, Was Bush Spy Pick on Agency Hit Team?, Mad Cow Morning News, Aug 24 2004

[10] Don Bohning, Indoctrination U, June 11, 2008. This article was access at the website "Washington Decoded" and contains interesting comments. http://www.washingtondecoded.com/site/2008/06/simkin.html

[11] NPIC Reunions Database, List of Deceased NPIC Employees, http://npicreunions.blogspot.com/

[12] Suzanne Goldenberg, The Guardian profile: Porter Goss, The Guardian, August 12, 2004

[13] Daniel Hopsicker, Porter & 'the boys:' Goss Made His 'Bones' on CIA Hit Team, May 6 2006

[14] Fabian Escalante, CIA Covert Operations 1959-1962: The Cuba Project, 2004 (pages 42 and 43)

[15] Interview of Frank Sturgis by Michael Canfield, http://www.jfklancer.com/cuba/links/Sturgis_Oper_40.pdf

[16] Larry Hancock, Someone Would Have Talked, 2006

[17] Alan J Weberman, Michael Canfield, Coup D'Etat in America: The CIA and the Assassination of John F. Kennedy, Quick American Archives, 1992

[18] Daniel Hopsicker, Porter & 'the boys:'

[19] Daniel Hopsicker, FINALLY! Rudi Dekkers Behind Bars for Drug Trafficking, Mad Cow Morning News, December 14, 2012

[20] Ibid

[21] Daniel Hopsicker, Welcome to Terrorland: Mohamed Atta & the 9-11 cover-up in Florida, MadCow Press, 2004, pp 31, 185

[22] Daniel Hopsicker, The Ultimate Hedge?: Venice Airport has a 60-Year History of Drug Trafficking, Mad Cow News, March 8, 2010

[23] Peter Dale Scott, American War Machine: Deep Politics, the CIA Global Drug Connection, and the Road to Afghanistan, Rowman & Littlefield Publishers, 2010

[24] Peter Dale Scott, American War Machine

[25] Robert Parry, How John Kerry exposed the Contra-cocaine scandal, Salon, October 25, 2004

[26] For the analysis of the House Intelligence Committee's report, see Robert Parry's article "CIA Admits Tolerating Contra- Cocaine Trafficking in 1980s" from Consortium news, June 8, 2000. For more on Bush's involvement in the Contra-supporting cocaine trafficking, see Gary Webb's book Dark Alliance, Seven Stories Press, 1998

[27] Village Voice, Questions About Porter Goss and His 'Terrorist Breakfast' Go Unanswered, August 11, 2004

[28] The Washington Times, Syria, Iran aiding Iraq insurgents, March 17, 2005

[29] Douglas Jehl, Questions Are Left by C.I.A. Chief on the Use of Torture, The New York Times, March 18, 2005

[30] Bob Drogin, U.S. Had Plan for Covert Afghan Options Before 9/11, The Los Angeles Times, May 18, 2002

[31] Suzanne Goldenberg, The Guardian profile: Porter Goss

[32] Steve Coll, Ghost Wars: The Secret History of the CIA, Afghanistan, and bin Laden, from the Soviet Invasion to September 10, 2001, Penguin Books, 2004

[33] Adrian Levy, Catherine Scott-Clark, Deception: Pakistan, the United States, and the Secret Trade in Nuclear Weapons, Bloomsbury Publishing, 2010

[34] Michel Chossudovsky, War and Globalisation: the Truth Behind September 11, Global Outlook, 2002

[35] Ahmed Rashid, Descent into Chaos: The U.S. and the Disaster in Pakistan, Afghanistan, and Central Asia, Penguin, 2008

[36] The Abbas conversation was recorded by Glass and was reported by multiple news sources including the Palm Beach, Florida television station WPBF Channel 25. See WPBF Channel 25, Informant: Terrorists Warned of WTC Collapse, August 5, 2002

[37] John Pacenti, Intelligence Panel Hears From Glass, The Palm Beach Post, October 17, 2002

[38] Mindy Belz, Prodigal president? World Magazine. January 26, 2002

[39] Luke Harding and Rory McCarthy, Sanctions lifted as US rewards Pakistan, The Guardian, September 23, 2001

[40] John King, White House says politics could hurt September 11 probe, CNN, May 17, 2002

[41] Wikimedia Foundation, September 11 Attacks (Google ebook), eM Publications, p 342

[42] Richard Leiby, A Cloak But No Dagger

[43] Bob Graham and Jeff Nussbaum, Intelligence Matters: The CIA, the FBI, Saudi Arabia, and the Failure of America's War on Terror, Random House Digital, Inc., 2004

[44] Report of the Joint Inquiry into the Terrorist attacks of September 11, 2001 – By the House Permanent Select Committee on intelligence and the Senate Select Committee on Intelligence, p 18

[45] See documents released via FOIA request to the 9/11 Working Group of Bloomington, http://data.911workinggroup.org/foia/FBI

[46] United States Senate Committee on Banking, Housing, and Urban Affairs, Counterterror initiatives in the terror finance program, U.S. G.P.O., January 2005

[47] Bob Graham and Jeff Nussbaum, Intelligence Matters, p 166

[48] Philip Shenon, The Commission: The Uncensored History of the 9/11 Investigation, Hachette Book Group, 2008

[49] Mary Jacoby, Bill Adair and Sara Fritz, Florida congressmen anger Sept. 11 panel members, St. Petersburg Times, September 29, 2002

[50] Ibid

[51] Congressional Record: October 28, 2003 (Senate) Page S13349-S13372

[52] Eric Lichtblau, Saudi Arabia May Be Tied to 9/11, 2 Ex-Senators

Say, The New York Times, February 29, 2012
[53] Kevin R. Ryan, Playing the "Get Into Saudi Arabia Free Card", Washington's Blog, August 28, 2011
[54] Greg Miller, 9/11 report reveals details, questions, The Los Angeles Times, July 28, 2003
[55] Greg Miller, Page After Page, the Mysteries of Sept. 11 Grow, The Los Angeles Times, July 27, 2003
[56] Murray Waas, Cheney's Call: The Vice President's Actions In 2002 Helped Set Events In Motion That Led To The Prosecution Of Scooter Libby, National Journal, February 15, 2007
[57] Richard Leiby, A Cloak But No Dagger
[58] Report of the Joint Inquiry into the Terrorist attacks of September 11, 2001, p 131
[59] Report of the Joint Inquiry into the Terrorist attacks of September 11, 2001, p 20
[60] History Commons Complete 9/11 Timeline
[61] History Commons Complete 9/11 Timeline, Profile: SunTrust bank
[62] Kevin R. Ryan, Muslims did not attack the U.S. on 9/11, DigWithin.net, March 17, 2012
[63] National Commission on Terrorist Attacks Upon the United States, The 9/11 Commission Report
[64] Susan Schmidt, Panel Looks Beyond Intelligence Failures, Into U.S. Government's Response, The Washington Post, July 27, 2003
[65] 9/11 Family Steering Committee response to the 9/11 Commission Report, http://911truth.org/downloads/Family_Steering_Cmte_review_of_Report.pdf
[66] David Ray Griffin, The Bush Doctrine & The 9/11 Commission Report: Both Authored by Philip Zelikow, Information Clearing House, April 10, 2008
[67] Thomas H. Kean and Lee H. Hamilton, Without Precedent: The Inside Story of the 9/11 Commission, Alfred A. Knopf, 2006
[68] Ibid
[69] Thomas H. Kean and Lee H. Hamilton, Without Precedent, pp 66-67
[70] Ron Nessen, It Sure Looks Different From the Inside, Playboy Press, 1978, p 59

[71] National Commission on Terrorist Attacks Upon the United States, The 9/11 Commission Report

[72] National Commission on Terrorist Attacks Upon the United States, The 9/11 Commission Report, p 172

[73] Kevin R. Ryan, Evidence for Informed Trading on the Attacks of September 11, Foreign Policy Journal, November 18, 2010

[74] Ibid

[75] Ibid

[76] National Commission on Terrorist Attacks Upon the United States, The 9/11 Commission Report, p 555

[77] National Commission on Terrorist Attacks Upon the United States, The 9/11 Commission Report

[78] Brent Mickum, The truth about Abu Zubaydah, The Guardian, March 30, 2009

[79] Ibid

[80] Zayn al Abidin Muhammad Husayn v. Robert Gates, Respondents Memorandum of Points and Authorities in Opposition to Petitioner's Motion for Discover and Petitioner's Motion for Sanctions. Civil Action No. 08-cv-1360 (RWR), September 2009.

[81] George Tenet, At the Center of the Storm: The CIA During America's Time of Crisis, Harper Perennial, 2007

[82] Peter Finn and Julie Tate, CIA Says It Misjudged Role of High-Value Detainee Abu Zubaida, Transcript Shows, The Washington Post, June 16, 2009

[83] George Washington, The Reason for the Cover-up Goes Right to the White House, Washington's Blog, March 18, 2010

[84] 9/11 Commission Report, page 146

[85] Kevin R. Ryan, Looking for Truth in Credentials: The Peculiar WTC "Experts", Global Research, March 13, 2007

[86] Graeme MacQueen, Waiting for Seven: WTC 7 Collapse Warnings in the FDNY Oral Histories, The Journal of 9/11 Studies, January 2008. See also Paul Joseph Watson, 9/11 First Responder Heard WTC 7 Demolition Countdown, Prison Planet, September 13, 2007.

[87] BBC acknowledged that it reported the collapse of WTC 7 prematurely. It would be difficult to deny, of course, because the reporter was announcing the collapse while viewers could see the still-standing building right behind her in the video. Years later, BBC's

answer that it was all just "confusing and chaotic." http://www.bbc.co.uk/blogs/theeditors/2007/03/part_of_the_conspiracy_2.html. Other networks prematurely reported the same unprecedented event, as described at RememberBuilding7.org. http://rememberbuilding7.org/foreknowledge/
[88] Kevin R. Ryan, Are Tall Buildings Safer As a Result of the NIST WTC Reports?, Dig Within, September 7, 2012
[89] Remember Building 7, Free Fall Collapse, http://rememberbuilding7.org/free-fall-collapse/
[90] For information on Battelle and the anthrax attacks, see Barry Kissin's article "The Truth About The Anthrax Attacks" (November 15, 2009, accessed at InformationClearingHouse,info). For Battelle's links to the DOE and nanothermite, see my article "The Top Ten Connections Between NIST and Nano-Thermites" in the Journal of 9/11 Studies, July, 2008
[91] Ibid
[92] The National Institute of Standard and Technology, NIST Releases Final WTC 7 Investigation Report, November 25, 2008, http://www.nist.gov/el/wtc7final_112508.cfm
[93] For discussion of one of these media attempts, see Kevin R. Ryan, "Finally, an apology from the National Geographic Channel", 911Blogger.com, August 22, 2009, and also Jon Cole's videos at 911SpeakOut.org, which demonstrate that the media source in question was not being honest.
[94] Ray McGovern, Cheney Cat's Paw, Porter Goss, as CIA Director?, Buzzflash, July 7, 2004
[95] Joel Brinkley and James Risen, On Other Side of the Aisle, Bruised Feelings Linger, The New York Times, August 11, 2004
[96] Julian Borger, CIA memo urging spies to support Bush provokes furor, The Guardian, November 17, 2004
[97] Ibid
[98] Suzanne Goldenberg, The Guardian profile: Porter Goss
[99] Empty Wheel, Rockefeller and the Torture Tape Investigation, July 27, 2010

Notes to Chapter 17

[1] The 9/11 Commission Report references this NSC email, from Clarke to Rice and Hadley, entitled Stopping Abu Zubaydah's attacks, May 29, 2001

[2] Richard A. Clarke, Against All Enemies: Inside America's War on Terror, Simon & Schuster, 2004, pp 7-9

[3] See CNN video footage of August 16, 2002

[4] Joint Chiefs of Staff, Aircraft Piracy (Hijacking) And Destruction of Derelict Airborne Objects, July 31, 1997, http://tinyurl.com/czn9hrd

[5] See 911Review.com, The 'Stand-Down Order', http://911review.com/means/standdown.html

[6] 9/11 Commission Memorandum for the Record (MFR) on John Hawley interview, October 8, 2003

[7] Stephen Pizzo, Family Values, Mother Jones Magazine Sep-Oct 1992

[8] In the summer of 2007, Congressman Peter DeFazio, a member of the U.S. Homeland Security Committee, was denied access to the White House's COG planning documents. This was after it was discovered that, in 2002, President Bush had hid the facts from members of Congress. For more details see Washingtons Blog, Do I Have to Obey Orders From an Unconstitutional Government?, September 11, 2008

[9] For details on the Lloyd's lawsuit against the Saudis, see Russ Baker's article "Saudi 9/11 Alert: Here's That Missing Lloyd's Lawsuit" at WhoWhatWhy.com, November 10, 2011

[10] Christopher Ketcham, The Israeli "art student" mystery, Salon, May 7, 2002

[11] James Mann, Rise Of The Vulcans: The History of Bush's War Cabinet, Viking Press, 2004

[12] Andrew Cockburn, Rumsfeld: His Rise, Fall, and Catastrophic Legacy, Scribner, 2007

[13] See, for example, Paul Alexander, Machiavelli's Shadow: The Rise and Fall of Karl Rove, Rodale, 2008

[14] The concept of Peak Oil is important in understanding one probable motivation for those behind 9/11. A good place to start learning about Peak Oil is the website of Richard Heinberg, http://richardheinberg.com/.

[15] Andy McSmith and Phil Reeves, Afghanistan regains its Title as World's biggest Heroin Dealer, The Independent, June 22, 2003

[16] Alissa J. Rubin, Opium Cultivation Rose This Year in Afghanistan, U.N. Survey Shows, The new York Times, November 20, 2012

[17] Kevin Phillips, American Dynasty: Aristocracy, Fortune, and the Politics of Deceit in the House of Bush, Penguin, 2004

[18] Peter Dale Scott, Who are the Libyan Freedom Fighters and Their Patrons? Global Research, March 25, 2011. Also see Joseph Wakim, Al-Qaeda now a US ally in Syria, The Canberra Times, September 11, 2012

[19] Edward S. Herman and Noam Chomsky. Manufacturing Consent: The Political Economy of the Mass Media, Random House, 1988 and 2002

[20] The idea that al Qaeda was working for the CIA and its allies was proposed shortly after 9/11 by Canadian professor Michel Chossudovsky. His book "War and Globalisation: the Truth Behind September 11" (Global Outlook, 2002) gives some of the details behind this theory.

[21] Glenn Greenwald, The FBI again thwarts its own Terror plot, Salon, Sep 29, 2011,

[22] Paul Harris and Ed Pilkington, 'Underwear bomber' was working for the CIA, The Guardian, 8 May 2012

[23] Wikipedia page - Casualties of the September 11 attacks

[24] Deborah Baum, Estimated cost of post-9/11 wars: 225,000 lives, up to $4 trillion, Brown University "Cost of War" Project, June 29, 2011

[25] Robert Dreyfuss, The $6 Trillion Wars, The Nation, March 29, 2013

[26] The more conservative estimates include that of Iraq Body Count (http://www.iraqbodycount.org/) which puts the number of civilian deaths at about 100,000. Others, including Just Foreign Policy (http://www.justforeignpolicy.org/iraq), estimate the deaths from the Iraq War at over 1.4 million. Middle range estimates include that of the British medical journal The Lancet, which in 2008 put the number near 700,000.

Bibliography

Ahmed, Nafeez Mosaddeq. The War on Freedom - How and Why America Was Attacked September 11, 2001. Tree of Life Publications, Institute for Policy R & D, 2002

Ahmed, Nafeez Mosaddeq. The War on Truth: 9/11, Disinformation, and the Anatomy of Terrorism. Northampton, Mass.: Olive Branch Press, 2005

Baker, Russ. Family of Secrets: The Bush Dynasty, the Powerful Forces That Put It in the White House, and What Their Influence Means for America. New York: Bloomsbury Press, 2009

Bamford, James. Body of Secrets: Anatomy of the Ultra-Secret National Security Agency. Anchor Books, NY, 2002

Bamford, James. A Pretext for War - 9/11, and the Abuse of America's Intelligence Agencies. Doubleday, 2004

Barrett, Wayne, and Dan Collins. Grand Illusion: The Untold Story of Rudy Giuliani and 9/11. HarperCollins, 2006

Beaty, Jonathan and Samuel C. Gwynne. The Outlaw Bank: A Wild Ride Into the Secret Heart of BCCI. Beard Books, 2004

Ben-Veniste , Richard. The Emperor's New Clothes: Exposing the Truth from Watergate to 9/11. Macmillan, 2009

Bremer, Lewis Paul. My Year in Iraq: The Struggle to Build a Future of Hope. Simon and Schuster, 2006

Briody, Dan. The Iron Triangle: Inside the Secret World of the Carlyle Group. John Wiley & Sons, 2011

Briody, Dan. The Halliburton Agenda: The Politics of Oil and Money,

John Wiley & Sons, 2004

Brzezinski, Zbigniew. The Grand Chessboard: American Primacy and Its Geostrategic Imperatives. Basic Books, 1997

Chandrasekaran, Rajiv. Imperial Life in the Emerald City, Random House, 2006

Chossudovsky, Michel. War and Globalisation - The Truth Behind September 11. Global Outlook - The Centre for Research on Globalisation, 2002

Chossudovsky, Michel. America's War on Terrorism. Global Research, Centre for Research on Globalization, 2005

Clarke, Richard. Against All Enemies - Inside America's War on Terror. Free Press, 2004

Cockburn, Andrew. Rumsfeld: His Rise, Fall, and Catastrophic Legacy. New York: Scribner, 2007

Coll, Steve. Ghost Wars - The Secret History of the CIA, Afghanistan, and Bin Laden, From the Soviet Invasion to September 10, 2001. Penguin Press, 2004

Creed, Patrick and Rick Newman. Firefight: Inside the Battle to Save the Pentagon on 9/11. Presidio Books, 2008

De-Haven Smith, Lance. Conspiracy Theory in America, University of Texas Press, 2013

Douglass, James W. JFK and the Unspeakable: Why He Died and Why It Matters. Orbis Books, 2008

Dubose, Lou and Jake Bernstein. Vice: Dick Cheney and the Hijacking of the American Presidency, Random House, 2006

Dwyer, Jim, and Kevin Flynn. 102 Minutes: The Untold Story of the Fight to Survive Inside the Twin Towers. Times Books, 2005

Farmer, John J. The Ground Truth: The Untold Story of America Under Attack on 9/11. Riverhead Books, 2009

Fenton, Kevin. Disconnecting the Dots: How CIA and FBI Officials Helped Enable 9/11 and Evade Government Investigations. Trine Day, 2011

Filson, Leslie. Air War Over America: September 11 Alters Face of Air Defense Mission. U.S. Air Force Publications Office, 2003

Frantz, Douglas and David McKean. Friends in High Places: The Rise and Fall of Clark Clifford, Little Brown & Company, 1995

Freeh, Louis J. My FBI: Bringing Down the Mafia, Investigating Bill Clinton, and Fighting the War on Terror. St. Martin's Press, 2005

Gaffney, Mark H. The 911 Mystery Plane and the Vanishing of America. Trine Day, 2008

Gaffney, Mark H. Black 9/11: Money, Motive & Technology. Trine Day, 2012

Giuliani, Rudolph W. Leadership. Hyperion, 2002

Glanz, James and Eric Lipton. City in the Sky: The Rise and Fall of the World Trade Center. Henry Holt, 2003

Gourley, James. The 9/11 Toronto Report: Issued from the International Hearings on the Events of September 11, 2001. Create Space, 2012

Graham, Senator Bob. Intelligence Matters: The CIA, the FBI, Saudi Arabia, and the Failure of America's War on Terror. Random House,

2004

Griffin, David Ray. The New Pearl Harbor: Disturbing Questions about the Bush Administration and 9/11. Olive Branch Press, 2004

Griffin, David Ray. The 9/11 Commission Report: Omissions and Distortions, Olive Branch Press, 2004

Griffin, David Ray. Christian Faith and the Truth Behind 9/11: A Call to Reflection and Action, Westminster John Knox Press, 2006

Griffin, David Ray and Peter Dale Scott. 9/11 and American Empire: Intellectuals Speak Out, Olive Branch Press, 2006

Griffin, David Ray. Debunking 9/11 Debunking: An Answer to Popular Mechanics and Other Defenders of the Official Conspiracy Theory. Northampton, Olive Branch Press, 2007

Griffin, David Ray. The Mysterious Collapse of World Trade Center 7: Why the Final Official Report About 9/11 Is Unscientific and False. Olive Branch Press, 2009

Griffin, David Ray. 9/11 Ten Years Later: When State Crimes Against Democracy Succeed, Interlink Books, 2011

Goldberg, Alfred, et al. Pentagon 9/11. Historical Office, Office of the Secretary of Defense, 2007

Hall, Anthony J. Earth Into Property: Colonization, Decolonization, and Capitalism: The Bowl with One Spoon. McGill Queens University Press, 2010

Heinberg, Richard. The Party's Over: Oil, War and the Fate of Industrial Societies. New Society, 2003

Herman, Edward S. and Noam Chomsky. Manufacturing Consent: The

Political Economy of the Mass Media. Random House, 1988 and 2002

Hicks, Sander. The Big Wedding: 9/11, the Whistle Blowers, and the Cover-up. Vox Pop, 2005

Hopsicker, Daniel. Barry and the Boys: The CIA, the Mob, and America's Secret History. Mad Cow Press, 2001

Hopsicker, Daniel. Welcome To Terrorland -- Mohammed Atta & the 9-11 Cover-up in Florida. Mad Cow Press, 2004

Huff, Mickey, Peter Phillips, and Project Censored, eds. Censored 2010: The 25 Top Censored Stories of 2008-2009. Seven Stories, 2009

Hufschmid, Eric. Painful Questions: An Analysis of the September 11th Attack. Ink and Scribe, 2002

Kean, Thomas H. and Lee H. Hamilton. Without Precedent: The Inside Story of the 9/11 Commission. Knopf, 2006

Klein, Naomi. The Shock Doctrine: The Rise of Disaster Capitalism. Henry Holt/Metropolitan, 2007

Kolb, Larry. America at Night: The True Story of Two Rogue CIA Operatives, Homeland Security Failures, DirtyMoney, and a Plot to Steal the 2004 U.S. Presidential Election--by the FormerIntellegence Agent Who Foiled the Plan. Penguin, 2008

Lance, Peter. 1000 Years for Revenge: International Terrorism and The FBI - The Untold Story. Regan Books/HarperCollins, 2004

Lance, Peter. Cover Up: What the Government is Still Hiding About the War on Terror. Regan Books, 2004

Lance, Peter. Triple Cross: How bin Laden's Master Spy Penetrated the CIA, the Green Berets, and the FBI-And Why Patrick Fitzgerald Failed

To Stop Him. William Morrow, 2006

Langewiesche, William. American Ground: Unbuilding the World Trade Center. North Point Press, 2002

Mann, James. Rise of the Vulcans: The History of Bush's War Cabinet. Viking Penguin, 2004

Marrs, Jim. Inside Job: Unmasking the 9/11 Conspiracies. Origin Press, 2004

Marshall, Johnathan, Scott, Peter Dale, and Hunter, Jane. The Iran Contra Connection: Secret Teams and Covert Operations in the Reagan Era. South End Press, 1987

McCoy, Alfred W. The Politics of Heroin: CIA Complicity in the Global Drug Trade. Lawrence Hill Books, 1991

Meyerowitz, Joel. Aftermath: World Trade Center Archive. Phaidon Press, 2006

Meyssan, Thierry. 9/11: The Big Lie. USA Books, 2002

Miller, Mark Crispin. Cruel and Unusual: Bush/Cheney's New World Order. Norton, 2004

Miller, Mark Crispin. Fooled Again: The Real Case for Electoral Reform. Basic Books, 2007

Monaghan, Aidan. Declassifying 9/11: A Between the Lines and Behind the Scenes Look at the September 11 Attacks, iUniverse, 2012

Morgan, Rowland, and Ian Henshall. 9/11 Revealed: The Unanswered Questions. Carroll & Graf, 2005

Naiman, Arthur. 9/11: The Simple Facts -- Why the official story can't possibly be true, Soft Skull Press, 2011

Napoleoni, Loretta; Modern Jihad -- Tracing the Dollars Behind the Terror Networks. Pluto Press, 2003

National Fire Protection Association. Guide for Fire and Explosion Investigations. National Fire Protection Association, 2004

Paul, Don. The World Is Turning: "9/11", the Movement for Justice, and Reclaiming America for the World, WireOnFire.com, 2009

Paul, Don and Jim Hoffman, Waking Up from Our Nightmare, the 9/11/01 Crimes in New York City, I/R Press, 2004

Phillips, Kevin. American Dynasty: Aristocracy, Fortune, and the Politics of Deceit in the House of Bush. Penguin, 2004

Prouty, Leroy Fletcher. The Secret Team: The CIA and Its Allies in Control of the United States and the World. Skyhorse Publishing, 2011

Rea, Paul W. Mounting Evidence: Why We Need A New Investigation Into 9/11. iUniverse, 2011

Ridgeway, James. The 5 Unanswered Questions about 9/11: What the 9/11 Commission Report Failed to Tell Us. Seven Stories Press, 2005

Risen, James. State of War: The Secret History of the CIA and the Bush Administration. Free Press, 2006

Rumsfeld, Donald. Known and Unknown: A Memoir. Penguin, 2011

Ruppert, Michael C. Crossing the Rubicon: The Decline of the American Empire at the End of the Age of Oil. New Society Publishers, 2004

Russell, Dick and Jesse Ventura, 63 Documents the Government

Doesn't Want You to Read. Skyhorse Publishing, 2011

Scott, Peter Dale. American War Machine: Deep Politics, the CIA Global Drug Connection, and the Road to Afghanistan. Rowman and Littlefield, 2010

Scott, Peter Dale. Deep Politics and the Death of JFK. University of California Press, 1993

Scott, Peter Dale. Drugs, Oil, and War: The United States in Afghanistan, Colombia, and Indochina. Rowan and Littlefield, 2003

Scott, Peter Dale. The Road to 9/11: Wealth, Empire and the Future of America. University of California Press, 2007

Scott, Peter Dale. The War Conspiracy: JFK, 9/11, and the Deep Politics of War. Mary Ferrell Foundation Press, 2008

Shenon, Philip. The Commission: The Uncensored History of the 9/11 Investigation. Twelve Books, 2008

Shorrock, Tim. Spies for Hire: The Secret World of Intelligence Outsourcing. Simon & Schuster, 2008

Sick, Gary. October Surprise: America's Hostages in Iran and the Election of Ronald Reagan. Times Books, 1992

Spencer, Lynn. Touching History: The Untold Story of the Drama That Unfolded in the Skies Over America on 9/11. Free Press, 2008

Suskind, Ron. The One Percent Doctrine: Deep Inside America's Pursuit of its Enemies Since 9/11. & Schuster, 2006

Swanson, David. War Is a Lie. Self published, 2010.

Tenet, George. At the Center of the Storm: My Years at the CIA.

HarperCollins, 2007

The Oklahoma Bombing Investigation Committee. Final Report on the Bombing of the Alfred P. Murrah Federal Building April 19, 1995. 2001

Thompson, Paul. The Terror Timeline: Year by Year, Day by Day, Minute by Minute: A Comprehensive Chronicle of the Road to 9/11- and America's Response. Regan Books/Center for Cooperative Research, 2004

Trento, Joseph J. Prelude to Terror: The Rogue CIA and the Legacy of America's Private Intelligence Network. Carroll & Graf, 2005

Trento, Susan B. The Power House: Robert Keith Gray and the Selling of Access and Influence in Washington. St. Martin's Press, 1992

Trento, Susan B. and Joseph J. Unsafe at Any Altitude: Failed Terrorism Investigations, Scapegoating 9/11, and The Shocking Truth about Aviation Security Today. Steerforth Press, 2006

Truell, Peter, and Larry Gurwin. False Profits: The Inside Story of BCCI, the World's Most Corrupt Financial Empire. Houghton Mifflin, 1992

Unger, Craig. House of Bush, House of Saud: The Secret Relationship Between the World's Two Most Powerful Dynasties. Scribner, 2004

Unger, Craig. The Fall of the House of Bush: The Untold Story of How a Band of True Believers Seized the Executive Branch, Started the Iraq War, and Still Imperils America's Future. Scribner: 2004

U.S. Army Medical Department. Office of Medical History. Soldiers to the Rescue: The Medical Response to the Pentagon Attack. Office of Medical History, 2004

Vogel, Steve. The Pentagon: A History. The Untold Story of the Wartime Race to Build The Pentagon—And to Restore It Sixty Years Later. Random House, 2007

Weiner, Tim. Legacy of Ashes: The History of the CIA. Doubleday, 2007

Weisman, Alan. Prince of Darkness: Richard Perle: The Kingdom, the Power, and the End of Empire in America. Union Square Press, 2007

Wright, Lawrence. The Looming Tower, Random House, 2007

Zarembka, Paul. The Hidden History of 9-11, Seven Stories Press, 2008

Zwicker, Barrie. Towers of Deception: The Media Cover-Up of 9/11. New Society Publishers, 2006

Documentary Films

9/11: Explosive Evidence- Experts Speak Out, AE911Truth.org, 2011

9/11: Press for Truth, Ryko Distribution, 2006

A Noble Lie: Oklahoma City 1995, Free Mind Films, 2011

Fahrenheit 9/11, Lions Gate Films, 2004

Loose Change 9/11: An American Coup, Microcinema International, 2009

Reports

9/11 Family Steering Committee Response to the 9/11 Commission Report, accessed at 911Truth.org

ASCE and SCI, The Pentagon Building Performance Report, January

2003

Federal Emergency Management Agency (FEMA) Region II, New York, and Federal Insurance and Mitigation Administration, Washington, DC. World Trade Center Building Performances Study: Data Collection, Preliminary Observations, and Recommendations. (Government Printing Office, Washington, DC, 2003)

National Commission on Terrorist Attacks Upon the United States. The 9/11 Commission Report: Final Report of the National Commission on Terrorist Attacks Upon the United States - Authorized Edition. W.W. Norton & Company, July 22, 2004

National Commission on Terrorist Attacks Upon the United States [Steven Strasser, ed.]. 9-11 Investigations - Staff Reports of 9/11 Commission, Excerpts from the House-Senate Joint Inquiry Report on 9/11, and Testimony from 14 key witnesses. BBS Public Affairs, 2004

OIG Report on CIA Accountability With Respect to the 9/11 Attacks, June 2005

Senate Committee on Intelligence & House Permanent Select Committee on Intelligence. Joint Inquiry into Intelligence Community Activities Before and After the Terrorist Attacks of September 11, 2001. Government Printing Office, Washington, DC, December 20, 2002

The National Institute of Standards and Technology (NIST), WTC Report, http://www.nist.gov/el/disasterstudies/wtc/wtc_finalreports.cfm

The Project For A New American Century. Rebuilding America's Defenses: Strategy, Forces, and Resources for a New Century. PNAC, 2000

U.S. Justice Department office of Inspector General's Inquiry into 9/11, http://www.justice.gov/oig/special/s0606/final.pdf

Scientific Articles

Brookman, Ronald H., A discussion of "Analysis of structural response of WTC 7 to fire and sequential failure leading to collapse," Journal of 9/11 Studies, Vol. 33, Oct. 2012.

Niels H. Harrit, et al., "Active Thermitic Material Discovered in Dust from the 9/11 World Trade Center Catastrophe." The Open Chemical Physics Journal, Vol. 2 (April, 2009), 7-31

Ryan, Kevin R., et al. "Environmental Anomalies at the World Trade Center: Evidence of Energetic Materials." The Environmentalist (9/08): 56-63.

Steven E. Jones et al., "Extremely High Temperatures during the World Trade Center Destruction," Journal of 9/11 Studies, January 2008.

Steven E. Jones, et al., "Fourteen Points of Agreement with Official Government Reports on the World Trade Center Destruction," The Open Civil Engineering Journal, Vol. 2, 2008, 35-40.

For additional information on the falsity of the official accounts for 9/11, see the *Journal of 9/11 Studies*, found online at www.journalof911studies.com.

26016010R00228

Made in the USA
Lexington, KY
13 September 2013